Christopher Isherwood

Christopher Isherwood

A Critical Biography

by
BRIAN FINNEY

New York
Oxford University Press
1979

Library of Congress Cataloging in Publication Data

Finney, Brian.
Christopher Isherwood: a critical biography.

Bibliography: p.
Includes index.
1. Isherwood, Christopher, 1904–   2. Authors,
English—20th century—Biography.
PR6017.S5Z65   823'.9'12   [B]   78-26622
ISBN 0-19-520134-5

Printed in the United States of America

Contents

Illustrations

Acknowledgements

My greatest debt is to Christopher Isherwood without whose friendly co-operation this book could never have been written.

I am also deeply indebted to those friends of his who lent me his letters which they had kept and spent time talking about him and his work, namely: Alec Beesley and Dodie Smith, Roger Burford, Eric Falk, John Lehmann, Fowke and the late Sylvain Mangeot, Humphrey, Stephen and Natasha Spender, James and Tania Stern and Edward Upward.

Two collectors of his work have also gone out of their way to help me: Alan Clodd and John Whitehead.

I am also indebted to the following, all of whom helped me obtain or shape much of the information and material which form the backbone of this book: Dennis Altman (University of Sydney); Don Bachardy; the British Broadcasting Corporation (especially Gwyniver M. Jones, Written Archive Centre); Michael Barrie; B. C. Bloomfield; Neville Braybrooke; the British Library; Mrs May Buckingham; Mrs Rosamira Bulley; Peter Burton; John Byrne (Bertram Rota); University of California at Berkeley, Santa Barbara and Los Angeles (Departments of Special Collections); Professor A. H. Campbell; Jonathan Cape Ltd; W. Caskey; Columbia University Libraries (Kenneth A. Lohf, Librarian of Rare Books and Manuscripts); Mrs D. Connolly; Curtis Brown Inc, New York (Perry H. Knowlton); Curtis Brown Ltd, London (Peter Grose); Spencer Curtis-Brown; University Library, Durham (David Burnett); William Empson; Eyre Methuen Ltd (John Cullen); Faber and Faber (Charles Monteith); Farrar, Straus & Giroux Inc (Robert Giroux); Jonathan Fryer; P. N. Furbank; Mrs M. E. Gardiner; Granada Television Ltd (Stephen Hosty); Ronald Hayman; Donald Hayne; Henry Heckford; William Heinemann Ltd; George A. Hilton; Hogarth Press Ltd; University of Hull; Mrs Laura Huxley; Julien

Jebb; King's College Library, Cambridge; Gavin Lambert; Richard Layard; Mrs R. E. de Lichtenberg; University of London; Los Angeles Times (Judith A. Wilson); Mrs J. and H. G. Mackenzie-Wintle; Miss A. C. McNaughton; Robin Maugham; Robert Medley; Edward Mendelson; Karl Miller; Elizabeth Monkhouse; Mr and Mrs Patrick Monkhouse; Mrs Rachel Natzio; Mrs Eileen Neale; New Directions Publishing Corporation (James Laughlin); New York Public Library (Henry W. and Albert A. Berg Collection, Astor Lenox and Tilden Foundations); Oxford University Press, New York (James Raimes); Alice Prochaska; John Reid; Repton School (W. B. Downing); Maurice Richardson; W. D. Robson-Scott; N. J. Sidnell; Simon and Schuster (Peter Schwed); Michael Sissons; Mrs B. Stimson; John Symonds; A. J. Taylor; Universal City Studios Inc; Gore Vidal; Alan Wallis; Colin Research Center); Theatre Museum, London; Twentieth Century Fox Film Corporation; University of Tulsa (Michael Blechner); Universal City Studios Inc; Gore Vidal; Alan Wallis; Colin Wilson; Wisconsin Center for Film and Theater Research, Madison, Wisconsin, Gore Vidal Collection (Julie D'Acci).

I am doubly indebted to Elaine Allen who not only typed the manuscript, but undertook much of my administrative work during two prolonged absences connected with the book.

I am grateful to the University of London for releasing me from my duties in the summer of 1976 and again in the autumn of 1977, and to the Arts Council of Great Britain for granting me a writer's award.

Permission to quote from copyright material is hereby gratefully acknowledged:

For extracts from Christopher Isherwood's work: Christopher Isherwood and the following publishers: Jonathan Cape and New Directions (*All the Conspirators*); The Hogarth Press Ltd and New Directions (*The Memorial, The Berlin of Sally Bowles/The Berlin Stories*); Eyre Methuen Ltd and New Directions (*Lions and Shadows*); Eyre Methuen Ltd, Curtis Brown Ltd, NY and Random House (*Prater Violet, The Condor and the Cows, The World in the Evening*); Eyre Methuen Ltd, Candida Donadio and Asso. and Simon & Schuster (*Down There on a Visit, A Single Man, Exhumations, A Meeting by the River, Kathleen and Frank*); Eyre Methuen Ltd and Farrar, Straus & Giroux (*Christopher and his Kind*); Vedanta Press (*An Approach to Vedanta*).

For extracts from W. H. Auden's and Christopher Isherwood's *Journey to a War*: Christopher Isherwood, the Estate of W. H. Auden (courtesy Professor Edward Mendelson), Faber & Faber Ltd and Random House.

For extracts from W. H. Auden's work: the Estate of W. H. Auden (courtesy Professor Edward Mendelson), Faber & Faber Ltd and Random House (*Poems 1930, The Orators, Collected Shorter Poems 1930–1944, Collected Poems*).

All previously unpublished writings by Christopher Isherwood are copyright © by Christopher Isherwood and printed by his permission.

All previously unpublished writings by W. H. Auden are copyright © by the Estate of W. H. Auden, and printed by permission of Professor Edward Mendelson.

December 1977

Who is that funny-looking young man so squat with a top-heavy head
A cross between a cavalry major and a rather prim landlady
Sitting there sipping a cigarette?
A brilliant young novelist?
You don't say!

(Opening stanza of an unpublished poem written by Auden
for and about Isherwood in 1937)

Introduction

I can think of few other writers whose work invites biographically informed criticism to the extent that Isherwood does. On the one hand he claims that all his novels constitute a kind of fictional autobiography, on the other hand that autobiography is always fiction.[1] Repeatedly in his books he has assumed the pose of a biographer in order to understand himself and his dealings with others in the past. All his books tantalise the reader with the ambiguous relationship that holds in them between the protagonists, the narrator and the author. Some critics have assumed that much of his best work is mere reportage, a collage of carefully selected extracts from diaries skilfully woven together by an expert craftsman. Others, ignoring the distance, at times admittedly small, separating the writer and his protagonists, have castigated him for the faults with which he has consciously imbued his fictional counterparts. The academic world has been content mainly to confine its attention to his contribution to British writing of the thirties. Yet, as his large following of readers on both sides of the Atlantic knows, he has continued to write fiction, biography and autobiography up to the present day. At least two of his novels of the sixties compare favourably in quality with his Berlin-based novels, just as his latest autobiography, published in 1976, can stand comparison with his first work of autobiography written in the thirties.

Nevertheless he has produced work of differing quality at different periods of his life, although I know of no book of his which does not offer some reward to the reader. Yet this unevenness in itself suggests that biographical investigation might well uncover the reason for the astonishing variations that characterise his literary career. Like his books Isherwood has himself been subject to radical changes. Until the age of thirty-five he was in rebellion against his mother, his native country, its religion and its politics. Then suddenly the wanderer has settled for life in California, espoused religion of a different variety, and, instead of subscribing to a united front of the Left, has turned pacifist. How is it possible to reconcile the author of 'The Nowaks', the apparent political champion of the oppressed, with the contributor to *Vedanta and the West*, with its advocacy of non-attachment, especially in the sphere of politics? His life and his work are more overtly interdependent than is usually the case, and both offer irresistible challenges to the literary biographer.

Leon Edel, the biographer of Henry James, and one of the first biographers since Lytton Strachey revolutionised the art of biography to write about the art of specifically *literary* biography, has suggested that 'the writing of a literary life would be nothing but a kind of indecent curiosity, and an invasion of privacy, were it not that it seeks always to illuminate the mysterious and magical process of creation.'[2] The present book rests largely on this assumption. My selection from the enormous amount of material that inevitably offers itself to the biographer of a still-living subject is primarily dictated by an interest in Isherwood the writer. The biographical sections are intended to inform the critical sections, to establish parameters within which meaningful criticism of Isherwood's different books can be pursued. James Clifford, another biographer who has more recently written about the problems of literary biography, quotes a friend who called life-writing the last major discipline uncorrupted by criticism.[3] Since my own approach to literary criticism is largely opposed to the highly theoretical responses to literature currently in vogue in many academic circles, while equally opposed to the ultimate subjectivity of the empiricist school for which the text exists virtually in a vacuum, a critical biography is the perfect vehicle for combining the objective discipline of research with the belief that each artist establishes his own criteria within which meaningful responses to, and criticism of, his work can take place.

I have therefore done my best to make this book appeal both to the general reader and to those who already know much of Isherwood's work. My hope is to attract the former to a desire to read some of Isherwood's books and to offer the latter greater understanding of his intentions. All but Chapter 19 and the last four chapters are exclusively devoted either to his life or to a critical consideration of one of his works, while in Chapter 19 and

I

Family

Christopher Isherwood, like most of his British literary contemporaries who came to prominence in the 1930s, was born into
a comfortably well-off middle-class family. In fact his father's side
of the family verged on the aristocratic, owning a large Elizabethan mansion, Marple Hall, in Cheshire with its own park and
small lake. At the turn of the century the Bradshaw-Isherwoods
were the largest landowners in the vicinity, leasing out, for
example, the farmland to which was attached Wyberslegh Hall
where Isherwood's parents began their married life in 1903.
Isherwood's father, Frank Bradshaw-Isherwood, however, had
the misfortune of being born the second son of the head of the
family, John Bradshaw-Isherwood. Traditionally this meant that
he had to find a suitably undemeaning way of earning his own
living in order that the family estate might pass undivided to his
elder brother, Henry. He chose to follow his father's example by
becoming a professional soldier, and was commissioned into the
York and Lancaster Regiment in 1892 at the age of twenty-three.
Isherwood's portrait of his parents, *Kathleen and Frank*, makes it
clear that, while he was a perfectly satisfactory officer, he was
temperamentally unsuited to the profession. Reticent and
sensitive, he preferred to spend his spare time reading, painting
and playing music, rather than drinking and exchanging dirty
stories in the officers' mess.

Until the publication of *Kathleen and Frank* in 1971 Isherwood
appears to have consistently underplayed his aristocratic family
connections on his father's side. For example, in a series of
lectures he delivered in 1960–61 at the University of California at
Santa Barbara on the subject of 'The Writer and His World', he
referred to the Bradshaw-Isherwoods as 'successful farmers' who
had bought a 'large house' (meaning Marple Hall) which entitled
the head of the household to be known by 'that curious English

appellation of Squire'. Isherwood was clearly still embarrassed at this time by the snobbery associated with his upbringing as a member of the upper middle class: 'it was always breathed into me,' he confessed, 'that this upper middle class was the real aristocracy of England.'[1] By whom? By his mother, Kathleen, herself the daughter of a wine merchant who was 'in trade' as the expression went. This form of occupation relegated Kathleen's father, Frederick Machell Smith, by some perverse logic, to a lower place in the English class structure of his day than that of the landed gentry, such as the Bradshaw-Isherwoods.

The father took his revenge on the class system by withholding his consent to his daughter's marrying Frank for as long as he dared on the grounds of Frank's inability to maintain her in the circumstances to which he had accustomed her. Kathleen, as so often happens in these circumstances, became more upper-class than the upper-class family into which she married at the age of thirty-five. Isherwood's fictionalised portrait of Kathleen as Lily Vernon in *The Memorial* includes a bitingly satirical depiction of her attempt to maintain the rights of the squire (her father-in-law) over his social inferiors. Ironically she poured her life's energies into the maintenance of English class distinctions at almost precisely that moment in history when they were finally in the process of disintegration.

Kathleen was in fact destined to live long enough to witness in person the demolition of the Hall by the local council to make room for a new secondary school and housing estate with roads called Bradshaw, Isherwood and Vernon among others. His mother's adopted snobbery eventually produced a strong reaction in Isherwood who only exorcised this particular parental demon with the writing of *Kathleen and Frank*. Even in 1975 it was still the 'big streak of hypocrisy in her nature', the fact that 'she was always thinking of what the Jones's thought', that still rankled most.[2]

Kathleen and Frank offers a fascinating portrait of the two families from which Isherwood stems. On Kathleen's side are the Machell Smiths—the father testy, selfish, hypocritical and tyrannical within his own family circle—and the Greenes—the mother, Emily, equally wilful but forced to win her own way in a more indirect manner by developing self-induced illnesses. He calls his grandmother 'a great psychosomatic virtuoso' (*KF* 8), who not only forced her husband to move the family to London on grounds of ill health, but then proceeded to outlive him by nineteen years. On Frank's side are the Bradshaw-Isherwoods, the father, John, the last true squire of Marple, a baby-faced gentleman of leisure whose recurrent strokes had reduced him to premature senility; the mother, Elizabeth, small and rather lost amidst the large Elizabethan mansion in which she spent her married life, dazed by her poor memory and exuding her own anxiety over the rest of the family. One is hardly surprised that Isherwood's father, Frank, should emerge from this background sensitive and retiring, an essentially private person whom circumstances would not allow to remain buried from the outside world. Similarly Kathleen's vigorously assertive character must surely be the result of both inheriting and withstanding her parents' wilful egotism.

Isherwood himself strongly believes that heredity plays a much more important part in the formation of personality than is currently held fashionable. In writing *Kathleen and Frank* he was forced to the conclusion that 'one isn't an individual so much as part of a *weave*',[3] because, as he explained, 'you are partly your mother and partly your father.'[4] Although this emphasis on the effects of heredity partly represents the later Isherwood's need to reconcile himself to his parents against whom he had reacted so violently in his youth, he did find, when he was reading their diaries in the late 1960s, similarities between them and him which he had not realised existed. For example, his father, Isherwood realised to his surprise, was at the turn of the century drawn to Theosophy, which Isherwood sees merely as a European version of Hinduism. By the time he first came across this interest of his father's he had already been himself a student of Hindu philosophy for over a quarter of a century. Similarly it turned out that Frank had always wanted to travel in the footloose fashion that his son was to do in the 1930s. Above all, his father's artistic temperament was inherited by the son whose ambition to write can be traced all the way back to his childhood.

What, then, does he owe to his mother who outlived her husband by forty-five years? A scrap of paper entitled 'Preliminary Statement' has survived, probably dating from the late 1920s, in which Isherwood and Auden were scribbling down their ideas on drama and psychology. One of the many epigrams reads 'Old age is believing that parents are ideal.'[5] *Kathleen and Frank* is a book written in his late sixties and, in spite of its occasional reservations, it does betray a tendency towards idealisation in its portrayal of Kathleen. Despite the fact that she mellowed as she grew older, there can be little doubt that she was a formidable woman in her prime who inherited all her parents' stubborn will-power. In particular her streak of obstinacy, which frequently manifested itself as a refusal to face current facts, was to be inherited by Isherwood, who in his turn was equally adamant in his refusal to conceal unpalatable truths from her. Spender and Auden have humorously recounted what a tyrant Isherwood could be in private life, Auden calling him at different times a strict little landlady and a Prussian drill sergeant. If Isherwood owes this ruthless streak to Kathleen, he also inherits her social poise and ability to win her way by tact and charm. Unconsciously reflecting these dual attributes in his mother, Isherwood con-fessed to one of his many interviewers: 'I must say my friends and acquaintances make me a rather complex creature: part despot, part diplomat. . . . I'm supposed to have an overpowering will. . . . Then again, I'm so sly.'[6] It is arguable, of course, how much he owed these traits to his mother. After all, just as Kathleen acquired much of her forcefulness not through any genetic inheritance but from her social conditioning, which necessitated her self-assertion in the face of two formidable parental authority-figures, so Isherwood acquired much of his own wilfulness from his similar need to withstand the despotic side to Kathleen's personality. Isherwood's emphasis on heredity throws most light on his own habit of making myths about his past. Ultimately it is impossible to separate the effects of heredity from those of childhood conditioning.

the final four chapters the same practice is adopted within the two sections of which each consists. But the biographical chapters or sections invariably include the evolution of his next book, while the critical chapters or sections embody, wherever relevant, remarks Isherwood has made in letters or interviews (many unpublished) which throw biographical light on his work. I have deliberately risked the appearance of creating a collage in the critical sections in the belief that a literary biographer owes it to his readers to include as much relevant biographical evidence as he can so that others can make use of it for their different readings of the texts. As for footnotes, I have always confined these to a description of the source of my information, so that there is no need for anyone but the committed scholar or the curious reader to consult them.

The present book could not have been written without Isherwood's help and co-operation. He gave me permission to approach any recipients of his letters with the one exception of his brother. Almost all his closest friends, as well as libraries, collectors and his publishers, have been remarkably helpful in lending me letters dating back to the twenties, manuscripts, rare publications and all the other paraphernalia which the biographer has to accumulate before he begins to sort and select. Isherwood also gave up whole days of his time to my endless questions and lent me manuscripts in his possession. Certain obvious gaps in the evidence remain—his letters to his mother and brother, his letters to Auden (who never kept anyone's letters), and his journals since 1939 (which will be published one day, though at present he tends to favour posthumous publication). None of these is likely drastically to alter the picture one can acquire of him from the main body of evidence, only to modify it a little.

Isherwood himself has been as near an ideal subject as any biographer could hope for—helpful, infinitely patient, friendly but always aware of the distance needed if hagiography is to be avoided. There is no time here to discuss the limitations of any biography of a living person. Sufficient to point out the fact that with so many of the protagonists still alive certain reticences have to be maintained. Isherwood has never requested any information about himself to be withheld; all his concern has been for others. The fact that he has been a homosexual all his adult lifetime also creates problems, since not all his homosexual friends have chosen to declare themselves as he has done. In fact I am frequently asked why, as a heterosexual, I have chosen to write about someone whose life and writings have been informed throughout in one way or another by his membership of the homosexual minority. Yet it should be obvious, especially in his most recent work, that his views are primarily addressed to the Others, which is the heterosexual majority in the sexual arena. Who better to react to his life and works than a member of that majority? On the other hand Isherwood has always maintained that his homosexuality originated in, and therefore symbolises his need to rebel against, a much wider range of majority attitudes, and in many of these parallel confrontations I find myself naturally in sympathy with the minority. I hope the resulting ambiguities allow me to adopt as objective a stance as is possible towards Isherwood and his work in what is ultimately a highly subjective genre.

2

Childhood

Isherwood's parents were married in 1903. The marriage was to prove a success, but the lack of any great passion on either part is evident from the fact that on the second day of their honeymoon in Cambridge they were joined by Kathleen's mother—at Frank's suggestion. After five days the couple went north to move into their new home at Wyberslegh Hall. Far less imposing than Marple Hall, Wyberslegh was nevertheless grand enough to warrant being called a Hall and was at least as old. Frank's father had divided up the house for the newly married couple, confining the existing tenant farmers, the Coopers, to the rear and separating off the grander front half for Isherwood's parents, inevitably creating a good deal of ill-feeling between the two families in the process. Wyberslegh was chronically damp, according to Isherwood, despite its location just above the village of High Lane on the Ridge, as the range of Cheshire hills was called. Marple Hall was only three miles away and both families visited one another regularly.

Seventeen months after their wedding Kathleen gave birth to Christopher William Bradshaw-Isherwood on 26 August 1904 at Wyberslegh. Her father-in-law told her at the christening that she had done her duty well, with which quaint words mother and son became accepted members of the Bradshaw-Isherwood family. Within two months a nanny was engaged, one Annie Avis, a little younger than her employers, who became a life-long member of the family. As a child Isherwood saw far more of Nanny, as he called her, than of his mother who was frequently called away from home to spend time with Frank or her mother. In *Kathleen and Frank* Isherwood mentions at different points the fact that his mother washed and dressed him for the first time when he was almost five and that he slept in a separate room from Nanny for the first time when he was nine and a half years old

(*KF* 197, 279). Such a delegation of maternal responsibilities was by no means abnormal among the middle classes at that time—Evelyn Waugh, John Lehmann and Graham Greene all mention their nurses among their earliest memories in their autobiographies. Nevertheless the prevailing presence of Nanny in Isherwood's childhood might well account for his unusual independence from his mother from a surprisingly early age. His only emotional dependence on his mother was to be a negative one. She was to become someone to be rebelled against.[1]

Isherwood's detailed account of his youth in *Kathleen and Frank* reveals little of real significance in his early years. Dividing his time between Wyberslegh and Marple (where he was visited by the family ghost) with occasional visits to his mother's family in the south or for a holiday in Wales, he spent most of his time in the company of his nanny, the servants at Marple Hall, and his parents when they were not away from home. One of the first books to have left its mark on him, he claims, was Beatrix Potter's *The Roly-Poly Pudding* in which Mrs Twitchit's home became identified in his mind with Marple and Wyberslegh. The Mortmere fantasies he was to concoct in his twenties with Edward Upward derive some of their features from Beatrix Potter's strange amalgam of animals and humans in the same social setting.

When he was three and a half years old Isherwood and his mother were forced to leave Wyberslegh, as his father, who had transferred to the Volunteers on getting married in order to go on living at Wyberslegh, had rejoined his old Regiment which was currently stationed at York. That the move was a temporary one, as the Regiment was due to move to Aldershot later that year, only added to his mother's determination to dislike their new house in Strensall, near York. Her diary entry for 29 February 1908, the day she left Wyberslegh, is heavy with nostalgia and self-pity: 'It seems like the passing away of Romance and Youth' (*KF* 240). Her growing tendency to mourn the past rather than live in the present is to be matched by her son's subsequent determination to turn his back on the past in all its forms—the ancestral home, class distinctions, the study of history, Cambridge, and finally England itself. Much of Isherwood's life and writing was determined by a compulsive reaction against selected aspects of his mother's personality.

In November 1908 the family moved again, to Frimley, to be near Frank's barracks at Aldershot. They spent the next three years there on the Surrey/Hampshire border with extended visits to Marple each Christmas and summer. During this period he first met the Monkhouse children who lived near Marple in the village of Disley. Their house was later to provide Isherwood with the model for the Scrivens's house in *The Memorial*. The eldest son, Patrick Monkhouse, was the same age as Isherwood while his sister Rachel was about a year and a half younger. Rachel remembers him as a confident young boy who was always taking the initiative in games, deciding which slope was best for tobogganning, when they would meet next, and tending if anything to lord it over them by virtue of his more opulent family home at Marple Hall.[2] At this stage of his childhood he was understandably still introjecting his mother's class distinctions.

In his sixth year his father took his education in hand, teaching him reading and writing by compiling an illustrated daily called 'The Toy-Drawer Times' which was intermittently kept up until Isherwood first went to boarding school four years later. He also shared his father's love for home theatricals, where he could write his own scenario and manipulate the characters at will. His erotic memories of watching his almost naked father exercise in the morning are given retrospective significance in *Kathleen and Frank*, but throw more light on the older Isherwood's penchant for mythologising his life as a homosexual than on the child, since he claims in *Christopher and his Kind* that his homosexuality was more the result of a deliberate choice on his part than the outcome of an irreversible biological condition (*CK* 16–17). In 1911 he began attending a local school for an hour a day with four other small boys. The same year his mother gave birth to his younger brother, Richard. Because they were separated by seven years the two brothers remained relative strangers to one another until Richard reached his late teens. Richard was always much shyer than his elder brother, and much less of a rebel where his mother was concerned. His unwillingness to complete his education beyond school or to make his own living was to make his mother all the more worried about her elder son's failure to adopt a respectable profession with a secure income, and this issue was to become a constant source of tension between them in the later 1920s.

During their Frimley period, Isherwood's father, recognising
his essential incompatibility with the army, tried without success
to obtain his release. A major by now, in late 1911 he was forced
to rejoin his Regiment which had been posted to Limerick in
Ireland. The rest of the family followed in the New Year. During
their first year in Ireland Isherwood, with a few other boys,
attended the local Girls High School where he quickly became
top of his class. The following year he was transferred to a Miss
Burns's school where most of the six or seven pupils were male.
The young Isherwood's fascination with dramatisation constantly
surfaces in Kathleen's diaries for this period. Given a toy theatre
for Christmas 1911, he was forever staging melodramatic versions
of Shakespeare's tragedies or sub-Sarah Bernhardt plays of his
own concoction. The most interesting of his mother's entries for
this period gives a new complexion to his passion for home
theatricals: 'he so easily gets overexcited and frightens himself
over the stories he tells himself, and he is always telling himself
stories', she complains (KF 272). It is hardly surprising to find
him taking equally enthusiastically to the cinema, which he
visited for the first time in Limerick, and which was to play such
an important role in his life and the development of his writing.

The schooling the young boy was receiving in Ireland was less
than satisfactory, so his parents decided to send him to preparatory
school in southern England as a boarder in 1914. They chose
St Edmund's School in Hindhead which was run by two of
Frank's cousins, Cyril Morgan Brown and his sister Monica,
together with his daughter Rosamira. On 1 May 1914 his mother,
full of misgivings, handed Isherwood over to Cyril Morgan
Brown at Waterloo station. A new, painful phase of Isherwood's
life had begun.

3

St Edmund's Preparatory School

'A private school,' wrote Cyril Connolly, 'has all the faults of the public school, without any of its compensations. . . . It is one of the few tortures confined to the ruling classes and from which the workers are free.'[1] Many of Isherwood's contemporaries shared Connolly's views. Among them George Orwell has written of his prep school with perhaps the greatest bitterness in 'Such, Such Were The Joys'.[2] But one has to turn to the milder tone of William Plomer to understand why Isherwood and his generation reacted so strongly against this particularly English institution. 'During the War,' he wrote, 'we were still being taught to believe in and serve the "ideals" that were destroying the generation a little older than our own, the generation of Wilfred Owen.'[3] In Isherwood's case his father's death in battle was to bring home to the bewildered young boy of ten this chasm between the school's ideology and his own experience in a painfully personal way. Time has healed the wound and in *Kathleen and Frank* Isherwood gives a rather bland account of his four years at St Edmund's. But in his earlier writings, *Lions and Shadows* and the short story based on St Edmund's, 'Gems of Belgian Architecture', there is no mistaking the note of underlying anger and resentment at the régime to which he was subjected.

The same note can also be detected in an early description of the school he quotes in *Exhumations* where he writes of an 'aggressive gabled building' with 'sham frontings', 'about the size of a private hotel', in front of which is 'a plantation of dwarf conifers, such as are almost always to be seen in the grounds of better-class lunatic asylums' (E 169). Actually the grounds in which the school stood were extensive and wild. They included a large number of gorse bushes into which boys earning their fellows' disfavour (like Dwight in Isherwood's story) were sadistically thrown. Although Isherwood came in for his fair share

of rejection and unhappiness at St Edmund's, he appears to have
held his own among his school-fellows despite the fact that his
physical timidity made him a poor performer at most of the
organised school games. In *Kathleen and Frank* he claims to have
found wrestling and boxing sexually exciting. As most boys,
especially when cooped up in an all-male community, experience
powerful homosexual feelings during their puberty, one needs to
view Isherwood's later assertion that he realised he was gay by
the time he went to St Edmund's at the age of ten[4] (which conflicts with his account in *Christopher and his Kind*) as the mythopoeic utterance of the militant spokesman for homosexuals that
he has become in the last decade. Both *Kathleen and Frank* and
Christopher and his Kind give the impression that behind Isherwood's militancy against the heterosexual majority lurks an
equally strong militancy against his past self whom he now hates
for covering up his earlier homosexual tendencies which he
consequently exaggerates by way of compensation.

What turned out to be the greatest source of his unhappiness at
school were paradoxically his own relatives, 'Ciddy', as the boys
called the headmaster, and to a lesser degree his daughter, Rosa,
neither of whom liked him, he claimed in *Kathleen and Frank*
(p 286). The only one who took to him, Mona, the head's sister,
left at the end of the first term after war had been declared to run a
soup kitchen in the East End. Both 'Ciddy' and Rosa might have
been over-compensating with the young Isherwood in that
peculiar way the British have for their blood ties by demonstrating
their complete impartiality towards him all too thoroughly. But
one suspects that there was a deeper divergence of temperaments
between their irritatingly precocious young relative and their own
traditionalist outlook, already becoming outmoded by the outbreak of world war. A brilliant classicist, the headmaster gave
many parents the deceptive illusion that he was the odd-job
carpenter, according to Rosa,[5] so dazed and dreamy was his
appearance, as Kathleen confirmed in her diary (*KF* 278, 283).
But both Isherwood and Harold Llewellyn Smith, who joined the
school the following year, agree that 'Ciddy' had a way of deflat-
ing boys whom he considered to have got above themselves so
effectively that they usually ended their cosy fireside chats with
him in a welter of tears.[6] The Morgan Brown ethos amounted to a
late-Victorian belief in normality and regularity, 'all the virtues',

as Isherwood summed it up, 'recommended by Kipling in *If*' (*KF* 286).

The curriculum was unchanged since Victorian times, concentrating on classics, mathematics, French and divinity. English was taught as part of history and geography, all three subjects being confined to four hours' teaching a week. Brainy but lazy according to the head, Isherwood during his first two terms managed to win, of all things, the Divinity Prize in both Forms I and II, besides passing his mid-term examination with honours.[7] His mother took him back to Limerick for the last time during the summer holidays. While there, war was declared and a little over a week later the young Isherwood witnessed the departure of his father with his Regiment for England *en route* to the Front. From this time on mother, nurse and children would spend school holidays either in Marple or with Emily, Kathleen's widowed mother, in her London flat in Buckingham Street off the Strand near Charing Cross Station. A month after he had started his third term at St Edmund's at the beginning of 1915, Isherwood went down with measles which was further complicated by a touch of pneumonia. When he was well enough, his mother took him away from school to recuperate in Ventnor on the Isle of Wight. What with lumbago and rheumatic pains, the ten-year-old Isherwood didn't recover properly for another month and a half and was kept at home on the doctor's advice for the remainder of the summer term. On 12 May 1915, the day after mother and son travelled up to Marple from Ventnor, a telegram reached her from the War Office informing her that Colonel Isherwood (his rank by this time) had been wounded. Although she had to spend agonising weeks in London ascertaining the fact, Isherwood's father had actually been killed on 8 May in the second battle of Ypres.

Isherwood spent most of that summer at Marple. Much of this time he was left in the hands of Nanny. On his return to St Edmund's after a term and a half's absence he wore a black armband and was treated with ritualistic respect by his schoolfellows on whom the Morgan Brown ethos had obviously left its stamp. During the summer he had not felt his father's loss too keenly, partly, he writes in *Kathleen and Frank*, because his mother was so much more grief-stricken herself and partly out of jealousy of the man who was distracting his mother's attention from himself. But once he was back at St Edmund's 'Ciddy' and Rosa seized on his father's death to force their eleven-year-old upstart cousin to conform to their glamorised vision of war, patriotism and death. His dead father became an heroic ideal with whom the son would be constantly compared to his disadvantage by his school teachers, as well as by his mother and the establishment at large. This subtle manipulation of the bewildered prep schoolboy's guilt feelings naturally made him begin to resent his father's memory which proved a further source of shame and guilt.

At the time Isherwood felt confused, resentful, scared and guilt-ridden. The father he had known, admired and loved had been turned into an heroic abstraction of unattainable perfection. If his father was willing to lay down his life for his country, the least his son could do, the older generation reiterated, was to comply with their codes of conduct. W. H. Auden, a new boy at St Edmund's that autumn term of 1915, gives a light-hearted illustration of this attitude in his 'Letter to Lord Byron' where he remembers how even the boys' failure to construe the Latin for war (*bellum*) correctly was instantly interpreted as an act of treachery:

> *But once when half the form put down* Bellus
> *We were accused of that most deadly sin,*
> *Wanting the Kaiser and the Huns to win.*

Similarly Stephen Spender recalls how his prep school house-master, on discovering that some of the boys out of hunger had eaten more than their allotted quarter of a slice of bread during the break, paraded them before the rest of the school to whom he announced: 'These boys are worse than huns, they're FOOD HOGS.'[8] Because his father was constantly invoked to give stature to such pettiness, Isherwood's later pacifism probably stems from his natural childhood rejection of everything his schoolmasters advocated.

In *Kathleen and Frank* Isherwood claims to have mythologised his personal dilemma at this period of his life by secretly rebelling against the Hero-Father who had been conjured up by what he calls The Others. In the process, he argues, he was compelled to reject the Flag, the Old School Tie, the Unknown Soldier, the Land That Bore You and the God of Battles (*KF* 357). The biographer, however, has to treat Isherwood's retrospective application of the myths he has constructed around his own earlier life with considerable care. Obviously his mythopoeic faculty has helped Isherwood understand and live at peace with himself. But just as he has found himself unable to write novels based on his own experience until he has sufficiently distanced himself in time from it, so his mythic constructs are invariably later interpretations and explanations of the raw material of his life that is all too anarchic at the time. The autobiographical kind of novelist he has aspired to be has naturally encouraged this search for order in his past life. The need for orderly explanation is further emotionally motivated because it helps him to accept his rearranged past, to see it in a much wider context, and to live happily with it. But the raw material for these myths is a great deal more unruly than they suggest.

Moreover, the myths are themselves subject to alteration with the passage of time. An earlier version of the myth of War, for example, to be found in *An Approach to Vedanta*, admits that, far from rejecting the War and all it stood for, Isherwood 'was horribly scared by the idea of War and therefore subconsciously attracted to it' (*AV* 7). Out of this came his concept of The Test that obsessed him all through the 1920s. An even earlier and more reliable version of the personal circumstances underlying this particular myth appears in *Lions and Shadows*. There he describes his psychological state on leaving St Edmund's where the headmaster had done his best to persuade him that he was 'in general more unpleasant than anybody else'. In the same passage he writes: 'I had arrived at my public school thoroughly sick of masters and mistresses, having been emotionally messed about by them at my preparatory school, where the war years had given full licence to every sort of dishonest cant about loyalty, selfishness, patriotism, playing the game and dishonouring the dead. Now I wanted to be left alone' (*LS* 13). That has more of the touch of authentic experience about it. The mythology was to come later. For his remaining three years at St Edmund's Isherwood was to remain confused, unhappy, angry even, but unable to discern that the reason for these feelings lay in the two quite different versions of his father that were fighting for supremacy within him. The Anti-Heroic Hero he describes in *Kathleen and Frank*, the heroic father who mocks the militaristic system he apparently subscribes to, is the mythic construct of an altogether more mature individual whose literary instincts have prompted him to employ paradox as a means of reconciling the two conflicting memories.

Isherwood's mid-term report that autumn of 1915 hints at the young boy's concealed emotional turbulence when it comments on his inattention and lack of interest in some subjects. As Orwell wrote of his own prep school days, 'a child which appears reasonably happy may actually be suffering horrors which it cannot or will not reveal', and he continued: 'It lives in a sort of alien underwater world which we can only penetrate by memory or divination.'[9] The records that have survived from this time, however, belong to the public world and show Isherwood adapting to its needs and echoing its shibboleths. Two poems parodying earlier writers which he wrote at St Edmund's illustrate how successfully the school had implanted in him its own xenophobic version of patriotism.[10] The earlier poem, which he wrote in April 1916, is called 'A Lay of Modern Germany' and crudely evokes the tone and metrical form of Macaulay's 'Lays of Ancient Rome'. 'Shame on the cowardly Prussian,' it reads, that sends over 'Billy's leaky gas bags' (Zeppelins) and then flees before the might of the Allied armies. In the finale of the poem Isherwood could not have been aware of the ironic undertones of his satirical portrayal of the Germans' resort to gas, which was actually first used by them at Ypres where his father was killed:

> Then out spoke fat Von Winklepop
> Who composed the 'Hymn of Hate'
> To everyone in all ze landt
> Death cometh soon or late;
> Then how can man die petter
> Than facing fearful odds
> And gassing vell dese English swine
> Who tink that they are gods.

Needless to say the use of gas doesn't succeed and the Allies win the battle.

The poem he wrote the following year is a more polished parody of Lewis Carroll's nonsense poem, 'Father William'. In the twelve-year-old Isherwood's version Father William is the Kaiser and the young man is the Crown Prince. However the young poet clearly still identifies with the jingoistic sentiments of The Others. For instance, the second stanza reads:

> *'In my youth,' Kaiser William replied to his son,*
> *'I slept every night without pain,*
> *But now that I think of the crimes that we've done*
> *I shall never slumber again.'*

The implacable morality inculcated by the school underlying both poems made a deep impression on Isherwood and his generation. Their subsequent revolt against the ethics which they held responsible for the catastrophe of the First World War was merely, it became clear in the 1930s, the substitution of one set of moral absolutes for another. As Samuel Hynes has suggested in *The Auden Generation* the new Myth of War epitomised by Wilfred Owen's poetry was not so much a rejection of former attitudes as a revision of them.[11] The identity of the Enemy had simply changed, although, in Isherwood's case, the Fascist Villain of the 1930s was to prove too crude a substitute for the Kaiser. Nevertheless he has retained a strong moral streak in his character that can be traced all the way back to the indoctrination of his prep school.

Isherwood didn't really make contact with W. H. Auden until his last year at St Edmund's, by which time Auden, his junior by two and a half years, had caught up with him in the fourth form. Auden was perfectly happy at St Edmund's and his jovial disposition, his laziness and untidiness, his self-confidence and his tendency to be insolent towards the masters must have earned Isherwood's admiration and provided him with a badly needed new perspective on the entire school ethos. Wystan Auden (or 'Weston' as he is called in *Lions and Shadows*) had a plump figure with fair hair and an anaemic complexion. He was precocious for his age and is alleged to have announced on his arrival at St Edmund's that he was looking forward to studying the different psychological types.[12] His status among the boys was much enhanced, Isherwood recalls in *Lions and Shadows*, by the knowledge about the facts of sex which he had illicitly learnt from the medical books belonging to his father who was a doctor. The admiration that sprung up between the two boys in 1918 was mutual. Auden later recalled that the first time he ever heard a remark which was witty was when he was taking a school walk with Isherwood who announced, 'I think God must have been tired when He made this country.'[13] Their mutual admiration even led to one abortive attempt at literary collaboration. Auden's schoolfriend, Harold Llewellyn Smith, remembers a school cricket match in 1918 when he, Auden and Isherwood jointly planned an ambitious historical novel set in Marple Hall which, however, came to nothing.[14]

In later life both Auden and Isherwood derived a great deal of fun from their memories of St Edmund's and it is probable that their attitude of humorous detachment originated in 1918 when the two friends were comparing notes and learning to laugh at some of the more obviously silly sides to school life. Both of them mention one of the more eccentric masters, Captain Reginald Oscar Gartside-Bagnall, who rewarded his favourites with beer and biscuits and read to them all from his own melo-drama, *The Waves*.[15] As Auden wrote in his 'Letter to Lord Byron', the War had emptied the school of its ablest masters, so that they were left with 'The remnant either elderly grey creatures/ Or characters with most peculiar features.' Both writers also had off pat the sermon that the Reverend Mr Richmond used to deliver every year on St Edmund's Day. Auden even parodied it in one of his earliest works, *The Orators*, in which the 'Address for a Prize-Day' opens with virtually the identical words used by this pompous old boy of the school. His sermon also used to contain a story about impossibly stagey patriotic exchanges between troops in passing trains, the whole absurd performance being concluded with a rhetorical question 'Is this mere senti-mentality?' to which the obvious answer was exactly the reverse of that intended.[16]

The friendship with Auden that was to be renewed seven years later must have helped Isherwood to begin the long and difficult task of detaching himself from the deeply implanted beliefs of an older generation. In particular Isherwood left St Edmund's full of resentment and hostility towards Cyril Morgan Brown and with a dread of authority verging on hysteria. Outwardly, how-ever, he conformed like the rest of his school-fellows, winning the form prize in both his final years and so ending his prep school career in the opinion of Rosa, the head's daughter, 'in a blaze of glory'.[17]

4

Repton

Like most of the British writers of his generation, Isherwood went on to public school, an institution (unlike its democratic namesake in the States) the raison d'être of which was, according to Auden, the mass production of gentlemen.[1] The influence that the great public schools had on those writers who went through them in the immediate post-war years was sufficiently disproportionate to produce the corporate myth first formulated in an anthology edited by Graham Greene in 1934 called *The Old School*. Traditionalist and élitist, the public school of this period was designed, as Harold Nicolson wrote in his contribution, 'to provide a large number of standardized young men fitted for the conquest, administration and retention of a vast . . . Empire',[2] happily unaware of the fact that the Empire was already in the process of disintegrating. Public schools commanded an entry into so many of the positions of power and influence in the kingdom that, for Anthony Powell at Eton, 'the government of the country was somehow made almost a personal matter.'[3] It is natural therefore that the post-war disillusionment of Isherwood's generation with the previous generation which had been responsible for the débâcle of the war should equally infect their attitude to their public school. As Auden wrote only half-humorously in the 1930s, 'The best reason I have for opposing Fascism is that at school I lived in a Fascist state.'[4]

In January 1919 Isherwood entered Repton, near Derby. His mother probably chose this public school on the advice of her brother-in-law, Jack, who was himself an old boy of the school. Founded in the reign of Mary Tudor, the school had a long ecclesiastical tradition. G. F. Fisher, the headmaster in Isherwood's time, like his predecessor, William Temple, went on to become Archbishop of Canterbury, as did Michael Ramsey who joined Repton the same year that Isherwood did. Repton was subdivided into eight different houses. Isherwood was in the Hall where the head was also his housemaster. Thirty-one years old on Isherwood's arrival, likeable and full of charm, yet brusque and physically unprepossessing, he had none of Temple's depth nor Ramsey's subsequent culture. Sixth-formers used to say that his religion was not Christianity but divinity.[5] Because in later life Fisher delivered a speech in the House of Lords defending homosexuals against state persecution, Isherwood seems to have forgotten his earlier resentment against his head's unimaginative and often oppressive regime.[6] The deputy housemaster for the Hall was Strickland, an ex-militarist who avoided conscription by running the OTC. His bullying manner made him a figure of hate for most of the boys, although Isherwood's friend, Pepper (called 'Dock' in *Lions and Shadows*) seems to have shown Isherwood how to deal with this particular manifestation of school fascism.

All public school authorities were haunted by the spectre of homosexuality. One ineffectual but time-honoured way of restricting it was to segregate the houses from each other so that boys in different houses rarely got the opportunity of making friends with one another until they reached the sixth form where this particular taboo no longer applied. For his first two years at Repton, consequently, Isherwood only got to know boys in his own house. There he met Eric Falk (the Eric of *Lions and Shadows*), a Jewish boy who early on showed a natural allegiance to the rebel element among his schoolfellows. Although he wasn't a victim of it, anti-semitism, like snobbery, lay just beneath the surface of school life. Another Jewish boy, Barnett, for instance, despite his muscular physique, had on one occasion a skewer driven up his arse.[7]

Despite their disparity in years, Falk befriended Vernon Watkins, another rebel, after he had entered the Hall in September 1920, but Isherwood didn't make real contact with this fellow writer until their paths met again at Cambridge. Another member of his house with whom Isherwood became friendly was Anthony Gross who, according to Isherwood, was marked out early on as a future artist and who even at Repton was constantly burning his boots with the acid he used for doing etchings in his study.[8] Each house was divided into daytime studies which normally contained from two to five fags (using the word, of course, in its

English schoolboy sense), from one to three seconds (neither fags nor studyholders) and one studyholder who could beat his fags at will. Isherwood was unusually lucky in having for his studyholder the head of house whose lazy benevolence saved him during his first year from the regular beatings which were so much a part of the average new boy's experience.

For the first two years at Repton Isherwood swam with the tide. He managed to survive by cunning, befriending the tough older Liverpudlian, Pepper, and relying on his own wits to balance Pepper's muscle. Eric Falk remembers Isherwood's deadly power of invective as the most potent weapon in his armoury of defences. One sycophantic boy in the Hall who got on the wrong side of Isherwood was instantly nicknamed 'Lubricant' by him, a sobriquet so appropriate that it stuck to the unfortunate boy for the rest of his schooldays.[9] In class Isherwood was no more than average, doing worse than most in maths and science (which he dropped in 1920) and better than most at classics and the Bible paper. But he did win the Distinction Prize in English Subjects twice in 1919 and once in 1920. During the Michaelmas term of 1920 he was marked 'partially absent' and spent the Lent term of 1921 catching up with special work. Nevertheless by the time he entered the History Sixth in May 1921 he was among the youngest of its eight boys.[10] This suggests that he was bright for his age from the start but that he had always had to compete with his elders for form places and prizes.

Isherwood's two years in the History Sixth between the ages of sixteen and eighteen mark the beginning of his long drawn-out struggle actively to liberate himself from the ideas and codes of conduct which had been drilled into him up to this date by both schools and the establishment they represented. In the first place he came under the direction of G. B. Smith (the 'Mr Holmes' of *Lions and Shadows*) who had joined the school the same year as Isherwood. Isherwood has left a vivid portrait of this, his most influential teacher, in *Lions and Shadows* where Smith emerges as a masterly psychologist of adolescence, encouraging individual eccentricities, provoking lazy sixth-formers to outraged protests at his deliberately wild generalisations and collecting about him a devoted following, some of whom were later to become his personal friends. Isherwood quickly fell under his spell and only realised during his last term at school that he really wanted to read English at Cambridge, so hypnotic had been his history master's effect on him.

The sixth form was allowed to do its private work in the library and it was here that Isherwood met two quite different boys from other houses who were to become life-long friends. One was Hector Wintle (called 'Linsley' in *Lions and Shadows*) who had entered New House in September 1916 and was studying Modern Languages in the sixth when Isherwood first came across him. Isherwood remembers him for his sheer amiability, the way he made one start to laugh the moment one saw him. In *Lions and Shadows* he describes how Wintle spent much of his time in the library writing a novel called *Donald Stanton* about public school life modelled on E. F. Benson's light novel, *David Blaize*. He submitted the manuscript to the mischievous scrutiny of his fellow sixth-formers and was quite unruffled by the howls of gleeful derision that greeted each newly discovered malapropism.[11]

Another aspirant writer whom Isherwood met in the sixth form was Edward Upward from Latham House (who is called 'Allen Chalmers' in *Lions and Shadows*). A short boy like Isherwood himself, nervous and excitable, he was much more secretive about, and dedicated to his art than Wintle, and immediately attracted the younger Isherwood by his combination of rebelliousness towards the school and his commitment to writing poetry. In *No Home But the Struggle*, the third volume of his autobiographically-based novel, *The Spiral Ascent*, Upward has described his unhappy early years at Repton which were responsible for his rejection of the entire institution in his final year there. By the time Isherwood (called 'Richard' in Upward's trilogy) became friends with him in 1921, Upward had refused to make use of fags as a studyholder, had had himself demoted in the school Officers' Training Corps by behaving with deliberate slovenliness, and had refused to be confirmed, telling his housemaster he was an agnostic. Isherwood, by comparison, had been confirmed the winter before they met, having been prepared by Dr Fisher. By the summer he already felt let down both by Fisher and by his own capitulation to the religious establishment.[12] Nevertheless Isherwood found that he could get by at Repton in a way that he had found impossible at St Edmund's.

Upward, who had been desperately unhappy during his early years at public school, admits in *No Home But the Struggle* that he deliberately prolonged the spirit of rebellion against Repton because the accompanying unhappiness this produced nurtured the poetry of Gloom which he was writing by 1921. Like Walt Whitman, whom he discovered at this time, his declared aim in life and literature was to 'nourish active rebellion' and the poem which won him the Howes Verse Prize, 'The Surrender of the German Fleet at Scapa Flow', contemptuously avoided its patriotic subject and indulged instead in decadent romantic images of pain and death. Upward recalls how all his poems of this time were filled with tombs, lichen, leprosy, toads, lych-owls and putrefaction.[13] When Upward first came to know Isherwood he found that his new friend had not only been writing poems himself for about a year before entering the sixth but that his poetry was more mature and technically more competent than his own. Each aspiring writer was attracted to the complementary qualities of the other—Upward to Isherwood's command of the medium, Isherwood to Upward's cult of gloom and rebellion. Within the year both of them were having their poems published in *The Reptonian*, Isherwood hiding behind the pseudonym of Cacoethes (meaning an itch to do something, presumably derived from Juvenal's 'incurable itch of writing'). Isherwood's earliest contributions to the December 1921 issue clearly show the influence of Pound's verse translations of the Chinese poet, Li Po, in *Cathay*. Though obviously a poor reflection of their original model, they do illustrate Isherwood's technical competence for his age. Later poems in *The Reptonian* are written under the influence of Wordsworth ('The self-same Force which fashioned Sun and Earth/Ordains the marvel of a pansy's birth')[14] and other poets equally recognisable to everyone but their teenage author. Isherwood's most successful poetic coup was to have another poem 'Mapperley Plains' published in an anthology, *Public School Verse*, Volume 3, 1921–1922 which Heinemann brought out in 1923. It is reprinted in *Exhumations* where he recalls how his friend Patrick Monkhouse from Disley suggested that in future he should sign his work Christopher (rather than C.W.B.) Isherwood (*E* 11).

What all the poems have in common is a positive attitude which removes them from the morbid gothic romanticism which marks Upward's poetry of the time. Isherwood's first published work, however, was not a poem but, appropriately, a short story, 'The

Hang-Yü Mysteries'. It is a heavy-handed parody of Sax
Rohmer's popular mystery stories featuring Dr Fu Manchu, the
inscrutable oriental villain, and his suave opponent, Nayland
Smith, the perfect English gentleman who never loses his cool.
Isherwood's portrait of the hero is a combination of Nayland
Smith and his prolific creator, who continues to write through a
series of increasingly bizarre interruptions. Here, for example, is
how Isherwood describes his appearance:

> The occupant of the study was tall and spare; in complexion,
> dagoesque. To look at him one would not have believed that
> here was the only man in Europe who had seen the ear-ring of
> the Prophet and lived. He had lost his scalp during a visit to the
> Sioux Indians and his nose while studying the habits of the
> Esquimaux. A trip to the Obi Gum had cost him a hand, and
> three of his toes had been the price of an encyclopaedic
> knowledge of the burial-customs of the Dormi Binos. It was
> characteristic of the man that, at the moment, he was engaged
> in a Chinese treatise on Brazilian cricket for the benefit of the
> Fiji Islanders . . .

This appeared in the only issue of the unofficial Repton School
humorous magazine, *The Phoenix*, in July 1921. Isherwood's early
literary outpourings by no means distinguish him from his public
contemporaries. 'What a ridiculous generation we are', wrote
Evelyn Waugh, for instance, in his diary at this time—ridiculous,
he explained, for their rush to get into print well before the age of
nineteen.[15]

Upward's influence on Isherwood was at its height when they
went to Cambridge in December 1921 to sit for their scholarship
examinations. Both of them saw Cambridge as a more insidious
extension of the school ethos, bribing them instead of disciplining
them into a continued subscription to the code of the establishment. Both of them entered Cambridge like spies penetrating
enemy territory (both the myth and its imagery are destined to be
transmitted through Isherwood to Auden whose debt to Upward
in his early poetry is enormous). Under the hypnotic influence of
G. B. Smith, Upward won a sixty-pound scholarship and Isherwood a forty-pound exhibition to Corpus Christi College. Two
terms after they met, Upward left Repton to spend the first five

months of 1922 learning French in Rouen before going up to Cambridge.

Isherwood stayed on for another year, compensating in part for his friend's absence by growing closer to G. B. Smith. Under Smith's teaching he became one of the school's brightest scholars, winning the English Literature Prize in the Lent term, and the F. W. Head History Prize (on the set subject of Mary Queen of Scots) in the summer term, as well as the Form Prize. This suggests that without Upward's subversive presence he reverted to a more orthodox attitude towards the school in his final year.

That summer Isherwood went abroad for the first time in his life, on a walking tour of the Alps arranged by G. B. Smith. Apart from Isherwood, there was Geoffrey Kingsford (called 'Queensbridge' in *Lions and Shadows*) and Upward whom they picked up at Rouen. Unchanged apart from a pipe and a moustache, Upward once again cast his spell over his friend. The actual landscape of France receded before the fantasy world they lived in when in each other's company. Because the Alps were conventional objects of admiration the two friends refused to admire them, just as they withheld their approval from Les Invalides because Upward had previously denounced it as a shrine of war. Instead they entered the imaginative world of Villon and Baudelaire whom Upward had discovered during his stay at Rouen. As Isherwood points out in *Lions and Shadows* both of them were still virgins at this time which encouraged them enthusiastically to adopt Baudelaire's diseased view of love as another way of undermining the establishment. It is ironic that Isherwood who was to spend almost ten years wandering all over the Continent should have returned home so upset by French food that he had to spend several weeks recovering.

Back at Repton that autumn for his last term there Isherwood kept in touch with Upward who had gone up to Corpus Christi. In *No Home But the Struggle* Upward recalls how at first he was unsure whether Cambridge would prove sufficiently disagreeable to sustain the mood of gloom he was cultivating for the sake of his writing. His imagination soon proved stronger than actuality and he promptly sent Isherwood a letter describing Cambridge as an 'insidious hell' and 'a blood-supping blasé monster' (*LS* 44). The decadent mood he was nourishing was fed with readings of Baudelaire and, a recent addition, Wilfred Owen, who became a cult hero for the Isherwood generation.

At Repton Isherwood was enjoying for the first time the powers of being a studyholder. Against his principles he gave in to the temptation his new-found power offered him and beat his fag (Austin Darling) on a trumped-up charge. Nevertheless Isherwood only appears to have gone through this humiliating experience once, unlike the majority of studyholders at the time. In a letter he wrote to Upward in June 1923 he mentions that 'the flame still burns brightly before Darling's altar', which suggests that the beating was an expression of both his desire for Darling and his need to repress the desire by punishing its object. Other more congenial positions of power included his editorship of the school magazine and his proposal of an anti-patriotic motion in the school debating society in which he argued that patriotism fosters ill-feeling between nations, hinders world peace and is therefore the bane of civilisation.[16] A more tactful version of this argument was offered by G. B. Smith whose intervention helped win the motion. Isherwood also records beginning his first novel this term, presumably a forerunner of the *bildungsroman* he refers to as *Lions and Shadows* in the autobiography to which he later gave the same title. At the end of term he resat his examination at Cambridge and, thanks to G. B. Smith, won an eighty-pound scholarship with flying colours. Isherwood remembers how Dr Fisher, when they were taking their leave, derogatively remarked that he supposed that Anthony Gross would no doubt become a famous artist and that Isherwood would write a book called *Essays on Style*. Nevertheless, in his own biting way, he was acknowledging the promise of real talent in both boys.[17]

Reviewing his own years at Eton in *Enemies of Promise*, Cyril Connolly produced what he called his 'Theory of Permanent Adolescence'. The theory propounded that public school so dominated the imaginative lives of the boys passing through it that it arrested their development and left the greater part of them 'adolescent, school-minded, self-conscious, cowardly, sentimental, and in the last analysis, homosexual'.[18] Considering what a wild generalisation this is, it is surprising how much of the early literature produced by Isherwood, Upward, Auden and his circle reflects many of these attributes. One finds them in the Mortmere fantasies, in 'Gems of Belgian Architecture' and 'The

Orators'. Fifteen years later Isherwood and Auden are still evoking the team spirit and rivalries of their schooldays in their jointly written play *The Ascent of F6*. The cast of characters is virtually all-male, the moral code, even where it is being satirised, is still based on the public school's concept of leadership and responsibility, and the scenario is most commonly a thinly disguised evocation of the football field or an OTC field day. Isherwood, Upward and Auden were to spend at least a decade struggling free from this highly selective microcosmic view of the world that their public schools had implanted in them.

On his return home he found his mother with Nanny and his grandmother, Emily, in a new house she had rented that autumn at 36 St Mary Abbot's Terrace near Olympia. When Emily had been told to move out of her Buckingham Street flat because the stairs were too much of a strain on her heart, Isherwood's mother had been forced to find a new London home for the family. During the Christmas holidays he would meet schoolfriends like Hector Wintle or Eric Falk for tea or to go to the pictures. All three were addicted to the cinema and would go anywhere to see their eight-year-old idol of the day, Jackie Coogan, who had achieved world fame playing opposite Chaplin in *The Kid* in 1920. In a letter to Upward early in 1923 he claims to have seen Coogan in *Oliver Twist* no fewer than seven times. Interestingly he comments: 'I think paiderastia is the lowest state of the human soul and the Film Industry the nadir of Commercial Prostitution.'[19]

Obviously Isherwood found Jackie Coogan wildly attractive but had also partially inherited his school's rigid moral attitude towards his own homosexual proclivities. He was to suffer from the emotional tensions this produced in him for most of the 1920s. Patrick Monkhouse remembers how Isherwood struck the Monkhouse family at this period as slightly odd. His parents, in particular, were aware of something about their son's friend that was off the track.[20] In 1922 Patrick's father, Allan Monkhouse, used Isherwood as a model for one of the principal characters in a novel he wrote called *My Daughter Helen*. Although the character concerned, called Marmaduke, soon takes on a fictional life of his own, he is characterised by an off-beat personality, someone about whom 'there was something unexpected' and who 'would shrink from emotion, secretly fearing and desiring it'.[21] That description seems to fit the Isherwood of this period.

Isherwood appears to have spent the first three months of 1923 at home. In April he followed in Upward's footsteps by going to stay for three months in the same pension, Le Vert Logis, at Rouen, run by an old schoolteacher, M. Morel, who worked his foreign students hard but in a sufficiently pedagogic manner to ensure that Isherwood forgot all the French he learnt there as soon as he left. Bored out of his mind, he spent his time corresponding at great length with masters and schoolfriends, especially Upward, Wintle, Falk and Patrick Monkhouse. His addiction to the cinema continued unchecked: he consumed at least three different film magazines a week besides rushing off to the cinema to see Jackie Coogan and a new French juvenile idol, Jean Forest. Half-way through his stay a Glaswegian called Stuart arrived at the pension. Despite Stuart's ugly appearance Isherwood developed a 'keenness' as they called it at Repton for him and spent most evenings with him tearing like bats out of hell through the dark forest-lined roads around Rouen on a Triumph motorbike which Stuart had bought out there.

Isherwood continued to write feverishly at Rouen—he mentions a 'spicy' play called 'One Man's God' and two stories, one a 'yarn for Homos' called 'The Wrong God':

It concerns a gent called Fryne—a real 'character', like Sherlock Holmes; the complete hunter of Boys, the subtle and patient Nimrod of London. Fryne meets a man who insists on taking him to see the films of Billy Brighteous, the Wonder Kid. The result is idolatry of the said Billy for six weeks, until Fryne's friend leaves for India; and Fryne, too late, discovers that he was keen on *him* all the time and enjoyed the films because of *his* presence. All this is set forth in 6000 words of sloppy flippancy.[22]

On his return to London he read the story aloud to Hector Wintle, which gave him enough insight into its true worth to end up throwing slippers at it. By way of compensation be began work in July on the first novel he was to complete, obtusely called *Lions and Shadows* (a quotation from C. E. Montague's *Fiery Particles*) simply because it sounded sufficiently mysterious. His appetite for films that summer remained voracious—he went, usually with Wintle, to at least six in just over two weeks that July, including *Intolerance* and *Doctor Mabuse*. During the first two weeks of August he went back to Repton at G. B. Smith's invitation to do library work.[23] An additional incentive was the fact that Upward might be there for the same reason during the second week. The two friends, however, were about to be more permanently reunited when Christopher went up to Corpus Christi College, Cambridge in October 1923.

5

Cambridge

Influenced by Upward's disenchanted reports of the history course at Cambridge, Isherwood had written the previous January to the college tutor of Corpus Christi, William Spens, asking to be transferred from the Historical to the English Tripos. As G. B. Smith had already forecast, he was refused. When Isherwood joined Upward in rooms above his at Corpus Christi in the Michaelmas term of 1923, his friend was already thoroughly disillusioned with the way history was presented at Cambridge—with what Upward calls 'its fact-grubbing passionlessness, its dull indifference to human suffering, its lack of love, generosity, beauty or poetry.'[1] Isherwood was fortunate enough to have for his history tutor Kenneth Pickthorn ('Mr Gorse' in *Lions and Shadows*), a veteran of the war still in his late twenties, who won the respect of both undergraduates despite the biting criticisms he levelled at each of them. Yet even Pickthorn was a poor public lecturer, while his colleagues completely failed to catch the imagination of either Isherwood or Upward. Upward knew that he had to get a degree if he was to find the kind of employment that would allow him time and energy enough to continue writing poetry. With Isherwood the compulsion was weaker, because there was the distinct prospect of an allowance from the Isherwood estate in the offing. Well before the end of his first term he had effectually abandoned his history studies for the social life of the university and the even more fascinating private world of Mortmere which he and Upward constructed between them during their two years together there.

In *Lions and Shadows* Isherwood recalls the way in which each of them exerted a subtle moral pressure on the other to abjure the company of rival friends. During his first year alone at Cambridge Upward had cultivated the acquaintance of a number of college 'hearties' whose addiction to games, girls, cars and cards constituted a half-hearted revolt against the university. Among them Isherwood mentions 'Black' (actually H. White), 'Sargent' (Christopher Orpen) and 'Queensbridge' (Geoffrey Kingsford) in *Lions and Shadows*; Upward disguises his original models more carefully in his composite character of 'Desmond' and 'Pearson' in *No Home But the Struggle*. Upward enjoyed his rowdy escapades with this gang during his first year, playing poker late into the night, taking town girls down 'fornication creek' under the nose of the Proctors (though Upward himself never got a girl to live up to the reputation of the place), and climbing back over the college walls in the early morning half-drunk. But when Isherwood arrived, his presence alone was enough to make Upward uncomfortably aware of his friends' lack of real interest in literature. Meanwhile Isherwood was being courted by that upper-class faction of undergraduates whom Upward had contemptuously dubbed 'the Poshocracy'. Like Upward with his group of 'hearties', Isherwood was unconsciously drawn to the poshocrats (after all, he theoretically qualified as one himself). Yet in Upward's company he felt shamed into making fun of them. It was a case of mutual jealousy. In *Lions and Shadows* the only two major quarrels he remembers having had with Upward were over his friendship with the poshocrats, and he admits that he might well have become a snob like them without Upward's vigilant eye and their invention of a corporate conscience which they personified as 'The Watcher in Spanish'. Ever alert, the Watcher ensured that both friends remained loyal to their rebellious faction of two, reminding them that they were still at secret war with the poshocracy, the history school, the college authorities, and in fact the entire institution.

It was at Repton, not Cambridge as Isherwood writes in *Lions and Shadows*, that they had first invented their own embodiment of the Enemy in the figure of Laily, who derived from the loathly worm of an early English ballad. Based on a caricature of a particularly serious-minded near-contemporary of theirs in the History Sixth, Laily quickly ceased to bear any resemblance to his original. Upward still has in his possession an introduction to their joint fantasies written by Isherwood around 1926 and called 'Mortmere: Introductory Dialogue'. In it Isherwood explains how originally Laily was conceived as 'the self-seeking scholarship-seeker', the book-worm whose name they used in their

letters to each other at school to represent the dull conformism of
the Enemy.[2] At Cambridge Laily became metamorphosed into a
comic history don with clod-boots, serge suit, pink flesh and
continual perspiration. In *No Home But the Struggle* Upward
points out how much of their satiric portrait of Laily relied for its
effect on public-school distinctions of dress that reeked of
snobbery, not to mention the schoolboy prejudice it betrayed
against physical disabilities of any kind. Upward portrayed
Laily in his unfinished poem, 'Tale of a Scholar'. Isherwood
matched his attack by a series of prose skits with titles like 'Letter
written to the Tutor of Corpus after a year's Historical Study' (in
which he purports to express his gratitude to his tutor for rescuing
him from the turbulence of life and literature and leaving him
becalmed in the haven of history), or 'Prefatory Epistle to my
Godson on the Study of History', which ironically recommends
the study of history for its rendering of 'the splendour and
solemnity of the Obvious'.[3]

Like the Enemy, their chosen literary allies also date back to
Repton days. But at Cambridge to Wilfred Owen and Baudelaire
they added Katherine Mansfield and Emily Brontë—a strange
amalgam, united possibly by their cult of strangeness and their
early deaths. Their practice of calling these ghostly allies by their
nicknames ('Wilfred', 'Kathy' and 'Emmy') they adopted from
Robert Nichols, a poet of the First World War who had read
some of his poems to the Repton Literary Society and habitually
referred to writers in this familiar way, calling Wordsworth
'Wordy' and so on.[4] Both young undergraduates entered the
battlefield of literature in what Isherwood has called 'a state of
raging cerebral excitement' only possible at that age.[5] Their
response to writers was extreme. Books would be burned or
ceremoniously thrown into the waste-bin. Writers of whom they
disapproved were nothing less than deadly enemies to society,
agents provocateurs despatched by the Enemy to destroy the world
of art. Yet at the same time, as the 'Introductory Dialogue'
wryly points out, the two rebels were leading an extraordinarily
secure existence at Cambridge: 'Even Wilfred Owen could not
wholly remind us that the tea-shops where we ate ourselves
miserable on the richest green cake were unlike dug-outs on the
Western Front.' Their literary tastes, it goes on, were at any rate
years behind the times: 'We endorsed every word of the *London*

Mercury's review of *The Waste Land*.' Similarly they treated all kinds of politics at the time with a mixture of contempt and indifference. Even Freud only made any impact on them in 1924, whereas Auden, for example, had been reading his works enthusiastically back at his public school.

Nevertheless, in dismissing the conventional values and benefits that Cambridge had to offer them, they created an amoral cosmos of the imagination in which they could explore their own individuality unimpeded by the traditional taboos of society. During their two years together at Cambridge they rapidly enlarged this world of fantasy, based on Upward's cult of the sinister, calling it first 'The Other Town', then 'Rat's Hostel' and finally 'Mortmere', each imaginary location becoming more remote from actuality than its predecessor. The Other Town was a night-time alternative to Cambridge located in the city itself, just as the Rat's Hostel originated in Garret Hostel Bridge in Cambridge. Within a year the Other Town had been removed to the edge of the Atlantic and renamed Mortmere, while the Rat's Hostel, according to the 'Introductory Dialogue', had become the Skull and Trumpet Inn at Mortmere owned by Sergeant Claptree where each night the drinkers turned into animals. 'Yes,' Isherwood adds, 'we had both read Beatrix Potter.'

From the beginning of their collaboration the two of them had assumed the pseudonyms of Edward Hynd and Christopher Starn, although the stories they wrote at first had nothing to do with Mortmere. Hynd and Starn began life as two pornographers who exchanged outrageous stories with each other. Isherwood and Upward would dash these stories off late at night in a state of great excitement and leave them on each other's tables to be discovered by the other in the morning. Upward explains in *No Home But the Struggle* that they chose to pose as pornographers not just in defiance of conventional morality but in order to expose 'the namby-pamby delicately indelicate pseudo-pornography— James Branch Cabell's *Jurgen* was an example of this—which was fashionable with some members of the poshocracy.' Upward goes on to summarise the plot of the first story he wrote in this genre, 'The Leviathan of the Urinals', in which a drunken young man is given syphilis by a fishlike monster which grows out of the urinal and touches him, much in the manner of the fisherman and the genie in the *Arabian Nights*.[6] The Hynd and Starn stories were a strange mixture of different influences—Beatrix Potter, Poe, Baudelaire, Conan Doyle, Lewis Carroll (Hector Wintle discerningly pointed out that debt to his friend), the *Arabian Nights*, Dürer, Sir Thomas Browne—the list is seemingly endless and reflects both writers' fascination with the surreal.

Soon the stories were flowing thick and fast. Frequently they were left unfinished once the original conception had been fleshed out sufficiently for the rest to be deduced. Two of the earliest stories to be finished were Upward's 'The Little Hotel' (a tale about necrophiles summarised in *Lions and Shadows*) and Isherwood's 'The Horror in the Tower' (a parody of the conventional detective story, summarised in *No Home But the Struggle*, in which the villain, a poshocrat, turns out to be a coprophagist). By 1924 they had already accumulated a formidable cast of characters in their stories many of whom also featured in the quite separate book on Mortmere they were planning simultaneously. Isherwood gives a brilliant description of the major characters in *Lions and Shadows* where he manages to make them actually more interesting than they are when one meets them in the stories that have survived in Upward's collection. Laily, who underwent two metamorphoses as Wrythe and then Mr Charles, is the archvillain and enemy of Mortmere. Its principal defender was Reynard Moxon, a successor to the Watcher in Spanish, with the appearance and habits of T. S. Eliot. He was originally invented to get their own back on Vernon Watkins ('Percival' in *Lions and Shadows* and 'Sugden' in *No Home But the Struggle*) for indiscreetly revealing their fantasy world to the mockery of an outsider. Other characters included Moxon's friend, Ronald Gunball, a drunken fisherman of the boasting variety who invarably remains imperturbed when faced with the impossible; the Rev Welken, the vicar of Mortmere who re-enacts his homosexual past while manufacturing angels in the belfry with the help of his beautiful choirboy, Boy Radnor (also lusted after by the curate, Harold Wrygrave); the local landowners, the Belmares (an obvious skit on the Poshocracy); Dr Mears, the village doctor with his own highly unorthodox views on medicine; Wherry, the architect responsible for the disaster recounted in Upward's 'The Railway Accident'; and a host of supporting characters.

The problem with the Mortmere material was that it remained necessarily private and inaccessible to a wider readership—

Upward recounts in *No Home But the Struggle* how one poshocrat, 'Cyril Ainger' (modelled on Charles Smythe, an ex-Repton history scholar), reacted with barely concealed disgust on the only occasion they showed one of their stories to an outsider.[7] By the time they left Cambridge the two friends were still planning to write Mortmere as a separate book which would incorporate these characters and which would be held together by the presence of the two fictitious narrators. As the 'Introductory Dialogue' explains: 'Hynd and Starn, the two pornographers, finding London too hot for them, come to Mortmere for quiet, and there meet with a series of adventures culminating in a disaster to the whole community.' Well after they had left Cambridge, both writers continued to produce stories offering different versions of the demise of Mortmere. Upward wrote 'The Convocation' in which Gunball, the original character, dies. The 'Introductory Dialogue' explains that since he had come 'to represent the whole Mortmere illusion . . . he would die. As Gunball sickened, so Mortmere would fade.' But it took a long time to fade. Isherwood wrote at least two more of these apocalyptic stories. In the first, 'Christmas in the Country', all the inhabitants of Mortmere perish in the village hall where the boiler is about to explode at the same time as the roof is due to collapse because of an error in its construction made by Wherry. In the other, 'The World War', Moxon turns traitor and demolishes the Rectory by bombarding it from an airship. The only published story in the canon, 'The Railway Accident', wasn't written by Upward until 1928. Isherwood was less held under its spell than Upward. This becomes clear when one reads in the 'Introductory Dialogue' (probably written in 1926) the clear-headed and detached manner in which he reviews their various attempts to reduce Mortmere to its prime factors of reality. All attempts were doomed to failure: 'There is nothing in our stories which could be used as a starting-point in sanity or objective reality,' he writes. 'There is always a further reservation in favour of strangeness. Every brick of Mortmere village is strange.'[8]

Apart from Mortmere, both authors were also producing work within their own chosen genre. Upward was trying to write a new positive kind of poetry; Isherwood was meantime engaged on his first full-length novel tentatively called *Lions and Shadows*.

Begun in July 1923, it was finished at the end of the Christmas holidays in January 1925. Concurrently Isherwood, like Upward, had been keeping a journal modelled on W. N. P. Barbellion's *Diary of a Disappointed Man*. A dedicated artist dying of an obscure disease, Barbellion spurred Isherwood (who was a hypochondriac for much of his life) into imagining himself equally afflicted, as illustrated in the amusing entries he reproduces from his journal of the time in the book he ultimately published as *Lions and Shadows*. The same obsession with ill-health obviously spilled over into his *bildungsroman* which describes how the hero, Leonard Merrows, grows up much in the same way as Isherwood had with one significant difference—he misses out on public school because his heart has been strained from a prolonged bout of rheumatic fever. This enabled Isherwood to re-write his own well-adjusted life at Repton in the image of Barbellion (not to mention 'Emmy', 'Kathy' and Baudelaire). Stylistically, however, as he confesses in *Lions and Shadows*, it was a pastiche of Hugh Walpole's *Jeremy* novels, Compton Mackenzie's *Sinister Street* and E. F. Benson's *David Blaize*—florid, 'literary' and extremely competent, to judge from the extracts he quotes in *Lions and Shadows*.[9]

From the perspective of the 1930s, Isherwood discerns lurking behind this early novel one of the myths that came to dominate his life and writings, that of 'the Test'. His detection of its presence involves a tortuous explanation. First the real Repton had to be transformed in his imagination into a battleground where individual heroism has a place. In *Lions and Shadows* he asserts that he achieved this by drawing on a day-dream he had been hiding from Upward's inevitable mockery in which he re-lived his schooldays at Repton in the heroic style, battling with immorality and finally winning through against all odds, thereby passing the Test. That Isherwood did make this imaginative conversion of his Repton schooldays at this time is confirmed by a story called 'The Hero' which he wrote shortly after he had finished the first draft of his novel and which was published by his old friend Patrick Monkhouse in *The Oxford Outlook* (an Oxford undergraduate literary review) for June 1925. The story is set in Rugtonstead, a literary version of Repton which incorporates all those opportunities for heroism and group accolade that Isherwood, especially under Upward's influence, had chosen ostensibly to ignore while he was there. Even more striking is the hero's failure to pass the test of heroism. He doesn't avoid it, like Leonard Merrows; he leaps into the river after a drowning friend to whom he is physically attracted only to panic and make for the shore. Nevertheless Isherwood ends the story with a double irony, as if to preserve himself from the criticism that he would invite by his otherwise overt acceptance of the public school games ethos. The hero becomes the toast of the school for his apparent bravery; this in turn loses him the friendship of the boy he tried to save. The Test is a private affair: the hero is the only one who knows he failed it, but he is also the only one to suffer for his failure. Isherwood actually wrote two stories for *The Oxford Outlook*, both tinged with homosexual romanticism. (No wonder Oxford undergraduates jokingly referred to it as 'The Yellow Fairy Book', or alternatively as 'Just So Stories'—'so' being slang for 'gay' in those days.) The other one called 'Two Brothers' Isherwood described to Upward at the time as 'a very "mortality" piece which I mistook for immortal, but now regard as tosh'.[10] Hardly surprisingly, he omitted both stories from *Exhumations*.

In *Lions and Shadows* his explanation of how his first novel reflects his own obsession with the Test at this time continues by suggesting that his hero's relief at not having had to face the Test offered by a glamorised version of public school reflects his own guilty feelings of relief at having avoided the Test which his immediate predecessors had had to face on the battlefields of the First World War. In *Lions and Shadows* he claims that the 'young writers of the middle twenties were all suffering, more or less subconsciously, from a feeling of shame that we hadn't been old enough to take part in the European war' (*LS* 74). Extraordinary as this might seem, it is a sentiment which Isherwood shared with many of his contemporaries. George Orwell, for example, told Richard Rees that his 'generation must be marked forever by the humiliation of not having taken part,'[11] and this communal sense of guilt is echoed by Cecil Day Lewis, John Lehmann, Michael Roberts and others.[12] It is obvious that Isherwood as an undergraduate had inherited from his two schools ideals of heroism (heavily illustrated by examples of self-sacrifice at the Front) that he and his schoolfellows had no chance of emulating (one had to die first to qualify). Nevertheless his writings at Cambridge suggest that the Test was confined to the games fields of his public school.

Only after he had met Auden did he manage to reconcile the concept of the Enemy with whom he and Upward were continually at war with his romanticised idea of the public school Test which he kept secret from Upward's inevitable derision. In some of Auden's earliest poetry mythic images of the War merge imperceptibly into images of school athletics, uniting his generation's guilt feelings at having escaped the Test of real war with its associated conviction that it never even passed the Test offered by public school. As for his first novel, as soon as he'd finished it, he knew it was no good, the usual kind of thing that a boy with a certain amount of talent burns out in order to get it out of his system. When he took it to his father's old novelist friend, Ethel Coburn Mayne (called 'Venus' in *Kathleen and Frank*) she confirmed his worst fears, telling him to put it away and start again. His next attempt, *Christopher Garland*, remained unfinished.

Isherwood's public life at Cambridge included joining the Film Club that was founded in 1924 by a new friend, Roger Burford ('Roger East' in *Lions and Shadows*) and helping to found a new literary society in 1925. Burford, who was additionally involved in making amateur films, was quickly attracted by Isherwood's instinct for play, his gift for dramatising the everyday and making it interesting with his powers of exaggeration.[13] In *Lions and Shadows* Isherwood also describes the fiasco of his short-lived career as a motor-cyclist who was terrified of his own machine (one of the brothers dies in a motor-cycling accident in 'Two Brothers'), and his escapades during the vacations with Hector Wintle who was reluctantly entering the long training required to become a doctor and with whom he would compare novels, discuss Mortmere, walk the streets, visit cinemas and the Wembley Exhibition and go roller-skating in Holland Park. In 1924 John Isherwood died, leaving Marple Hall to his Uncle Henry (no great friend of Kathleen's) and so ending the constant visits to Cheshire. The same year Kathleen's mother died. (After the funeral, Isherwood told Upward, the infatuated clergyman pursued him in a taxi.) More isolated than ever before, his mother inevitably concentrated more of her attention on her two sons just when Isherwood in particular needed a greater sense of freedom. That year he announced to his churchgoing mother that he was an atheist (*AV* 12).

The following year he delivered a far more shattering blow

to her ambition that he should become a don. Having done virtually no work of his own since he had miraculously obtained a Two One in the Mays examinations at the end of his first year, he decided that his only way out of the impasse was to end his career prematurely by answering his Tripos papers facetiously, which he proceeded to do. (By coincidence Vernon Watkins had simultaneously decided to leave Magdalene College, Cambridge, after only a year, unable to stand the pedagogic approach of his tutors in Modern Languages.)[14] Summoned back by telegram after the end of term, Isherwood was allowed to withdraw his name from the college books to avoid public expulsion. Fantasy had finally proved stronger than normality. Shortly after leaving Cambridge for good Isherwood wrote a long poem called 'The Recessional from Cambridge' in which he and Upward (who obtained a Second) leave their history tutor to his arid academic life in Cambridge while they travel through the night to the poetic life in Mortmere accompanied by its principal inhabitants:

> *Therefore, we leave you, snug in Cambridge town*
> *With your cigar, your glass of old dry sherry,*
> *Your smirking and plump-busted secretary,*
> *Curtly dictating with closed eyes and frown:*
> *'Dear Starn, the master has removed your name*
> *From the college books. Personally, I will not blame . . .'*[15]

6

London

Turning his back with relief on Cambridge, Isherwood temporarily evaded his family as well by taking a holiday at Freshwater Bay in the Isle of Wight in July 1925. A letter he wrote Upward at this time reveals his escapist mood of the moment. Refusing even to do any writing, he passed the time converting everyone at the Bay into characters from Mortmere:

> They are all here. I met Gunball strolling under the cliffs with a gun over his shoulder, a curious three-pronged spike projecting from the barrel. We embraced with tears. Moxon, Welken and Miss Dogbeer arrived in a crimson char-a-banc with oblong parcels. You should see Claptree's new hat.[1]

Back in London for August, he made a joint application with Roger Burford to work in films with both the Stoll Studios and George Pearson's smaller company. Although their efforts were initially unsuccessful, Pearson held out hope of work for the spring, which induced Isherwood to take a temporary job in the meantime. He continued to demonstrate his feelings of irresponsibility and defiance by blowing most of his savings on a second-hand Renault which was antiquated even for that time. It was through owning the Renault that Isherwood came to know the Mangeot family (called the 'Cheurets' in *Lions and Shadows*). Eric Falk had just returned from a holiday at Port Louis in Brittany. There he found himself staying in the same hotel as the Mangeots and was at once attracted by the younger son, Sylvain ('Edouard' in *Lions and Shadows*).[2] While at Port Louis Sylvain cut his knee to the bone in a bicycle accident. Back in London Eric Falk arranged wheelchair outings for his new twelve-year-old friend, commandeering Isherwood and his car to take them to Richmond Park. Afterwards Isherwood had tea with the whole family and before he had left the father, to his delight, had offered him a job as part-time secretary of his string quartet at one pound a week.

The family lived in a mews house in Cresswell Place, Chelsea, and consisted of André and Olive, both in their early forties, Fowke ('Jean') their eldest son aged fourteen, Sylvain, and Hilda ('Rose'), the cook. A gifted French violinist, André had settled in England early in the century and married his English wife, Olive, fifteen years before Isherwood met them.[3] The atmosphere of the household was the opposite to Isherwood's own—casual, friendly and chaotic. Olive's calm temperament balanced André's excitability, while in the background Hilda, a Rubenesque country woman from Hoxne, ran the household and kept everyone in their place. The large downstairs room served as an office and rehearsal room for the quartet. First called the Music Society String Quartet, then the International String Quartet, it consisted of André, first violin; Boris Pecker ('Kurella'), second violin; Harry Berly ('Tommy Braddock'), viola; and John Barbirolli ('Forno'), 'cellist.

Within two days Isherwood had begun work for André, attempting the impossible task of catching up with his correspondence and arranging future engagements. In *Lions and Shadows* Isherwood offers a glimpse of a typical concert tour in October 1925 with the quartet which was made even more hazardous than usual by their use of the ageing Renault. On their return Isherwood sold the car at a considerable loss. He remained secretary to the quartet for a year and a friend of Olive Mangeot, in particular, for life. He introduced his friends to the family which he treated as a much-preferred alternative to his own home. Fowke remembers numerous escapades which they shared with Isherwood and Auden, among them letting off fireworks from Auden's hat, escaping from a policeman in the fog, and breaking into the family home when they had left their keys behind and nearly being arrested for housebreaking.[4] The influence that the Mangeots' life-style had on him soon spilled over into his work. Almost a year after abandoning his earlier novel *Christopher Garland* he wrote six chapters of a new novel based on his vision of life with the Mangeots called *The Summer in the House*. In lighter vein he also wrote to order a series of nonsense poems to accompany a hand-made book of animals which Sylvain had painted and bound as a present for his parents. Called *People One*

Ought to Know[5] and dated January 1926, it contains humorous portraits of the Mangeots disguised as animals. André is portrayed as a football-playing horse, Olive as a snail whose rests are continually being disturbed by the telephone ('I never have a wink of slumber—/Somebody always gets my number'), Fowke as a seal dressed in a cricket blazer, Sylvain as (among others) a badger who is a fearful cadger, and Yvonne Arnaud, the patriotic actress and friend of the family alluded to in *Lions and Shadows* (*LS* 178) as a giraffe who 'was mascot/To a regiment quartered at Ascot'. Auden printed one of these, 'The Common Cormorant', in his anthology *The Poet's Tongue* in 1938, which is reprinted in *Exhumations*.

In *Lions and Shadows* Isherwood recalls how he fell possessively in love with the whole family and 'wanted . . . to be acknowledged by them as elder brother and son' (*LS* 153). Soon he was inventing reasons for staying on at Cresswell Place late into the evening even though he was only being paid to work mornings. The contrast between the warmth and liveliness of the Mangeot household and the cold respectability of his own home is reflected quite closely in the difference between Mary Scriven's chaotic house and Lily Vernon's pristine flat in *The Memorial*. Olive, in particular, came to represent for him everything that his own mother was not and before long he was treating her like an adopted mother and signing letters to her 'Ever your loving eldest'.[6]

Because Isherwood grew closer to his mother as they both mellowed in later life he has unconsciously modified his memories of how he felt about her during this earlier period. Apart from his aggressive portrayals of Mrs Lindsay and Lily Vernon (who are both modelled on his mother) in his first two novels, there is enough circumstantial evidence to conclude that his relations with her were at their worst during the years between his leaving Cambridge and settling in Germany. Upward remembers that her son's hostility to her reached a crescendo at this time. Everything she did enraged him. The more she worried about him and tried to organise things to make life easier for him, the more he felt she was interfering with his life.[7] Sylvain Mangeot has also recalled what a formidable woman Kathleen was in the late twenties and how claustrophobic her effect was on Isherwood, who would frequently be driven from the house in a fury by her indirect

criticisms and snide remarks so amiably slipped in.[8] There is an
unpublished poem of his from this period which appears to be
addressed to his mother in particular, part of which reads:

> *Marvelling, I might have learnt life fickle, thievish*
> *And naked as the scourge drawn on bare shoulders,*
> *Yet not have feared the knowledge.*
> *But you, with stupid love and your wan kindness*
> *Smeared the old wounds with lies.*[9]

It was this complex combination of love and hypocrisy in her that
confused and infuriated him so much at this time. Moreover the
situation was further complicated for him by his financial
dependence on her. Although he began receiving a small allowance from his Uncle Henry shortly after his twenty-first birthday,
this had to be supplemented by a further allowance from her.

His recoil from Kathleen took a number of different forms.
Apart from spending as much time at the Mangeots as possible, it
was around this date that he told her quite frankly that he was
homosexual. In *Christopher and his Kind* he writes of his first real
homosexual experience at Cambridge where he was seduced by
his more determined—or experienced—partner. But in the same
chapter he confesses that his choice of homosexuality was heavily
motivated by his need to rebel against the conventional majority
epitomised by his mother: 'She is silently brutishly willing me to
get married and breed grandchildren for her. Her Will is the will
of Nearly Everybody, and in their will is my death.' He goes on
wittily but revealingly to conclude: 'If boys didn't exist, I should
have to invent them' (*CK* 17). *Christopher and his Kind* leaves one
with the strong impression that Isherwood, more naturally a
bisexual at this time, was partly propelled into homosexuality by
his need to defy his mother (and not to retain her love by a
complex series of role changes, as Freudian orthodoxy would
have it). In *Kathleen and Frank* he has cast the part she played in
his life in the later twenties in a positively optimistic light; she
becomes 'the counter-force which gave him strength' (*KF* 361).
But at the time he could not foresee this and many of his actions
were determined by his need to fight away from her powerful
presence and beliefs.

Even his belated response to the General Strike in May 1926,
volunteering for work on a sewage farm (hardly a gesture his

family could boast about), constituted a complex protest against
the system represented by his mother ('my female relative' as he
distantly refers to her at this point in *Lions and Shadows*, p 179).
Not content with absenting himself from home from Mondays to
Saturdays, he also spent almost every Sunday of the last months in
1925 visiting Upward who was then living at his parents' home in
Romford, Essex, trying to lead the life of a dedicated artist. The
two friends continued to develop the Mortmere fantasies during
the year Isherwood was working for the Mangeots, inventing a
Mortmere Tarot pack (inspired by the Hanged Man in *The Waste
Land*) with titles like 'Wormhouse Gate' and 'The Rat Catcher';
amalgamating Hynd and Starn into a composite narrator, Hearn;
and creating an apocryphal Mortmere canon with elaborate
parallels between stories written or planned and different books
in the Bible.[10]

Simultaneously both of them continued with their own writing.
In 1926 Upward took a private tutoring job at Carbis Bay in
Cornwall. When Isherwood joined him there *en route* for an
Easter holiday in the Scilly Isles, he arrived with his incomplete
novel based on life with the Mangeots. He was saved from having
to continue with this latest pastiche of Henry James and Romer
Wilson by Upward's discovery of E. M. Forster's anti-heroic
approach to the modern novel. Having just read *Howards End*, he
announced that 'a tragic view of life . . . had ceased to be possible
during the period since the ending of the 1914 to 1918 war.'[11]
Life since the war could only be treated comically. 'The whole of
Forster's technique is based on the tea-table', he told an excited
Isherwood; 'instead of trying to screw all his scenes up to the
highest possible pitch, he tones them down until they sound like
mothers'-meeting gossip' (*LS* 173–4). In fact, Upward suggested,
Forster's tea-table technique involved a reversal of conventional
fictional stress; life's horrors and tragedies should be given *less*
emphasis than everyday trivialities. Forster was to remain the
most influential figure in Isherwood's literary life. When they
reached Hugh Town he began to discuss with Upward the outline
of his next neo-Forsterian novel set in the Scilly Isles and
provisionally called *Seascape with Figures*. From these early
excited talks was eventually to emerge Isherwood's first published
novel. By the time their week's holiday was over, the first chapter
was already under way.

In December 1925 a mutual friend brought Wystan Auden to tea. The two had not met since Isherwood left St Edmund's and soon found common ground recalling the more ludicrous aspects of their prep school. Eighteen years old, Auden had just finished his first term at Christ Church, Oxford, and gave Isherwood the impression that he had not quite decided whether to strike the pose of an undergraduate aesthete or of the unkempt bohemian he naturally was. Spender recalls him as he was at Oxford with his 'almost albino hair and weakly pigmented eyes set closely together',[12] his preference for darkened rooms even when the sun was shining and his utter self-confidence verging on arrogance. Isherwood adds his own mildly caricatured portrait of Auden's short-sighted boyish scowl, his ink- and nicotine-stained stumpy fingers, his disrespect of Isherwood's obsessive neatness, scattering ash and opened books all around him. But one innovation in Auden involuntarily drew these two acquaintances into a much closer relationship. To Isherwood's surprise he had become a poet. Still curiously imitative, his poetry was nevertheless extremely competent and immediately won Isherwood's respect.

During the summer vacation of 1926 Auden joined Isherwood on holiday at Freshwater Bay in the Isle of Wight. Arriving in a foppish black felt hat that, to his delight, drew attention to him wherever they went, he announced his conversion to a poetry of 'austerity' under the influence of Eliot whom he had recently discovered. Isherwood's response was to write 'Souvenir des Vacances', a parody of Eliot at his most obscure, which Auden, not in the least put out, proceeded to publish in *Oxford Poetry 1927* which he edited with Cecil Day Lewis. When he cast his friend in the role of literary elder brother, Isherwood felt flattered and showered him with advice. Nevertheless one needs to treat with a great deal of caution Isherwood's much-quoted assertion in *Lions and Shadows* that Auden's celebrated obscurity was due to his habit, bred of laziness, of scrapping whole poems except for Isherwood's favourite line in each—'until a poem had been evolved which was a little anthology of my favourite lines, strung together without even an attempt to make connected sense' (*LS* 191).

Spender has written that 'Auden's life was devoted to an intellectual effort to analyse, explain and dominate his circumstances.'[13] By comparison Isherwood's was a far more intuitive intelligence which Auden recognised at once and valued because intuition was what he knew he lacked. According to Spender, it was Auden's policy arbitrarily to cast his friends into particular roles. He chose to make 'that severe Christopher'[14] the principal critic of his early poetry, but he never for a moment believed himself to be less than his equal. In fact he once told Spender that he invariably ranked people in order of their cleverness and added, looking very coy, 'I've always known that I was brighter than anyone else.'[15]

In the poem Auden wrote later to Isherwood on his thirty-first birthday he recollects how on this holiday in 1926:

> *Our hopes were set still on the spies' career,*
> *Prizing the glasses and the old felt hat,*
> *And all the secrets we discovered were*
> *Extraordinary and false.*[16]

He is referring to their extension of the Myth of War to link up Auden's love of Icelandic sagas with their joint memories of prep school and Isherwood's and Upward's Mortmere fantasy (Isherwood had introduced Auden to Upward earlier that year at a Soho restaurant).[17] The effect Mortmere had on Auden was probably greater than that which the saga material had on Isherwood, and when Auden sent Upward his *Poems 1930* he wrote: 'I shall never know how much in these poems is filched from you via Christopher.'[18] Nevertheless the idea of embodying the Test in a school context which is imbued with the mythic qualities of the Icelandic sagas did spur Isherwood into writing 'Gems of Belgian Architecture' the following year. Its mode of fictional realism however prevents this early story from achieving that air of mystery and archetypal significance that still makes Auden's charade 'Paid on Both Sides' fascinating reading today.

In *Lions and Shadows* Isherwood is not quite accurate when he asserts that Auden left him in such emotional turmoil that he could not bear to see anyone, even Upward (*LS* 195). In fact he went on holiday to France the following month with Upward. However Auden's uninhibited attitude to sex had had its effect as he eventually abandoned Upward at Bourg-Saint-Maurice in pursuit of a boy he had met on the train.[19] Back in London Isherwood became more restless than ever. The claustrophobic effect of living at home made him indulge in a series of dramatic gestures: running away to Wales, buying a revolver and threatening suicide (like Graham Greene and Evelyn Waugh), taking a tutoring job in St John's Wood to acquire more financial independence and finally moving out of the family home altogether in September 1926. He wrote to Roger Burford, who had recently met an artist called Stella Wilkinson ('Polly' in *Lions and Shadows*) and departed with her for Milan: 'By the time you return I shall have gone mad. I am leaving home, a pauper with incipient St Vitus' dance, sans hope, sans virtue, sans a Cambridge degree', and ending up 'everything here is vile, vile, *vile*, vile, vile, VILE, *VILE*.'[20] Burford bequeathed Isherwood his rooms at 26 Redcliffe Road, Chelsea, including Mrs Clarke ('Mrs Partridge' in *Lions and Shadows*), its permanently debt-ridden landlady.

The autumn he moved into Burford's flat he had finished *Seascape with Figures* and taken it to Ethel Coburn Mayne for her verdict. When she had approved it he had sent it to two publishers both of whom had rejected it. Discouraged, he put it aside and spent his first six months of 1927 in Burford's old room planning an ambitious new novel to be called *The North-West Passage*. Like other large-scale projects for novels he was to dream up during the following decade, this Balzacian conception was destined to remain unrealised. But the myth underlying its elaborate plot was to become a dominant motif in his early works. It was concerned with the neurosis which is implicit in a concept of heroism that constantly needs to be tested. The Truly Strong Man doesn't need to prove his heroism; but the Truly Weak Man spends his life seeking out the Test:

> The Truly Strong Man travels straight across the broad America of normal life, taking always the direct, reasonable route. But 'America' is just what the truly weak man, the neurotic hero, dreads. And so, with immense daring, with an infinitely greater expenditure of nervous energy, money, time, physical and mental resources, he prefers to attempt the huge northern circuit, the laborious, terrible north-west passage, avoiding life; and his end, if he does not turn back, is to be lost for ever in the blizzard and the ice. (*LS* 207–8)

This new myth is of central importance to much of Isherwood's

work. Philip Lindsay in *All the Conspirators* and Edward Blake in
The Memorial are both examples of the Truly Weak Man who fails
the Test. Similarly *Goodbye to Berlin* and *Down There on a Visit* are
littered with neurotic heroes lost on the huge northern circuit.
Auden was obviously much attracted to Isherwood's new conception of modern heroism, as it fitted into his own private
iconography. One of his earliest 'Shorts' is a thumb-nail sketch of
the Truly Weak Man:

> *Pick a quarrel, go to war,*
> *Leave the hero in the bar;*
> *Hunt the lion, climb the peak:*
> *No one guesses you are weak.*[21]

In the second of their later collaborations the two writers were to
construct an entire play around this idea of the neurotic hero who
conceals his weakness from the world by killing himself in his
attempt to scale F6. A. L. Tolley has suggested that these concepts of the Test and of the Truly Strong and Weak Man are
surprisingly fascist preoccupations.[22] This probably derives from
the fascist ethos of their public schools, whose division into
'hearties' and 'aesthetes' is unconsciously paralleled in Isherwood's more complex division into the Truly Strong and the
Truly Weak. His own mildly neurotic state at this time induced
him to empathise with his truly weak modern heroes and probably
blinded him to the essentially fascist nature of the Test which they
all inevitably failed.

At first it seems that Isherwood's move out of the family home
helped to liberate him from some of his inhibitions. He began going to bed with Auden, for example, during this period, although
he soon found Auden too much like himself to provide the sexual
frisson which only his opposite in type could give him. 'The love
remains,' he has since explained, 'but it's a love without tension,
a different kind of love.'[23] During the summer of 1927 at Freshwater Bay possibly under the same impulse he started learning
German and rewrote *Seascape* in its final form, although the final
title, *All the Conspirators*, was only concocted towards the end of
the year with Upward's help. Nevertheless, like Philip Lindsay's
attempts to escape from Bellingham Gardens, Isherwood's break
from home didn't survive beyond the late summer. Just as Philip
was too fond of his home comforts to sacrifice them easily, so

Isherwood found life at Burford's old lodging house too anarchic in the long run.

But once he was back at home in the autumn of 1927 the old syndrome returned and he was soon ricocheting off in all directions. An example is his wild, drunken car trip almost to Cape Wrath on the north coast of Scotland with a friend he met through the Mangeots, Bill de Lichtenberg ('Bill Scott' in *Lions and Shadows*). An artist some eleven years older than Isherwood, he was trying to decide whether to marry a girl 'cellist called Ruth, which he did the following August.[24] This escapade is ironically echoed in Auden's early poem 'Missing', where he insists that genuine revolutionaries 'must migrate: 'Leave for Cape Wrath tonight'.'[25] Isherwood was not yet ready to migrate. Instead he announced his intention to enter medical school. The idea had been planted in his head by someone he had met at the Bay that summer called Mander ('Lester' in *Lions and Shadows*), and, despite Hector Wintle's discouragement, Isherwood allowed his romantic fantasies of a doctor's life to carry him away. His mother quickly saw to it that he was enrolled at King's College Medical School for the next course starting in October 1928.

During the intervening months Isherwood did part-time private tutoring jobs (which he obtained from 'Rabitarse and String' as he nicknamed the scholastic agency, Gabbitas and Thring), and, as he confesses in *Lions and Shadows*, prayed for a miracle to save him from the reality of a second undergraduate career. He saw much of Upward at this time, introducing him to Olive Mangeot and assisting him in his search for relief from his pent-up sexual urges.[26] They were together again at Freshwater Bay when *All the Conspirators* was finally published by Jonathan Cape (on Edward Garnett's advice) in May 1928.[27] Isherwood has confessed that he was so excited by the arrival of the advance copies that whenever Upward was out of the room he would furtively peep at his name on the title pages. In the event the novel received a sprinkling of varied notices and sold less than three hundred copies (*LS* 273–5). By this time Upward had written his last Mortmere story, 'The Railway Accident', and both friends were developing other modish writing techniques like the automatic writing Isherwood gives examples of in *Lions and Shadows*. Hector Wintle, still a seemingly interminable medical student, visited them for a weekend. Once again he was in love, and Isherwood and Upward both teased him unmercifully and tried to fix him up with a local girl as consolation prize. This incident is the basis for the prose extract he omitted from *Lions and Shadows* called 'An Evening at the Bay' (which was published in *New Country* and *Exhumations*), although the outcome was less satisfactory for Wintle than the story suggests.

In late May, Isherwood's continuing mood of escapism prompted him to accept an invitation from an elderly cousin of his called Basil Fry who had invited him to visit him in Bremen where he was British consul. The incident is reflected in the first episode of *Down There on a Visit*, where Fry is called 'Mr Lancaster', although Fry didn't commit suicide and the episode with the 'braut' was pure invention. One can judge how much of the rest of the 'Mr Lancaster' episode is based on fact by comparing it to part of a letter he wrote Upward from Bremen:

> . . . the tramp steamer had a Chinese cook and a Welsh cabin boy. Its captain appeared drunk on the bridge as soon as we entered the Weser. His barely credible insults to important German officials on the quay. 'Now then, Tirpitz—show a leg.' They merely smiled . . .
>
> Proust, also, would have rewritten a volume if he'd attended the consular dinner. The ices had coloured lights inside them. There is a kind of brandy liqueur which you drink out of a beer mug. It makes you speak French better than English. My cousin is a prig, a fool and a neuter. Hatefully tall. His Oxford titter.[28]

Signed jocularly 'Marco Polo', the letter reveals an adolescent yearning 'never to remain more than a week in any country'. But if he was hoping for a miracle there it never happened and his first visit to Germany had none of the symbolic importance he attaches to his first stay in Berlin the following year. Nevertheless he did note gleefully in the same letter how 'the whole town is full of boys'—a promise of things to come.

That summer Auden introduced Isherwood to Stephen Spender with whom he was to form a life-long friendship. He portrays Spender '(Stephen Savage')' at this time as 'an immensely tall, shambling boy of nineteen, with a great scarlet poppy-face, wild frizzy hair, and eyes the violent colour of bluebells' (*LS* 281). Spender, with similar artist's licence, recollects Isherwood as he was in 1928, seated beside Auden in his traditionally darkened room, giggling and looking 'like a schoolboy playing charades'.[29] What attracted Spender to Isherwood was his 'peculiarity of being attractively disgusted and amiably bitter',[30] a feature which he had partly inherited from Upward. Within a year of their first meeting Spender had, according to Isherwood, 'decided that I was the healer who was going to lead him out of his puritan captivity'[31] and unquestioningly accepted his advice to put the manuscript of his first novel (which he had sent him) to one side for a year.[32]

In October 1928 Isherwood entered King's College full of misgivings. The two terms he spent there were a repetition of his experience of Cambridge. Bored and mystified by the lectures, he soon took to his old habit of cribbing from a fellow-student's work. His account of this period in *Lions and Shadows*, however, lays responsibility for his failure as a medical student firmly on himself. The entire episode represents his last fling at making a success of life in his mother's understanding of the term, and even then he had only persuaded himself to submit to it by fantasising madly about leading the life of a police surgeon or becoming a second Chekhov. His true energies were meanwhile being poured into writing the rough draft of his second novel which explored the origins of his generation's obsession with War and the Test. Even in this respect he was simply repeating the pattern of his years at Cambridge. Conceived well before, and not during his sailing trip on the Weser with his consular cousin in the late spring of 1928 as he suggests in 'Mr Lancaster', the first draft of *The Memorial* was completed by December 1928 as stated in *Lions and Shadows*.[33]

By the Christmas holidays a combination of factors forced him to face the impossibility of ever completing his medical studies. His poor examination results and his success in getting on with the draft of a new novel both indicated where his genuine interest lay. All that was needed was for him to give conscious recognition to the unconscious choice he had already made. The impetus came with the return of Auden from Berlin full of the psychoanalytical theories of Homer Lane which he had acquired at first hand from a follower of Lane's called John Layard ('Barnard' in *Lions and Shadows*). In a sense Layard had only revived for Auden the psychosomatic teachings he had already adopted at Oxford from

Freud and Groddeck. The letter from Layard to Auden which Isherwood quotes in *Christopher and his Kind* gives some idea of the tremendous sense of liberation that Isherwood must have experienced on first hearing about Layard's ideas. To link up the Devil with reasonable behaviour (and its consequences—disease) while associating God with unreasonable, often anti-social impulses (leading to health) was precisely the message Isherwood wanted to hear. And where better to put the new uninhibited life into practice than Berlin with Auden, Layard, its boy-bars, and its reputation for homosexual promiscuity. How better to repudiate his mother than to emigrate to the capital of the country which had deprived her of her husband and her happiness?

Before the end of the holiday Isherwood had broken the news of his decision to leave King's to his mother. Having paid a year's fees on his behalf, she persuaded him to compromise by staying on for one more term. But his mind was made up and he did even less work during the spring term of 1929 than during his first term. Concealing his real motives from the college authorities, he excused his sudden departure on the extraordinarily inappropriate grounds that he was getting married. Armed with almost £50 from a recently discovered War Loan certificate, Isherwood left for Berlin on 14 March 1929.

All the Conspirators

Although Isherwood's first published novel reads like one, it is none the less extraordinarily competent considering that he began it when he was twenty-one and finished it at twenty-three. In fact some of its features originated even earlier in those rambling teenage *bildungsromans* which he describes with such humour in *Lions and Shadows*. The hero of his first full-length novel, also called *Lions and Shadows* and written between the ages of eighteen and twenty, suffered from rheumatic fever and consequently missed going to public school, like Philip Lindsay in *All the Conspirators*. Both heroes also console themselves by reflecting how much more comfortable it is at home. The hero of Isherwood's next unfinished novel, *Christopher Garland*, is an artist like Philip, who also treats art as a neurotic alternative to life. *All the Conspirators* itself is the product of two writings, the earlier version being a much closer approximation to Upward's idea of depicting real domestic tragedies but stripping them of any suggestion of grandeur. However, in the process of rewriting it, Isherwood eliminated both the major tragic actions, cutting out the girl who dies from a rock-fall in the earlier section and 'tea-tabling' Allen's murder of Victor Page at the end by reducing it to an inconclusive tussle. Although he claims in *Lions and Shadows* that he finished the revised novel in July of 1927, the last page of the manuscript, which he gave to Roger Burford as a wedding present, is dated Armistice Day (i.e. 11 November) 1927.[1]

In describing his first unpublished novel, Isherwood writes of his 'fatal facility for pastiche' (*LS* 79) and this imitative streak is still present in *All the Conspirators*. Only the models have altered: in place of E. F. Benson and Compton Mackenzie he detects, in his Preface for the 1957 edition, echoes of Forster, Virginia Woolf and Joyce. The influence of Virginia Woolf is the least obvious of the three, although Isherwood's use of stream of consciousness owes as much to her way of rendering a character's inner throught-stream as to Joyce's. In his Preface he particularly criticises his more obvious imitation of Joyce's style because of its obtrusive nature. He has subsequently explained that from *The Memorial* onwards he has always subscribed to the idea that 'style is like the perfect suit of clothes: you hardly know whether you've got it on or not.'[2] *All the Conspirators* is a determined attempt to be *avant-garde*, to compete with the leading Modernists of the day in its technique and its consequent obscurity. The concept of the novel as a contraption with elaborate rules of its own derives from a young man's excited but deluded interpretations of the way Joyce worked. As the *TLS* review put it, 'Mr Isherwood has collected various parts of a machine, but he has not succeeded in putting them together.'[3] Less consciously, perhaps, Isherwood was also writing his own anti-heroic *Portrait of the Artist as a Young Man* in which a pseudo-artist fails to elude the nets of family and class and is outmanœuvred by his mother's superior use of the modern artist's defences, silence and cunning.

Forster's influence is far more profound, as Isherwood has been the first to admit. Above all Forster's informality of approach struck him at the time with the force of a revolution: 'One of the most revolutionary sentences to a working novelist', Isherwood has explained, 'was "One may as well begin with Helen's letters to her sister", the way *Howards End* begins. This was dynamite; it was much more [so] than the first time we wrote "fuck".'[4] *All the Conspirators* dutifully opens with a relatively trivial exchange about the direction of the wind; but this cultivation of extreme informality is carried even further in *The Memorial* which opens in mid-sentence (' "No, not really," Mary was saying.'). This in turn is responsible for *All the Conspirators'* curious combination of violence and bathos. It is, as Cyril Connolly wittily remarked, 'a novel . . . of atrocities witnessed at tea in the drawing room, or over Sunday night supper.'[5] The use of understatement determines the tone and nature of Isherwood's first novel. Forster's 'tea-tabling' meant more than a mere device to him. It profoundly affected his moral vision. By deliberately underplaying scenes and events in *All the Conspirators* which the traditional Edwardian novel would have treated as most significant, Isherwood was able subtly to undermine conventional moral values even while the narrative was ostensibly tracing their triumph over a younger generation's unsuccessful revolt.

K. W. Gransden has pointed out how *All the Conspirators* belongs to a genre which includes Forster's *The Longest Journey*, Maugham's *Of Human Bondage* and Butler's *The Way of All Flesh*. Just as Forster's Rickie Elliot is foreshadowed by Butler's Ernest Pontifex, so Philip Lindsay is a successor to both anti-heroes. They are all victims of the wills of others and assert their own wills only when it no longer matters. Gransden also suggests Isherwood's indebtedness for his portrayal of Mrs Lindsay to Forster's Mrs Failing in *The Longest Journey* and to Mrs Hamilton in *Where Angels Fear to Tread*.[6] Isherwood himself admits that Victor is largely modelled on Henry Wilcox of *Howards End* (*LS* 175). Even the jerky narrative sequence, the use of time jumps and flashbacks, and the omission of major scenes (like Mrs Lindsay's ugly outburst offstage near the end) are over-eager applications of Forster's methods, according to Isherwood.

Yet *All the Conspirators* is more than merely a clever pastiche of modernist influences. Many of the characters originate in some of the principal figures in his own life. Philip is partly based on Hector Wintle (who had rheumatic fever as a child and whose home in Ladbroke Gardens is used for Bellingham Gardens), but owes far more of his inner nature to Isherwood himself. Similarly Mrs Lindsay looks like Wintle's mother but acts like his own mother (Isherwood has called it a hostile view of Kathleen). Allen Chalmers is of course based on Upward, although the constant friction between Allen and Philip is not so much a reflection of the two friends' relations at this time as a dramatic necessity, a means of forcing Philip to befriend Victor, a poshocrat he would otherwise have disliked.[7] It is above all the undeclared warfare between mother and son, between an older and a younger generation that infuses the novel with a curiously claustrophobic and overpowering feeling of genuine passion. This surcharge of emotion without any apparent objective correlative is partly the result of 'tea-tabling' the genuinely tragic moments; yet it is even more the product of Isherwood's own complex emotional feelings towards his mother which can only be given concealed expression. As he wrote in the American Preface of 1958, the author himself 'makes not the smallest pretence of impartiality. His battle cry is "My Generation—right or wrong!" ' (*E* 92).

All the Conspirators, whatever its literary failings, does offer a key to the attitudes of the intellectual younger generation of the 1920s. Its assumptions are virtually identical to those underlying Auden's earliest poetry. The enemy is the same for both writers, epitomised by the Loathly Lady of myth and saga. Auden's concluding moral in the final chorus of *Paid on Both Sides* (published the same year as Isherwood's first novel) is equally applicable to *All the Conspirators*: 'Though he believe it, no man is strong . . . he is defeated. . . . His mother and her mother won.'[8] Much of the imagery is also common to both writers—the guerilla warfare that is being waged between young and old; the concept principally derived from Groddeck of psychologically determined illness (consider, for instance, Allen's 'Boredom belongs to the group of cancerous diseases', p 26); the symbolic use of islands to represent the isolation of the self (Philip in the Scilly Isles is like Auden's 'castaways on islands', who dream away their lives instead of 'rebuilding our cities').[9] In *All the Conspirators* this 1920s myth is still in embryo, the private property of the Auden group, still veiled in obscurity, private jokes and personal references. Yet its partial concealment is the source of much of the emotional power emanating from these early works of not just Auden and Isherwood but of Upward (in 'The Railway Accident') and C. Day Lewis (in *Transitional Poem*). When one also remembers the half-buried literary borrowings and the heavily camouflaged presence of Isherwood's own domestic drama, the title of his first book is not as inappropriate as he claims in *Lions and Shadows*.

All the Conspirators is, for its time, a subtle exploration of various forms of sickness and health. The 'Old Gang' understand this dichotomy in purely physical terms. To his mother Philip is delicate and prone to get ill more easily than most, and to Mr Langbridge, the family friend, the way to cure his office blues is through physical exercise. Simultaneously it quickly becomes apparent that the older generation uses physical exercise to conceal from itself a deeper malaise of the psyche. Victor has quite transparently inherited his attitude from his uncle. 'You know,' he confides to Philip, 'if I don't have heaps of fresh air and exercise, I get most frightfully morbid (p 35). Yet for all his use of his uncle's dumb-bells and his sleeping on the floor he is obviously maimed emotionally, cut off from his feelings by his family and his school. In particular his capacity for sexual love has been stunted by, it is suggested, the public exposure at school of his homosexual feelings for another boy. Having thoroughly repressed his feelings at the time in accordance with the ethos of his elders, he is left sexually crippled, asphyxiated by his first really passionate kiss, looking to marriage for 'the jolly outdoor sort of friendship of a pair of boys' (p 184), and destined to end up like his perverted uncle who gets his sexual thrills photographing mating puffins. By conforming to the codes of his society Victor provides an indication of the nature of that society's illness. He and it are suffering from a repression so fundamental that their life has become one gigantic lie. As Isherwood explains in his American Preface, what particularly angered him and his contemporaries was that 'a Freudian revolution had taken place of which they [Victor and the older generation] were trying to remain unaware' (E 92).

Mrs Lindsay is the principal member of the reactionaries and she ostensibly adopts a pre-Freudian attitude to Philip's poor health. Yet it becomes clear as the novel progresses that at a less conscious level she is herself responsible for his ill-health, both physical and psychological. Although she tells him how anxious she is to see him 'safely launched . . . before anything happens' to her (p 79), and believes it, the demon mother below the surface has spent a lifetime plotting the exact reverse. Beneath her hypocritical protestations lies a deep desire to prolong Philip's dependence on her indefinitely. Wanting him to remain her child for life, she actively encourages his more puerile urges. She admires Victor ostensibly because he is 'splendidly sane', but less consciously because he is himself an arrested adolescent. So whenever Philip shows signs of asserting his independence as an adult, his mother instinctually engineers a breakdown in his health, after which he reverts to his acceptably childish behaviour.

This pattern is repeated twice in the course of the novel. On the first occasion, after his return from the Scilly Isles, she operates what Philip calls a 'blockade' (p 73) which quickly reduces him to a neurotically-induced state of ill-health. His capitulation produces the first sign of real passion on her part and a psychosomatic bilious attack on his:

His weakness moved her. She emitted a primitive, glabrous sound as they embraced.

'My darling boy.'

As soon as possible, Philip went up to his bedroom and lay down. Ten minutes later, he was vomiting. (p 80)

Philip's second attempt at rebellion is a more complex affair. He accepts the post in Equatorial Africa not in order to escape his family but in order to punish his mother for forcing him back to his hated office job in the City. Allen shrewdly points out to him how his motive for going to such an unsuitable climate is similar to his own childish motives when, as a boy of seven, he hoped that his castor oil would kill him in order to punish his Nannie. Philip, in other words, is not even rebelling against his childish enslavement. Rather he is the Truly Weak Man for whom Africa constitutes the North-West Passage which he dare not attempt. When his mother calls his bluff and fails to stop his going, he runs away from home and the prospect of Africa in a panic. This poses a real threat to Mrs Lindsay who significantly loses her temper (offstage) and is forced to take to her bed for the only time in the novel. But Philip soon proves the weaker. After being reminded by an unemployed ex-serviceman he meets of the ultimate Test of War he and his generation have evaded, he catches rheumatic fever, precisely the same illness which helped him escape the worst moments of his life at prep school. In fact he reverts to the age he was at prep school on his return home. 'It was so necessary to keep him constantly amused', Mrs Lindsay explains to Victor. 'He mustn't be put out or crossed in the least thing' (p 243). Mrs Lindsay has also become years younger, radiant, confidently gay. Like the old men who (according to the 1920s myth) sent their sons off to die in the War to prolong their positions of power, she has unknowingly sacrificed her son to preserve her own *raison d'être* as a mother and head of the family.

Perhaps the sanest character in the book is Allen who is significantly training to become a doctor. With his ironic detachment, he is the only person who really understands Philip's neurotic behaviour and motivation. Isherwood uses Allen's medical knowledge to state authoritatively that Philip can enjoy normal health if he wants to. All that is needed is for him to stop believing his mother who has convinced him that he is an invalid. Yet although Allen comes closest of the characters to voicing his author's opinions, he is himself suffering from a disease of the psyche which afflicts all the younger characters in the book, including Joan. When we first meet him he is experiencing boredom so acutely that it makes him feel physically sick (p 15). Boredom also drives him to drink, and only when he is drunk is he able satisfactorily to express his antagonistic feelings towards Victor and the adult world whose values he parrots so accurately. Allen is in fact suffering from a similar though less acute case of sexual repression to Victor's. He is out of touch with his feelings; his 'callousness is diseased' (p 89). Ultimately he fails himself and Joan. When Philip, in the concluding lines of the book, has the nerve to accuse Allen of refusing to venture into life, the irony is double-edged because the accusation is not without truth even though it is truer of the accuser than of the accused.

All the major characters in the novel, then, are infected by the cancer of a pre-war ethos. However, one is left in no doubt about the author's opinions. Isherwood controls his reader's reactions by a skilful use of irony. Walter Allen has called *All the Conspirators* 'a montage novel' in which the irony emerges from the frequent and sometimes shocking juxtaposition of scenes and images[10]—Joan, on the eve of Victor's arrival, driven out of the chaste atmosphere of her room for a walk by the piercing cries of mating cats (p 156), Philip's dream of his paralysis in a train in the midst of his supposed flight from home (p 215), or Philip's and Victor's flashbacks to the formative moments of their schooldays.

All the Conspirators is constructed like a collage in which the author shares with his readers insights unobtainable to the characters. What all the characters lack is self-knowledge, and an awareness of the unconscious operations of the psyche is what Isherwood offers any reader acute enough (he implies) to penetrate the modernist obscurity of his ironical juxtapositions. Despite his employment of what he has called its 'secret language', despite its obvious echoes of Joyce and Forster, its obtrusive technique and its tendency towards caricature, Isherwood's first novel has a strange power of its own. Behind the author's ironic detachment simmers a personal emotional involvement and a militant partiality of viewpoint which transfuses it with an unintended autobiographical interest, an interest which is only openly admitted into his fiction towards the end of the next decade.

Berlin

By the end of the 1930s Isherwood's name had become in-dissolubly linked with Berlin in the public imagination. His two best-selling Berlin books set during the final years of the Weimar Republic were, of course, primarily responsible for this associa-tion; but the myth of Isherwood, the beleaguered reporter, warn-ing a deaf world of the dangers of Nazi-ism was reinforced by Auden, Spender and other friends in his circle. Take, for example, Auden's melodramatic portrayal of him in *The Orators*:

> *And in cold Europe, in the middle of Autumn destruction,*
> *Christopher stood, his face grown lined with wincing*
> *In front of ignorance—'Tell the English,' he shivered,*
> *'Man is a spirit.'*[1]

Whether Auden was wholly serious or not, the image stuck.

Because Isherwood, however, had pressing personal reasons for abandoning England for Berlin, he has tended to over-react against this myth in his autobiography of the 1930s, *Christopher and his Kind*, and stress that for him 'Berlin meant Boys' (*CK* 10). Berlin certainly offered him a society in which homosexuality of all kinds was more publicly accepted than probably anywhere else in Europe at the time. But his need to explore a new persona in a new language was not just sexually motivated. In fact he has admitted to more than one interviewer that his dramatic plunge into what looked like the depths of depravity turned out in the long run to have been an extremely prudent move after all. As Auden once remarked to him, he always knew when to clear out.[2]

The Berlin in which he found himself in 1929 was in an economic and political turmoil which was to be exacerbated in October when Stresemann, the strong moderate Chancellor, died and the Wall Street Crash precipitated the Germans into a polarisation of political parties. The Communists and the Nazis gradually emerged as the only hopeful alternatives to a humiliated and impoverished population. For the four years Isherwood was in Berlin the issue hung in the balance. Both parties had private armies and frequently took to the streets in their battle for power. 'In Berlin', Claud Cockburn wrote of this period, 'you felt that the deluge was always just round the corner.'[3] Isherwood was obviously as much stimulated by the atmosphere of permanent crisis as he was by the boy-bars and one therefore needs to treat *Christopher and his Kind* with caution, as perhaps over-compensating for his earlier excessive discretion about his personal and sexual life in the Berlin books.

On his arrival Isherwood was met by the twenty-two-year-old Auden (he was spending a year there before starting a teaching career) who introduced him to his new friend, the anthropologist, John Layard. They visited the Hirschfield Museum and the Cosy Corner in Zossenerstrasse, Auden's favourite boy-bar. These notorious *Nachtlokals* were at first sight just 'very cosy' according to Isherwood, 'like parlours where everyone came to relax around a nice warm stove'.[4] But for the initiate from puritanical England the overt manner in which the boys offered themselves for sale (prospective purchases could be visually inspected in the lavatory and handled through cut-off pockets at the tables[5]) was a revelation. There Isherwood met Berthold Szczesny, who was called 'Bubi' (Baby) by everyone. Like many of the unemployed bar-boys, he was a heterosexual willing to practise homosexuality for the money. Isherwood instantly projected all his upper-middle-class homosexual fantasies on to this beautiful young Czech boy from the working class with whom he could barely communicate at all except in bed, and he spent much of his time as a tourist in his company, quarrelling with him out of jealousy on more than one occasion and paying for him wherever they went.

John Layard did not unduly impress him during his first brief visit to Berlin. This was hardly surprising as Layard was in a state of morbid depression, ostensibly at Auden's failure to reciprocate his passion, but more fundamentally because his mentor and analyst, Homer Lane, had died half-way through his analysis, at which Layard had transferred his feelings of dependence on to Elta, a beautiful Italian patient of Lane's, who refused to have any

contact with him. Six days after Isherwood left Berlin, Layard
tried to commit suicide by shooting himself through the mouth.
Miraculously he survived. Stuffing a hat over his blood-stained
head he took a taxi to Auden's place and asked Auden to finish
him off. Instead Auden called an ambulance.[6] Isherwood only
learnt of this episode subsequently from Auden and Layard himself, but it struck him forcibly enough for him to transplant it
into *The Memorial*, where Edward undergoes virtually the
identical experience.

Back in England after barely two weeks in Berlin, Isherwood
spent his time learning more German, sending letters (and money
of course) to Bubi and working on the second draft of *The
Memorial*. In mid-June he returned to Germany to join Auden and
his current boyfriend who were staying at Rotheheutte in the
Harz mountains. When Bubi failed to turn up as arranged
Isherwood rushed off to Berlin to try to find him only to learn
that he was wanted by the police and had vanished. On his
return to Rotheheutte he received a letter from Bubi announcing
his impending departure for South America from Amsterdam.
Only stopping to borrow enough money for the trip from John
Layard, he raced off to Amsterdam with Auden. Bumping into
Bubi and a friend almost immediately, Isherwood found that
Bubi had less than £5 left. As he reported to John Layard:

> 'Shall you go back to Germany one day?' I asked Bubi. 'No.
> Never. When my money is gone, there's this.' He produced a
> small revolver from his pocket. I examined it and saw that the
> ammunition was blank. A purely compensatory weapon. Very
> interesting. I merely said, well, don't fire through the roof of
> your mouth—and showed him where.[7]

He could make a joke of this kind at Layard's expense as Layard
had firmly declared on his recovery that one did not try to kill
oneself twice.

After celebrating a prolonged farewell in Amsterdam, Isherwood returned to London at the end of June. By this time his
mother had moved from St Mary Abbot's Terrace now shaken by
the increasing volume of traffic using the Kensington Road to the
seclusion of a smaller house in the same area at 19 Pembroke
Gardens off Edwardes Square. When Auden also came back to
England that summer, he and Isherwood began the first of their

dramatic collaborations, *The Enemies of the Bishop*, an amazing hotchpotch that includes most of their current obsessions and which, not surprisingly, never saw the light of day. Auden also obtained for his friend a commission to translate Baudelaire's *Journaux Intimes*. The mother of the children whom Auden was tutoring on his return to London had established her own small publishing business called the Blackamoor Press for which Isherwood did his amateur translation. Her husband, Colonel Solomons, was paralysed from the waist down and once earned one of Layard's devastatingly honest remarks when he was inveighing against pornographic writers (like Lawrence) who hit below the belt: 'That's hardly surprising that you take that attitude', he told the Colonel, 'considering what you've done to yourself below the belt.'⁸ Auden alludes to Colonel Solomons in the Prologue to *The Enemies of the Bishop* where one stanza starts: 'Will you wheel death anywhere/In his invalid chair.'⁹

In August Isherwood was in a remote seaside village in Sutherland where he was earning some extra money as a private tutor. *The Memorial*, he informed Roger Burford, 'has been written twice and will have to be written again as soon as I get away from this hell-hole.'¹⁰ There he had one of the two heterosexual experiences he ever had in his life with the mother of his attractive pupil.¹¹ 'It was quite workable', he told an interviewer. 'But I preferred boys and I already knew that I could fall in love with them. . . . If my mother was responsible for it, I am grateful.'¹² Auden accused him at this time of being a repressed heterosexual, and his extraordinary statement in *Christopher and his Kind* that only boys, not girls, can be romantic and so find a place in his personal myth of love (*CK* 17) only emphasises the element of choice where his own homosexuality is concerned. Stephen Spender has pointed out that much of the homosexual chauvinism Isherwood displays in *Christopher and his Kind* stems from his need to justify his choice of homosexuality to the exclusion of the heterosexual side of his nature. This is why, Spender claims, 'he advances as treachery on the part of a homosexual or bisexual, if he doesn't choose to be homosexual but chooses to be heterosexual. And he thinks it especially bad if he continues to have a homosexual life.'¹³ This militant homosexual stance also surfaces in *A Meeting by the River* and its stridency and lack of argumentative clarity does suggest the presence of a very

personal motive perhaps based on the early rejection of his
bisexual proclivities.

On 29 November 1929 Isherwood, his German much improved, left for an indefinite stay in Berlin. The previous June
Auden had told him to look up an English archaeologist friend
of his, Francis Turville-Petre, who had helped him search for
Bubi in the boy-bars of Berlin he knew so well. His only contact
now that Layard was also back in England, Francis was living
next door to Dr Magnus Hirschfield's famous Institute for Sexual
Science. Isherwood immediately moved into a vacant room in the
same large apartment where Francis rented two rooms and was
soon introduced to the Institute: Dr Hirschfield, his lover-cum-
secretary, Karl Giese, and a friend of Karl's, Erwin Hansen, an
ex-gymnastic instructor for the army who did odd jobs around
the Institute. The Institute and Francis between them brought
Isherwood face to face with the most extreme members of the
homosexual spectrum. The Institute, founded in 1919, was concerned with investigating and helping sexual deviants of all kinds.
Francis was attending it for the VD which he suffered from for
much of his adult life. Until Francis left Berlin in the New Year,
Isherwood spent much of his time in his company, touring the
working-class boy-bars in the evening where Francis (known
there as 'Der Franni', anglicised to 'Fronny' by Auden and
Isherwood) would spend half the night bargaining with the boy
of his choice. But early every morning Isherwood would go to a
café in In Den Zelten where he would work steadily at the third
draft of *The Memorial*. It took him a year to complete it.

In February of 1930 he was forced to return to London when
his Uncle Henry quixotically withheld his quarterly allowance.
There he was plunged into a family row between his mother and
his brother, Richard, who had tried to lie his way out of being
tutored for Oxford by pretending he had a job. On his own
admission Isherwood avenged himself on her for her past
attempts to mould him in the image of the Others by siding with
Richard (*CK* 35–36). He also called in John Layard who found
her as unreceptive to analysis as to her son's arguments. He saw a
lot more of Layard during his three-month stay in England and
this time felt more strongly attracted both to the man and his
ideas than he had done the previous year.

On his return to Berlin in May 1930 he found his working-class German friends even more impoverished since Dr Brüning, the new Catholic Chancellor, had introduced emergency decrees cutting wages and restricting social insurance. Shortly after his arrival he met and fell for a German boy to whom he refers by his fictionalised name of 'Otto' in *Christopher and his Kind*. The model for Otto Nowak in *Goodbye to Berlin*, he was young, good-looking, and sufficiently poor to earn his living selling himself to homosexuals, although like many of the bar-boys he was more hetero- than homosexual by nature. His bisexual promiscuity caused so much jealousy and anger on Isherwood's part that, as he admits in *Christopher and his Kind*, his artistic need for emotional stimulation must have provided an unconscious motivation for entering into this masochistic, drama-filled relationship.

In late June Auden came to stay bringing with him his *Poems* (1930) dedicated to Isherwood. He also wrote an unpublished poem celebrating his friend's new affair with 'Otto', the first stanza of which reads:

> *Dear Christopher, you old old bugger*
> *Here in this land of fear and rugger*
> *Where love is mostly hugger mugger*
> *Your letters quoted*
> *By jealous ladies make us eager*
> *To be devoted.*[14]

Isherwood himself quotes the penultimate stanza in which love has awarded him 'most of "Otto" '—Auden could obviously read the signs (*CK* 42). In mid-August he spent a weekend in Hamburg with Stephen Spender and during the last week of August Upward came to stay. Upward's recent conversion to Marxism heightened Isherwood's awareness of the German political scene. When Brüning called elections for that September rather than abrogate his emergency decrees, the meteoric success of the Nazi party (which obtained six and a half million votes compared to less than a million in the previous election) awakened Isherwood to the menace of fascism. A life-long left-wing liberal, he could never, however, wholeheartedly commit himself to the Communist Party. In fact the following year he was writing to Spender: 'I'm through with the Communists. All politicians are equally nasty. We must work for our own sort of revolution all by ourselves.'[15] That epitomises Isherwood's attitude to politics throughout the thirties.

Temporary poverty[16] and not politics induced him to move at 'Otto's' suggestion into his family home, a slum tenement in Hallesches Tor, for the month of October. Isherwood was to draw on this brief experience to produce one of his most admired Berlin stories, 'The Nowaks'. Forced to leave when 'Otto's' tubercular mother was sent to a sanatorium, he moved first to a neighbouring slum area, Kottbusser Tor for November, and then again in December 1930 to the more respectable Nollendorf-strasse 17, where he took a room in the flat belonging to the landlady on whom the now famous Frl Schroeder was modelled, Frl Thurau.

Frl Thurau's household has been portrayed so vividly in *Goodbye to Berlin* that it is difficult to distinguish the original from this heightened, fictionalised account of it. 'Frl Kost', the prostitute, 'Frl Mayr', the unemployed Nazi sympathiser, and 'Bobbi' (actually called Willy) the bar-tender all existed in fact. So did 'Sally Bowles', although Isherwood now confesses how impossible he finds it to distinguish between his own character, 'Sally', and Jean Ross on whom she was modelled. One of the most important contemporary witnesses was Stephen Spender, whom Isherwood had invited to join him in Berlin that winter. But, apart from his own tendency to produce brilliant caricatures, Spender confesses to a similar difficulty in distinguishing himself or their mutual friends from their counterparts in the Berlin books.[17] Isherwood emerges from Spender's account far more in control of all their joint lives than the faceless narrator of the novels. As Isherwood admits, he was keeping a detailed diary all this time with the firm intention of using it later as the raw material for his books, and he obviously cultivated potential 'characters' for his fiction and encouraged them to act up to the roles he had cast them for.

What can be pieced together of the real Jean Ross? Spender recalls her dishevelled appearance, 'her eyes large onyxes fringed by eyelashes like enamelled wire, in a face of carved ivory'.[18] The daughter of a wealthy Scottish cotton merchant, she had been brought up in Egypt surrounded by servants. At seventeen she had rebelled against her parents' bourgeois standards and had left home to 'learn about life' in Berlin, as she put it.[19] There she had drifted into occasional appearances as a singer (with little talent but tremendous charm) at a small run-down club. Although she enjoyed acting up to an exaggerated image of her own depravity, she nevertheless tended to end up in bed with the men she met, however casually, including, on one occasion, the Pope's publisher.[20] Paul Bowles, the American musician turned novelist, recollects that her most characteristic pose at Frl Thurau's was 'stretched out in bed, smoking Murattis and eating chocolates' entertaining one or more German friends whom she would frequently address as 'Du Schwein'.[21] She did meet Isherwood at the flat of a mutual friend, Franz Ullman (called 'Fritz Wendel' in *Goodbye to Berlin*), just as she did get pregnant by Kurt ('Klaus') and did have an abortion in the summer of 1931 (which so impressed Spender that he refers to it in the penultimate stanza of his poem 'The Prisoners'). But according to Spender it was he and not Isherwood who sent Paul Rakowski ('George P. Sanders' in the novel) to her and it was he also who accompanied her to the police station. After she left Berlin she went to stay with Olive Mangeot and continued to feature in Isherwood's life whenever he returned to England.[22]

Through Spender Isherwood also met Gisa Soloweitschik, a wealthy young Russian Jewess on whom he very remotely based 'Natalia Landauer' in *Goodbye to Berlin*. She was not in fact related to Wilfred Israel, who provided an even more remote model for 'Natalia's' cousin, 'Bernhard Landauer'. The Jewish owner of Berlin's largest department store, Wertheim's, he fought a continuous rearguard action against the Nazis until he was forced to leave Germany in 1939, quite unlike his passive fictive counterpart.

On 10 March 1931 Isherwood returned to London to receive Cape's verdict on *The Memorial* which he had finished at the end of the previous year. When they turned it down, he took it to Curtis Brown, the literary agents. He travelled back to Berlin on 21 March with Archie Campbell (Spender's friend from Oxford) who remembers Isherwood's perplexed state of mind at having just received an irate letter from André Mangeot whom Olive had just divorced that January on the grounds of his adultery with Ann McNaughton. In fact André's peccadillos began much earlier than this. Finally, after he had fallen for and gone on tour to France with a former pupil of his, Rachel Monkhouse,

Patrick's sister whom Isherwood had introduced to the household, Olive had made up her mind to find suitable grounds for a divorce which Ann McNaughton obligingly provided. Now that Olive had moved out to Gunter Grove where she ran her own lodging house, André quite unjustly accused Isherwood of introducing Rachel to the family in the certain knowledge that he would fall for her and so provide Isherwood with material for his writing. André was sufficiently unbalanced at the time to write in his letter to Isherwood that his failure physically to seduce Olive deprived him of the excuse to thrash him. Olive's house at Gunter Grove now became the centre for Isherwood's group when in England. Jean Ross stayed there on her return from Berlin, as did Christopher Cornford and Gabriel Carritt who, with Upward, was possibly responsible for Olive's and Jean's conversion to Communism.[23]

Back in Berlin Archie Campbell introduced Isherwood to John Blomshield (called 'Clive' in *Goodbye to Berlin*), an American artist friend of his who was spending as much of his wealthy wife's fortune as he could before she obtained a Mexican divorce. He had an entire suite at the plush Adlon Hotel where he would order a bottle of champagne on waking up with the excuse 'I just can't drink tea on an empty stomach.' Stephen Spender, mistakenly convinced that he was in need of a girl, set Jean Ross up for him one evening at a dance hall, after which a hothouse romance bloomed briefly until Blomshield left abruptly for America. Nevertheless he was in fact accompanied by an eighteen-year-old Norwegian boyfriend with whom he was constantly quarrelling. They did all see Hermann Müller's funeral from the Adlon (as described in 'Sally Bowles') during which the half-drunk Blomshield was irreverently throwing coins from the balcony to the street-boys below.[24] Brüning's death spelt doom for German social democracy and the domination of the centrist coalition. That July the Darmstädter und Nationbank failed and Isherwood wrote to his agent that a revolution was imminent. In September Britain abandoned the gold standard, the pound was devalued (much to his discomfort) and German unemployment topped four million.

Meanwhile Isherwood went for the summer to Sellin in Ruegen Island on the Baltic accompanied by 'Otto' with whom he spent the time quarrelling over his affairs with the local girls, much in the same way as 'Peter' does in *Goodbye to Berlin*. They were joined there by Spender and Auden who recalls this holiday in stanzas 6 and 7 of his 'Birthday Poem' where he mockingly remembers how they all believed at this time that the solution to all the world's troubles was Love: 'Surely one fearless kiss could cure/The million fevers, a stroking brush/The insensitive refuse from the burning core.'[25] Isherwood's jealous tantrums over 'Otto' were the living disproof of this optimistic thesis. As for writing, his future plans, he informed Roger Burford, included 'a book of stories and a novel about Berlin. Politics, Pox and Prostitution—very strong tobacco, suitable for Knopf, 200 copies numbered backwards and bound in brass.'[26]

Early that summer he met Gerald Hamilton on whom he was to base 'Mr Norris'.[27] Forty years old at the time, Hamilton was running the Berlin office of *The Times*, a job which ended when news of his support for the Communists reached Times Square. Born in Shanghai, of Irish extraction, he had early on learned to make a precarious living from his aristocratic and political connections. In 1914 he published under a pseudonym *Desert Dreamers*, a homosexual romance set in Biskra recounting the hopeless passion of an Englishman for his young Arab guide who dies at the end of the book. Isherwood turned this into *Miss Smith's Torture Chamber* in the novel, a more appropriate title for Hamilton's fictive heterosexual counterpart. He was twice imprisoned during the First World War, first for an act of gross indecency with a male (he was inveterately homosexual), and then for anti-British activities.

By the time Isherwood met him he had helped steal a Greek millionaire's wife's jewel case from the Blue Train, been arrested and imprisoned by the Italians for fraud in connection with a pearl necklace and become an associate both of Willi Münzenberg (cf 'Bayer'), the leading Communist organiser in Berlin and prominent Nazis.[28] Moore Crosthwaite, a friend of Spender who was in Berlin the same summer, remembers how Isherwood was so obviously fascinated by Hamilton's potential as a character for his fiction that, unlike his friends, he remained wholly indifferent to his new friend's more sinister aspects. It was even alleged that Hamilton was not above resorting to blackmail, for instance.[29] His father summed him up with the epigrammatic remark, 'Gerald has no wounds that can't be cured by a cheque poultice.'[30]

Isherwood wrote jubilantly to Spender that autumn: 'I shan't starve. Because I've made friends with the mammon of unrighteousness.'[31] Gerald Hamilton was probably harbouring the same thoughts about him. In fact each was to prove a source of revenue to the other.

That summer he also met Paul Bowles, a young American musician who found that Isherwood and Spender when together were like 'two members of a secret society constantly making references to esoteric data not available to outsiders'[32]—one more example of the group solidarity of the members of Auden's cabinet of emerging artists.

At Spender's suggestion, John Lehmann, who had joined the Woolfs' Hogarth Press early in 1931, asked to see *The Memorial* which had already been rejected by three more publishers beside Cape, possibly due to the risqué homosexual element in the second half of the novel. He liked it and finally persuaded Leonard and Virginia to accept it. The acceptance came only just in time to forestall his mother's plan to lure him home on the grounds that he was obviously not able to earn his living as a writer. As he wrote to Spender prior to paying a lightning visit home in early October, 'Mater's preparing some nice little rat-trap for me, I know, but I'm too old and whiskery a rat to be tempted by the rather musty bit of Pembroke Garden cheese.'[33] *The Memorial* came out on 17 February 1932 and, despite some good notices, sold poorly.

On his return to Berlin he was forced by the devaluation of the pound to move into a cheaper back room at Frl Thurau's. Hamilton's finances were in an even worse state and his dealings with the bailiff were a general source of amusement. His failure to raise much income from the tight-fisted Communist Party may have led him to open bidding with their Nazi rivals. He introduced Isherwood and Spender (who had returned to Berlin in November) to Aleister Crowley who outdid even Mr Norris at living off what Hamilton drily termed 'involuntary contributions from his friends'.[34] That autumn Isherwood also met William Robson-Scott who had come out to lecture at the University. He remembers Isherwood as detached, even reserved, but alert and observant as a bird, and completely committed to his writing. Isherwood was to borrow some of Robson-Scott's external features (like the way he rubbed his knees when pleased and the fact that he was undergoing analysis in Berlin) for 'Peter Wilkinson' in *Goodbye to Berlin*, partly to disguise the fact that this is a self-portrait at a more fundamental level.[35]

While *The Memorial* was doing the rounds that year, Isherwood was writing his first version of what would eventually become *Lions and Shadows*. Simultaneously he was formulating the idea of a *magnum opus* about Berlin called *The Lost* which he would try out in conversation on Spender and other close friends. By the following July he had abandoned his autobiographical book for his first attempt to write *The Lost*. 'It is written entirely in the form of a diary,' he wrote to John Lehmann that July, 'without any break in the narrative. It will have lots of characters and be full of "news" about Berlin.'[36] This must have been a false start as he dictated a new draft outline of the entire novel to his brother Richard a month later. At this stage it was modestly enough based on events surrounding only Jean Ross and 'Otto's' family. His only work to be published that year consisted of a 'pot-boiler' article on 'The Youth Movement in Germany' for *Action*, Mosley's short-lived periodical edited by Harold Nicolson, which he had already disparagingly labelled 'the rankest John Bull stuff'.[37]

Ever since 'Otto' had played fast and loose at Ruegen Island the previous summer their affair had been coming to a good-natured end. In March 1932 Isherwood met Heinz, a young German boy of seventeen, whom he fell for immediately and more seriously than with anyone else until then. Francis Turville-Petre, who had returned to Berlin that January, had taken a house in the country at Mohrin, north-east of Berlin, and had invited Isherwood to join him there. He had hired Erwin Hansen (from the Hirschfield Institute) as cook and housekeeper and Erwin, on Francis's instructions, had engaged Heinz to help him. Frequently left to themselves, Isherwood and Heinz each found in the other complementary qualities that drew them closer together. Although Isherwood claims in *Christopher and his Kind* to have filled the role of elder brother to Heinz, subsequent events show that he acted more like his father than his brother, assuming an increasing responsibility for Heinz as he unwittingly deprived him of his independence and legal status in his passionate desire not to lose the first real love of his life.

Isherwood stayed at Mohrin until late June and spent July on Ruegen Island with Heinz, Stephen Spender and his brother Humphrey, William Robson-Scott and Wilfred Israel. Meanwhile the German political situation was deteriorating further. During the Presidential election that spring, Hindenburg had only defeated Hitler on the second ballot in which Hitler nevertheless attracted almost thirteen and a half million votes. In the July elections the Nazis won 230 seats out of 609 to become the largest party in the Reichstag. When Hindenburg refused to make Hitler Chancellor violence flared up again on the streets. On Ruegen Island Isherwood wrote to Upward (now a member of the Communist Party) of the menacing presence of the Hitler Youth: 'Only beyond, in beach-pyjamas—hakenkreuz village hog-necked Nazis in their khaki bus-driver's uniform remind the Marxist that we are witnessing the opening stages of the last and most appalling fascist reaction.'[38] Later that summer at Berlin airport, advocates of rearmament bombarded him from aircraft with leaflets printed 'If this had been a bomb, you'd be dead.'[39]

On his return to London for the months of August and September Isherwood was badly worried by the mood of apathy and ignorance about the rising Nazi menace that prevailed except among a few of his friends. Few Englishmen seemed to have heard of the New Hitler Youth Movement. Naturally he talked endlessly about this with his Communist friends like Jean Ross and Olive Mangeot whom he saw much of at this time. Apart from seeing most of his old friends like Hector Wintle (now qualified and about to make his maiden voyage as a ship's doctor), Upward, Auden, et al., he made several new friends during this visit. He met John Lehmann, the manager of his new publishers, although he only came to know him closely when Lehmann visited him the following winter in Berlin. In his autobiography Lehmann recalls Isherwood at this time as a dominating presence despite his short stature, capable of inventing absurd comic fabrications, yet essentially serious, and constantly at war with anything tainted by the English establishment.[40] Through Auden he met Gerald Heard and his close friend, Chris Wood. At this time Heard was Science Commentator for the BBC and a council member of the London Society for Psychical Research. In 1929 he had published The Ascent of Humanity, a philosophical view of history as 'the shadow cast by man's evolving conscious-

ness' to use his own words.[41] But Isherwood was not yet
receptive to these semi-mystical ideas and spent most of his time
with Chris Wood while Auden and Heard locked themselves
away to discuss abstruse scientific and philosophical topics of
mutual interest.

An equally important introduction was made by a fellow-
writer, William Plomer, with whom he became friends at this
time through Spender. Plomer took Isherwood to meet E. M.
Forster, his literary mentor. Forster had been impressed by *The
Memorial* which naturally delighted his disciple. Isherwood
remembers his babylike appearance, his light blue eyes and
vulnerability. Forster's memory of their meeting focused incon-
sequentially on the bowler hat his young admirer was wearing
and Plomer's reference to Isherwood's mother as a grey iron-
clad.[42] After this meeting the two novelists started corresponding
and seeing each other whenever they both found themselves in
the same country.

That September Isherwood and Spender quarrelled sufficiently
seriously to prevent Spender from returning to Berlin as planned
that autumn. Ostensibly a quarrel over Spender's indiscreet
revelations about Isherwood's life in Berlin, it was really
motivated, according to Isherwood, by his fear that Spender
would scoop him in writing about their joint Berlin experiences
which he was patiently attempting to fictionalise in *The Lost*.
When one thinks of the way he appropriated Spender's meeting
with 'George P. Sanders' and utilised Spender's presence at
Ruegen Island for the first-person narrator he calls 'Christopher
Isherwood' in *Goodbye to Berlin*, one can understand why he felt
that this process could easily be reversed by Spender in his own
writing. On the other hand, Spender himself feels that Isherwood
was becoming overwhelmed by his own claustrophobic admiration for him and his preference for Isherwood's company to that
of anyone else in Berlin. Besides, Spender has observed, the fact
that he was witness to Isherwood's active social life annoyingly
belied the image of the ascetic and lonely novelist which he had
created for their joint friends at home.[43]

Once Spender had renounced his intention of returning to
Berlin, Isherwood's fears were allayed and the friendship was
restored to a new basis of equality. Nevertheless, during the
period in which Spender had treated Isherwood as his literary

mentor, Isherwood had been of real help to him, mixing criticism with encouragement and genuine admiration. 'Really,' he had written to him the previous autumn, 'your work is the most astounding *tour de force*. Because you are absolutely "modern" in feeling and yet get your effects with all the old words and associations.'[44] Maybe he did not feel so threatened by Spender's poetry as by his prose, but generous praise of this kind was obviously written with conviction and must have given the young poet what he most needed, a belief in his potentiality as a writer.

Back in Berlin in October, Isherwood renewed his liaison with Heinz whom he saw regularly three times a week (he makes it sound like a business appointment). His letters during his last winter in Berlin are strewn with references to the worsening political situation. They mention the translation he did for Münzenberg's IAH Communist front organisation (like 'William Bradshaw'), the Nazis' attack on an opponent he witnessed within sight of the police, the impending imprisonment of a Communist friend, Willi Müller, for attacking a policeman (like 'Werner'), the tram strike and the election, called by von Papen to lessen Nazi power following the street violence, in which the Nazis were reduced to 196 seats and the Communists gained 100 seats in the Reichstag.

Meanwhile he was struggling with *The Lost*, 'an indecent unctuous stupid sort of novel,' he wrote to Forster, 'which I fear you won't like.'[45] He was also invited by Michael Roberts to contribute to *New Country*, a sequel to *New Signatures*, that was to include prose this time. Just how little he subscribed to any left-wing group orthodoxy can be seen from a letter he wrote Lehmann: 'Have just heard from Roberts, who wants something showing "the new spirit" in literature, politics, etc. But what is the new spirit? Search me. Poor old Marx could hardly be described as new.'[46] 'It's like being asked to a party,' he wrote Plomer, 'where one doesn't know if one's supposed to dress.'[47] Initially he sent Roberts the first ten thousand words of *The Lost* which was based on the 'Nowaks'' sanitorium experience. 'It's full of sex and not a word about Communism so far', he informed Spender.[48] Roberts must have objected (possibly to the sexual content) as *New Country* when it was published in March 1933 contained 'An Evening at the Bay', an extract from the autobiographical novel Isherwood was at work on in the first half of 1932 which had even less to do with politics than the 'Nowaks' material.

During the Christmas holidays Auden came to stay for ten days. That autumn he had been asked by an old school-friend, Robert Medley and his friend Rupert Doone to write the scenario for what eventually became *The Dance of Death* for the new experimental Group Theatre they had formed in London. During his visit at Christmas Auden talked this over with Isherwood who provided a few ideas but did not enter into any closer collaboration with him on this occasion.[49] Lehmann, who had abandoned the Hogarth Press that autumn, paid Isherwood a brief visit on his way to Vienna in October and a longer one starting in late January 1933. Isherwood performed much the same introduction to the working-class boy-bars of Berlin for his new friend as Auden had done for him four years earlier. They also tentatively discussed starting a new magazine, but political events overtook Isherwood so rapidly that literary projects were forced to give way to the need for both of them to leave Berlin—first Lehmann, then Isherwood accompanied by Heinz who was threatened with imminent conscription.

At the end of January Hitler forced Hindenburg to appoint him Chancellor after the Nazi deputies had withdrawn their support from Hindenburg's appointee, Schleicher. Isherwood reported the immediate results of Hitler's new power to Plomer: 'Nazis are to be enrolled as "auxiliary police", which means that one must now not only be murdered but that it is illegal to offer any resistance. In the summer all out-of-work boys will be rounded up and sent off in squads to work on the land.' Since most of his German friends were either Communists or out-of-work or both, Isherwood began to become seriously worried for them, and especially for Heinz. Hitler next called new elections and used the Reichstag Fire as an excuse to arrest leading Communists and to increase his party's vote in the elections of 5 March in which they became the controlling power with 288 seats. After the Enabling Act of 22 March had given Hitler's cabinet power to legislate on its own authority, after boy-bars had been closed down and Isherwood had witnessed at first-hand the opening of the anti-Jewish campaign with the boycott of Jewish businesses, he faced the inevitable and made plans to

leave Berlin for good. First he took back to London all his
belongings which he did not want to take with him on his
travels. He spent the last three weeks of April 1933 in London
seeing Gerald Hamilton (who had fled Berlin after being arrested
by the police for his supposedly Communist activities), E. M.
Forster (who spent a day with him in the country at Charltons
and lent him the typescript of his homosexual novel, *Maurice*, to
read), Bubi and Upward. He showed Upward the first part of his
second draft of *The Lost* which he had told Lehmann in late
March he was rewriting 'more with "Memorial" technique—
much better.'[50] In fact its sheer scope was destined to defeat him.

Back in Berlin at the beginning of May, Isherwood learnt from
Frl Thurau that the police had been asking questions about him
in his absence. This helped make up his mind for him and he
wrote back to Francis accepting his friend's invitation to join
him on an island off the east coast of Greece with Heinz and
Erwin Hansen. Erwin gave him a first-hand account of the
Nazi raid on the now empty Hirschfield Institute where he was
still living as caretaker, and Isherwood himself witnessed with
Robson-Scott the Institute's books being publicly burnt a few
days later. On 13 May 1933 he left Berlin with Heinz and Erwin
by train on what was to become a seven-year odyssey in search of
an unknown homeland.

9

The Memorial

All the Conspirators is an indictment of the Edwardian family in general and barely conceals its writer's personal vendetta against his own family in particular. *The Memorial* is an indictment of British society at large and sees even the threatening mother figure as herself a victim of a diseased civilisation. The war is symptomatic of a wider malaise affecting old and young alike. In fact the post-war generation is seen to suffer as much damage from the war as the previous generation which participated in it directly. Isn't it familiar—that 'land you were once proud to own',[1] 'those handsome and diseased youngsters'?[2] Of course, it is the landscape of Auden's early poetry; it is also Upward's vision of doomed youth which struck him so forcibly during his holiday with Isherwood at Freshwater Bay in 1928.[3] It is a myth about the 1920s shared by the writers of the 1930s, not quite the myth built up by Huxley and Waugh in their satirical portraits of the Gay Twenties, but more that of Graham Greene and the so-called Auden Group for whom post-war England is an embattled country where nobody is well.

Isherwood has said that his idea for the novel certainly pre-dates his visit to Bremen in the spring of 1928 when he claimed in 'Mr Lancaster' to have conceived it.[4] The previous summer he had met 'Lester' at Freshwater Bay, shell-shocked, a relic of the war, a ghostly reminder of the past. This crucial meeting with 'Lester' provided the initial impetus for Isherwood's novel in which all his characters are suffering from psychic shell-shock of one kind or another. They, as much as 'Lester', belong to 'the nightmare Never-Never-Land of the War' (*LS* 256). Isherwood suggests as much in his description of his first conception of *The Memorial*:

It was to be about war: not the War itself, but the effect of the idea of the 'War' on my generation. It was to give expression, at last, to my own 'War' complex, and to all the reactions which had followed my meeting with Lester at the Bay.

(LS 296)

'Lester' appears to have uncovered certain neuroses in Isherwood which he then found were shared by many of his contemporaries. Out of the corporate myth which they constructed around this complex of neuroses concerning heroism and the Test, each of these writers was able to forge his own works of art at one further remove from the raw emotion. The superiority of *The Memorial* to *All the Conspirators* owes much to this process of distillation.

Isherwood goes on to describe his initial idea of *The Memorial* as 'an epic disguised as a drawing-room comedy' (*LS* 297). Although this suggests the influence of Forster, it is in fact Virginia Woolf more than any other writer who leaves her mark on this book, and her influence has been variously discerned by such commentators as Hena Maes-Jelinek, Goronwy Rees and Angus Wilson.[5] Nevertheless *The Memorial* is the last novel Isherwood wrote which owes a debt either to Modernism in general or to specific modernist writers, like Virginia Woolf, in particular. Far more significant is its rejection of the more disjunctive neo-Joycean techniques that obtrude in *All the Conspirators*. Such difficulty or obscurity as survives in his second novel is a necessary element of its fragmented vision of British society, not a modish imitation of the *avant-garde* as it is in the earlier novel. Even his use of interior monologue is integral to his conception of the isolation of the individual in the post-war world.

The episodic nature of *The Memorial*, then, was dictated by its theme. At the same time it anticipates the solution he finally evolved to the problems of how to extricate himself from the highly complicated plot of *The Lost*. His idea of making 'an album of snapshots' (*LS* 297), modelled perhaps on cinematic 'takes', is very similar to his method of construction in two of his most successful books, *Goodbye to Berlin* and *Down There on a Visit*. Quite apart from the time scheme, characters are invariably presented as if the reader had already been introduced to them. As happens in life one learns about their past as and when an appropriate occasion arises for them to reminisce. In this way characters are not simply isolated from each other but remain partially inaccessible even to the reader privileged to overhear their interior monologue.

Ultimately, as one American reviewer observed, 'his characters are always, in one sense, social symbols.'[6] Each of the three generations of the Vernon family represents a phase in the history of British civilisation. There is John Vernon, the last Squire of the Hall, who represents for Lily the Victorian world of social order for which she yearns. But he has degenerated into a second childhood (symptomatic of the decline of Victorian society), slobbering over his food and behaving in public 'like a baby being naughty' (p 89). Lily belongs to Edwardian England and has become fixated in her pre-war past which she equates with her brief period of happiness in Richard's company. She blames the war in which her husband was killed for her un-happiness, quite unable to see that the war was simply a violent expression of the values she had allied herself with. Lily also has adopted 'the look of a child' (p 23). Yet her 'childish innocence' (p 134) is made to appear culpable when the novel concentrates on the devastating effects the war has had on the youngest of the three generations. Eric, Maurice and Anne are all victims of their time. Eric is a mass of neuroses. He finds 'a certain satis-faction in doing injury to his health' (p 208), while his mother speaks of him 'as if she were talking of someone who had died' (p 26). Maurice is not so much dead as a dealer in death. He is 'thoughtless, like a child' (p 201), and his irresponsibility im-plicates him in the death of Stewart-Baines and numerous other near-fatalities. Anne meanwhile masochistically opts for the death of love by agreeing to marry the inhibited Tommy Ramsbotham.

Yet to talk of Isherwood's characters in this book solely as social symbols gives a false impression of their impact. Most of them are recognisably modelled on individuals whom he knew intimately and to whom he had already allotted roles in his private mythology. In *Kathleen and Frank* he has called John Vernon a 'candid . . . portrait' of his grandfather, John Isherwood, and Lily and Richard 'dull substitutes' for his parents, Kathleen and Frank (*KF* 184–5). The Hall is recognisably Marple Hall (just as the Scrivens' house in Gatesley is modelled on the Monkhouse family home in Disley). Even Major Ronald Charlesworth is based on a distant maternal cousin called Major Raymond

Smythies.[7] At the time Isherwood confessed to Hector Wintle's wife, 'I libelled the whole of our family pretty severely in *The Memorial*',[8] and many of the portraits were close enough to their originals to incur the displeasure of some members of the family. He also informs us in *Christopher and his Kind* that Olive Mangeot was a model for both Margaret and Mary (*CK* 81). One could go on: Maurice is modelled on Upward's friend at Cambridge, Christopher Orpen; Edward's attempted suicide is closely modelled on Layard's; Ramsbotham derives from the owner of a jute mill near Marple called Scott; and so on. The point is that he is abstracting from his own immediate experience of life and people, not fleshing out ideas in the manner of Aldous Huxley, for example. In relying so heavily on models about whom he knew so much more in reality than could be revealed in the book, there was always the danger of assuming that the reader knew things which had not in fact been told him. Judging from the confused reactions of some of the reviewers he may not have entirely avoided this pitfall.

Perhaps some of the confusion arose from Isherwood's studied refusal to allow the reader to identify with any one character. The time jumps and the constant transfer of narrative viewpoint from one character to the next focus attention firmly on the thematic and symbolic qualities of the novel. At the level of plot the various characters are all connected by ties of blood or friendship to the Vernon family, whose decline is symbolised by the gradual decay of the Hall, which by 1929 had gone 'quite dead' (p 246). But what unites them all far more meaningfully is the harmful effect which the war has had on them. The War Memorial after which the book is called looms like a dead weight over all the survivors from the war, both those who had faced the Test in battle, like Edward, or those who were too young at the time to be tested, like Eric. Alan Wilde has suggested that Edward and Eric are the first of Isherwood's 'doubles' and originate in two projected characters in his unwritten novel, *The North-West Passage*, in which one character is the embodiment of his double's 'dream of himself as an epic character' (*LS* 211).[9] Both are examples of the Truly Weak Man, he argues; but Eric avoids attempting the North-West Passage altogether whereas Edward is constantly attempting it and failing.

However, it is not Edward whom Eric emulates, but his dead

father, Richard. Eric's neurosis, like Isherwood's own, derives from the impossibility of emulating his father's heroism or of filling his place in his mother's eyes. Out of the obsessive guilt which this situation creates come his endless attempts to prove himself in the post-war battle of the classes. But his social and political commitments are the products of his neurosis and it is therefore no surprise that he turns back from the huge northern circuit by means of which the Truly Weak Man avoids life, and ends up in the arms of the Roman Catholic church, a mere substitute for his mother who was the source of most of his neuroses. As at least one reviewer has seen Edward's conversion as a sign of redemption,[10] it is worth pointing out how throughout the book references to Christianity invariably associate it with the denial of life (Lily finds there is no prayer asking for happiness—p 96) and of love (Major Charlesworth turns himself into a 'martyr' at the shrine of a beatified Lily— pp 254 and 261). Lily appears even to Eric as a boy 'like an angel' (p 73) which only emphasises his reversion to the mother-child relationship on his conversion to Roman Catholicism.

Edward, on the other hand, has faced the Test of war and acquitted himself bravely from all accounts. But his Edwardian schooldays conditioned him before the war to accept a code of honour which could only produce inhibition and neurosis:

> He dared refuse no adventure—horribly frightened as he often was. He would have fought any boy in the school, would have got himself expelled for any offence, rather than admit to being afraid. (p 131)

It is this upbringing which convinces him that he had failed the Test of war when he once faked illness to get sick leave from active duty. By comparison his friend Richard had no need to prove his courage, being an example of the Truly Strong Man. Yet even Richard lets Edward down when he submits to Lily's snobbish refusal to have any contact with Mary after she has absconded from home. Perhaps the Truly Strong Man never existed? Certainly no character in *The Memorial* is left unflawed. Lily's reverence for Richard is sufficient to make him suspect in the reader's eyes. As the next squire of the Hall, wasn't he the inheritor of an upper-class ethos which made the war an inevitability? Doesn't his memory cast a deathly shadow over the lives of both Eric and Edward? Perhaps the Truly Weak Man is only brought to life by the existence of a Truly Strong Man. Didn't Maurice irresponsibly dare Eric to enlist prematurely out of sheer devilment? Yet had he been killed, wouldn't Maurice have been cast in the role of Hero, and couldn't Eric have survived like Edward, destined to spend a lifetime seeking out substitutes for war?

The same sense of ambiguity hovers over all the characters in the book. On the one hand Lily is an enemy of youth; according to Eric 'she doesn't feel' (p 51); she ignores her son and lives in the past; to Edward she is 'a wax doll' (p 135), to Mary she 'could be exceedingly cruel' (p 112). On the other hand she is far more sympathetically portrayed than was Mrs Lindsay, her predecessor. Her love for the Past is not a purely negative quality: 'She challenged the future with an extraordinary passion of quiet resentment' (p 30). She is also capable of self-criticism and admits to Major Charlesworth later in the book that she often wonders how much of her interest in the past is genuine (p 256).

In the same way Mary, who comes nearest to the writer's viewpoint in the novel, is by no means given his unqualified approval. A rebel against her family and the outmoded values it represents, a champion of the Present in its traditional fight with the Past, she is nevertheless a victim of her need to rebel. In the first chapter of the book Anne levels the identical charge against Mary that Eric had made against Lily: 'Had she ever really felt anything at all?' (p 15) Mary's excessive toleration of everyone and everything, itself a reaction against the Hall, conceals a Bohemian ethic quite as destructive in its way as the ethic which it has replaced. Mary only has to respond to Anne's sincerely expressed wish to make nursing her vocation with an 'indulgent, ever so faintly amused smile' for Anne to abandon the idea out of sheer embarrassment (p 15). On her final appearance in the book she is agreeing to play Queen Victoria for positively the last time. 'Liar!' shouts Maurice (p 288), and the point is ever so subtly made that Mary will continue to turn life into a game and to re-live the Past from which she has never fully escaped.

Maurice suggests the Truly Strong Man manqué. Had he been old enough to fight in the war, his dare-devil attitude (itself an indication of how little he values life) would have probably won him a Victoria Cross and/or death. Instead he risks his own and others' lives in mad journeys which symbolise his desire to escape from the Present and remind one of his Irish father who also escaped from his commitments by absconding from his family. It is entirely appropriate that Maurice should end up selling his escapist dream symbols to others. Nevertheless Maurice is no villain. His complete lack of responsibility is accompanied by an absence of guilt and the neurosis it gives rise to in characters like Eric and Edward. His childishness, unlike Eric's, is that of a 'thoughtless' child (p 201), one who has never grown up, as opposed to one who has reverted to a second childhood. He is an indiscriminate force of life, vital, destructive, wholly amoral.

A further sense of confusion is the book's time scheme. Isherwood only inserted the dates at the beginning of each section at the suggestion of his publisher.[11] Even then one American reviewer recommended his readers to read the book in its chronological rather than its narrative order if they were to make any sense of it.[12] In fact the time scheme is deliberately circular, as Isherwood explains with some humour at his own expense in Lions and Shadows (pp 297-8). Time is irrelevant to these victims of the war. Where the large number of separate scenes emphasises the isolation of all the characters from one another, the circular chronology of the sections emphasises the stasis which overrides their frenetic attempts to escape from the past. The past imprisons the present both in their lives and in the structure of the narrative which gives them life. Frank Kermode, who much admires this book, points out that one unfortunate result of its Conradian time scheme is that for much of the book 'people remember rather than act', which he finds 'becomes noticeable and irritating'.[13] Yet it is part of Isherwood's main strategy to show present action paralysed by memories of the past, a further means of ironically undercutting any positive moves his characters might appear to be making.

The Memorial is so hedged in by qualifications of all kinds that it is difficult to see the stance that Isherwood is adopting from which to criticise his entire cast in one way or another. The postwar world might be doomed, but what is the pre-lapserian ideal? V. S. Pritchett has suggested that Isherwood has offered the reader a possible response in the characters of Margaret and Edward at the end: 'They are making a virtue of being lost. They are thought of as people who have "faced up".'[14] This makes them sound very much like Hemingway heroes, or even an anticipation of George, the stoic hero of *A Single Man*. In fact their stoicism is narcissistic and infused with self-deception. Margaret's last letter voices her conviction that sex will matter less and less to them. The narrative disproves her assertion by showing Edward reading it to his latest homosexual pick-up. Similarly Edward's continuing death-wish is ironically placed in proper perspective by his working-class boyfriend's down-to-earth refusal to believe that anyone who has money should wish to shoot himself. The only assertion which is given narrative authority (albeit in a rather heavy-handed manner) by its position at the end of the novel is a negative one: 'that War . . . it ought never to have happened' (p 294).

In fact there are no absolute positives in *The Memorial*. Isherwood was himself the product of the same repressive upbringing that has been the undoing of his characters and inherited the puritan conviction that all men were in a fallen state. Everyone is doomed and it is the task of the novelist to portray this with as little interference as he can manage. Here are the origins of Isherwood's cultivation of the impartial stance of the reporter which Auden was to celebrate in his mock-serious poem, 'The Novelist'. The dedicated novelist, according to Auden,

> *Must struggle out of his boyish gift and learn*
> *How to be plain and awkward, how to be*
> *One after whom none think it worth to turn.*[15]

But the more Isherwood attempted to sink his personality into that of the objective observer the more false his position became. No sooner had he invented that ventriloquist's dummy, 'William Bradshaw', than he felt the necessity to own up to his identity by renaming him 'Christopher Isherwood'. The culmination of this process came with his abandonment of both 'impartiality' and the disguise that accompanied it in *Christopher and his Kind*.

The Early Wander Years

Isherwood, Heinz and Erwin took a week to get to Athens, stopping off on the way at Vienna to look up John Lehmann. In Athens they were met by Francis (once again suffering from syphilis) and a Greek boy called Tasso. On 21 May they left for the island of St Nicholas which Francis had leased from the villagers of Chalia on the Greek mainland. The island lay north of Chalkis between Chalia and the island of Euboea and was completely uninhabited apart from a small church. Isherwood has fictionalised his stay there between May and September in the 'Ambrose' section of *Down There on a Visit* in which he has mixed up fact and fiction in his usual way. There he characterises the island as 'a tiny crumb of land in the midst of the unthirst-quenching sea' on which invariably 'the sun is shining with an appalling vertical intensity'(*DTV* 99). In the novel Francis becomes 'Ambrose', Heinz 'Waldemar' (an amalgam of Heinz and 'Otto'), Erwin 'Hans Schmidt', and Tasso 'Aleko'. 'Geoffrey' and 'Maria' are inventions. In actual fact Francis was also accompanied by what he grandly called his 'chauffeur', Mitso and two other Greeks (called 'Theo' and 'Petro' in *Down There on a Visit*). Each day the masons came over from the village on the mainland to get on with the construction of the house Francis was having built for himself on the island.

Life under canvas, which suited Francis's temperament, soon got on Isherwood's nerves. Water had to be brought over from the mainland in benzine tins and tasted accordingly. Francis's Greek retainers proved hopelessly inefficient and unhygienic. The most sensational example of this—when one of the Greeks raped a duck which they were due to eat (the incident is mirrored in 'Ambrose')—may well have reminded Isherwood of *The Orators* in which Auden makes reference to 'the fucked hen', a phrase which Eliot as his publisher suggested replacing by 'the

June bride' much to Auden's amusement.[1] There was no privacy. Isherwood's work on *The Lost* eventually tailed off rather in the way that his fictitious diary in 'Ambrose' dries up. 'I believe', he wrote in an early draft of 'Ambrose', 'on that island, I came as near as I have ever come to losing my identity.'[2] Much of the same feeling surfaces in his letters of the time: 'I don't know how long we shall stay here. The heat obliterates all will, all plans, all decisions.'[3] In fact he couldn't leave the island before the autumn because he had invested so much money in paying for his own, Heinz's and part of Erwin's fares there. In view of the fact that he was to portray the island in 'Ambrose' as a microcosmic homosexual dictatorship (albeit run by an anarchist), one of his comments in a letter to Spender is interesting: 'Talking it over this morning with Heinz, we came to the remarkable but simple conclusion that what we lack on this island are one or two really nice women. . . . How I long for a little gaiety, a little innocent fun, instead of all this stale winey talk about boys and brothels and the best way of building the lavatory.'[4]

Although 'Ambrose' suggests otherwise, Isherwood did succeed in getting some work done on his draft novel. On 28 July he wrote to Olive Mangeot: 'I am just finishing off Jean in my novel and couldn't resist having a scene at a party at Lady Klein's. You appear for a moment, in the background.'[5] Nevertheless he was destined to abandon this version of *The Lost* and start again within the year. Otherwise he kept his diary going, fled to Athens on at least three occasions when he couldn't bear life on the island a moment longer, and gradually worked himself up into a frenzy of jealousy over Heinz who had adapted happily to life on the island and got on well with all the Greeks despite the language barrier. Finally, when he could afford to leave, he staged a quarrel with Heinz, whom he forced into making the decision to split up. They left the island on 6 September and took a boat to Marseilles. It appeared to be the end of his life with Heinz: 'He's sitting about with a face like death and won't speak', Isherwood wrote in his diary. 'I shall have to get rid of him as soon as I'm in Paris' (*CK* 113). Instead they were reconciled in Marseilles (restored to sanity most likely by their return to civilisation) and spent the last two weeks of September at Meudon, a suburb of Paris, where

Dr Rolf Katz lived. Katz was still an energetic Communist propagandist whom Isherwood had first met in Berlin. In 1933 Hitler's putsch had forced him to flee to France. He features frequently in Isherwood's life throughout the 1930s and provided the model for 'Dr Fisch' in the 'Waldemar' section of *Down There on a Visit*, besides turning up under his own name in *The Condor and the Cows*.

He brought Heinz home with him to London on 30 September where his mother's instinctive recognition that Heinz was from the working classes caused her to patronise him ever so slightly, much to Isherwood's discomfort. In *Christopher and his Kind* he admits to a feeling of relief when Heinz's tourist visa ran out and he had to return to the Continent, as he had become a hostage to fortune in Isherwood's continuing guerilla warfare with his mother. While Heinz was in England Isherwood took him to Oxford to see Archie Campbell who was at the university. Campbell remembers how singularly unimpressed Heinz was with all things English. When asked what he thought of anything he would invariably reply, 'Nicht besonders' (nothing special).[6]

In mid-October 1933 Jean Ross telephoned Isherwood with a proposition. She had just met a Viennese-born Jewish film director called Berthold Viertel whom Gaumont-British had lured over from Hollywood to make three films in their London studios. The first of these was *Little Friend*, the story of a little girl who reconciles her parents after they had quarrelled by attempting to commit suicide. The producer had hired Margaret Kennedy to work on the screenplay because of her recent success with *The Constant Nymph*, a novel with a similar subject. She had just walked out on the studios to concentrate on *Escape Me Never*, a play of hers that was in rehearsal at the time. Jean had suggested Isherwood as a replacement to Viertel who had asked to see his latest novel. Could she have a copy of *The Memorial*? Sceptical of Jean's story, Isherwood suggested that she buy a copy of *The Memorial* herself. If Viertel hired him then, Jean countered, would he agree to give her half or all of his first week's salary?[7] Done, Isherwood said: Viertel read Edward's suicide scene and was sufficiently impressed to hire him within the week.

His first experience of working in the film industry provided him with the material for his post-war novelette, *Prater Violet* (although he dreamed up the plot for the musical comedy in it with the help of John van Druten). In it Dr Friedrich Bergmann is quite closely modelled on Berthold Viertel. A forty-eight-year-old Austrian poet-turned-director, he had moved out to Hollywood in 1928 where he lived with his family in Santa Monica canyon. His homesick descriptions of life in California and of the family's glamorous friends (like Greta Garbo) must have implanted in Isherwood a dream of life on the West Coast that was to be realised six years later. Like his fictional counterpart, Viertel carried what Isherwood has called 'his psychological "weather" ' around with him (*CK* 119), and reduced the normally talkative novelist to the role of passive confidant and pupil. However, Viertel has recalled how he found in Isherwood 'a dialogue writer of unusual finesse and tenderness'.[8] Isherwood for his part has said: 'Working with Viertel was totally unlike any other movie work I've done since. In fact, I can't remember the physical act of writing at all, because it seemed to me that we talked the whole film into existence.'[9] *Prater Violet* also provides fictionalised sketches of Chan Balcon, the executive alluded to in *Christopher and his Kind* (p 127) (although 'Chatsworth' also slightly caricatures Victor Saville whom Isherwood worked for in 1940), Lydia Sherwood ('Anita Hayden') who played the mother's part in *Little Friend*, and Robert Stevenson, the associate producer, in 'Sandy Ashmeade'. However 'Ashmeade' also incorporates features borrowed from his contemporary at Repton, Sir Basil Bartlett, whose writing is again alluded to in 'Ambrose', where 'Isherwood' reads a glowing review of 'Timmy's' new society novel with growing disgust (*DTV* 144–5).[10]

In mid-December the studio asked Isherwood to stay on, officially as dialogue director, unofficially as a mediator between the volatile Viertel and the studio executives. Missing Heinz badly and repressing all memory of how unsuccessful his last stay at home had been, Isherwood wrote to him sending enough money for him to come over to London with enough to spare, he explained, to convince the immigration officials that he could support himself. On 5 January 1934 he went to Harwich with Auden to meet Heinz off the boat. Totally guileless, Heinz had brought Isherwood's letter enclosing the money with him and had shown it to the immigration officers as proof that the money was his. They promptly sent him back by the next boat. Auden was convinced that he hadn't a chance from the start because one of the immigration officers was himself a homosexual and recognised the situation at once. All Isherwood could do was first to complete the screenplay and then in late January to collect Heinz from Berlin and put him in lodgings in Amsterdam. Isherwood admits that he was principally motivated by the need to show his mother that Heinz's safety came before every other consideration. In scoring this point against her, he ironically contrived to threaten Heinz's safety in the long run far more seriously, eventually turning him into a fugitive from German justice.

Back at the studio in February for the shooting, Isherwood was soon lost in the drama of studio life. He has subsequently claimed that the two months' experience of filming *Little Friend*, doing rewrites on the spot and hearing them spoken almost immediately, permanently affected his writing: 'You have suddenly the most tremendous sense of immediacy, from being a kind of introvert, shut up in this room, you're terrifically extroverted. . . . I think this had a lasting effect on me, starting with *Mr Norris*. . . . I took to hearing much more clearly what the speeches would sound like that people said.'[12] He enjoyed the extrovert role in the studio and invited many of his friends to visit the set, including Forster. He also needed the large sums of money it earned him if he was to go away somewhere with Heinz and get *The Lost* written. When his friends' wisecracks at the expense of *Little Friend* began pouring in from all sides the following summer Isherwood adopted a rakish air: 'After all,' he wrote to Plomer, 'if I sold myself, I did at least make them pay handsomely for me.'[13]

As soon as filming was finished he rejoined Heinz in Amsterdam. On 4 April they left Holland for the Canary Islands, having had insufficient time to catch a boat to Tahiti where Isherwood most wanted to go, because of French formalities.[14] He spent two months in the servants' penthouse quarters of the Towers Strand Hotel in Las Palmas looking out across the bay towards Tenerife. He had once again started writing a new version of *The Lost* on the boat journey to Gran Canaria, but, by 9 May he was informing Spender, 'It won't do and I'm back for the hundredth time on a book of memoirs about Germany.'[15] Isherwood has summarised the elaborate plot of *The Lost* in *Christopher and his Kind* (pp 135–6). It amounted to an intricate network of relationships which brought Peter Wilkinson, the neurotic English hero (another Truly Weak Man) into contact with Otto Nowak, the Landauers, Sally Bowles and Klaus, Baron von Pregnitz, Olga and Mr Norris. In Las Palmas Isherwood finally faced up to the fact that there was no advantage to be gained from having all these characters meeting one another. 'But it was a bitter moment', he has recollected, 'when I disentangled all this stuff. I felt I was tearing the thing to bits and I was really scared.'[16] At the end of May accordingly he put aside his book of German memoirs and began writing *Mr Norris Changes Trains*, a far less ambitious version of *The Lost* (as it was still called) which concentrated exclusively on Mr Norris because, he has explained, 'he was the only character in *The Lost* . . . who was purely heroic',[17] and therefore worth a whole book to himself.

On 6 June he and Heinz moved to the adjacent island of Tenerife where they stayed at a pension near Orotava (Pavillon Troika) on the lower slopes of Mount Teide. There he rapidly completed *Mr Norris Changes Trains* by 12 August. He described it variously in letters to friends as 'a portrait of a traitor',[18] 'a sort of glorified shocker'[19] and 'more or less knockabout farce . . . chiefly about the Underworld of Berlin'.[20] In the meantime he had taken time off from the novel in mid-July to climb Mount Teide, the twelve-thousand-foot volcano that dominates Tenerife, in the company of Heinz and a German schoolmaster who turned out to be pro-Nazi. Heinz was far too delighted to have a German-speaking companion to worry about his political convictions while Isherwood projected on to him all the vague threats which Nazi Germany held poised over Heinz's unsuspecting head. Both this expedition and one they had made in Gran Canaria to El Nublo at the beginning of June are reflected in Stephen's similar trips with Michael in *The World in the Evening*. Isherwood also made literary use of a trip they both made around the smaller islands of La Palma, Gomera and Hierro in late August once he had finished *Mr Norris Changes Trains*. He wrote 'A Day in Paradise' at Upward's instigation for *The Ploughshare*, the organ of the Teachers' Anti-War Movement, in which he crudely contrasts the tourist view of one of these islands with the barely concealed poverty and accompanying presence of communism. A letter to Forster tells of his meetings with 'The Spanish Explorer-Captain, Don Ramiro Sanz' as his card read, and his rival in the professional begging stakes, a Hungarian who invariably demanded money as of right from the mayors of all the larger towns. Both figures feature in 'The Turn Round the World', a sketch that appeared in *The Listener* the following year. The two sketches were written early in 1934 and are reprinted in *Exhumations*.[21]

Although Isherwood wanted to return to England, Heinz's father had written begging him to keep him out of Germany.[22] As a compromise Isherwood settled on Copenhagen where the immigration laws were reasonably flexible and German was a second language. He and Heinz spent the whole of September travelling through Spanish Morocco, Spain and then by boat to Copenhagen. There he met Spender's young Danish friend, Paul Kryger, and Spender's elder brother, Michael who was living in Classensgade with his German wife Erica. They helped him find and move into a minute flat in the same modern block as they were in. There they stayed throughout the winter until mid-April 1935. Erica Spender told Isherwood that whenever she saw the two of them together she would think to herself: 'My God, they must bore each other to death, how can they *bear* it?' (*CK* 147) Apart from doing a lecture in Sweden about his experience with Gaumont-British and translating the odd article for Katz, he spent his time working on his book of Berlin reminiscences which he had begun again in late August out in the Canaries.[23]

The Berlin book was already stuck, however, when early in November Auden sent him the typescript of *The Chase*, a play he had written for Doone's Group Theatre and which was an amalgamation of the reformatory sub-plot from their former collaboration, *The Enemies of a Bishop*, and *The Fronny*, a play about the search for a missing heir which Auden had written on his own in 1930.[24] The two friends drifted into collaboration when Isherwood started making a whole series of suggestions for new scenes as well as for the elimination and revision of existing ones. When it became clear that the entire conception of the play was undergoing transformation Auden persuaded

Faber, who had already accepted *The Chase* for publication, to advance him the air fare to fly out for a personal consultation with Isherwood. After Auden's brief visit to Copenhagen from 10–13 January 1935 Isherwood wrote to Spender of the play that was now retitled 'Where is Francis?': 'It has gradually turned into a completely new work, but keeping the best things from the old version.'[25] By the end of January Isherwood had finished typing the new version which was subsequently renamed *The Dog Beneath the Skin* at Rupert Doone's suggestion. T. S. Eliot, Auden's publisher at Faber, was most reluctant to bracket Isherwood's name with Auden's as joint author and only agreed to after Auden had written to him pointing out that Isherwood had been responsible for outlining the plan of most of the scenes and further listing the scenes which were entirely written by his collaborator.[26]

Ever since he had turned his back on Berlin Isherwood had grown increasingly concerned at the threat of war that the new Germany posed. As early as August 1933 he was asking John Lehmann 'Is there going to be a war?' and then adding 'This question may well be answered before you read it.'[27] Prompted by Katz's alarmist predictions, Isherwood lived throughout most of the 1930s quite sure that war would break out at any moment. He begged Leonard Woolf to publish *Mr Norris Changes Trains* earlier, convinced that by 1935 it would 'no longer have any meaning whatever'[28] because, as he wrote to Spender in November, 'what with Yugo-Slavia and the Saar, I have the gravest doubts whether my novel will ever see the light at all.'[29] In this respect he was typical of his literary generation almost all of whom felt 'hounded by external events' like Spender[30] and 'intensely conscious that war was coming' like Upward.[31] In March 1935 Hitler introduced conscription. Isherwood, determined not to be forcibly parted from Heinz for the next five years, left Denmark on 13 April for Brussels to discuss with Gerald Hamilton who was living there ways of having Heinz's nationality changed. At the end of April he left Heinz in the uncertain care of Hamilton to spend a fortnight in London where *Mr Norris Changes Trains*, which had come out in February, had been received with great enthusiasm by most of the critics and had gone into a second printing within two weeks of publication.

Geoffrey Grigson has described how at a party of this time

Jonathan Cape asked to be introduced to the author of the successful *Mr Norris* and proceeded to ask Isherwood whether he could publish his next novel. Isherwood naturally took some satisfaction in reminding the forgetful old man that not only had they met before, but that Cape had actually published his first novel only to reject his second one.[32] Courted by publishers and praised by critics, Isherwood had at last achieved recognition as an important young novelist of his day.

Mr Norris Changes Trains
(The Last of Mr Norris)

In an interview he gave in 1961 Isherwood has suggested that his fiction divides itself into 'constructed novels' on the one hand and 'dynamic portraits' on the other. In the first category he placed *All the Conspirators*, *The Memorial*, *Mr Norris* ('I suppose') and *The World in the Evening*; in the second, *Goodbye to Berlin*, *Prater Violet* and *Down There on a Visit*.[1] The 'I suppose' expresses a doubt about the status of *Mr Norris* which is evident in later remarks he has made about this novel. Even after he had decided surgically to remove the figure of Mr Norris from the main body of *The Lost*, he was still 'under the spell of writing a contrived novel with a plot and all kinds of . . . tricks and surprises', whereas what he 'was trying to do . . . was to draw portraits'.[2] *Mr Norris* is a transitional work within this context, a book that set out to be a portrait but reverted to a plotted thriller-cum-spy story.

According to Isherwood this is a major flaw in the novel because the Eric Ambler element in the second half of the book lured him outside the limits of his own experience. Yet it was in order to approximate more closely to life as he experienced it that he had introduced a first-person narrator into *Mr Norris*. If he was to be true to the Germany he had come to know as a foreigner mixing with foreigners as often as with Germans, he argued, then it would be a form of dishonesty to identify with any character but himself as observer. But in making Mr Norris engage in international espionage he involved his narrator in a milieu about which he knew nothing at first hand. Moreover he trapped his fictional self into behaving with a naïvety quite alien to his real self who, he claims, 'would have seen right through these people and had nothing to do with them'.[3]

Other criticisms follow thick and fast. Having introduced a first-person narrator in order to concentrate on his dynamic portrait of Mr Norris, he had constantly to shut up William Bradshaw, 'because otherwise', he has explained, 'he becomes so interesting that he upstages the characters.'[4] In particular he felt compelled to keep hidden from the reader his homosexuality which, apart from other effects, would have turned his narrator into another 'evil monster' like Mr Norris and interfered with the novel's focus. The result has been, according to Isherwood, 'a kind of void in the books'[5] about Berlin in the form of a faceless, sexless narrator, whom he also accuses of heartlessness: 'The only genuine monster was the young foreigner who passed gaily through these scenes of desolation, misinterpreting them to suit his childish fantasy' (E 87).

Over the years, in interviews, in his preface to Gerald Hamilton's memoir Mr Norris and I, in lectures and finally in Christopher and his Kind, Isherwood has evolved an interlocking set of critical responses to this book that have more to do with his own development in later life than with the novel he wrote in his thirtieth year. The militant Isherwood of the 1970s wishes that he had had the courage to have become an underground writer who admitted to his narrator's homosexuality, since it was his own homosexuality, he claims, which provided him with such special insights as he had. Whether this would have produced a better novel than Mr Norris is a matter for speculation. But the Mr Norris he wrote is the product of the experience and inhibitions of a much younger Isherwood and much of its subtlety and irony derives from the compromises he felt compelled to reach at the time. Gore Vidal, who has been faced with parallel problems in his own work, has rightly written of Mr Norris that 'what might have been a limitation in a narrator the author, rather mysteriously, made a virtue of.'[6]

Part of the explanation for this paradox lies in Isherwood's recognition at other moments of the fact that subjective truth necessarily allows for the distortion of objective fact. 'When I started writing about Berlin', he has recalled, 'I found that the story would be more coherent and indeed truer if I fictionalised it to some degree.'[7] He is alluding there to Mr Norris but the same principle can be extended to the narrator. Just as Mr Norris is separated from Gerald Hamilton by 'Gerald-as-I-chose-to-see-him' according to Isherwood (E 85), so William Bradshaw is separated from Isherwood by his own mental image of himself that is likely to be as much of a caricature as those he constructs of others. In his fictionalisation of life as he experienced it in Berlin his criterion was not whether the originals of Mr Norris or Bradshaw actually underwent each experience described in the novel but how they would have behaved had they done so. This is the narrative technique he employed in all his fiction in which biographical fact and imaginative fantasy are woven together to produce a fabric of subjective truth.

Furthermore his narrator's anonymity and passivity positively encourage the reader to project himself into Bradshaw's position and to see Mr Norris through his gradually opened eyes. The entire novel is concerned with the problem of deception, and obviously the secretive Arthur Norris with his wig and his equivocal habits of speech is the most complex example of the tissue of lies, evasions and deceit which also characterises the sexual and political underworlds of Berlin in the novel. Bradshaw's first sight of him is 'of a schoolboy surprised in the act of breaking one of the rules' (p 7), although the narrator goes on innocently to underestimate which rule he is breaking. This initial underestimation is characteristic of Bradshaw throughout the book. On every occasion he is outwitted by Norris into placing a less sinister interpretation on events surrounding him than is in fact the case. He unconsciously assists Norris in his elaborate game of self-deception by turning him into a romantic criminal for his friends' benefit, 'a most amazing old crook' (p 58) whom he did not actually credit with the ability to break any but the most petty laws. Bradshaw is therefore used by Isherwood to trap the reader into the same fallacy, to suspend his normal moral judgement, despite the warnings he and Bradshaw have received from the opinions of hard-bitten characters like Helen Pratt and Fritz Wendel, and despite Bradshaw's own self-confessed prejudices in favour of an image of Norris that is clearly as much of a distortion as was that earlier creation of Isherwood's fantasy-life, Reynard Moxon.

Norris is at any rate a very unusual combination of charm and wit balanced by a complete absence of moral principles. As Gerald Hamilton said of himself, 'I am not everybody's cup of tea. But I am certain people's liqueur.'[8] His aestheticism neatly illustrates how he contrives to turn questions of morality into matters of taste. His morning toilet (itself a ritual of disguise), his habit of travelling first class, of eating at the best restaurants and drinking champagne at the smallest excuse, of happily pawning the sitting-room carpet to finance his birthday party add up to the picture of a lovable eccentric, a gentleman of the old sort fallen on hard times, someone who deserves one's sympathy and understanding. But Norris uses the same appeal to aesthetic values to justify actions and commitments that properly belong to the sphere of ethics. He gives as his reason for joining the Communist Party his childhood hatred of tyranny and injustice, which, he explains, 'offends my sense of the beautiful. It is so stupid and unaesthetic' (p 83). But as beauty is in the eye of the beholder, he actually reveals the egotistical and subjective nature of his moral vision, although Bradshaw chooses to ignore this fairly obvious deduction from the facts Norris gives him.

The more one examines Norris's explanations of his conduct, the more one realises how gullible Bradshaw is. He justifies Schmidt's function to Bradshaw by a characteristic appeal to his own need for gentility and decorum:

'It is very painful for anyone of our own class to say certain things to certain individuals. It offends our delicate sensibilities. One has to be so crude.' Schmidt, it seemed, experienced no pain. He was quite prepared to say anything to anybody. . . . He followed Arthur's wildest shots, and returned with money like a retriever bringing home a duck. (p 67)

Bradshaw has made the necessary deductions here but seems incapable of coming to the obvious conclusion that Arthur is a crook who conceals his criminal activities from the world by adopting a mask of snobbery and aestheticism, both of which attributes he can make to seem attractive by his undoubted wit and charm. Meanwhile Schmidt, who is in fact only his assistant in the crimes he perpetrates, bears all the odium attached to such immoral activities as blackmail and treachery. In an interview with Alan Wilde in 1964 Isherwood revealed the fact that Schmidt is 'quite literally a familiar',[9] the double of Arthur Norris. Bradshaw might choose to distinguish between the smiling face of Arthur and the snarling features of Schmidt;

but the reader is intended to realise by the end of the book that both faces belong to a modern Janus whose associations with war are appropriate in view of the connections Isherwood simultaneously makes between Norris's amateur intrigues and the far more sinister manipulations of Hitler and the Nazis whose rise to power by the end of the book presages world war.

What is it that neutralises Bradshaw's normal moral judgement, blinding him to the sinister aspects of Norris so blatantly apparent in his alter ego, Schmidt? David Thomas has suggested that Bradshaw is a successor to Eric Vernon, another Truly Weak Man who 'attempts to purge himself of neurotic fears . . . by the familiar Baudelairian descent into the nether world—the society of criminals, sexual eccentrics, and revolutionary politics.'[10] A victim of puritanical English social and moral norms, he is compelled to suspend all judgement in these areas to effect his own cure. But Isherwood tells us virtually nothing about Bradshaw's past. What he does suggest, as John Whitehead has pointed out, is a filial relationship between the narrator and Mr Norris, who becomes for him 'a disreputable Father-figure', reminiscent of the relations connecting Hal to Falstaff.[11] Even Bradshaw's feelings of possessiveness towards Arthur are reminiscent of a child's jealous love for its parents, just as his occasional paternal scoldings echo a child's imitation of its parents' normal behaviour towards it. Mr Norris actually refers to his status with Bradshaw as *'in loco parentis'* on one occasion, to which Bradshaw teasingly replies 'Pardon, Daddy' (p 187).

For as long as he is fixated by Mr Norris as a parental substitute, Bradshaw is incapable of sufficient detachment from him to read the signs which are liberally provided for him and the reader by Isherwood. Not until Bayer reveals the extent of Norris's duplicity does the narrator achieve sufficient distance from him to see him in his true colours. In his review of *Mr Norris* in the *New Statesman*, Cyril Connolly suggested that Bradshaw does undergo a form of education in the course of the book by the end of which he has grown up.[12] Certainly during his interview with Bayer he is compelled to realise his gullibility in his past dealings with Norris. After his humiliating confession to Bayer he is at best purged of his romantic fantasies about the criminal underworld to which he was so neurotically drawn at the beginning of the novel. On the other hand he only substitutes one father-figure for another; Bayer replaces Mr Norris as parental substitute and mythic hero. His tone to Bradshaw is 'kind, almost paternal' (p 232) as he tells him not to blame himself too much for his past foolishness. Bradshaw's subsequent dealings with Norris are like those of Hal with Falstaff once he has assumed the trappings of responsibility. Nevertheless, by the end of the book Bayer himself is dead, and Bradshaw is deprived of the Truly Strong Man whose presence had obscured his own need to confront the Test now posed by the rise of Hitler to absolute power.

Samuel Hynes has suggested that the invasion of the private by the public world is the central theme of Mr Norris.[13] Even if one questions its centrality, this theme does give the portrayal and unmasking of Arthur Norris a significance which lifts the novel above the level of 'a glorified shocker' to which Isherwood relegated it in one of his many moments of self-effacement. From the opening pages Mr Norris lives in fear of the public world and its authorities. He only expands in private and much of the earlier part of the novel concentrates on his personal life and friends, his private reading tastes, and his kinky sexual practices. Bradshaw, himself an exile from the public life of his home country, is fascinated by his friend's cultivation of his own pleasures in his circle of acquaintances, a circle which almost parodies conventional society and its rigid regulation of how its members may behave in public. At Olga's anything goes and even Norris appears completely at home there. Nevertheless the public world is not so easily evaded. Schmidt glowers in the background, creditors shout through locked doors and soon, to Bradshaw's immense surprise, Arthur has joined the Communist Party, admittedly hardly establishment politics, but nevertheless a clear sign of his dependence on the external world for the means by which he pursues his private pleasures.

Arthur's self-centred hedonism in fact parallels the attitudes of the Berlin population at large during the final years of the Weimar Republic. His sexual masochism is like their political self-abasement. His distortion of language to conceal the truth from Bradshaw and everyone else is paralleled by the debasement of linguistic meaning by the politicians and the press as the political confrontation between the right and the left

heightens. And like them he is made to pay for his abandonment of responsibility by the escalating intrusion of public
affairs into his private life. The police summon him for question-
ing; Schmidt finally shows his claws over the pawn-money for
the sitting-room carpet; and mid-way through the novel he is
forced to flee the country in just the same spirit as the German
song-writers were advocating private escape: 'Find a dear little
sweetheart, they advised, and forget the slump, ignore the
unemployed' (p 131). But like the Baron's imaginary island,
the private world proves an illusory dream, as the march of
events overtakes all the characters in the novel.

It is the winter of 1931–2, half-way through the period covered
by the novel (late 1930 to spring 1933), and Isherwood seizes
the opportunity of Norris's long absence to bring the political
situation to the forefront of the narrative for the first time.
From this point on the reader is never allowed for long to forget
the violent events leading up to Hitler's accession to power.
There are frequent authorial interjections describing the political
scene like those at the beginning of Chapters 11 and 16. Almost
all the characters become embroiled in the political maelstrom,
ending up with Bayer and Kuno dead, Otto on the run and Anni
and Olga (like most Berliners) changing their allegiance to
survive. In the foreground are the bumbling machinations of
Arthur Norris, whose attempts to control the public world
for his personal financial betterment are eventually foiled and
exposed. But Isherwood uses his double-dealing as a comic
inversion of the far more skilful and successful machinations by
which Hitler is simultaneously usurping political power. This
identification between Norris and Hitler is finally given ironic
expression in two of the letters he sends Bradshaw from South
America after Hitler has succeeded in his bid for power by the
use of just those methods which Norris himself had employed in
his small-scale life of crime:

> It makes me positively *tremble* with indignation to think of the
> workers delivered over to these men, who, whatever you may
> say, are nothing more or less than *criminals*.

and again:

> It is indeed tragic to see how, even in these days, a *clever* and
> *unscrupulous liar* can deceive millions. (p 277)

Norris is incorrigible, but Bradshaw has finally realised to what extent Norris is the Jekyll to Schmidt's Hyde and, by implication, how similar these two are to the two faces of Hitler whose sinister shadow darkens the closing pages of the novel.

When one compares *Mr Norris* to *The Memorial* one is at once struck by the difference in style and tone between the two novels. They could almost have been written by different authors. Isherwood ascribes the change to his experience of working on *Little Friend* immediately prior to writing this novel. Script-writing forced him to visualise his scenes to a much greater extent than before, ruthlessly to prune his prose and to treat his dialogue with a dramatist's economy.[14] Isherwood's astonishing new command of what Cyril Connolly called 'the colloquial style' (in contradistinction to the more ornate 'Mandarin style' of the previous generation)[15] deservedly earned him praise from many of his reviewers and critics alike. Its apparent simplicity however is highly deceptive and caused even such an admirer of his as Connolly to write ambiguously of his 'fatal readability'.[16] A more perceptive and thorough-going examination of Isherwood's stylistic characteristics has more recently appeared in Alan Wilde's critical study of Isherwood's writing.[17] Wilde examines at considerable length the pervasive presence of an ironic vision in Isherwood's work which continually undercuts conventional narrative expectations and has a cumulatively reductive and deflationary effect.

Open *Mr Norris* at random and one is first struck by the brevity of the clauses or sentences which remain firmly distinct from one another, by his normal avoidance of metaphors and sparing use of similes, and by his choice of a vernacular vocabulary. On the other hand one quickly becomes aware of an elegance of diction and a sophisticated sense of wit which appears to run counter to his espousal of stylistic simplicity. The ironies that result from these seemingly opposite pairs of attributes are in fact equally due to another technique he learnt from his spell at Gaumont-British Studios, the art of juxtaposition. All his novels are structured by a series of contrasts, humorous and violent, comic and tragic. Richard Mayne further claims that in all his novels since *The Memorial* 'humour has been used as a screen for their serious purpose.'[18] This confirms the impression that with *Mr Norris* Isherwood has finally hit upon his own highly personal way of 'tea-tabling' experience. Forster, who had considerable reservations about this novel,[19] has been left firmly behind, and Isherwood has at last found his own voice to become, according to Connolly, 'a hope of English fiction'.[20]

12

The Last Years with Heinz

During his brief visit to London in early May 1935 Isherwood was invited by Joe Ackerley, the new arts editor of *The Listener*, to become a reviewer for him. This, in addition to the royalties from *Mr Norris*, was to provide him with a useful supplementary income over the next two years during which he wrote some forty reviews. According to Francis King, Ackerley came to consider Isherwood 'the most consistently brilliant of the reviewers, then anonymous, that he employed in the decade before the war'.[1]

On 12 May Isherwood rejoined Heinz in Brussels. The following day they crossed into Holland to renew Heinz's Belgian permit. When this was refused they settled in Amsterdam instead, taking a room at Emmastraat 24. Sharing the same pension was Klaus Mann, the son of Thomas Mann, who was editing an anti-Nazi refugee periodical called *Die Sammlung* and writing a book on Tchaikovsky. The entire family had fled from Germany in 1933 and, that May, Klaus's sister Erika arrived in Amsterdam with her company, The Peppermill, which was touring Europe with a revue satirising the Nazis mainly written by Erika. When she asked him to help her acquire a new nationality by a marriage of convenience, Isherwood reluctantly refused. His main reason, he has claimed rather puzzlingly, was a disinclination to associate Heinz through him with a prominent opponent of the Nazi regime. 'As things turned out', he told Carolyn Heilbrun in 1976, 'it might well have made trouble for him later, when he got arrested by the Gestapo.'[2] At this time, however, Heinz was breaking no law, since Germans living abroad were not due to be conscripted into military service until 1936. As Isherwood was ostensibly planning to remove Heinz from Europe before the end of the year, his concern for Heinz does suggest a subconscious fear or wish that Heinz was bound to end up back in Germany sooner or later. As an alternative, Isherwood suggested that Erika Mann approach Auden who readily obliged, marrying her on 14 June only a day before she was deprived of her German citizenship. Auden briefly informed Spender: 'I didn't see her till the ceremony and perhaps I shall never see her again. But she is very nice.'[3]

In June Isherwood began his next novel, *Paul is Alone*. Like *The Lost* it was an attempt to amalgamate his disparate experiences, in this case of Francis in Greece, Franz Ullmann from Berlin, Viertel in London, the Nazi schoolmaster in Tenerife and an Erika Mann type of character in Copenhagen. Paul, the hero, a romantic thief and a liar, is based on a kleptomaniac he knew in Berlin in 1929.[4] Since he was really trying to write about his own life between 1933 and 1935, Paul and all his other inventions were eventually to prove too great an obstacle and the novel was to be abandoned after a frustrating year.

Simultaneously another literary project was being planned that was to prove richly productive. On 7 July John Lehmann visited Isherwood on his way back to London from Vienna, his head full of a new magazine he wanted to launch for the writers who had contributed to *New Country* and foreign writers of a similar inclination. During this visit their discussions convinced Lehmann that the idea 'was no longer a pleasant daydream, but something about to become real'.[5] Among other things, the new magazine was to provide an outlet for stories considered too long by most periodicals. In *Christopher and his Kind* Isherwood claims that Lehmann's subsequent demand for shorter fiction of this kind for *New Writing* was 'responsible for the informal form of *Goodbye to Berlin*' (p 161). This statement could be misinterpreted to mean that *Goodbye to Berlin* is a happy accident, a mere gathering of individually conceived stories collected under a convenient generic title. In fact a postcard he sent Lehmann that winter categorically states that the first of his stories that he prepared for *New Writing*, 'The Kulaks' (as 'The Nowaks' was originally called), was 'to be part of a larger book', a fact which he has confirmed in more than one interview.[6]

In between giving private tuition, reviewing and struggling with *Paul is Alone*, Isherwood was helping Gerald Hamilton write the first of his many autobiographies, *As Young as Sophocles*, in return for Hamilton's help in obtaining for Heinz a permit to stay in Belgium and, more importantly, a change of nationality. During the summer he was also visited in Amsterdam by Humphrey Spender, his mother, Robson-Scott, E. M. Forster and his policeman friend, Bob Buckingham, Stephen Spender, and Brian Howard with his German boyfriend, Anton Altmann. Brian Howard, a leading Oxford aesthete in his day, has already become part of literary legend as the most outrageous member of what Martin Green has called the 'Children of the Sun'.[7] A devotee of pleasure and a talented poet without application, his life with the vacuous, semi-alcoholic Anton (who had been refused entry to even more countries than Heinz) offered Isherwood a warning of the dangers inherent in his own relationship with Heinz. That Isherwood was aware of these dangers is apparent from his constant efforts to find Heinz an occupation and his refusal to set up house with Brian and Toni in Portugal where they went in October.

In September Isherwood contrived to obtain a permit for Heinz to enter Belgium by the simple device of going first to Luxembourg. At the beginning of October they were joined by Spender's new boyfriend, Tony, called 'Jimmy Younger' in *World Within World*, followed by Spender himself. Tony was an ex-guardsman from Cardiff who was in much the same dependent relationship to Spender as Heinz was to Isherwood. Both writers perversely tended to blame their boyfriends for their enforced idleness. During this visit plans were hatched to go that winter to Portugal, which Isherwood saw as 'a waiting room for South America'[8] where Heinz would be beyond the reach of the German authorities. Apart from revising Gerald Hamilton's books of memoirs, Isherwood spent the time before their departure canvassing friends for contributions to the first number of Lehmann's *New Writing*, besides preparing his own contribution, 'The Nowaks'.

After Isherwood had paid a brief visit to London at the beginning of December 1935, the party of four friends left Brussels on 10 December, taking a boat from Antwerp to Lisbon which they reached on 17 December. By 21 December they had moved into a five-bedroomed house on the outskirts of Sintra called Alecrim do Norte. Isherwood soon added a whole collection of animals to the household mainly to give Heinz some occupation, as Tony had been given responsibility for supervising the two Portuguese servants and keeping the accounts. Apart from seeing much of Anton, whom Brian Howard had deposited at Sintra, they soon become part of the rather weird set of British emigrés resident in the area. These 'members of this psychic fringe', as Isherwood calls them (*CK* 173), failed to supply material for his writing, although they do survive vividly in the joint diary kept by Spender, Isherwood and Tony during their first month together.

On 16 January 1936 Humphrey Spender, Stephen's younger brother, arrived for a month's stay. He remembers Isherwood as a magnetic personality with endless resources of wit and humour. His relationship with Heinz, Humphrey Spender felt, was a strange mixture of genuine attachment alternating with periods of boredom with his company.[9] Humphrey also kept a diary during his stay that provides a valuable insight into the paradoxes inherent in this phase of Isherwood's life:

> The relationship between Christopher and Heinz is complicated. C makes no apparent effort to bring him into conversations . . .; it is therefore difficult to know exactly how much notice to take of him. He is obviously anxious to keep any external influences from him as much as possible, for should Heinz be taken from him—by a woman, for example—he would lose the decisive factor in his life, the reason for all his wanderings from country to country.[10]

Stephen Spender, meanwhile, Humphrey's diary records, was under the mistaken impression that Isherwood was trying to manage him, while Tony was so intent on proving his intellectual equality with the two writers that he bored everyone with his unending conversation and tended to boss and look down on Heinz. Rows flared up about nothing. When gambling fever overtook them all at the Lisbon Casino there were endless recriminations over the inevitable losses they all sustained. By mid-February, when Humphrey Spender left, he could already foresee the split-up of the quartet and in mid-March Stephen Spender and Tony retreated from the group ménage. Stephen Spender blames the break-up on his own inability to handle a homosexual relationship without identifying so closely with the other person that this became an unbearable burden on his partner.[11] In fact all four of them had some point of friction and Heinz and Tony in particular were temperamentally incapable of peacefully cohabiting for long.

Two days after Spender left, Auden arrived to collaborate on their next play, *The Ascent of F6*. Although the press reactions to the published text of *The Dog Beneath the Skin* had been largely dismissive, the Group Theatre production of a shortened version that opened in January 1936 had been more of a success, and Rupert Doone and Robert Medley had both urged Auden and Isherwood to write another play for them. During Auden's month-long stay the two of them managed to concoct, write and type the play which Isherwood felt was 'much maturer than Dogskin; and far more of a unity'.[12]

The following month he was back at work on *Paul is Alone* from which he had cut Fronny because 'he acted Paul off the stage.'[13] Nevertheless on 29 May he dramatically scrapped the novel and decided to begin a book of autobiographical pieces provisionally called *Scenes from an Education* that would include 'An Evening at the Bay' (his contribution to *New Country*), 'The Nowaks' (which had appeared in the first number of *New Writing* that spring amid wide acclaim) and a revised version of his Greek diary (that had been cut from the abortive novel).[14] His diary entry for 29 May shows that he also planned to include two other autobiographical episodes from the 1920s destined to be incorporated in *Lions and Shadows*, four other episodes that, with 'The Nowaks' and 'The Landauers', were to constitute *Goodbye to Berlin*, and his experiences at Gaumont-British which he finally used for *Prater Violet* (CK 182). Once again he was burdening himself with an excess of material and the book he planned had to be abandoned later that year. What is interesting is that five of the six episodes of *Goodbye to Berlin* were planned as part of an autobiographical rather than a fictional work.

The previous autumn (1935) he had worked hard on 'A Berlin Diary (Autumn 1930)' only to abandon it as 'too messy and diffuse'[15] in mid-November for 'The Nowaks' which he sent to Lehmann at the end of that month. By mid-January 1936 he had written a draft of 'Sally Bowles' which, he wrote, was too like Anthony Hope for him to release it as it stood.[16] The final version of 'Sally Bowles' was not completed until the third week in June. Endless delays followed. Upward finally urged Isherwood to release it in October and it took him almost another three months to contact Jean Ross and persuade her to allow him to publish the story, abortion and all. Then Lehmann attempted to persuade him to shorten the story for magazine publication, and to cut the abortion episode for fear of printers' objections. When Isherwood resisted, Lehmann accepted instead 'A Berlin Diary (Autumn 1930)' for *New Writing* No 3, and persuaded the Woolfs to publish *Sally Bowles* separately (it appeared in October 1937). The 'Berlin Diary' had been completed by the end of April 1936 and had been sent to Lehmann for the second number of *New Writing*. But when *Paul is Alone* dried up Isherwood asked him not to publish it as he had committed himself to produce a book for Methuen in a fit of pique at the Woolfs' standoffish behaviour. When it became clear that he was contracted to the Hogarth Press he felt fewer scruples about pre-releasing the Diary, which he did without further alteration at the end of December 1936.

On 25 June 1936 the German Consulate at Lisbon wrote to Heinz instructing him to report for military service. Isherwood's worst fears were realised and he entered into an abortive correspondence with Gerald Hamilton in an attempt to have Heinz's nationality changed. At the height of the crisis his mother came to stay for two weeks. Isherwood's continuing desire to seek her approval matched by an equally strong need to reject her tendency to run his life for him are apparent in his diary entry during her stay:

> It is amazing—the barrier, even now, between us. Mostly of shyness. But, in getting older, she seems to have got heavier and harder. I'd imagined myself falling on her neck, appealing to her to forget and forgive the past, to regard Heinz as her son—but all that, in her presence, seems merely ridiculous.

(CK 185)

Her condescending attitude to Heinz was also partly responsible for Isherwood's subsequent peremptory treatment of her as the crisis over Heinz's nationality reached a climax.

In mid-July William Robson-Scott arrived and introduced Isherwood to two friends of his, James and Tania Stern. James

Stern was an Irish writer whose first book of stories, *The Heartless Land*, was about life in Rhodesia. Tania was a German who had fled in 1933 and settled in Paris where they had met and married. When Isherwood found that he and Heinz got on with the Sterns he invited them to move into Alecrim do Norte and split the expenses. Initially the presence of Robson-Scott and the Sterns helped reduce Isherwood's near-hysterical reactions to Heinz's call-up. Then on 18 July civil war broke out in neighbouring Spain and quite soon the postal delays had reduced Isherwood's negotiations with Hamilton and his mother over Heinz's change of nationality to an exchange of telegrams. Isherwood brusquely instructed his mother to pay Hamilton's lawyer in Brussels. When the lawyer demanded money without guaranteeing any results Kathleen in her turn cabled Isherwood to return to London.

Isherwood and Heinz duly took a boat to Ostend, stopping in Vigo harbour on the day monarchist flags were being substituted there for Republican ones. Leaving Heinz at Ostend, Isherwood reached London on 21 August where he spent several days persuading his mother to pay Gerald Hamilton's lawyer £1,000 to obtain Mexican nationality for Heinz. (It is doubly ironic that Auden, in one of his letters from Iceland which he was still visiting with MacNeice at this time, should be writing, 'We are all too deeply involved with Europe to be able or even wish to escape.'[17]) By mid-September Isherwood had established his base in Brussels, although he spent six days back in England at the beginning of October (when he canvassed Auden and MacNeice for contributions to *New Writing*). In mid-October he spent a week in Spa after Heinz had had the first of two operations on his nose to improve his breathing. According to Heinz the town was absolutely dead but just might prove the right place for Isherwood to work in.[18] Although Spa in fact proved too much of a provincial dead-end, it was there that Isherwood jettisoned the over-ambitious *Scenes from an Education* and started writing the first draft of *Lions and Shadows*, initially called *The North-West Passage* (cf *CK* 192–3). Back in a Brussels pension by 22 October, Isherwood was also busily at work revising *The Ascent of F6*. After its publication in late September 1936 Spender published a highly critical review of the play in the November issue of the *Left Review*. This stimulated

Auden and Isherwood to make extensive revisions to the galleys of the first edition, 'cutting out', Isherwood informed Spender, 'the worst bits of priggishness and reversed-collarisms and schoolmaster's smiles'.[19] These alterations were incorporated in the first American edition of the play and a few further revisions appeared in the second Faber edition. Both editions came out in March 1937.

The autumn and winter of 1936 saw the formation of the Rome–Berlin axis, the Anti-Comintern Pact between Germany and Japan and the Abdication of Edward VIII. The worsening political situation became personalised for Isherwood when first Auden and then Tony (now separated from Spender who had married that autumn) announced that they were going to Spain in the New Year. At Christmas Tony joined them in Brussels accompanied by a fellow-volunteer, Giles Romilly, a nephew of Winston Churchill. As well as Gerald Hamilton and Heinz the company also included Robson-Scott and Humphrey Spender. No sooner had they seen Tony and Giles off on their way to join the International Brigade than Stephen Spender wrote that he too was off to Spain with T. C. Worsley as correspondents of the *Daily Worker*. On 12 January Isherwood met Auden in Paris where they spent a drunken day with Brian Howard before seeing Auden off to Spain the following day. He was determined to finish the first draft of *Lions and Shadows* before committing himself to going to Spain and confronting the Test of War, an event which he had been dreading since his school-days. Besides, Hamilton's lawyer was still no nearer to acquiring Mexican papers for Heinz. Isherwood succinctly described their situation at this time to the Sterns: 'I am busy and poor H is bored.' Poor Heinz was both an excuse for avoiding the Test and a burden preventing Isherwood from joining his friends in their public stand against Fascism.

However, at the beginning of February Isherwood had to go to London to attend the Group Theatre's rehearsals of *The Ascent of F6* at the Mercury Theatre in the absence of Auden in Spain. As he had been in Portugal during the rehearsals for *The Dog Beneath the Skin*, this was Isherwood's first experience of the theatrical world. He seems to have thoroughly enjoyed it, despite the authoritarian way in which the temperamental Rupert Doone directed the production, peremptorily omitting the chess scene and offending Benjamin Britten (whom Auden had met at the GPO Film Unit and introduced to Doone) by attempting to make cuts in his score for the incidental music as late as the dress rehearsal. In his biography of Forster, P. N. Furbank records the high state of excitement into which Isherwood had worked himself on the opening night of 26 February: ' "Oh dear! Oh dear!" he kept saying, "What shall I do? I don't think I can sit down." '20 The following day Forster, who had been present at the opening night, wrote Isherwood a long letter criticising especially the *dénouement*: 'The summit ought to seethe with visions as soon as R goes wompy', he suggested. Also, 'James *must* be put back . . . and I should have thought the Abbot back too', while the villains ought to be allowed to speak with dignity rather than being made ridiculous by squabbling amongst themselves.21 In an attempt to meet these criticisms a different ending was tried out each night for about a week. On his return from Spain on 4 March Auden went to see the play with Isherwood and appears to have been as thrown as Isherwood was the year before with the changes that had been made in his absence.

On 17 March Isherwood returned to Heinz who had been kicking his heels in Brussels and three days later brought him to Paris where Tania Stern had offered to introduce him to a silversmith who could start teaching him the trade. In Paris Isherwood saw much of Cyril Connolly, his American wife Jean and their American friend and disciple, Tony Bower, the latter two of whom were destined to feature as Ruthie and Ronny in the last episode of *Down There on a Visit*. In fact Isherwood had met Connolly earlier that year, as Connolly has recalled first meeting Auden in Spain with a written introduction from Isherwood.22 On 1 April Isherwood returned to London on a short business trip where, however, he fell ill with an infected mouth which kept him in London until 25 April. In the meantime, Heinz had got himself into trouble with the police in Paris and had been told his permit would not be renewed when it ran out on 19 April. Tony Bower volunteered to escort him to Luxembourg where Isherwood joined them as soon as he was well enough to travel. There they waited while Hamilton's lawyer held out false hopes of obtaining for Heinz a Mexican passport within a matter of days. Then on 12 May the inevitable happened. Heinz was told by the police that he must leave Luxembourg immediately and the lawyer insisted that he had to re-enter Germany before he could obtain a new short-term visa for Belgium. Heinz duly crossed the border to Trier where he was promptly arrested for draft evasion on 12 May. In mid-June Heinz was convicted of reciprocal onanism with Isherwood and draft evasion for which he was sentenced to six months in prison, a year's labour service for the state, followed by two years' military service.

Isherwood was not destined to see Heinz again until he returned to Berlin in 1952. In 1938 Heinz got married and a son was born in 1940. He served on the Russian and Western fronts during the war without getting wounded and ended up willingly surrendering to the Americans only to escape from his prisoner-of-war camp in Le Havre in July 1946 in order to look after his wife and child who were living in East Berlin.[23] Back in Brussels Isherwood was devastated. His *raison d'être* for the last five years was gone and it would take him some time to realise that at least a part of him had long since recognised that Heinz was not just a source of joy to him but also a liability (cf *CK* 215). Spender, who has testified to the absolute reality of the relationship that existed between Isherwood and Heinz, has further suggested that 'it was also in some ways a destructive relationship, partly in the sense that it couldn't have gone on indefinitely —as a matter of fact somewhere there is a consciousness there [in *Christopher and his Kind*] which is perfectly aware of all this and is rather grateful to Gerald Hamilton for having cut the Gordian Knot.'[24] While it appears unlikely that Hamilton was guilty of arranging Heinz's arrest, Spender's comment does help to explain Isherwood's otherwise inexplicable failure fully to realise how closely Hamilton had imitated his fictive *alter ego* by unhesitatingly seizing the opportunity to make some easy money at his friend's expense. But at the time he was too numbed to do anything but bury himself in Brussels where he forced himself to complete the first draft of *Lions and Shadows* which was rapidly rewritten in its final form by 15 September 1937.[25]

Lions and Shadows

Isherwood made his first attempt at writing an autobiography when he was still only twenty-six years old. This was to have covered his educational career from St Edmund's to Cambridge. When he abandoned this project in the spring of 1932 it was in favour of an early version of *The Lost* which was 'written entirely in the form of a diary. . . . Frank journalism, in fact.'[1] During the next four and a half years he continued to combine reportage, biography and autobiography in the books he was working on. *Scenes from an Education* was intended to incorporate three episodes from his life that he subsequently used in his first published autobiography as well as other material that was to supply him with the subject matter for part or all of three subsequent novels.

What made him separate these experiences into *Lions and Shadows* on the one hand and various fictional works on the other was the realisation that *Scenes from an Education*, apart from its over-ambitious scope, incorporated two literary genres: the true autobiography and the volume of memoirs. Whereas a true autobiography, he has explained, 'presents a central character to whom all other characters and all events are directly related, and by whose mind all experiences are subjectively judged', memoirs 'should ideally be written by an insignificant, almost invisible observer, with the utmost possible objectivity'.[2] Although *Goodbye to Berlin* is not strictly a volume of memoirs, its handling of the narrator is very similar, unlike the treatment of 'Christopher Isherwood' in *Lions and Shadows*. So in the autumn of 1936 Isherwood was able to divide much of *Scenes from an Education* between these two books and, despite the upset over Heinz, to complete both drafts of *Lions and Shadows* in less than a year. A letter to Leonard Woolf on 15 October 1937 reveals the fact that he made a last-minute cut in Chapter

One and had been compelled to remove 'The Railway Accident' from Chapter Seven, presumably at Upward's request because his communist view of literature no longer squared with this essentially escapist fantasy.[3]

When it was first published in March 1938 most of the reviewers complained about the confusion between its intention, as spelt out in the preliminary note 'To the Reader', and its achieved effect. As the *Times Literary Supplement* expressed it:

> The fault of the book lies in its method, in its lack of co-ordination. What it is not is what it is intended to be—an objective account of 'an Education in the Twenties' of a young English novelist. What it is, more than anything, is an intensively personal, subjective account of Mr Isherwood's own adolescent trials and tribulations.[4]

Although the *TLS* reviewer reacted too strongly, it was discerning of him to realise what Isherwood has subsequently confessed, that in the prefatory note he was 'trying to cover up a bit in case people would think it was indiscreet'.[5] Despite what the prefatory note asserts, according to Isherwood *Lions and Shadows* is 'factually . . . quite accurate', apart from occasionally 'telescoping similar incidents and situations into each other so as not to weary the reader'.[6] For Isherwood, at any rate, the distinction between fiction and autobiography is more a matter of technique, of point of view than of any objective significance. In one representative interview he claimed that all his novels 'are a kind of fictional biography' just as, up to a point, 'autobiography is always fiction.'[7] What interests him most is the interpretation of experience, whether his own or that of others seen through his eyes.

Seen in this light, *Lions and Shadows* constitutes an important stage in his development as a writer. The insight it gave him into the effect of bringing the first-person narrator to the centre of the stage had a noticeable effect on his more confident use of 'Christopher Isherwood' in *Goodbye to Berlin* compared to William Bradshaw in *Mr Norris*. *Lions and Shadows* proved to him just how detached it was possible to be from his past self whom he attempted to treat as much like a character as his friends who appear in the book. This is why he used assumed names for almost everyone, he explained to Spender at the time, 'because it seems so much easier to write objectively if you don't use the real ones'.[8]

This essentially novelistic approach to autobiography equally affected the selection he made from the material constituting his past life. He has willingly agreed to the suggestion that *Lions and Shadows* was 'romanticised', because, he has explained, 'it represented the past as I wished to remember it.'[9] Rather like his autobiographically-based novels, *Lions and Shadows* recreates the past in more glamorised form. In the Berlin novels, for example, he omitted the long stretches of boring routine which were a part of his life-style during those years. In just the same way *Lions and Shadows* has some glaring omissions, the most obvious of which are the absence of sex and of his relations with his mother and family. Although in *Kathleen and Frank* (p 346) he somewhat unbelievably claims that *Lions and Shadows* was an 'indirect apology' to his mother, his off-hand references to 'my female relative' or 'my family' were, he has since confessed, 'intended as a put-down',[10] and hint at the presence of a neurotic component in the book which was not wholly under the control of its thirty-three-year-old author. Isherwood half-humorously used an interesting metaphor in a letter he wrote to the Sterns while in the middle of writing *Lions and Shadows* which obliquely suggests this undercurrent of neurotic compulsion:

> My autobiography is getting on quite nicely. You're right; it *is* like a cancer. All books are. I hope to finish cutting mine out of myself by the end of January. But it will grow again. All of them do.[11]

Neurosis, of course, is also an ostensible theme, perhaps the dominant theme, in *Lions and Shadows*. But this is where the note 'To the Reader' is helpful rather than misleading. The neurosis Isherwood traces from his schooldays to its potential cure in self-exile is deliberately presented as a neurosis afflicting an entire generation of middle-class intellectuals. What he searches for in himself are the generic traits which mark him out as 'a young man living at a certain period in a certain European country . . . subjected to a certain kind of environment, certain stimuli, certain influences' (*LS* 7). For all his use of Audenesque 'clinical' language, this is no pose. As he explained to Spender while in the middle of writing the book, 'I try to be very objective and as far as possible impersonal, just speaking for my epoch, class, income, nationality, background, etc.'[12] This is his chief principle of selection, and at least one Englishman with a similar background but of a younger generation has endorsed its accuracy as a *mémoire pour servir*: 'England changes, but very slowly', Hugh Brogan wrote in 1976. '*Lions and Shadows* will long remain a valuable guide to her character; and when the tourist at last finds it out of date, the historian will be able to use it, confidently, as a source.'[13]

In order to highlight the representative nature of his own experiences, Isherwood has created an entire gallery filled with portraits of his fellow neurotics. All of his friends are transformed into larger-than-life embodiments of the disinherited post-war generation of writers. Like Isherwood, perhaps more so, Chalmers' development as an adult is heavily conditioned by his traumatic experience of school. He is even more dependent than the protagonist on the Mortmere fantasies with which they seek to compensate for personal inadequacies. Another Truly Weak Man faced by the Test, he is typical of many of his generation in seeking a collective response by joining the Communist Party. Weston is similarly portrayed as the victim of his class and education, a neurotic who seeks to overcome his inhibitions by exposure and self-analysis. When his hat invites laughter from the locals, he capitalises on it by claiming that 'laughter . . . is the first sign of sexual attraction' (*LS* 189). His pipe-smoking he attributes to 'insufficient weaning'. For him sex appears to be unrelated to love, merely an appetite that requires slaking. Consequently the literature that both Chalmers and Weston produce are seen to be the products of their neuroses—Chalmers' obsession with the Enemy, Weston's determination to make his poetry as 'austere' (and emotionally restrained) as his favourite subjects at school, geology and mining engineering.

Isherwood's characterisation hovers between biographical portraiture and outright 'caricature' (his own term in the prefatory note). Caricature is the novelist's licence and is the means by which Isherwood has been able to convert his own circle of friends into archetypal case-histories sufficiently dramatic to interest the reader. Alan Wilde has further pointed out the degree to which all the remaining characters can be seen as projections of the protagonist's personality: 'Everyone whom the young Isherwood meets throughout the course of *Lions and Shadows* is in some way an objectification of a quality, good or bad, that is inherent or potential in him; each is what he might be, what he revolts against, or what he is.'[14] This is not to charge Isherwood with egomania. It is part of his intended strategy in the book, which is above all to portray himself as the central 'exhibit in the vast freak museum of our neurotic generation' (*LS* 217). No character is more caricatured than 'Isherwood', the young protagonist. Although he might have felt subconsciously that he could only make free with his friends in the book if he made even freer with himself, this self-caricature is his principal symbol for the phenomenon he is describing in *Lions and Shadows* —a generation that has been psychically damaged by that 'tireless Sense of Guilt' (*LS* 217) that haunts the young Isherwood throughout the seven years covered by the book.

That the Sense of Guilt was deeply implanted not just in 'Isherwood' the protagonist but Isherwood the narrator is vouched for by the severity with which he exposes himself to ridicule in this, as in all his subsequent autobiographical writings and interviews. In his review of *Lions and Shadows* for the *Spectator*, Evelyn Waugh shrewdly suggested that Isherwood 'seems to take such relish in the exposure that the reader may at moments doubt whether the transformation has been complete.'[15] Wilde has also questioned whether the ending of the book represents an escape from his neurotic earlier self or sheer escapism.[16] Within the limits of the book it has to be seen as the former, since otherwise how could the thirty-three-year-old author-narrator acquire the necessary detachment with which to portray his earlier self, Isherwood the Artist, as that bogey of the socially committed writers of the 1930s, the Truly Weak Man of the previous decade, compensating for his inadequacies by posturing to the end as an austere ascetic, a latter-day Byron 'striking an attitude on his lonely rock'? (*LS* 304)

In this last chapter where he compares himself to Byron, he singles out a major difference between himself at Cambridge and himself at the crucial moment of decision in the winter of 1938:

But his black Byronic exile's cloak failed to impress me any longer. I knew what was inside it now—just plain, cold, uninteresting funk. Funk of getting too deeply involved with other people, sex-funk, funk of the future. . . . Why had I ever become a medical student? Largely, I had to admit, because of a vague, hardly defined fear—a fear that somehow, somewhere, I should one day be isolated and trapped, far from the safety of the nursery and Nanny's apron, and compelled to face 'The Test'. (*LS* 304–5)

At the same time, if this is an advance, it is by no means a release from the neurosis he shared with his literary contemporaries. The Test is itself part of that neurosis and there is a world of difference between self-analysis and cure. Both in his book and in his life he had a long way to travel before he could write, as Forster wrote to him after his departure for China, '*Bother the Test*—am so certain I shall fail mine that I can't think about it.'[17] This is where that less conscious neurotic undercurrent in the book surfaces disconcertingly and reminds one that Isherwood as author continues to attack himself as protagonist with at least as much puritan zeal forty years later in *Christopher and his Kind*.

Consequently, as Samuel Hynes has suggested, 'escape from the neurosis of the twenties . . . becomes a matter of style.'[18] Psychological abnormality is exposed by the normality of the language Isherwood employs, just as caricature implies the sane presence of the writer who shapes and controls that caricature. If the prevailing mode of *Lions and Shadows* is one of irony this only proves the degree of detachment which the writer has acquired from his earlier evasive form of existence. 'As long as I remained a sham', Isherwood writes in the last chapter of the book, 'my writing would be sham, too' (*LS* 305). What separates the older writer from his twenty-four-year-old protagonist at the end of the book is primarily the irony with which he dissociates himself from his earlier self's neurotic concealments. By the repeated use of bathos, humour tinged with mockery and caricature, Isherwood the writer demonstrates the distance he has travelled since his departure for Berlin. It is the maturity of style and vision that ultimately guarantees that the journey on which he embarks at the end of the book is not the flight of an escapist, but the beginning of a search for greater honesty and self-knowledge that characterises both his writing and the conduct of his life from this time on. Perhaps this is what he meant when he wrote in his prefatory note 'To the Reader':

Because this book is about the problems of a would-be writer, it is also about conduct. The style is the man. (*LS* 7)

The Break with Europe

In July Isherwood was back in London working on a screenplay for Alexander Korda that never came to anything. In the middle of August he went down to Dover with Auden for a month where E. M. Forster was taking a holiday. Apart from completing *Lions and Shadows*, he was collaborating with Auden on the first draft of *On the Frontier*, their third jointly written play for the Group Theatre. When they completed it by 11 September,[1] Isherwood described it to Rupert Doone as 'strong melodrama, with just the tiniest whiff of Barrie (in his "Mary Rose" mood).'[2] Back in London twelve days later they were already rewriting the lovers' scenes in response to criticism from Spender and others.[3] By 9 October the last scene had also been rewritten.[4] J. M. Keynes had agreed to subsidise the Group Theatre production of the play tentatively scheduled for that season, when first a possible visit to Spain and then their planned trip to China in the New Year necessitated postponing the production until their return to England the folllowing summer.

In point of fact Isherwood narrowly missed joining the tidal wave of artists sweeping across Republican Spain that year on not less than three occasions. Graham Greene invited him to fly to Bilbao, but in the end the Spanish government never provided the plane.[5] Then in late June 1937 he (like Auden and Spender) had accepted an invitation 'to talk tripe at a congress' in Valencia,[6] but decided not to go when the Foreign Office refused all of them visas[7] (typically, Spender went regardless on a forged passport provided by André Malraux[8]). Finally he was almost dragooned into joining another delegation to Spain in late November (mainly because Auden agreed to go) and was only saved from going by the Spanish government's repeated delays which brought the date into conflict with their planned departure for China (*CK* 217–19). Earlier that year Auden's publishers had made a contract with both of them to write a travel book based in the Far East. The Japanese invasion in July had made up their minds for them: at least China, as Auden put it, offered them a war all of their very own. In *Christopher and his Kind* Isherwood, with typical frankness, highlights the insincerity of his motivation at this time by recalling an evening in the company of Forster and other friends when someone asked Forster why he wasn't going to Spain. 'Afraid to', Forster cheerfully replied, exposing precisely the same motive force that was impelling Isherwood to confront the Test of War he dreaded so much (*CK* 218).

In fact 1937 and 1938 show Isherwood in a peculiarly schizophrenic state. On the one hand he is leading a particularly ephemeral kind of existence, socially pretentious and sexually promiscuous (Humphrey Spender recollects his going off with the bride's brother at his wedding in August, for instance);[9] on the other hand he is doing some of his best work, completing *Lions and Shadows* and hurriedly writing up the three remaining episodes of *Goodbye to Berlin*, because, he explained to Spender, he thought he 'might be killed in China and wanted to leave everything tidy'.[10] He only just managed to complete 'On Ruegen Island', 'The Landauers' and 'A Berlin Diary' (Winter 1932–33)' before he left for China, leaving Lehmann to collate the typescripts of the various stories in his absence.[11] When 'The Landauers' appeared in *New Writing* No 5 during the spring of 1938 Spender wrote him an emotional letter accusing him of ingratitude to Wilfred Israel and Gisa Soloweitschik, the original models for Bernard and Natalia Landauer, besides anti-semitism. 'The stories are a cheap cartoon, nothing more', Isherwood replied. 'As for my being anti-semitic: . . . the very idea is . . . absurd.'[12] Nevertheless he was stung by Spender's remarks into removing a short passage describing the various kinds of Jews at Bernard's Wannsee villa party from the story when it reappeared in *Goodbye to Berlin*.

On 18 January 1938 Rupert Doone arranged a party at Julian Trevelyan's Chiswick Studio to send off Auden and Isherwood. Also present were Forster, Rose Macaulay, Brian Howard and Benjamin Britten who accompanied Hedli Anderson (Louis MacNeice's wife-to-be) singing some of Auden's lyrics.[13] The following day Auden and Isherwood left on the boat-train for Dover. On 21 January they sailed from Marseilles on the French liner *Aramis* for Hong Kong and began taking turns at keeping a travel diary. At Port Said Francis Turville-Petre met them and drove them to Cairo, 'that immense and sinister Woolworth's', they wrote, 'where everything is for sale' (*E* 145). It was their last glimpse of Francis who died in Egypt in 1942. At Djibouti they paid fifty francs to see three girls demonstrate their inability to do the belly dance (*E* 147). Colombo they compared to 'an abandoned international exhibition' (*E* 170). Meanwhile they spent their spare time on board rewriting *On the Frontier* and learning about the weird life-style of colonial rubber planters.

They reached Hong Kong on 16 February where they stayed with the Vice Chancellor of the University and met various local dignitaries including William Empson who has claimed that Auden stole the limelight to such an extent that Isherwood hardly left any impression on him.[14] On 28 February they left for the north-eastern war front, travelling by boat, train and even (despite bad consciences) rickshaw to get there. The travel diary in *Journey to a War* takes up the story from the moment of their departure from Hong Kong and offers a detailed account of their adventures in China until they left Shanghai on 12 June. Their experiences of front-line warfare were confined to two days with the Nationalists fighting on the north-eastern front at Han Chwang, where they were hustled away as soon as a bombardment got under way, and a brief glimpse of the Communist forces on the south-eastern front at Meiki where they spent a night before being evacuated only ten hours before the Japanese occupied it. They met both the Chiang Kai-sheks and Chou En-lai besides Agnes Smedley, the English champion of the Communists, and Peter Fleming, *The Times* correspondent who accompanied them to Meiki.

Most of their time was spent meeting officials, attending receptions, waiting on trains and acting like any other tourists in a foreign country—they even spent the first two weeks in April in a vain attempt to reach Chung-king, 'as the gorges are said to be magnificent', Isherwood explained to Lehmann without any apparent sense of incongruity.[15] Especially in *Christopher and his Kind* Isherwood has virtually portrayed the two of them as a professional comedy act, Auden trailing around the Chinese countryside in a woollen balaclava helmet, shapeless overcoat and slippers because of his corns, Isherwood dressed up as a chi-chi foreign war-correspondent in a Spanish beret, a polo-neck sweater and riding boots. Then there is the Laurel and Hardy attitude to danger. While Isherwood is ultra-cautious, sleeping in his clothes in case he needs to make a quick escape and opening windows before a possible bombardment to avoid flying glass, Auden, as Isherwood wrote to Spender at the time, 'knows that he won't be killed, because Nanny would never allow it, and It Can't Happen Here. So whenever we get into any danger . . . he sulks and fusses: "Why can't they SHOOT?" or "It's not nearly LOUD enough".'[16]

On 25 May they reached Japanese-occupied Shanghai on the east coast where they stayed with the British Ambassador in the International Settlement, which Isherwood described as 'like an island in the moon—surrounded on all sides by a lunar wilderness of ruins, the suburbs where the terrible fighting of last autumn took place'.[17] There they had their first contact with the bland Japanese who claimed that they were only saving the Chinese from themselves and the menace of Communism. After obtaining twelve-month multiple-entry visas to the United States by revealing to a short-tempered immigration official the fact that they were staying at the British Embassy, they sailed from Shanghai on the *Empress of Asia* on 12 June. They took sixteen days to reach Vancouver and had the disorientating experience of calling at three ports in Japan (hitherto the enemy) and witnessing a hysterical mob send off a troop train in Tokyo. During the voyage they completed their revisions of *On the Frontier* which, Auden wrote to Spender, 'improve it' but still left them feeling uncomfortable: 'The subject is too contemporary for a semi-realistic play', they decided.[18] Meanwhile Isherwood had time to digest his experiences of the past five months on the long journey to New York. He realised that the Test had been rendered redundant by his experience of the reality of war. And because he had lost much of his neurotic fear of war, he was able to contemplate for the first time the possibility that because war itself is so indiscriminately destructive the only genuine response to it for himself might be a refusal to participate in it at all. He came to no firm conclusions at this stage but it was in China that he first realised 'in the simplest way that war involves a most awful lot of people who never asked for it, didn't want it, and have been simply dragged into it'.[19]

On 2 July they reached New York. During their nine-day stay there they were accompanied by George Davis, a novelist whom they had met in London the year before and who was now literary editor of a New York fashion magazine which had published some of their articles on China. They both fell for New York and before their departure Auden had decided that he would almost certainly return there and take up American citizenship.[20] George Davis introduced Isherwood, at his request, to a new young blond American boyfriend to whom he gives the pseudonym of 'Vernon' in *Christopher and his Kind*. Although 'Vernon' was as much the recipient of Isherwood's sexual fantasies as 'Bubi' had been, he was to be a significant factor in Isherwood's decision to return to the States with Auden six months later. Perhaps Isherwood's success with 'Vernon' was the cause of Auden's uncharacteristic outburst on the voyage back to England in which he confessed his conviction that he was a failure sexually (*CK* 227).

By contrast Isherwood's numerous sexual conquests in the period which followed his return to England on 17 July betray an underlying spiritual *malaise* which he has perceptively diagnosed in the 'Waldemar' section of *Down There on a Visit*. This highly autobiographical episode also relates the deepening international crisis over Czechoslovakia to Isherwood's own mounting tension: 'This time we're living through now—this doom-heavy summer—is *un jour sans lendemain*, or my fear whispers that it may be; and everything one does seems to have a tomorrowless quality about it' (*DTV* 155). He had tomorrowless affairs with Spender's old boyfriend, Tony, whom he took to Ostend towards the end of August, with 'B' and 'G' as he calls them in 'Waldemar' (*DTV* 174 and 193), and no doubt others. A letter he wrote Spender in late August gives an accurate impression of his state of mind at this time:

> I'm horribly scared by the Prague–Berlin crisis. No war, says Katz; and Harold Nicolson (I was at Sissinghurst, this weekend, with D— N—, and saw him) says: 'Well, if I were forced to bet a thousand pounds . . . I suppose I'd bet on peace. But it's going to be a very close thing.' My own chief scare follows on the discovery that, if there is a war, I haven't the faintest idea what I'd do.[21]

Simultaneously he was spending as much time as he could with all his old friends. In July he went for a few days with Lehmann to the Isle of Wight where he outlined plans for a trilogy of novels based on the fate of various refugees from Nazi Germany.[22] In August he saw Virginia Woolf, not for the first time, at a party given by Lady Sybil Colefax on 1 November at which Somerset Maugham, perhaps by way of excusing Isherwood's gauche behaviour, made the startling claim that 'that young man . . . "holds the future of the English novel in his hands"' (CK 242).

In London he relied on Dr Katz ('Fisch' in 'Waldemar') for informed opinion on the worsening crisis over Czechoslovakia, and found the strength which Upward and Olive Mangeot drew from their Communist conviction a source of sanity amidst the growing signs of panic—the issue of thirty-eight million gas masks, practice air-raids, trenches dug in the London parks, food shortages and a widespread conviction that London would be obliterated within days by the German *Luftwaffe*. Isherwood himself was a ready victim to each succeeding scare, and his behaviour at this time (his volunteering for propaganda work should war break out, his plans for sharing a flat with Lehmann, his compulsion to buy each new edition of the newspapers) reflects his confused sense of personal values. On the day that Hitler agreed to a four-power Munich conference (28 September) Auden returned from a holiday in Belgium, and as the crisis subsided Auden, in place of Hitler, became the determining factor in Isherwood's life when he agreed to accompany him back to New York in the New Year for an indefinite stay.

Throughout the autumn of 1938 Isherwood was writing up the 'Travel-Diary' for *Journey to a War*, as well as lecturing on China for the BBC and to various groups including Upward's sixth form. Because the Munich crisis made his account of a far-off war appear almost meaningless to him, he did not finish his contribution until 2 December, and it was not until 17 December that he and Auden completed the book by abandoning two proposed dialogues called 'Hongkong-Macao' and substituting Auden's two sonnets 'Macao' and 'Hongkong' in their place.[23]

On 14 November the Group Theatre gave the first performance of *On the Frontier* at the Arts Theatre, Cambridge. Both the theatre and the production were funded by J. M. Keynes. Doone directed; Robert Medley designed the divided stage set; and Benjamin Britten composed the music and accompanied the singers for no fee throughout the run.[24] To emphasise its topicality after Act III Scene 2 an interlude was added in which four journalists commented on events in Spain (where the civil war was drawing to a close), Ethiopia and elsewhere.[25] Despite the fact that, technically speaking, this was the most accomplished of their three joint plays, it was judged a failure. As C. Day Lewis wrote of it in *The Listener*: 'it possesses neither the vitality and invention of *The Dog Beneath the Skin* nor the deeply realised moral conflict of *The Ascent of F6*.'[26] The fact that the play transferred to the Globe Theatre, London, on 12 February 1939 says more for the reputation that Auden and Isherwood had acquired by this time than for the quality of the play itself.

In mid-December Auden and Isherwood (accompanied by his latest boyfriend) joined Gerald Hamilton in Brussels for a month. On New Year's Eve Auden threw a riotous party at which he read out his specially composed 'Ode to the New Year (1939)', one stanza of which was addressed to each guest in turn. The octet of the stanza to Isherwood reads:

> *Dear Christopher, always a sort of*
> *Conscience to which I'd confess*
> *In the years before Hitler was thought of,*
> *Or the guinea-pig had a success;*
> *Now reviewers are singing your praises,*
> *And lovers are scratching your back,*
> *But, O how unhappy your face is,*
> *So I wish you the peace that you lack.*[27]

Despite the presence of his new boyfriend Isherwood induced Auden to make a brief trip to Berlin to cope with Heinz before their return to England on 9 January.[28] On 18 January Forster saw them off on the boat-train from Waterloo and the following day they sailed from Southampton on the *Champlain*. A year later Cyril Connolly was to call their departure 'the most important literary event since the outbreak of the Spanish Civil War'.[29] The thirties—at least for them—had come to a premature end.

Goodbye to Berlin

In an introductory note to the first edition of *Goodbye to Berlin*, Isherwood calls his book a 'loosely-connected sequence of diaries and sketches' (p 287). Many readers and critics have taken him at his word and have either mourned his decision to abandon *The Lost* in favour of mere 'fragments', as even John Lehmann did at first,[1] or castigated him for his failure to mature into a novelist, like Frederick Karl for instance.[2] But one can quote Isherwood against himself. In *Christopher and his Kind* he explains that one of his reasons for falsifying the chronology in 'The Nowaks' was that 'from a *structural* point of view', he needed to introduce one or two major characters before dividing the reader's attention between the various Nowaks (*CK* 44). In an interview he offered a more comprehensive defence of the fragmented form of *Goodbye to Berlin*:

> *The Lost* would have been like Balzac's *Splendeurs et Misères des Courtisanes*—very complicated, all sorts of absurd contrivances to bring it all together, hundreds of characters. . . . And then I fell upon the understanding that as far as I was concerned you can get just the same effect by little broken bits of something, that the gaps are not worth filling in, that's all just plotting. And so what I did was I took up all the broken bits and put them into *Goodbye to Berlin* just as slivers of something. And you got just the same effect, that you've met a whole world.[3]

Here Isherwood appears to be offering an essentially modernist justification for the form of a book which in most other respects constitutes a reaction against Modernism. At the same time he confirmed the fact that he had a book in mind from the moment he started writing the first story.

If *Goodbye to Berlin* is more integrated, then, than the self-deprecating introductory note suggests, on what principles is it structurally organised? In the first place there is the time element. Section 1 is dated 'Autumn 1930', just as the last Section is subtitled 'Winter 1932–33'. The other four sections progressively span the intervening time gap: 'Sally Bowles' covers October 1930–autumn 1931; 'On Ruegen Island' summer 1931; 'The Nowaks' winter 1931–2; and 'The Landauers' recapitulates by starting in October 1930 and looks forward to the period covered by the final diary, ending as it does in May 1933. The book, therefore, is a portrait of Berlin and its inhabitants during the final two and a half years or so of the Weimar Republic. All the episodes, as Carolyn Heilbrun has suggested, are 'constructed around the disintegration and dehumanisation of a modern city'.[4]

There is also an internal contrapuntal organisation that balances the light-hearted opening Berlin Diary against the doom-laden Diary at the end, heterosexual against homosexual outlaws of society in 'Sally Bowles' and 'On Ruegen Island', and an under-privileged working-class family against a wealthy family of Jewish capitalists in 'The Nowaks' and 'The Landauers'.[5] These formal polarities reflect the real polarisation of attitudes that characterised the final years of democracy in Germany. The only connective principle is the presence of the narrator who is appropriately a foreigner and outsider, an artist who observes but rarely participates, someone who can and does leave Berlin when the situation becomes too unpleasant.

Any discussion of the function of 'Christopher Isherwood' within the novel is bedevilled by an unintended ambiguity that attaches itself to him. Isherwood has repeatedly explained his reasons for creating what he has called this 'demi-character' (*CK* 142)—his artistic need to be true to his own intuitive perception of life, his decision to use his pseudo-self as a scanning device, and his consequent need to avoid drawing attention to the narrator as a character in his own right (and to his homosexuality in particular). The narrator consequently hovers on the edges of the dramas he has witnessed like a character in limbo. Whenever he seems about to enter the action as a participant, Isherwood closes the scene or extricates his fictive counterpart from self-exposure, as if it was he (which for the main part it was) and not a narrator within his control who was about to reveal himself in his true colours. This 'convenient ventriloquist's dummy', as he called him in his introductory note (p 287), consequently affects the reader in ways unintended by Isherwood. Invited by the author to identify with 'Christopher Isherwood', yet constantly thwarted by his passivity and reticence, the reader tends to project on to the narrator feelings outside the control of his creator. Moreover, far from drawing no attention to himself, the narrator's enigmatic withdrawal from any commitment positively invites the reader to concentrate on 'Christopher Isherwood's' hidden responses and attitudes to the bizarre life he is witnessing. The more Isherwood represses him, the more out of his control the narrator becomes.

At one end of the spectrum of critical responses stand those readers who have seized on one sentence of the narrator ('I am a camera with its shutter open, quite passive, recording, not thinking'—p 289), and cited it as evidence of a new school of fiction. G. S. Fraser, for instance, saw Isherwood as the leading practitioner of the 'documentary' novel of the 1930s, parallel in intention and achievement to the British documentary film movement of this period.[6] Yet his use of a first-person narrator is an open declaration of his search for subjective rather than objective truth. The only facts to be found in his novel are those which impinged on the narrator's consciousness. This is why, for example, political events only surface towards the end of the time span covered by the novel—because Isherwood himself only became politically conscious during the last part of his Berlin sojourn. In fact, Isherwood has explained, this much-quoted sentence was intended to express the narrator's (not the author's) mood at a particular moment of time only.[7] When John van Druten turned part of the novel into I am a Camera one of the few lines Isherwood wrote for the play was right at the end where the narrator says, 'The camera's taken all its pictures, and now it's going away to develop them.'[8] If the narrator is a camera at times, the author is the cameraman who selects his subjects, his viewpoint, the degree of exposure and who proceeds to develop and print his film with all the further choices this process presents. It is only by failing to distinguish between author and narrator that one can dismiss Goodbye to Berlin as a series of snapshots where, as Norman Friedman has naively suggested, 'the aim is to transmit, without apparent selection or arrangement, a "slice of life" as it passes through the recording medium.'[9]

An alternative response to the enigmatic presence of a narrator who is continually intruding into and withdrawing from the action is for critics to read far more significance into the personality and function of 'Christopher Isherwood' than is justified within the context of the novel. David Thomas, for example, sees the narrator's comparison of himself with a camera as 'a defensive mask' which he clearly longs to abandon from the start: in the third paragraph of the novel, Thomas asserts, 'he yearns for a "call" to the "human" from his hiding-place in art.'[10] Both David Thomas and Alan Wilde see the narrator as the embodiment of the neurotic withdrawal of the artist (diagnosed at length in *Lions and Shadows*). But whereas Wilde feels that Isherwood implicitly condemns his fictive counterpart for his failure to make meaningful human relationships,[11] Thomas reaches precisely the opposite conclusion, that *Goodbye to Berlin* 'attempts to cure the neurotic hero by tapping springs of human sympathy, substituting people for the artificial sanctuary of art, religion or politics.'[12] Such conflicting interpretations are the result of projecting on to the narrator a meaning and function beyond that intended by Isherwood. Nevertheless Isherwood is at least partly to blame for such misunderstandings by continually drawing attention to the narrator but withholding much of the information he would supply as a matter of course in the case of his other characters. As the reviewer in the *Times Literary Supplement* observed at the time, 'his imagination tends to stop short at the contemplation of himself.'[13] Isherwood was the first to recognise this defect. In a letter he wrote to Spender after the publication of 'The Landauers' in *New Writing*, he called the narrator 'an evasion and altogether too harmless and too knowing', a literary device he was determined to avoid using again![14]

Since he is a writer for whom 'everything starts with autobiography',[15] the decision to keep this element to a minimum rode counter to Isherwood's natural inclinations. We are certainly given occasional glimpses of a more fully realised autobiographically-based character whose implied existence, at least in the author's mind, ensures that these glimpses do cohere. Cumulatively they contribute to a shadowy persona who is not so unlike the neurotic artist of *Lions and Shadows*. Both Natalia and Bernhard Landauer accuse the narrator of suffering from English inhibitions. In one of his rare moments of frankness Bernhard turns on 'Christopher' and implicitly condemns his emotionally frigid response to Bernhard's revelations about his childhood: 'It disgusts your English public-school training, a little—this Jewish emotionalism' (p 531). Similarly when 'Isherwood' tells Natalia that 'No Englishman ever laughs when he's amused', she rightly concludes that 'your Englishmen are mad' (p 493). In each instance, however, 'Isherwood' sidesteps the issue with evasive replies and the author refocuses our attention on the other character.

Clearly such revelations about the narrator are a means of telling the reader something further about the other character in question; but the device is distracting and invites the kind of speculation that has been mentioned already. One reaches the same conclusion when one considers similar occasions in the novel where the narrator's mask of reticence slips for a moment. On at least two occasions he betrays a strong fear of death— when Frl Schroeder lists all her previous lodgers and 'Herr Issyvoo' rushes off to the lavatory in an involuntary spasm of panic at the prospect of his own mortality (pp 295–6); and the long sinister dream he has during his visit to the sanatorium which culminates in his imagined murder by the inmates (pp 483–5). In both cases the narrative ends abruptly and one is left with disembodied *angst* lingering in the mind.

And yet isn't this part of Isherwood's artistic strategy in the book—to leave certain emotions lingering in the air of Berlin itself? Isn't the narrator's fear of death something he shares with most of the inhabitants of Berlin? Are his inhibitions really so different from those exhibited by both Natalia and Bernhard? When Sally Bowles makes him 'feel a sham' (p 379), isn't he reflecting her own sham responses to life? When, for example, she informs 'Christopher' that she is in love with Klaus, she at once adds 'At least, I think I am' (p 340). Like Otto Nowak she plays at love. In fact most of the inhabitants of Berlin during these final anarchic years of the Weimar Republic are playing at living, playing with life very much in the way that the artist does (and the narrator is, of course, an artist). One remembers 'Isherwood's' first visit to the Troika when the entire place leapt into simulated life and gaiety as soon as a party of rich customers entered: the page-boy's voice became 'mocking, clear-pitched like an actor's' (p 305), while the dancers showed 'in their every movement a consciousness of the part they were playing' (p 307). The entire performance is described in terms of a grotesque 'pantomime'.

The theatrical metaphor is extended as the novel progresses to embrace every aspect of Berlin. Even the political parties indulge in their own form of charade. The communist bar near the zoo with its back-slapping waiter and conspiratorial customers is 'thoroughly sham and gay and jolly' (p 564), just as the Nazi demonstration on the Bülowplatz and the counter-demonstration by the local inhabitants 'was too much like a naughty schoolboy's game to be seriously alarming' (p 577). Yet it is precisely because no one really takes the Nazis seriously enough that they are able to seize power at the climax of the book by staging what is in effect a gigantic *coup de théâtre*. With this Isherwood brings the curtain down on the sham world of Berlin that has been so sympathetically observed all this time by the narrator with his own penchant for the sham and the lost.

At one point in the novel 'Isherwood' almost joins the ranks of the lost himself. When he and Sally Bowles agree to join Clive on his world trip to nowhere 'Isherwood' realises that he is about to forfeit 'all kinship with ninety-nine per cent of the population of the world'. 'Yes', he concludes, 'I've done it, now. I am lost' (pp 356-7). In fact Clive saves him from himself and he returns to his normal state of limbo in which he associates with the lost but is never one of them. Each of the principal dynamic portraits in the novel, however, represents one of Berlin's misfits. They might be sexual outcasts like Sally Bowles or Frl Kost, or psychological outcasts like Peter Wilkinson, or social outcasts as the Jewish Landauers become, or economic outcasts like the Nowaks, or political outcasts like Rudi and his fellow-communists. Cumulatively the novel becomes a portrait of a city of the lost.

His choice of characters alone is peculiarly indicative of his overall intentions. As John Lehmann has pointed out, he always avoids the normal or even the idealised: 'He almost invariably prefers, on the contrary, to take eccentric and fantastic characters as his central pivots, the extreme products of the anarchy and pathological condition of modern society.'[16] These he shows from a variety of angles in order to give a three-dimensional effect by the accumulation of partially conflicting two-dimensional images. And just as he surprises the reader by juxtaposing apparently conflicting aspects of the one personality, so the various sections of the book juxtapose seemingly contrasting portraits which ultimately are seen to be all variations on the central theme of the lost. What lures Sally to Berlin, for example, is manifested in characters like Otto whom she never meets. Nevertheless they both are gold-diggers; both are prepared to use their considerable powers of sexual attraction for their own ends; and both are in the final analysis victims more often than victimisers, failures in the game of love for money from which only Frl Kost, the professional, seems likely to win any permanent betterment for herself. Yet perversely it is their vulnerability that attracts Isherwood (and us) because their failures signify the triumph of humanity in them over the profit motive.

Sally Bowles is probably the most peripheral of the major protagonists in the novel. She is a foreigner, like the narrator, living on an allowance from her upper-class mother, and, rather than having to face the consequences of her actions, she can, like him, escape from Berlin when she tires of her life there. The story, according to Isherwood, is both 'an attempt to satirise the romance-of-prostitution racket'[17] and yet 'to show that even the greatest disasters leave a person like Sally essentially un-changed'.[18] The two aims tend to conflict as the satire is undercut by Sally's unflagging powers of recovery after each successive set-back. The satirical intention emerges most clearly in her economic progress. The three hundred marks Clive leaves her have to be spent on the abortion necessitated by her first affair with Klaus, while she is made to pay even more heavily for her third attempt to persuade herself she is in love when 'George P. Sanders' leaves with the large sum of money she had in her bag. But her continuing emotional naïvety runs counter to the hard financial lessons she has been taught. Her abortion, which should have linked her to the images of disease and death that attach themselves to the remaining representatives of a dying society, leaves her virtually untouched, the most ephemeral member of the lost.

Peter Wilkinson, who is also a rich foreigner who returns to England when life abroad turns sour for him, is nevertheless quite clearly at home in the Germany of 1931. He displays its own neuroses and even seeks its own unsatisfactory cures, substituting Otto for his expensive Berlin analyst. 'On Ruegen Island' uses the metaphor of mental illness and disease to make a complex statement about German society at large. As always Isherwood works through the actual and the particular. Otto represents the best and the worst of Germany during the final years of the Weimar Republic. He has the health and vitality of an animal and 'like many very animal people, he has considerable powers of healing—when he chooses to use them' (p 406). Also, like an animal, he is utterly selfish, seeking his sustenance and his pleasure with a complete indifference to those around him. Peter seeks to cure his own neurosis by buying Otto and in doing so resembles all those other foreigners who were flocking to Berlin at the time for similar reasons. But if Peter Wilkinson and his kind parasitically seek to cure their psychological disorders at the expense of the Otto Nowaks of a decadent Germany, there are other Germans, like the Nazi doctor, who have a very different concept of health care. His approach is strictly 'scientific', and if it fails to work with Peter (when he tries to teach him how to throw) he has no doubts about what ought to be done in Otto's case: 'I believe in discipline. These boys ought to be put into labour-camps' (p 415). When one remembers Peter's own wilful attempts to discipline Otto it becomes apparent that Isherwood is also peripherally suggesting how closely fascism resembles English imperialism. Both are products of repression and disease, and both seek to cure an illness in others that in fact underlies their own love of power.

The next episode, 'The Nowaks', explores the economic origins for the sickness afflicting Otto and his kind. 'If', as Alan Wilde writes, 'Otto is an animal, he is a sick animal.'[19] He lives in a slum where poverty breeds disease, tuberculosis in the case of his mother, contempt for life and the business of living in his own case. In the final scene at the sanatorium Frau Nowak is explicitly compared to 'a desperate injured animal' (p 484): Otto's injury is psychological. Poverty and unemployment have turned him into a life-long actor who can believe in nothing beyond the scene in which he is participating at any one moment. His mercurial changes of mood subtly suggest the degree to which he has become alienated from himself. He can shamelessly persuade himself that Peter Wilkinson left him in the lurch, just as he can contradict himself between one sentence and the next:

'Nobody understands me here. Nobody's good to me. They all hate me really. They wish I was dead!'

'How can you talk such rubbish, Otto! Your mother certainly doesn't hate you.'

'Poor mother!' agreed Otto. He had changed his tone at once, seeming unaware of what he had just said. (p 450)

The fate awaiting Otto is clearly foreshadowed in his parents: either physical disease and premature death like his mother, or drunkenness and escape back into the world of his childhood like his father. The only other alternative is represented by Lothar who, like the doctor, seeks a cure to the ills surrounding him in Nazi-inspired self-discipline. For Otto the black hand of his nightmares beckons and he even makes an amateur attempt at slashing his wrists in a heightened moment of self-pity. Clearly his circumstances have turned him into one of the lost whose resemblance to his dying mother makes Isherwood on at least one occasion see both of them as 'creatures demoniacally possessed' (p 470).

The Landauers are also among the damned, victims of the inequalities of capitalism. Wealth has inhibited them in their upbringing and isolated them from the majority of their fellow human beings. Natalia is physically inhibited (she won't share 'Isherwood's' spoon), prudish in her response to Sally Bowles, and a culture snob who elicits infuriated animal noises from the usually restrained narrator. She escapes the fate of her cousin only by leaving Berlin for Paris, exchanging her rich Jewish family environment for the cosmopolitan existence of a Parisian artist. But Bernhard is a more advanced case of the neurotic inhibition that characterises Natalia and Peter Wilkinson. Barricaded behind four sets of doors, he has cut himself off from life so thoroughly that he feels compelled to ring up his own department store to reassure himself that it—and he—exist. He is a case of extreme alienation, someone who describes himself as 'a quite unnecessarily complicated piece of mechanism' (p 533), who is constantly conducting experiments on himself, rather in the spirit of a surgeon on a corpse.

He is doubly damned, by his capitalist wealth and by virtue of being a Jew. In the latter capacity he is representative of all his fellow-Jews who are destined to meet a similar end. The garden party at his Wannsee villa culminates in a vision of horror at the fate awaiting these Jewish representatives of the lost:

> However often the decision may be delayed, all these people are ultimately doomed. This evening is the dress-rehearsal of a disaster. It is like the last night of an epoch. (p 539)

The combination of the theatrical metaphor with premonitions of death and disease is yet another example of the consistency of Isherwood's diagnosis. The lost have been playing at life for so long that finally they have become fatally separated from their impulse to live. Like his mother who died of cancer, Bernhard's denial of life induces him virtually to commit suicide, although the weapon in his case is the Nazi terror that overtakes Berlin in the final section of the novel.

The threat of a political disaster has been present from the opening pages of the book where the antagonism between the Nazis and the Jews was given comic expression in the domestic battle waged between Frl Mayr and Frau Glanterneck. Nevertheless politics are firmly subordinated to the private lives of the characters, although none of them remains unaffected by the deteriorating political scene. Even Sally Bowles is momentarily troubled by the failure of the Darmstädter und National Bank. 'Everything Collapses!' screams the headline of the evening paper, and immediately this economic disaster is seen to belong to a wider breakdown of German society which lies at the centre of the novel. On Ruegen Island even the beaches are segregated between Jewish and Nordic races. The Nowak household breeds its own recruit to the Nazi cause. In 'The Landauers' politics cannot help but loom large in the lives of these public enemies of the Nazis. But only in the final 'Berlin Diary' do political events usurp the private domain. As the economic situation degenerates traditional moral values break down. Frau Krampf will demean herself to her sexually perverted butcher to obtain cutlets or a steak. The reformatory school boys no longer have a choice between the engineering works and prison when the former goes bankrupt. One of the most vivid images of Berlin on the eve of Hitler's putsch is of the jaded decadence of the Salome, appropriately decorated to look like hell, where 'stage lesbians', as part of the performance, imitate 'the laughter of the damned' for the sake of their clientele (p 562). Both actors and audience participate in this tragic farce. The whole of Berlin society (and not just the capitalists and Nazis) is corrupt, Isherwood implies.

'Christopher Isherwood exhibits values without stating them by illustrating their absence', the usually acerbic Geoffrey Grigson asserted approvingly in his review of the novel in *New Verse*.[20] Up to the final section, Isherwood has been showing the vacuum in the lives of the lost which made the Nazi takeover possible. One remembers Hippi Bernstein to whom politics were quite unreal, or Frau Nowak who did not understand politics and wanted the Kaiser back or, above all, Frl Schroeder who voted Communist in November 1932 and yet readily accepted Hitler's takeover of power in March 1933. Talking about Frl Schneider, her counterpart in *I am a Camera*, Isherwood called her 'the well-meaning but unwary landlady who symbolises the whole German public'.[21] He does not blame her. She too is a victim of a universal disease. Besides, she and thousands like her, 'whatever government is in power, are doomed to live in this town' (p 582), while 'Isherwood', in the last segment of the book, takes leave of Berlin. It is a significant gesture by the narrator who has maintained such sympathy and understanding for his cast of characters throughout the book. Who is he to judge Frl Schroeder and her kind when he can quit Berlin at will? Who also are we, Isherwood implies, to pass judgement when our experience is even more remote than his?

Colin Wilson, like others before him, has ·complained that Isherwood's objectivity is 'a little *too* cold and detached'.[22] In fact his detachment is essential if he is to maintain our sympathy for the lost. To prevent the reader from pre-judging his characters, it is necessary to show the distance which separates the reader's from their traumatic experience. Nevertheless he cannot always hide his own tendency to romanticise characters like Sally and Otto, and in the final Diary he momentarily reveals his own love for Berlin and all its doomed inhabitants: 'Berlin is a skeleton which aches in the cold: it is my own skeleton aching' (p 553). In fact the novel ends with 'Isherwood' himself subscribing to the universal hallucination among Berliners that nothing has really happened. Caught smiling at himself in a shop mirror while mourning over the fate of friends like Rudi, he epitomises at that moment the tragi-comic predicament of the lost to whom he too spiritually belongs.

The Collaborations with Auden

In the wake of anthologies like *New Signatures* and *New Country* and of magazines like *New Verse, Left Review* and *New Writing*, literary collaboration acquired a new respectability in the socially conscious thirties. Auden, in particular, collaborated not just with Isherwood but with Louis MacNeice and T. C. Worsley in the space of that one decade. Much the most celebrated of these literary partnerships was Auden's with Isherwood, and the works they jointly produced branded them as Marxist-orientated writers in the public mind. Since Isherwood first came to wider public notice with their jointly written plays, the Marxist label stuck to him despite the fact that none of his own novels could be read even remotely as an example of the socially committed genre of writing so favoured in the thirties. In fact even Auden's and Isherwood's collaborations, being the by-products of their own close friendship during those years, reflect if anything more their shared private mythology than the fashionable left-wing ideology of that period.

Auden's and Isherwood's first dramatic collaboration in 1929 was an extremely private affair. Dedicated to Otto Küsel and Berthold Szczesny, their current boyfriends, *The Enemies of a Bishop or Die When I Say When (A Morality in Four Acts)* was inspired by a play they had both seen in Berlin, Peter Martin Lampel's *Revolt in a Reformatory*.[1] A third-rate social documentary attacking life in reformatories, it amused them (perhaps —because of the language barrier—more than was intended) sufficiently to embark on an imitation that also incorporated the use of a Doppelgänger (borrowed from Henrik Galeen's *The Student of Prague*, a film they also saw together in Berlin),[2] not to mention a hero, Bishop Law, based on Homer Lane, their cult figure of that period, and various characters lifted from Mort-mere. 'The play was no more than a charade', Isherwood has

written, 'very loosely put together and full of private jokes.'[3] It
was never intended for production or publication. Many of
Auden's best poems that first appeared in *Poems 1930* are
arbitrarily introduced into the play, followed by flippant remarks
like, 'Well, I'm afraid all that's a bit above my head' or 'Oh, do
be quiet. I'm so tired.'[4] The poems themselves often originated
in private circumstances: 'Before this loved one', for example,
originated as a poem about Bubi which is simply put in the
mouth of Spectre, the Doppelgänger of one of the major
characters, Robert Bicknell (whose surname is Auden's mother's
maiden name). The intensely personal nature of their first collaboration is a feature which becomes less obtrusive with time.

The *Enemies of a Bishop* also indicates that their collaboration
began as between a talented but uneven poet and his admirer,
critic and literary elder. During the evolution of their subsequent
joint plays a more egalitarian relationship developed in which
Isherwood assumed the function of librettist and Auden that of
composer. According to Isherwood they were yin-yang in their
working partnership, first one then the other assuming the
initiative.[5] Auden, asked about their collaboration, explained
that 'when a collaboration works, the two people concerned
become a third person, who is different from either of them in
isolation.'[6] Whether this third persona or 'dual personality' as
Isherwood has called it[7] is the sum of the best or the worst of
both individual writers is a matter of opinion. Stephen Spender
had his doubts from the beginning, observing that 'most of the
poetry in these plays is inferior to the poetry of Auden's single
poems; no character in them has the subtlety and profundity of
characters in Mr Isherwood's novels.'[8] Certainly all of their
plays were written in far from ideal circumstances and usually
had to be completed in record time. This meant that, after
agreeing a rough scenario, the two writers would simultaneously
undertake different scenes with the inevitable result that their
plays lacked continuity of mood, tone and inspiration. Yet the
loose episodic structure, the startling changes between one
scene and the next, and the use of poetry, doggerel, dance and
song did offer a welcome relief from the conventional theatrical
offerings of the West End stage in the 1930s.

In fact Auden was first drawn into serious theatrical writing
by the formation of a group of actors, directors, designers and

musicians held together by their dissatisfaction with the established theatrical world of London. On 4 February 1932 the Group Theatre was founded by thirteen members. The prime mover and principal director was Rupert Doone who had been a professional dancer under Diaghilev, a choreographer for Max Reinhardt in Berlin and an actor and director for the Festival Theatre at Cambridge. His aim in building up the Group Theatre, he claimed, was to create 'a theatre which would be self-sufficient and independent of purely commercial considerations'.[9] It was to be a co-operative enterprise in the expressionist mode of drama: 'Theatre art is the art of co-operation. I want the theatre to be a social force, where the painter and the author and the choreographer . . . and the actor . . . and the stage producer combine with the audience to make realism fantasy and fantasy real.'[10] Despite this democratic ideology Rupert Doone was in fact highly dictatorial as a director, a talented if eccentric *prima donna* who was most arrogant and demanding when his ideas were most silly. This did not prevent him from attracting a growing band of dedicated actors, writers, musicians and artists including Tyrone Guthrie (a founder member), Michael St Denis, Robert Speaight, most of the so-called members of the Auden Group of writers, Robert Medley, Henry Moore and Benjamin Britten. At first the Group Theatre staged plays wherever it could find suitable premises. Then Anmer Hall made his recently acquired Westminster Theatre available and offered the Group Theatre a season of its own from 1935 onwards.

Auden was first introduced to Doone by his old schoolfriend Robert Medley in 1932 and was commissioned to write a ballet scenario and a short play. He combined the two forms in *The Dance of Death* which was staged by the Group Theatre early in 1934 and received a generally poor press. By November 1934 Auden had written a new verse play *The Chase* for Doone which he sent to Isherwood for his opinion. *The Chase* might have evolved from *The Fronny*, a play Auden wrote in 1930[11] (although Isherwood claims that *The Fronny* was an early draft of *The Dance of Death*).[12] This version of the play included a strike at Pressan which is brought to an end by the use of armed force during which Alan dies.[13] From Copenhagen Isherwood sent Auden a series of letters and a suggested scenario that required changes sufficiently drastic to induce Auden to delay Faber's publication of the play and to fly out to rewrite *The Chase* as *Where is Francis?* in January 1935. With Isherwood's help his earlier rambling verse play was stripped of its reformatory sub-plot and given structural coherence. Auden's indulgence in lyrics for their own sake was largely eliminated and numerous satirical prose scenes, mostly written by Isherwood, were inserted to turn Alan's brief search into a parabolic quest through the waste land of modern Europe. In adopting Doone's new title, *The Dog Beneath the Skin*, the two authors must have been aware of the allusion to T. S. Eliot's 'the skull beneath the skin' in 'Whispers of Immortality'.

Because the play began life entirely as Auden's creation critics have tended to discuss *The Dog Beneath the Skin* as if it were still mainly Auden's work. In fact not only was the political scenario Isherwood's, as he informed Spender,[14] but many of the scenes were written by him and others were his idea. A letter Auden wrote to Spender in late June 1935 provides much the most authoritative breakdown of their respective contributions. Apart from the Choruses, all of which Auden wrote, he claims that Isherwood wrote I.2 (except the song), II.1 (except the leader's speech), II.2 (except the song), II.5 (the dialogue between the feet only), III.2 (the Destructive Desmond episode), III.3, III.4 (from Francis's discovery on) and III.5 (apart from the Vicar's sermon). Moreover, although Auden wrote I.4 (the Ostnia Palace scene) and II.3 and 4 (Paradise Park), Isherwood outlined these new scenes in considerable detail in his letters to Auden on 23 November and 11 December 1934.[15] Isherwood was also responsible for substituting a dummy for the actress Miss Lou Vipond, modifying the character of the journalists, and suggesting the idea for lyrics like that between the journalists with its refrain, 'They're in the racket, too!' (pp 40–42)

In *The Chase* George who has escaped from the reformatory disguises himself in a dog's skin for a time to accompany Alan on his brief search for Francis (whom he finds on his return to Pressan in the infirmary at death's door). In turning this device into a central feature of the play Isherwood was borrowing the idea from *Peter Pan* and *Dick Whittington*. This fitted Auden's declared view that 'the music hall, the Christmas pantomime and the country house charade are the most living drama today.'[16] Act I Scene 1 'suggests the setting of a pre-war musical comedy' (p 17) and opens with a pastiche of Gilbert and Sullivan's *HMS Pinafore*. Rupert Doone in fact advocated a form of drama analagous both to modern musical comedy and the pre-medieval folk play.[17] This second element enters with the introduction of Alan's quest in search of the missing heir, Francis, and the prize of his sister to whoever finds him. The quest is common to the Icelandic sagas which so fascinated Auden and to the classic fairy tale.

Both Isherwood and Auden have explained how this fairy tale element necessitated an extremely crude form of characterisation. For Auden 'the subject of drama . . . is the commonly known, the universally familiar stories of the society or generation in which it is written.' This means that 'drama is not suited to the analysis of character, which is the province of the novel. Dramatic characters are simplified, easily recognisable and over life-size.'[18] This approach particularly penalised Isherwood whose strength lay in the acute observation and subtle portrayal of human behaviour. All of the characters in the play are representative of moral abstractions and most of them are no more than caricatures—of fascists, capitalists, aesthetes, the press, exploiters and exploited. As Spender, as usual the most percipient critic among Isherwood's friends, pointed out, such figures are already such stuffed dummies in actuality that something has to be done to give them life on stage and prevent them from looking like battered Aunt Sallies set up only to be predictably knocked down in the course of the performance. 'The scene', he wrote in 1938, 'in which the inmates of a lunatic asylum of Westlanders applaud a broadcast speech by the Leader and behave in the way that Nazis behave is inept because the alarming fact about Nazi Germany is that the Nazis are *not* lunatics.'[19]

The peculiar mixture of comic revue, light verse, popular song and serious political commentary in *The Dog Beneath the Skin* obviously owed its inspiration partly to Brecht. Auden and Isherwood have both acknowledged the influence which Brecht's *The Threepenny Opera* and *Rise and Fall of the City of Mahogonny* had on them when writing their first play.[20] Isherwood has specifically pointed out how Act III Scene 2 in the restaurant of the Nineveh Hotel was inspired by Scene 13 of *Mahogonny*, where in a scene of extreme gluttony a character dies of overeating.[21] But more generally the satirical treatment of the

European political scene derives from Brecht. In his letter to Spender of June 1935 Isherwood took personal responsibility for the political scenario, although Auden had embodied some crude satire of the English class struggle in the last act of *The Chase*. In *The Dog Beneath the Skin* the canvas is wider and includes Ostnia governed by a corrupt monarch and Westland ruled by a fanatical fascist. There are travesties of Dolfuss and his wife's behaviour during the Vienna uprising (I.4), of Hitler and the Nazis (II.2), references to Clemenceau (p 43), Churchill (p 179) and the discovery at the end of the play of a religious-fascist organisation in the midst of rural England reminiscent of Mosley's supporters in the mid-thirties.

Somehow neither of the writers appears to have put his heart into the political satire. Much the most successful satire is directed against various manifestations of misdirected love (Auden's obsession) or against the aestheticism of the artist (Isherwood's *bête noire*). As Auden explained to Spender at the time, the moral he tried to draw was always 'You have the choice. Yes you can make the world or mar it. Free will means you can choose either to fear or love.'[22] At its subtlest this theme is given magnificent poetic expression, as in Auden's lyric 'Enter with him/These legends, love' where the conflict is internalised. At its crudest, as perhaps it is in the Epilogue, Auden produces what Barbara Everett has called 'an amalgam of Dante's Paradise, the Communist Manifesto and the close of a romantic film'.[23] Between these extremes come Isherwood's scenarios for Paradise Park and the stuffed mannequin, Miss Lou Vipond. But when Isherwood is given his head with Francis's denunciatory speech in Act III Scene 5 he betrays the same heavy-handed didacticism that mars the Epilogue. 'Francis', he explained to Spender, 'is condemning his old attitude toward the villagers, condemning his "dog's view" as superficial, condemning his diary. In fact, the whole allegory of the dog-skin disguise is "Proust is not enough".'[24] Isherwood's anti-intellectualism combined with his feelings of guilt at remaining on the sidelines of the intensifying political struggle produced an arbitrarily imposed revolutionary ending to the play that is quite as ill-fitting as Auden's Marxist conclusion to *The Dance of Death*.

Nevertheless *The Dog Beneath the Skin*, uneven as it is, contains

1a. Wyberslegh Hall, Christopher
   Isherwood's birthplace

1b. Christopher Isherwood
   at seventeen

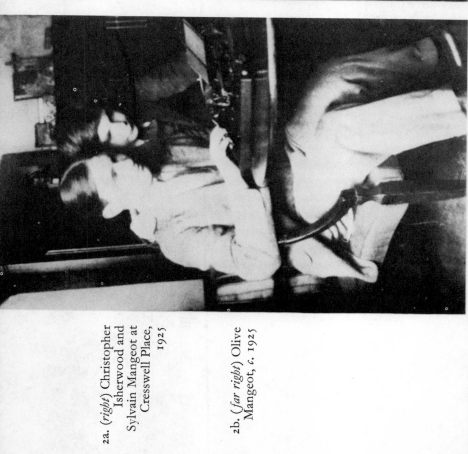

2a. (*right*) Christopher Isherwood and Sylvain Mangeot at Cresswell Place, 1925

2b. (*far right*) Olive Mangeot, *c*. 1925

Here, Mr. Z—, a crocodile
Boards the boat-train for Carlisle.
Living is cheap there, that's the reason
So many are visiting it this season.
The cars too shopmen leave large chops
hanging outside the butchers' shops;
And if you're clever, you can lunch
without paying, off a bunch
of two savages, a maybe
a stupid nursemaid's left a baby
unprotected in its pram —
(Babies are very nice with ham) —
Hence the sleek and jolly smile
On the face of this crocodile.

3a. (*right*) Sylvain
Mangeot's illustration
to 'Here, Mr Z—', from
*People One Ought to
Know*, January 1926

3b. (*far right*) 'Here,
Mr Z—', one of
Isherwood's poems
written for *People One
Ought to Know*,
January 1926

4a. 'Otto' and Christopher Isherwood on the Wannsee, 1930

4b. Heinz in Ruegen Island, summer 1932

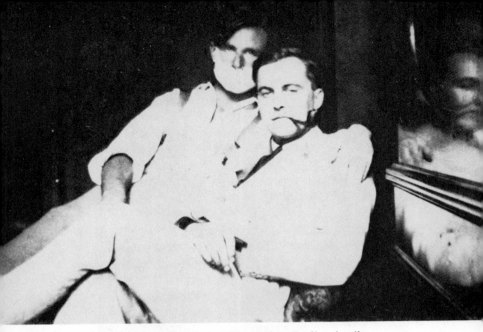

5a. Christopher Isherwood and Edward Upward in Berlin, April
1932: a humorous joint portrait during shaving

5b. W. H. Auden, Stephen Spender and Christopher Isherwood
in the early 1930s

6a. Jean Ross in the 1930s

6b. Gerald Hamilton in later life

7a. William Robson-Scott, Christopher Isherwood, James and Tania Stern, and Heinz in Portugal, 1936

7b. A scene from the Group Theatre production of *The Dog Beneath the Skin*, 1936

8. Christopher Isherwood, his mother and his brother Richard, photographed by Bill Caskey in the late 1940s

9a. Dodie Smith, Alec Beesley and Christopher Isherwood at Malibu Beach, Christmas 1945

9b. Christopher Isherwood with Bill Caskey and the Beesleys' Dalmatians, *c.* 1945

10. Christopher Isherwood and Swami Prabhavananda at the Vedanta Temple, Hollywood, 1944

11. Christopher Isherwood and Don Bachardy in 1953, the year they first met

12a. E. M. Forster and Christopher Isherwood in Forster's rooms at Cambridge, March 1970

12b. Christopher Isherwood on the deck of his house in Santa Monica, taken by the author in 1976

examples of Auden's finest early poetry, especially in some of the Choruses, his *tour de force* in prose, the Vicar's sermon (originally published in *Life and Letters* as 'Sermon by an Armament Manufacturer') and one or two brilliant satirical scenes penned by Isherwood such as the episode featuring Destructive Desmond. Because the play is about the same length as *Hamlet* Doone was forced to cut it savagely for its first public performance at the Westminster Theatre on 30 January 1936. It is ironic that all the outstanding features of the published play were either cut or severely pruned. Doone decided to omit Act I Scenes 3 and the first half of 4 depicting the execution of the workers, due to George V's death on 20 January 1936. The censor requested the omission of the Destructive Desmond episode and parts of the Vicar's sermon according to Robert Medley.[25] The play's length dictated the curtailment or omission of many of the Choruses. Many of the remaining satirical scenes, especially those parodying religious practices, were drastically shortened, whether at the request of the censor (as Cyril Connolly suggested at the time)[26] or for reasons of space remains uncertain.[27]

Moreover the authors kept on rewriting the end of the play. In an undated letter to Auden that he must have written after their consultation in mid-January 1935, Isherwood outlined a revised version of the last scene in which Mildred Luce shoots Francis and the journalists hush the matter up by claiming that only a dog has been killed.[28] This version was used for the Group Theatre production the following year. Nevertheless, according to Robert Medley, the unmasking of Francis, however it was done, was impossible to bring off successfully on the stage.[29] The press notices were mixed. Cyril Connolly dismissed it as 'undergraduate satire';[30] Derek Verschoyle discerned 'a genuinely dramatic talent';[31] while *The Sunday Times* claimed that 'on its merits, compared to the average London production, this play ought to run for five years.'[32] It ran for a derisorily short period, although it was revived briefly in the autumn of 1936. Perhaps Isherwood was right when he confessed that, although it was written for performance by the Group Theatre, its sheer length indicated that 'it was really written more to be read than to be necessarily acted.'[33] It still reads extremely well, a pot-pourri of slapstick, satire, legend and magnificent poetry that is only badly marred by the politically didactic ending.

The Ascent of F6, their second collaboration, is at once more workmanlike and less ebullient, nearer to conventional theatre in its concentration on psychological motivation and in making less use of dance, light verse and music.[34] Isherwood has given a detailed breakdown of who was responsible for what in this in *Christopher and his Kind* (p 180). Essentially, once they had agreed on the overall scenario, they divided the scenes up between them with almost mathematical precision. As Isherwood wrote revealingly in his diary, 'The only scene on which we really collaborated was the last' (*CK* 180). Since Auden wrote all the poetry as well as some of the prose (Michael Ransom's opening soliloquy in particular) he was probably responsible for more of the text than Isherwood, although, as with *The Dog Beneath the Skin*, Isherwood undoubtedly fed him with a number of the ideas which he then turned into poetry. Ostensibly *F6* is far more structurally integrated than *The Dog Beneath the Skin* with its loosely connected sequence of scenes more reminiscent of a revue or the music hall than of straight drama. Yet at a more fundamental level there is an aggravating sense of discontinuity in *F6* that must reflect in part the method by which it was put together.

Isherwood has repeatedly confessed the degree of irresponsibility which they both showed in their approach to the play. He told one interviewer:

We were serious, and yet not serious. . . . It was extremely aggressive towards a whole theatrical convention (ie traditional realist drama) and, yet again, it was making use of that convention. It was about nothing, and yet it was about something, very, very definite and clear. The play certainly has a theme, and yet, mixed up in it are definite obscurantist elements which seem designed simply to confuse critics, professors, members of the audience.[35]

In revolt against the neat mechanical plotting of the conventional theatre, Auden and Isherwood tended to resort to double-talk. This obscurantist element surfaces in just those scenes which received most revision—the mother's interior monologue in Act I Scene 3, the Abbot's speeches in Act II Scene 1, and the last scene of the play which they rewrote repeatedly, some of the versions being completely at odds with others. 'The end of the play was always a terrible mess', Isherwood has admitted, 'and we never really solved it.'[36] Part of the problem was that they gave lines from earlier passages in the play to different characters in the final scene which, according to Isherwood, was 'theatrically effective' in that it 'produced an extraordinary sense of meaning without (meaning) very much'.[37]

Their first version, written at Sintra and published by Faber in September 1936, elicited critical reactions both from Spender in the *Left Review* and Forster in the *Listener*. Spender wrote that 'Ransom is a colossal prig, a fact of which the authors seem insufficiently aware' and felt that his priggishness should have been made 'the final tragic realisation of the last act'.[38] Forster was less severe. But he perceptively diagnosed four separate levels on which the play operated, the heroic, the politico-economical, the ethical and the psychological, implying that there was a conflict between them.[39] In October Isherwood informed him that they were revising the play in an attempt to meet both his and Spender's criticisms:

> We are doing this partly by attempting to show more clearly how Ransom was, at the critical moment in the Monastery, forced into going up the mountain by his followers, like every dictator. And we are also making Mrs Ransom more like a dictator's public; submitting to him and yet preying on him.[40]

What Auden and Isherwood do not seem to have appreciated at the time was the radical nature of the alterations they were proposing. Many of the changes, which were incorporated in the first American and second English editions of March 1937, flatly contradict the meaning of the passages they replace. In the Abbot's speech in II.1 the first version reads 'You wish to be perfect' where the revised version reads 'You know, as I do, that Life is evil' (p 57). An additional passage in the second version contains the Abbot's confession that his visitation from the Demon means that he is already among the lost (p 59). Yet, as in the first version, it is the Abbot who still sits in judgement on Ransom in the final scene. Another example of the authors' complete *volte-face* is to be found in the last scene. In the first version an additional last scene showed all the representatives of the establishment mourning Ransom's loss in a radio tribute. These speeches are quite inappropriately transferred to refer to

James's death at the hands of his Demon Mother in the revised text (p 91).

After it opened at the Mercury Theatre on 26 February 1937 not only Forster but Doone expressed his dissatisfaction with the evasive nature of the final dream scene.[41] Besides the nightly changed endings during the first week's run, the production at the Arts Theatre, Cambridge on 23 April 1937 brought the play to a conclusion with Mr and Mrs A's line 'Die for us',[42] while the New York production by the Drove Players of 21 April 1939 considered, but abandoned, the introduction of a scene in which Mr and Mrs A., picnicking under Ransom's statue, declare 'He's one of us now.' But it did adopt the suggestion of Burgess Meredith, a friend of the two writers, who was simultaneously planning a Broadway production with himself as Ransom that never came off. He insisted that Ransom should reach the top of the mountain on his own. So the mother was made the last of the phantoms opposing the climb whom her son brushes aside lower down the mountain.[43] The Old Vic revival of 27 June 1939 with Alec Guinness in the lead part had James leap off the peak, cut Ransom's dream interview with his mother, jumbled up the final chorus, and reintroduced in altered form the radio tribute that followed Act II Scene 5 in the original version. Also in this version Ransom confessed that what he saw written in the crystal was: 'Man is an animal that has to love or perish. There is no Demon', which smacks strongly of Auden.[44]

This failure of the two collaborators to find satisfactory endings for both their first two plays prompted the acute observation from Spender that 'where an ending cannot be found, one may suspect that there is a lack of organic growth throughout the play and something is wrong from the start.'[45] Instead of organic growth *F6* exhibits the accumulated debris of all Auden's and Isherwood's obsessions of that period. Their favourite authors are pillaged, especially Ibsen, Eliot (in particular *Sweeney Agonistes*) and Dante. Ransom's climb up F6 becomes so heavily symbolic that it eventually loses all coherent meaning in the phantasmagoric climax on the peak where, as Spears has remarked, the political and psychological conclusions mutually conflict.[46] In addition each conclusion contains its own radical ambiguity. Is Ransom, as the *Group Theatre Paper* for December 1936 suggested,[47] a sympathetic portrait of a

dictator, or is he the victim of a capitalist society? Louis Mac-
Neice pointed out a similar internal contradiction in the psychological aspect of the play: 'Auden, while regarding so many of
our neuroses as tragic . . . yet believes . . . that neurosis is the
cause of an individual's development.'[48] Does Ransom acquire
self-knowledge when he recognises the Demon as his mother or
does he die because of his continuing oedipal dependence on
her?

Perhaps Auden and Isherwood relied too heavily on the
model they admit to having used for Ransom, T. E. Lawrence,[49]
to impose a meaningful pattern on the heterogeneous ideas they
were seeking to express in the play. Isherwood wrote of Lawrence
that 'he suffered, in his own person, the neurotic ills of an entire
generation' (E 24). But just because he did assume such large
symbolic proportions he offered Auden and Isherwood too
many opportunities to add to his significance and universality.
His appeal to writers of the thirties was in large part due to the
ambiguity surrounding his actions and motivation. When
Auden was reviewing Captain Liddell Hart's book on Lawrence
in 1934, he read into Lawrence's life an interpretation that was
completely at odds with his subsequent portrayal of him in F6.
'To me', he wrote, 'Lawrence's life is an allegory of the transformation of the Truly Weak Man into the Truly Strong Man.'[50]
Yet a year later he was depicting his fate as that of the Truly
Weak Man lost on the northern circuit (cf CK 193). But if he
represented for both writers a neurotic hero who, as Isherwood
has explained, fought the entire war for quite private reasons,
then he was quite inappropriate as a vehicle for the political
allegory. In making his ascent a political quest they were negating
the significance of his psychological pattern of behaviour.
Ultimately all these confusions are attributable to the irresponsible
attitude which the collaboration encouraged in both writers.
F. R. Leavis tended to indict the entire Auden group for protect-
ing its members from all contact with serious critical standards
in the case of F.6[51] But Spender's and Day Lewis's outspoken
public criticisms of the play at the time show this charge to be
groundless.[52] Spender was surely closer to the truth when he
suggested that 'each seemed secretly resolved not to put his best
efforts into a collaboration.'[53]

Perhaps Auden and Isherwood were becoming conscious themselves of their tendency to act irresponsibly in their collaborations by the time they came to write *On the Frontier*, the last of their three plays. Was it for this reason that there is more of Auden's work in their last joint play than the others? According to Isherwood, Auden took more charge of the construction and wrote not only all the poetry but 'a big share of the prose'.[54] The presence of a single controlling hand in this collaboration probably accounts for the greater sense of overall unity. But what was gained in structural terms was lost in other ways. According to Isherwood the irresponsibility they displayed in the earlier plays lent them a certain charm, whereas 'this one was too reasonable, perhaps too sensible.'[55] It is certainly the least innovatory of the three, closer to naturalistic than expressionist dramatic conventions. Even Auden's poetry is at its least inspired in it; he never reprinted any of the poems from it in the various subsequent editions of his collected poems, a fact which indicates his own later evaluation of the play.

On 14 November 1938 *On the Frontier* was premiered by the Group Theatre at the Arts Theatre, Cambridge. It was generally considered to be a flop—'not a narrowing disaster', Isherwood explained in *Christopher and his Kind*; 'it passed away painlessly' (p 244). The play that was performed at Cambridge was virtually identical to the published text apart from various small alterations demanded by the censor to make the parallels between Westland and Nazi Germany less obvious. Scandinavian names were substituted for German ones, and synonyms had to be found for phrases like 'Shock Troops' and 'labour camps'.[56] Such alterations are sad testimony to the dishonesty underlying the official British policy of appeasement in 1938. Not that anyone in the audience was unaware of the parallels being drawn between the Leader and Hitler: the grotesque caricature of the Führer was all too obvious. As T. S. Eliot wrote to Maynard Keynes the day after the opening night, 'I am afraid that Hitler is not the simpleton that the authors made him out to be.'[57]

Auden and Isherwood called *On the Frontier* a melodrama, and the crudity of its characterisation and political morality has been the subject of adverse criticism from the appearance of the first press reviews onwards. Part of the problem stems from the play's topicality which has dated it more than the others for readers today.[58] Even on its opening night, as Day Lewis pointed out, it suffered a 'dwarfing effect from the recent (Munich) crisis.'[59] This made it appear, as the *TLS* commented, to be 'annotating something "off",' so that the audience felt as if it were present at a running commentary of world affairs.[60] Both Auden and Isherwood thought that 'it was too near to the reality of the contemporary situation' to acquire a life of its own in the theatre;[61] the drama of actual international events was too compelling an alternative.

There is general agreement that *On the Frontier* is far inferior to the earlier two plays. Although, when they revised it, Auden and Isherwood substituted an indecisive ending for the original one in which the people actually succeeded in seizing power from their rulers,[62] the play still showed a clumsy left-wing bias that lacked any of the compensatory ebullience of *The Dog Beneath the Skin* or the moral complexity of *F6*. However justifiable their stance was, the fact remains, as Louis MacNeice pointed out, that 'a play cannot live by morals alone.'[63] When one considers how much more politically committed both authors were in the plays on which they collaborated than in any of their own work, it becomes apparent that each felt obliged to subscribe to current left-wing views with which privately each of them was growing increasingly disenchanted.

The play is at odds with some of their deepest convictions. It subscribes to the ideological position of the Popular Front at a time when they were so disillusioned with British society that they were on the point of leaving their native country for good. In the final scene, Eric, their pasteboard spokesman, rejects his earlier pacifist stance just when Isherwood is becoming aware of his own pacifist convictions. Similarly Valerian authoritatively pronounces the replacement of the church by industry (pp 116–18) when Auden is on the point of rediscovering his belief in Christianity—in fact Eric's last speech in the play where he foresees the construction of the just city caused at least one reviewer at the time to suggest how 'uncommonly like a Christian hymn to a better world' it sounded.[64] So much are Auden's and Isherwood's convictions in conflict with their ostensible intention that Valerian, the central villain of the play, is, rather like Milton's Satan, much the most lively and attractive of all the characters.

One might be inclined to argue that Auden's and Isherwood's

attempts at collaboration proved increasingly disastrous, had they not gone on to produce *Journey to a War*, their last joint effort in the quite different genre of the travel book. Much of the poetry Auden wrote for it is equal to his finest work, while the 'Travel-Diary' exhibits Isherwood's normal stylistic skills and avoids the blundering left-wing dogma that mars the plays. One could argue that the collaboration succeeds primarily because there is so little collaboration. Evelyn Waugh expressed this view in his own forceful manner when he reviewed the book, declaring: 'it is two books which for purposes of commercial convenience have been issued as one.'[65] In fact the prose section is collaborative as it is based on a diary which Auden and Isherwood took turns at writing on alternative days. When Isherwood rewrote this as the 'Travel-Diary' he made a point of crediting Auden with any especially witty remarks or acute observations that he had made during his turns at keeping the diary.

It is also collaborative in its overall approach to the subject of war. The book opens with Auden's sonnet to Forster whose promise—'still the inner life shall pay' (p 11)—provides the perspective from which both writers proceed to view China at war. Like Forster they insist upon a creed of personal relationships and see China in wartime not as the battleground of political and economic forces, but as the condition of modern man, an image of mankind overtaken once more by the indiscriminately destructive forces of war. Whereas Auden generalises from the particular, taking a wide historical view of his subject, especially in the 'Sonnet Sequence' at the end, Isherwood remains strictly within the limits of their personal experience of China. The 'Foreword' makes a point of emphasising the authors' lack of knowledge about China and their complete reliance on the distortions of interpreters. Neither writer pretended to know more than he did. Both accepted Auden's dictum in 'Hongkong': 'For what we are, we have ourselves to blame' (p 23).

Out of this insistence on the importance of the personal and the fallible comes much of the strength of the 'Travel-Diary'. Isherwood has subsequently written that the visit to China brought him 'back from a world of political principles to a world of human values' which he had 'temporarily lost' (*AV* 8). Forced by the near impossibility of reporting on life at the battle front to view the war from a beleaguered civilian's point of view, Isherwood naturally focuses on the personal relationships they made during their trip and quite unashamedly places Auden and himself at the centre of the book. The reader is made to see the Chinese through the uninformed but receptive eyes of the two Englishmen who are not even entirely sure why they are in China—apart from the fact that Bennett Cerf of Random House persuaded Fabers jointly to commission them to do a travel book and they could not resist so good an offer. As the *New Statesman* commented, 'what makes their book so different from a hundred others of the moment is that it avoids omniscience and brilliantly records first impressions.'[66]

Perhaps it is this Forsterian insistence on the validity of personal experience which gave Isherwood the strength to abjure political dogma. Strangely enough Auden is also being true to his innermost feelings by drawing back from the particular fray in his 'Sonnet Sequence' much in the same way as he had done so successfully in 'Spain' the year before. The 'Travel-Diary' also remains doggedly true to the anarchic sequence of events befalling the two writers. In other words the disconnected form of the diary accurately reflects the chaos they encountered in a war-torn country. Nor was the chaos purely external to either writer. Both of them were experiencing fundamental doubts about their convictions of a decade. Auden's verse 'Commentary' ending in a prayer points in the direction he was moving. Similarly Isherwood was groping towards his subsequent realisation that he was a pacifist: 'War starts with principles but it ends with people', he discovered (*AV* 8).

Journey to a War succeeds to the extent that it does because it allows both collaborators to exploit their own particular strengths and avoids any joint subscription to an ideology about which neither of them cared deeply enough to write with genuine feeling. Nevertheless one cannot help feeling that Auden emerges from this final work of collaboration the more successful of the two. As Evelyn Waugh pointed out, the 'Travel-Diary' suffers from a certain flatness. This might be due to Isherwood's cultivation of Forsterian understatement, but Waugh attributes it to the fact that 'he is far too individual an artist to be a satisfactory reporter.'[67] His insistence on subjective truth is responsible for some of the least satisfactory passages in which he portrays Auden and himself at their most puerile moments, attaching in this way an altogether false importance to their least significant actions. Yet Isherwood is essentially an intuitive writer and his instinct to give priority to his subjective responses imbues the 'Travel-Diary' with what life it has. *Journey to a War* was Auden's and Isherwood's last collaboration. Coming at the end of the thirties, a decade in which joint ventures and literary factions proliferated, the book symbolically anticipates in its strict division of responsibilities between its two authors the retreat from group solidarity and the return to individualism that also overtook so many other writers of this period during the war years that followed.

17

The War Years

What made Isherwood decide to emigrate to the States in January 1939? It is important to understand the circumstances surrounding his departure from Europe if one is to avoid the moral prejudices which have prevented a number of his readers and critics from appreciating his post-war fiction. In the first place he left after the threat of war had receded with the Munich agreement. Secondly he had long since become what he calls in *Christopher and his Kind* 'a chronic wanderer' (p 246) who had spent most of his adult life in voluntary exile from England. Besides, patriotism, like Christianity, was something he had learnt to hate in his prep school days when it was used by the Others to turn his father into a heroic ideal by comparison with which they repeatedly berated the bewildered young boy. In the third place the decision to settle in the States only formed gradually some time after his arrival there. He did not apply to become a permanent US resident until the beginning of May 1939[1] and in November of that year he was still sufficiently undecided to write to Spender: 'Shall I come back? I don't know. If I am really needed, yes.'[2] Throughout 1940, by which time his pacifist convictions had hardened, he fully expected to go to the war in the east as an ambulance driver. Under these circumstances there are no grounds for accusing him of leaving Europe to avoid conscription.

But he certainly was in an emotional and spiritual turmoil at this time. One small indication of the panic he was undergoing was the way in which he left his English boyfriend badly in the lurch, only announcing his break with him after his arrival in New York. Yet symptoms of this kind suggested a much deeper underlying *malaise*. As he recounts in *Christopher and his Kind*, on the boat journey to New York he and Auden finally admitted to one another their mutual disenchantment with 'the

Popular Front, the party line, the anti-fascist struggle' (p 248). Unlike Auden, Isherwood was to remain a liberal in his political sympathies throughout his life. But neither writer cared passionately about politics as such and their subscription to political commitment in their public talks and jointly written plays had been inducing a schizophrenic state of mind in them both. After his arrival in New York on 26 January Isherwood had still to discover even more fundamental elements in his personality which he had held repressed since his childhood. He had yet to learn that behind his hatred of Christianity lay a deeply religious attitude to life and that behind his neurotic talk of the Test lurked a profound contempt for war and the values it represented.

During the three months he spent in New York he was experiencing the doubts and despair that accompanied this radical division within himself. Despite the presence of 'Vernon', the blond American art student with whom he had had a brief affair the previous year, he felt strangely alienated by New York. He shared rooms with Auden, first in the George Washington Hotel, then in an apartment on East 81st Street in the Yorkville area of Manhattan. Both gave readings and lectures about China and Europe at which they were expected to follow the old left-wing line in which they no longer believed. But nevertheless Auden took to New York. Within ten weeks he had met Chester Kallman, with whom he was to spend the rest of his life, at a symposium of English writers held on 6 April at the Keynote Club. By comparison Isherwood has recorded how he 'suddenly felt very inadequate, . . . and that Wystan was the dominant figure who was going to succeed there, . . . as indeed proved to be true.'[3]

Although he was surrounded by old friends like the Manns and Paul Bowles, as well as making a new friend of Lincoln Kirstein, a poet and choreographer who was a friend of Spender, he felt that he was accepting their hospitality under false pretences, because, as he explained, 'the Christopher Isherwood they wanted to see was no longer myself—for he represented those very attitudes and beliefs I had just abandoned' (*AV* 15). In *An Approach to Vedanta* he claims that he couldn't write a line. This is not strictly true, as he wrote a joint article with Auden on 'Young British Writers On The Way Up' for *Vogue*, another one on 'German Literature in England' for the *New Republic*, and a review of Steinbeck's *Grapes of Wrath* for the *Kenyon Review*. But in creative terms Isherwood had reached an impasse that he was to be unable to overcome until he had resolved the conflicts raging within him. New York turned to dust in his mouth, a succession, he wrote to Upward, of 'press interviews, photographs, dinners for Spain, lunches for China, lectures, crooked publishers, long-haired Trotters and stern Reds'.[4]

In a letter to Spender on 28 April Isherwood admitted for the first time:

> I have suddenly realised that I am a pacifist, pure and simple. I can't kill the Germans or the Italians, and I won't. I get no further than that, yet I don't know the answers to all the objections about Liberty etc. And maybe there'll be no time to think them out before the Test is popped on us.[5]

As he has explained in *Christopher and his Kind*, the fact that Heinz had been compulsorily conscripted into the German army was initially the highly emotive cause of his new attitude. Behind his rejection of the Popular Front line, he realised, lay his rejection of the militarist stance it embraced. But if he was prepared to reject the revolutionary beliefs of the left because of his personal allegiance to Heinz then he obviously needed to attempt a revolution within himself if he was to substitute a personal for a political idealogy. So his mind turned to Gerald Heard whom he had met in London seven years earlier and who had subsequently involved himself in the Peace Pledge Union with Aldous Huxley. In 1937 Heard with Christopher Wood and Huxley with his wife and son had crossed the Atlantic and eventually settled in Los Angeles. There Huxley and Heard had continued to advocate pacifism and were drawing for some of their arguments on the teaching and practice of Eastern religions, Hinduism in particular. They, at least, had given to the entire question a great deal more reasoned thought than Isherwood had. So he wrote to Heard from New York. Heard replied, advising that he might make a start by joining the Red Cross, since he believed that 'creative accuracy must be opposed to disorder and destruction' (*AV* 16). Lured by the prospect of acquiring greater self-knowledge at first hand from Heard's own example, of meeting Huxley and seeing Christopher Wood again, and of

exchanging the Golden West for New York which only bred in
him 'the feeling of pure despair, values dissolving, everything
uncertain',[6] he decided to leave for California. Early in May
Isherwood and 'Vernon' began a three-week trip by Greyhound
to Los Angeles via Washington, New Orleans, El Paso, Houston,
Albuquerque and Flagstaff.

Despite spending his first hot Saturday night in Los Angeles in a
squalid hotel down-town, he was quickly captivated by the city
as it was in 1939, small, sleepy, spread out like a garden suburb,
dotted with orange groves and almost virgin hills, a meeting-
place between man and the wilderness. He felt at home in what
he called its 'theatrical impermanence'.[7] 'I love California more
than ever', he wrote to Lehmann the following year; '—it is
without nostalgia or regret or apprehension of the future—
you are free here, you can be anything you make yourself.'[8] On
his arrival Christopher Wood lent him two thousand dollars
to help him until he could find work in one of the Hollywood
studios. Berthold Viertel, whose family lived in Santa Monica,
had promised to effect introductions but was not due back from
the East Coast until July. In the meantime Isherwood rented a
house in the Hollywood hills (7136 Sycamore Trail) with
'Vernon' who spent the weekdays attending art school.
    Nevertheless within himself Isherwood was still in a turmoil.
'I am so sick of being a person', he wrote to Lehmann. 'I'm
tired of strumming on that old harp, the Ego, darling Me.'[9] For
his first two months in California he spent much of his time in
the company of Gerald Heard whose most recent book, *Pain,
Sex and Time* seemed to speak to his condition. An Irishman of
fifty and a spell-binding talker, Heard had spent his life attempting
to correlate historical and scientific truths with his interest in
psychical research which had persuaded him that consciousness
does exist outside the space-time continuum. When Heard
finally settled in California he met Swami Prabhavananda, a
Hindu monk from Calcutta who had established a centre for
the study of Vedanta philosophy in Hollywood in 1929. The
Reality which Prabhavananda believed in struck Heard as
identical to the consciousness he had posited for himself. Vedanta
offered him not just the philosophical framework he was seeking
but the discipline needed to make contact with the unchanging

consciousness. Heard's studies of history had convinced him that man's evolution pointed towards a new phase of consciousness, a psychic revolution. The individual ego is bound to the physical world by its attachment to pleasure and aversion from pain. To free oneself from the bondage of the self and make contact with the Real one needed to rid oneself of addictions, possessions and pretensions. Positively he adopted from Swami Prabhavananda the practice of meditation, the act in which one sought union with 'this thing' as he wisely called it when talking to the supposedly atheistical Isherwood.[10] Heard meditated obsessively six hours a day and Isherwood began practising meditation himself on a trial basis.

Towards the end of July he was sufficiently interested to ask Heard to introduce him to Swami Prabhavananda. Prabhavananda lived in a secluded house on Ivar Avenue, just off brash Hollywood Boulevard. The year before a small onion-domed temple had been built in the garden. Prabhavananda proved to be quite the opposite to Heard, small in stature, boyish in appearance although in his mid-forties, completely unaffected in manner, and with an inward simplicity that made the most complicated elements of Vedanta appear clear even to the novice. This meeting was to prove one of the decisive events in Isherwood's life. To the influence Forster had exercised over him up till now was gradually added the teaching of the Swami. Isherwood's conversion was entirely intuitively based. Just as he had become a convinced pacifist because of his feelings for Heinz, so he became a Vedantist through coming to know Prabhavananda. The Swami simply convinced Isherwood over a period of time that he was in contact with the Real within and outside himself, by a process of self-knowledge, meditation and prayer. 'The Swami doesn't impress you', he tried explaining to Forster, '—sometimes he is ridiculous—but when you are with him you know that God exists.'[11] 'How he does go on about God!' Forster was to write later to Plomer, adding more charitably, 'I suppose it wouldn't matter in conversation.'[12]

Vedanta means the end or goal of the Vedas. The four Vedas or scriptures forming the basis of the Hindu religion pre-date Christ by some thousand years. They teach that there is one reality or Godhead who is both within the individual (the Atman) and without (the Brahman), which remains unchanging

amidst the transience of life on earth (Maya). Since Brahman-
Atman can be known by man, one's purpose in life is to realise
the godhead within one, to make contact with one's essential
nature. Union with the Atman can be achieved by one of four
yogas or disciplines—through devotion, through intellectual
discrimination, through selfless work or through meditation.
Vedanta philosophy permits a wide choice of religious cults. In
other words, instead of meditating on the impersonal Brahman
one can subscribe to a particular devotional cult. Isherwood
became a student of Vedanta philosophy who subscribed to the
cult of Ramakrishna, the nineteenth-century Indian avatar (or
incarnation of Brahman) whose teachings Prabhavananda had
acquired directly from one of his two principal disciples,
Brahmananda. Like great artists, Isherwood has claimed, religious
exemplars such as Ramakrishna 'restate what is eternal, but
nevertheless do so in a new language'.[13] In fact Vedanta specifically appealed to Isherwood's artistic *dharma* (or vocation): 'In
the religious outlook on life, you try to see individuals *sub specie
aeternitas*, as children of God, rather than just as tiresome and
often rather hostile freaks. Isn't that exactly what you do in
writing really? You see them as children of art, and, in the eye
of art, everything is ultimately forgiven.'[14] Yet in his post-war
fiction, as in his life, even if the quality of compassion is the same,
the perspective is radically altered by his conversion to a belief
in a religious dimension. The more immediate effect on him was
to reassure him that his instinctual rejection of political solutions
and his pacifist stand made sense within the wider philosophical
framework that Vedanta offered him.

By July Heard had also introduced Isherwood to Aldous
Huxley and his wife Maria. They were renting a house in Amalfi
Drive, Pacific Palisades at this time. Huxley was just finishing
After Many a Summer, a book about the illusive nature of
quantitative time, which was to feature in one of Isherwood's
own novels, *A Single Man*, twenty-five years later. That August
Huxley began working on a screenplay of *Pride and Prejudice*
for M-G-M for the princely sum of $1,500.00 a week.[15]

Initially Isherwood, rather intimidated by Huxley's immense
erudition, tended to think of him as 'bookish and inclined to be
pontifical.'[16] When he got to know him better, however, he
grew to respect his fearless intellectual curiosity, and also found

him lovable and gregarious. Huxley was equally interested in Prabhavananda's teaching at this time, even becoming his disciple for a period.[17] But then he was a tireless researcher into so many para-psychological movements before they had achieved a popular following. In fact his later experiments with mescalin and LSD were opposed to Prabhavananda's teaching.[18] Isherwood soon came to know the Huxleys' circle of friends, which included Anita Loos, in whose *Diary* Isherwood was subsequently to feature, and Krishnamurti, the self-renounced Messiah of the Theosophical Society.

The other circle into which he was drawn was that of the Viertels and their friends (mainly German emigrés) in the world of literature, music and the movies. At the Viertels, who lived in Santa Monica Canyon, he met Thomas and Heinrich Mann, Schoenberg, Max Reinhardt, Greta Garbo and Chaplin. To earn some money while he was waiting for Berthold to return and help him to find employment in Hollywood, Isherwood wrote a pot-boiler for the *New Yorker*, 'I am Waiting', a story about a psychic time-traveller. He confessed to James Stern (by then living in New York), that it was not very good but elicited showers of letters from readers who thought it was genuine.[19] On Viertel's return, so as to be closer to him, Isherwood moved into the same road as the Huxleys, just a few minutes' walk away from the Viertels' house. There he began working with him on a film for Sam Goldwyn, a Chinese spy story developed out of *Mr Norris* (the film rights for which he parted with for a derisory sum). In January 1940 Gottfried Reinhardt, Max Reinhardt's son, an M-G-M producer who was living in the Viertel household at this time, employed Isherwood to write the dialogue sections for the screenplay of James Hilton's *Rage in Heaven*. Partly due to differences that arose between one of the lead actors and the director the film was poorly received, the first of many disappointments for Isherwood.[20]

Nevertheless in May 1940 M-G-M offered him a year's contract which, much to their consternation, he insisted on altering to allow him as well as them, an option to terminate, an option that in the event he, not they, took up.[21] During the year he wrote bits and pieces for *A Woman s Face*, based on a French thriller and produced by Victor Saville on whom he was to base part of the character of Chatsworth in *Prater Violet*; *Crossroads*,

a mixture of mystery, romance and blackmail; a film about
the life of Chopin that never materialised; *Free and Easy*, an
adaptation of Ivor Novello's play, *The Truth Game*; and *Forever
and a Day*, a family saga of England made in aid of wartime
charities that took seventy-eight actors, twenty-one writers and
seven directors three years to make. Apart from *Forever and a
Day*, Isherwood's name does not even appear on the screen
credits of any of these films. Rather like Huxley, Isherwood has
always seen movie work as an easy means of earning sufficient
money to get on with his own work. Because it is such a co-
operative enterprise in which the producer is in overall control
he has never been much perturbed by the fate of his scripts.
'The studio', he explained to Stern in 1940, 'is just an office I
visit in the daytime,'[22] a spectacular example of the world of
maya, one might say.

Throughout 1940 Isherwood's life was split between his
M-G-M job and the circle of Huxley, Heard and Prabhavananda
which used to meet regularly for lunch on Tuesdays at a market
where everyone could eat their vegetarian and faddist medical
foods under olive trees in the open.[23] On Sundays they would
meet for lunch at Anita Loos's ocean-front house at Santa
Monica, or go for picnics. She has described one especially
bizarre picnic where the company included Krishnamurti and
some fellow Theosophists (weighed down by uncontaminated
pots and crockery), Chaplin, Paulette Goddard and Greta
Garbo (both disguised to avoid their fans, the former bearing
caviar and champagne, the latter raw carrots for her diet),
Bertrand Russell (currently teaching at UCLA), the Huxleys and
Isherwood. No sooner had this distinguished gathering begun
preparing its various elaborate meals than a sheriff appeared and,
flatly refusing to believe that the film stars were who they were,
ordered them to leave because they were trespassing.[24]

In 1940 Isherwood with others came under attack in the English
press. *Reynolds*, for instance, accused Huxley, Heard and Isherwood of going to California merely to contemplate their navels.
A highly ambiguous defence of Isherwood and Auden (who had
also been attacked in Mosley's *Action*) appeared in the second
number of *Horizon*, the new periodical which Spender and
Connolly, financially backed by Peter Watson, had launched at

the beginning of the year. Among other things, Connolly had written in his 'Comment' that the two emigrés, Auden and Isherwood, 'are far-sighted and ambitious young men with a strong instinct of self-preservation, and an eye on the main chance'.[25] Unmoved by the other attacks, Isherwood was hurt and angered by these remarks and sent off a heated protest to Spender before Connolly had had time to explain to him that the editorial was his work and was meant to be a defence of his two friends. In April Harold Nicolson launched a further ill-informed attack on Auden, Isherwood, Huxley and Heard accusing them of retreating 'into the gentler solitudes of the Wisdom of the East . . . when Western civilisation is bursting into flame'.[26] In the next issue Spender rallied to their defence.[27] On 13 June Sir Jocelyn Lucas MP asked in the House of Commons whether men like Auden and Isherwood would be summoned back from the States for call-up. This elicited in *The Spectator* later that month a particularly nasty anonymous epigram, 'To Certain Intellectuals Safe in America'.[28] This time Forster replied, scenting unconscious envy behind the attacks and asking 'whether there could not now be a close time for snarling at absent intellectuals'.[29] For his part, Isherwood could see no point in adding a further unwelcome pacifist to Britain's problems. As for the attacks, with the exception of the *Horizon* 'Comment', they only helped to make him feel better, he claimed.[30] Klaus Mann, who had a long conversation with him that June, has recorded what a convinced pacifist Isherwood had become by this time, motivated by an utter horror of war.[31]

During the year in which he was contracted to M-G-M Isherwood also saw three of the principal individuals whom he was to use as models in 'Paul', the final section of *Down There on a Visit*. Tony Bower (cf 'Ronnie'), Cyril Connolly's American disciple whom Isherwood had met in Paris and who had recently found himself a job as film-correspondent for a New York paper, visited him in May with all the latest news from England and New York. He was the same brilliant gossip in life as in the novel and, like his fictional counterpart, he was drafted into the US army early on in the war. Sometime in 1940 Isherwood also met Denham Fouts ('Paul'), whom he had first met in London in 1938. He was the son of the owner of Safeways, and was currently in the company of Cyril Connolly's wife Jean

('Ruthie'). Denny's earlier career has been colourfully sketched
in by Truman Capote in one of the published episodes of his
huge, still unpublished scabrous novel, *Answered Prayers*. According to Capote Denny eloped to Europe from his home in Florida
at the age of sixteen in the company of a cosmetics millionaire.
His bisexual prowess ensured him a living with a succession of
wealthy patrons. In 1938 Peter Watson (the backer of *Horizon*)
fell for him and when the blitz began in London in 1940 sent
him for safety's sake to the United States, chaperoned by Cyril
Connolly's wife, Jean.[32] For a short period in the late spring
of 1941 he and Isherwood shared a place as described in *Down
There on a Visit* and became involved in Heard's seminars. In
February 1941 Isherwood met Somerset Maugham again,
resting for a few weeks in the midst of a lecture tour. 'He reminds
me of an old Gladstone bag', Isherwood wrote to Forster,
'covered with labels. God only knows what is inside.'[33]

All this time Isherwood was being drawn closer to Heard,
Prabhavananda and the life of the spirit. When his Uncle Henry
died in July 1940, leaving him Marple Hall and Wyberslegh,
Isherwood renounced his rights in favour of his brother Richard.
A year later his mother returned to Wyberslegh where she was
to spend the rest of her long life with Richard and Nurse Avis
(cf *KF* 349–51). In the autumn of 1940, after attending the
Vedanta Centre for some fifteen months, Isherwood underwent
an initiation ceremony in which he became the disciple of
Prabhavananda, now his guru (*AV* 40–41). In late February
1941 he and 'Vernon' gave up their house (by then in Los
Angeles proper) and split up amicably. As soon as his M-G-M
contract was up in May 1941 he planned to volunteer for a
labour camp. In the event only Denny Fouts went to a forestry
camp for conscientious objectors—at San Dimas, Chailas Flats.
In the long term Isherwood still hoped to join a Quaker ambulance unit and go to one of the war-fronts. From 7 July to
7 August 1941 he joined twenty-five like-minded enthusiasts
(many of them Quakers) for a retreat organised by Gerald Heard
and the Friends' Service Committee at La Verne College, thirty-
five miles inland. There they divided their time between meditation, readings and discussion. Isherwood returned radiantly well
and eventually sent a brief account of the month's ascetic
proceedings ('just a parish magazine summary', he wrote

apologetically[34]) to a somewhat bemused John Lehmann who nevertheless published it in *Penguin New Writing* the following year.[35] Subsequently Isherwood also modelled the section of 'Paul' at Eureka Beach on the La Verne retreat, though with considerable fictive additions and changes. The only other writing he did at this time, apart from maintaining his diary, was a review of Hemingway's *For Whom the Bell Tolls* and an obituary of Virginia Woolf, both at Klaus Mann's instigation.

Impelled by a lingering sense of guilt at having opted out of the European war, in October 1941 Isherwood obtained through some Quaker friends who were with him at La Verne a job at the Co-operative College Workshop in Haverford, Pennsylvania. At the time he justified his move as an exchange of raja for karma yoga, that is of meditation for selfless work. Later on he recognised the true motivation behind his decision—'the terrible psychic restlessness which a war-situation generates' (*AV* 45). The Quaker school had been specially established to help the enormous influx of mainly German refugees to learn the language and to adapt to the American system of education. The school was run by an Irish directress called Caroline Norment and contained some twenty-five German and Austrian refugees, all teachers and lecturers who hoped to continue their profession in the States. Apart from coaching them in English, Isherwood's job, he wrote to Forster, was 'social, menial, confessional, advisory, interpretative, consolatory, apologetic.'[36] The refugees studied teaching methods at the neighbouring Haverford College. Isherwood soon became friendly with a lecturer in French and Spanish there called René Blanc-Roos whose drinking habits and irreverent attitude to life offered him a welcome relief in the evenings from the claustrophobic and pious atmosphere of the school. Blanc-Roos urged him to try his hand again at writing something creative. The result was 'Take It or Leave It', a contrived story which was published by the *New Yorker* in October 1942 and which he subsequently disliked as much as 'I am Waiting'. René Blanc-Roos later served as a physical model for Lawrence Dwight in *Prater Violet* which was dedicated to him.

At intervals during the nine months he was at Haverford he took the train to New York where he let his hair down with friends like the Sterns, Benjamin Britten until he left in February

1942 for England, and of course Auden. After Pearl Harbor in February 1942, registration began for Isherwood's age group. He had registered as a conscientious objector with the minimum of difficulty, as Pennsylvania had long since learned to respect the large community of Friends in the neighbourhood. The following month Auden sent Spender his impressions of Isherwood's transformation since his sojourn in California:

> What he is trying to do must seem meaningless unless one believes, and I do, firstly that there is such a vocation as the mystical contemplative life, and secondly that of all vocations it is the highest, highest because the most difficult, exhausting and dangerous. . . . Christopher felt that he is called, and is certainly taking it very seriously. I think his friends should have enough faith in him to trust his judgement for himself.[37]

Huxley offered a similar defence of the stance Isherwood and like-minded individuals were taking at this time: 'The world', he wrote to a friend, 'would be even more horrible than it is, if it were not for the existence of a small theocentric minority working along quite other lines than the anthropocentric majority.'[38] By July 1942 the call-up had created enough vacancies to absorb the refugees at the hostel and Isherwood returned to a rented house in Alto Cedro Drive, Beverly Hills fully expecting to be drafted to a forestry fire-fighting camp for conscientious objectors at Santa Barbara. 'Some day', he wrote to Forster on the train carrying him back west, 'I will write about Haverford.'[39] Twelve painful years later a pale distillation of his experience of the Friends' way of life was to surface in *The World in the Evening*.

Back in California he found the Huxleys had recently moved to a house at Llano in the Mojave Desert. Gerald Heard, who with Chris Wood had moved to Laguna about a hundred miles to the south of Hollywood in October 1941, was currently nearing the end of building Trabuco College some miles inland, his monastery, as Huxley, temporarily disillusioned by his friend's assumption of the role of guru, insisted on calling it.[40] Denny was still cook at his work camp, but was already studying to become a psychiatrist and hoped to be released soon on medical grounds. Later that year John van Druten, the successful play-wright and director whom Isherwood already knew, took him to meet Dodie Smith, a fellow playwright from England and her husband/manager Alec Beesley (a fellow CO) who had just moved to Beverley Hills from Carmel. With so much in common they quickly took to one another and Isherwood settled into the habit of spending most Sundays with them, a custom which he continued on and off until 1952. While he was waiting to be drafted that autumn he began his first serious attempt to write fiction since *Goodbye to Berlin*, 'a study of Berthold working at Gaumont-British, which I intend to call *Prater Violets*' he wrote Lehmann.[41] However, the writing had to be laid aside in December 1942 when Lesser Samuels (the scriptwriter with whom he had worked on *A Woman's Face*) asked him to write a CO tribunal scene for a Paramount film version of Somerset Maugham's *The Hour Before Dawn*. In the event the scene was scrapped. But Isherwood's renewed contact with Lesser Samuels, who had also worked at Gaumont-British in the thirties, was to prove invaluable in helping him recreate the technical jargon of that time in *Prater Violet*. That December the age limit for conscription was lowered to thirty-eight and he was free to plan his own future.

As soon as the film writing was over (in February 1943), Isherwood moved into the Vedanta monastery in Hollywood at the invitation of Prabhavananda who had asked him to col-laborate on a new translation of the *Bhagavad-Gita*, a text which was of particular interest to him as it contains the teachings of Krishna on the subject of war and pacifism. From spring 1942 to March 1944 he helped the Swami translate this Sanskrit classic first into prose, then, after Huxley reacted unfavourably to it, into a mixture of poetry and prose. For Isherwood it was an intense education in Vedanta philosophy at the hands of a man whom he grew to respect more the more contact he had with him. One catches an authentic glimpse of his life in the monastery in *Batter My Heart* by Donald Hayne, a lapsed Roman Catholic priest whom Isherwood invited to the monastery in the spring of 1943 where he lived until the summer. Apart from sleeping in two houses some four men and eight women lived together sharing the same table, household chores and ritual worship in the small temple. 'Apart from the ochre robe

worn by the swami in the temple', Hayne writes, 'the monks and
nuns . . . dressed as casually as any other Californians.' Like
Prabhavananda himself, the inmates combined celibacy and
spiritual dedication with a relaxed gaiety typical of Hindu
religious communities.[42] That summer Tennessee Williams
arrived at the monastery with an introduction from Lincoln
Kirstein and was rather put out to find himself joining one of
the daily sessions of meditation. But the relaxed atmosphere of
the monastery emerges more clearly when one learns from
Williams that subsequently he and Isherwood would frequently
go out for fish dinners on the Santa Monica pier,[43] and equally
when one realises that Isherwood continued to see Dodie Smith
and Alec on Sundays throughout his stay at the monastery.[44]
Nevertheless as late as February 1945 Isherwood, still at the
monastery, was contemplating undertaking the lengthy training
required to become a swami himself.[45] By the spring of that year,
however, he finally decided that his true vocation or *dharma* was
that of a writer, not a monk. Meanwhile he had been assisting
Prabhavananda in editing *Vedanta and the West*, the Vedanta
Society's bi-monthly magazine to which Heard, Huxley, van
Druten and he, among others, had been periodically contributing. At the suggestion of Marcel Rodd, who brought out the
joint translation of the *Gita* in August 1944, Isherwood edited a
selection of articles culled from the magazine since its inception
in 1938 which was published late in 1945 as *Vedanta for the
Western World*. It contains an introduction by him and three of
his articles reprinted in *Exhumations*. His monastic life was also
responsible for a poem 'On his Queerness' and a story 'The
Wishing Tree' both collected in *Exhumations*.

During Isherwood's two years at Ivar Avenue Denny Fouts
featured frequently in his life. Although Denny was reclassified
as medically unfit, before he was given a medical discharge he
ran into trouble with the Quaker authorities over his homosexual activities and left prematurely, turning up at the Beesleys'
house unexpectedly one day in the spring of 1943.[46] Soon he had
moved into a beach house in Entrada Drive, Santa Monica and
began studying for a career in psychiatry. That August Isherwood
sent Gerald Hamilton a brief sketch of the new Denny:

Denny has two jobs: one daytime one, as a janitor, during

which he studies algebra, Shakespeare and German for his high school diploma, which, in the rush of getting educated in other ways, he never stopped to take—and an evening job at a bookstore. We go swimming together every Saturday.[47]

By 1944 Denny had enrolled at the local university on a crash course for his pre-medical examinations. Like his fictive counterpart, Paul, he had the Picasso he owned jointly with Peter Watson shipped over from the Museum of Modern Art in New York and installed in the living room. But unlike Paul, Denny was living in Santa Monica enjoying his penchant for little boys who even queued up for him at times. It was not until 1945 that he left for New York to continue his medical studies there.

An indication of Isherwood's ambivalent feelings towards the religious life is the fact that he wrote both versions of *Prater Violet* while residing at the monastery. After completing the *Gita* translation in March 1944, he turned his attention to the novelette he had begun and abandoned in the autumn of 1942. He approached it as historical fiction and was faced with the problem of having 'to *allow* for the war, without mentioning it'.[48] By the end of July 1944 he had a rough draft ('triumph of will rather than literature', he wrote to Forster).[49] By the end of the year he had rewritten it and sent it off to his publishers. The encouraging reactions he received from friends on both sides of the Atlantic in the spring of 1945 must have been a factor in his decision to leave the monastery and pursue his literary vocation.

Besides, he was earning virtually no money during this period. During the first half of 1944 he tried to make himself enough money by collaborating with Aldous Huxley on an original screen story called 'Jacob's Hands'. Their treatment traces the career of a faith healer who discovers the dangers of applying his healing powers to adults (one young woman in particular) when he has no way of knowing the consequences.[50] Based on a ranch-hand with a gift for healing animals who lived near Huxley's house at Llano, it was greeted enthusiastically by James Geller, the story editor at Warner Brothers, only to be turned down for fear of offending the powerful medical profession to whom psychosomatic medicine was still a dirty word at the time. Many years later when the climate of opinion had altered, their treatment was turned into a screenplay for American television.[51]

Unable to make himself money this way, in the early spring of 1945 Isherwood went back to working for Warner's—'It's more anonymous than writing potboilers', he explained to Lehmann,[52] thinking of his *New Yorker* stories. He spent most of the rest of the year at Warner's writing a screen version of Maugham's *Up at the Villa* for Gottfried Reinhardt's brother, Wolfgang, which was never made, and also contributing scenes to an adaptation of the Wilkie Collins novel, *The Woman in White*, almost nothing of his reaching the screen in the event.

But his return to the Hollywood scene resulted in his departure from the monastery in the summer of 1945 when he moved into the departed Denny's apartment above a restaurant close to the beach in Entrada Drive, Santa Monica. In fact Isherwood appears to have undergone a spontaneous reaction against the religious life, telling Maria Huxley that May, for example, that he was not joining Heard's group at Trabuco because he was 'fed up, sick and tired of hearing them yacking about God'.[53] Not that he ever abandoned his Vedantist beliefs or his attachment to Prabhavananda and what he represented. But with the end of the war Isherwood did recognise that his particular *dharma* lay with writing and the secular life.

Prater Violet

Although *Prater Violet* makes use of similar narrative conventions to those successfully employed in the central four episodes of *Goodbye to Berlin*, Isherwood confessed to Auden and James Stern at the time that he was suffering from stage-fright, in the opening scene in particular: 'Making a comeback after so long, I was unsure of my audience', he explained.[1] Part of the problem was purely linguistic. Realising that the language of theology or Vedanta would alienate most of his readers, while the language of *Goodbye to Berlin* was no longer adequate for expressing the religious dimension, he found that he would have to 'invent a new way of writing'.[2] *Prater Violet* does employ a new language, although this is due more to the nature of Bergmann/Viertel's volatile Austrian personality and the specialised nature of studio terminology than to any fundamental stylistic revision on Isherwood's part. Despite his apprehensions *Prater Violet* caused what *Time* called a 'mild critical flurry' when it first appeared in *Harper's Bazaar* in the summer of 1945.[3] Diana Trilling gave it a glowing review in *The Nation* ('gay, witty, sophisticated, but wholly responsible')[4] and Edmund Wilson claimed in the *New Yorker* that it kept up the same high level of excellence as *Goodbye to Berlin*.[5] Isherwood himself subsequently came to prefer it to any of his pre-war novels.[6]

Like *Goodbye to Berlin* this novelette is set firmly in a relatively brief historical period (October 1933 to March 1934) and is based broadly on a selection of Isherwood's own experiences during this time. Its major departure from fact is the substitution of an absurd musical comedy called 'Prater Violet' for the film he actually worked on with Viertel called 'Little Friend'. John van Druten helped concoct the intentionally sickly plot of 'Prater Violet'[7] which forms a far more effective contrast (and parallel) to the drama surrounding the Austrian uprising and its ruthless suppression by Dolfuss than *Little Friend* would have done. The same first-person narrator ('Christopher Isherwood') controls the narrative viewpoint as in *Gooddye to Berlin*. Or is he quite the same? We learn more about his private life than before. We are given intimate glimpses of his mother and brother in their Pembroke Gardens house. And in the final pages Isherwood reveals for the first time in his fiction that his autobiographical hero does have a sex life of his own. Isherwood has remained far more satisfied with his use of the narrator in *Prater Violet* than in any of his other works, mainly, he has explained, because his passivity is for once perfectly natural in the company of such a dominating scene-stealer as Bergmann.[8]

In *Prater Violet* 'Isherwood' also continues the self-education he began in *Mr Norris*. An artistic novice himself, he learns at the hands of a master the true nature and limitations of the artist in modern society. Before he meets Bergmann 'Isherwood' gives himself all the airs of a temperamental artist while betraying an underlying insincerity that his credulous brother unwittingly exposes whenever he accepts what 'Isherwood' says at face value. Richard honestly admires his brother's apparent indifference to the offer of a filmwriting job (which is purely a charade) just as he genuinely suggests not answering the 'phone when the studio rings back, in both cases exposing the narrator's hypocritical pose.

Opposed to this representative of the neurotic artist is Bergmann who, even before one sees him, gives the impression of someone who is victimised by his strong emotions and quite incapable of concealing anything. He is a 'tragi-comic clown' (p 13), a 'Jewish Socrates' (p 31), a mass of contradictions exposed for all the world to see. Bergmann combines the emotional directness of a child with the authority of a parent and quickly diagnoses 'Isherwood's' case as that of 'a typical mother's son' (p 22). In their first meeting on their own Bergmann, when he praises 'Isherwood's' novel, is compared to 'a proud parent who listens to his son being praised by the headmaster' (p 21), and the relationship of father and son, so reminiscent of Arthur Norris and William Bradshaw, is explicitly applied to them on a further three occasions (pp 40, 97 and 102). As father-cum-diagnostician Bergmann mercilessly exposes the neurotic nature of 'Isherwood's' artistic position. A declassed intellectual like 'Isherwood', he tells him,

'. . . is unable to cut himself free, sternly, from the bourgeois dream of the mother, that fatal and comforting dream. He wants to crawl back into the economic safety of the womb. He hates the paternal, revolutionary tradition, which reminds him of his duty as its son. His pretended love for the masses was only a flirtation, after all. He now prefers to join the ranks of the dilettante nihilists, the bohemian outlaws, who believe in nothing, except their own ego, who exist only to kill, to torture, to destroy, to make everyone as miserable as themselves—'

'In other words, I'm a Nazi and you're my father?' (p 40)

Bergmann here represents the force of political events which turned so many writers of the thirties towards political commitment. To maintain the ivory tower position of the twenties, he demonstrates, is to condone the spread of fascism. The artistic ego cannot be separated from external events or from empathy with all classes of its fellow humans.

The novelette moves from the psychological to the political and philosophical examination of the place of art in that low, dishonest decade. Isherwood's neurotic artistic isolation reflects Britain's political isolationism in the face of Hitler's mounting aggression. As Theodore Purdy suggested in his review of the book in *The Saturday Review of Literature*, what distinguishes it is Isherwood's 'ability to see the studios and their denizens as significant and alarming symptoms of the world's present malaise'.[9] Bergmann's apparently paranoid reaction to British Bulldog in fact reveals a subtle criticism of the fascist assumptions underlying British society in general. He and 'Isherwood' are fellow-prisoners (p 22), criminals 'dragged into court to hear the death-sentence' (p 47), tortured when they have nothing to confess (p 51), permanently threatened by legislation (p 66). The executives of the studio are the 'enemy' who conspire against the artist (p 89), spy on him, persecute him and betray him (p 90), just as Goering and his fellow Nazis were concurrently hounding van der Lubbe, Torgler and Dimitroff in the Reicnstag Fire Trial. Bergmann identifies himself with Dimitroff (the Communist leader who defied Goering in court and was finally acquitted); by implication Ashmeade is Goering, head of the 'secret police' (cf p 46). For Bergmann there can be no separation

of art from politics. His is 'the face of a political situation, an
epoch. The face of Central Europe' (p 12). His struggles with
'Prater Violet' are like Dimitroff's fight against the Nazis: both
are 'fighting for Truth'.

When the Christian-Democratic Chancellor of Austria, Dolfuss,
puts down the workers by force, Bergmann feels as if he had been
suppressed too and detects the defeat of Truth not just in his
home country but in the film he is making:

> 'The picture! I s— upon the picture! This heartless filth! This
> wretched lying charade! To make such a picture at such a
> moment is definitely heartless. It is a crime. It definitely aids
> Dolfuss . . .' (p 77)

But the artist has to compromise with the society in which he
lives. Bergmann allows himself to be manipulated by Chatsworth
into re-making the last part of the film which he had put together
with such contempt the first time around. While art is inseparable
from the circumstances affecting the life of the artist (and his
relatives and friends), it can, however temporarily, triumph over
the anarchy amidst which the artist lives. Although Lawrence
Dwight lacks Bergmann's tempestuous involvement with everyone and everything around him, he does express a view of art
which Bergmann draws on in re-shooting the ruined last section
of the film. When 'Isherwood' asks him what the incentive is
for doing any job, Dwight replies:

> 'The incentive is to fight anarchy. That's all Man lives for.
> Reclaiming life from the natural muddle. Making patterns.'
> (p 55)

But to make his patterns Bergmann abandons Dwight's ivory
tower of technical perfection and his own feelings of political
disillusionment to extract the best from everyone on the set by
sheer emotional magnetism. Art and life prove inseparable.

What is so extraordinary about this short and apparently
inconsequential novelette is the manner in which Isherwood has
fused naturalistic depictions of character and dialogue with a
density of texture and meaning that one would normally expect
to have made it too ponderous, too burdened with significance.
Yet it retains its light touch flawlessly from start to finish. It is a
small marvel of artistic control. Look, for example, at its structure,

and it divides itself into two halves with a final coda that in itself supplies an added dimension within which one retrospectively views anew the rest of the book. During the first fifty pages 'Isherwood' is closeted with Bergmann and is compelled to learn the difference between his own neurotic conception of art and Bergmann's passionately committed relation of his art to the world around him. Then overnight they are transferred to the studio where their work of art is exposed to all the contingencies of an imperfect society—temperamental actors and actresses, interfering studio executives, defective equipment, in fact everyday human fallibility. This second half of the novelette is deliberately disorderly, a simulcrum of the anarchy with which art has to come to terms. Chronology is abandoned; present tense is now alternated with past tense; even more chaotic events in Austria temporarily usurp the apparent anarchy of the studio. Yet the film somehow does get made in the end.

Isherwood uses this structural division to distinguish two phases in his narrator's education. In the first movement 'Isherwood' learns the nature of true art at the hands of his artistic guru, Bergmann. In the second movement 'Isherwood' is swept up in the creative process itself. He is forced to abandon his self-importance, to recognise that 'this was simply a job' which he was doing as well as he could (p 51), a compromise between the desirable and the attainable. Finally, in the coda (pp 98–103) Isherwood allows us a glimpse of the narrator's ego which has proved such a formidable obstacle in his progress towards artistic maturity. Even in the first movement Bergmann's apocalyptic vision of the coming world war, which English society at large and 'Isherwood' in particular chose to ignore, gave rise to a passage in which war and the extinction of personality become imagistically fused in the narrator's mind (pp 33–4). The flicker of fear 'Isherwood' occasionally experiences when he contemplates his own death is shown in the coda to have been responsible for his neurotic attitude to art. The egotistical pose of the artist as the Truly Weak Man originates in 'Isherwood's' 'private fears of childhood', especially 'the arch-fear: the fear of being afraid' (p 101).

The novelette has cleverly developed the situation to a point where everything naturally points towards the necessity of self-renunciation on the narrator's part. If fear of fear is responsible for all that is wrong with his art then only a form of non-attachment from the ego can save him from this fear. Written after his conversion to the teachings of Vedanta philosophy, the novelette subtly suggests the inevitability of such a move. But as it is strictly confined to a moment in time when he was firmly committed to a materialist view of existence he has the narrator reject this possibility of release from his fear, paradoxically out of a fear of making such a momentous move:

'No,' I think, 'I could never do it. Rather the fear I know, the loneliness I know . . . for to take that other way would mean that I should lose myself. I should no longer be a person. I should no longer be Christopher Isherwood. No, no. That's more terrible than the bombs. More terrible than having no lover. That I can never face.' (p 101)

It constitutes a marvellously ironic ending after which the few paragraphs outlining the fate of 'Prater Violet' and its director seem superfluous. The functional end of the novelette comes when Isherwood catches a momentary glimpse of the reality underlying his relationship to Bergmann, of the genuine love that exists between an anonymous son and his impersonal father (p 102). Within the context of the book genuine love, like genuine art, presupposes a renunciation of the superficial self, a renunciation to which Isherwood himself was dedicated by the time he wrote it.

Travelling: *The Condor and the Cows*

The contrast between the studied tranquillity of life in the monastery and the crowds of returning servicemen thronging Hollywood Boulevard less than five minutes' walk away was at its peak in the summer of 1945. A major factor in Isherwood's decision to move out of the monastery was his meeting that summer with a Kentucky Irish boy called William Caskey. Caskey had been raised on a stud-farm and had worked with the photo-finish of a racecourse where he had acquired his first skills as a photographer. He was short, young, good-looking, pleasant, obstinate, and a great drinker. Part of his attraction for Isherwood lay in his natural self-sufficiency. Since his enforced separation from Heinz (whom he finally heard from again in March 1946), Isherwood took care to encourage all his subsequent boyfriends to pursue a vocation of their own. He had helped launch 'Vernon' as an art student and he did everything in his power to turn Caskey into a successful professional photographer.

Caskey moved into Denny's beach apartment with Isherwood that summer of 1945. Once his film work for Warners was finished in November Isherwood turned his mind to the two other novelettes about refugees he wanted to write as companion pieces to *Prater Violet*. One was to be about his experiences on the Greek island of St Nicholas. The other, which he began work on first, was to be based on his experiences at Haverford. At first he still thought of using the same ventriloquist's dummy, 'Christopher Isherwood', he had manipulated so successfully in *Prater Violet*, although from the start he was filled with doubt as to its continuing efficacy. 'The problem is always', he told James Laughlin of *New Directions*, 'how to handle Christopher Isherwood, that tiresome but, to me, unavoidable character.'[1] By April the novelette had become a full-length novel 'about the Quakers, Hollywood, pacifism, a psychopathic liar, jealousy,

refugees, sex, etc. . . . It plays in 1941.'² Work on the novel,
however, was interrupted first by having to move house and then
by the necessity to earn money at the studios. In April 1946
he and Bill Caskey moved into an apartment intended for the
chauffeur over the Viertels' garage at 165 Mabery Road in Santa
Monica. Almost immediately he was forced to do two months'
work on the original story for *Adventure in Baltimore*, a vehicle
for Shirley Temple that was subsequently transformed for the
worse.³ That summer he continued work on the novel which
by then he regarded as 'a sort of parent book, which will split up
into two or three novels eventually'.⁴ 1946 was also the year in
which both he and Auden were granted American citizenship.
Isherwood has repeatedly explained that, having been in exile
from England since 1929, he preferred to formalise his status as
a foreigner, since he can only write out of a sense of foreignness
and alienation.

Once again that autumn he was forced to lay the book aside
to collaborate with Lesser Samuels on an original film story
which Samuels had thought up called 'Judgment Day in Pitts-
burgh'. When they sold this for fifty thousand dollars (which
Samuels insisted on sharing fifty-fifty), Isherwood felt sufficiently
in funds to plan a three-month trip to England for early in 1947.
Meanwhile he celebrated the windfall by spending Christmas
with Bill Caskey in Mexico City. Their brief visit may well have
planted the idea in their heads of a more extended trip to South
America the following year, especially after they managed to sell
an article, 'Notes on a Trip to Mexico', illustrated with Caskey's
photographs, to *Harper's Bazaar*.

Yet beneath Isherwood's successful reversion to the flesh-pots
of Hollywood lay a continuing deep conviction in the truths of
Vedanta philosophy which he had acquired at first hand from
Prabhavananda. One sign of this is the translation he and
Prabhavananda completed during 1946 of Shankara's *Crest-Jewel
of Discrimination*. 'What is most to be feared?' asks Shankara in
his *A Garland of Questions and Answers*. 'To become possessed by
your own wealth', comes the answer.⁵ Isherwood was in little
danger of this pitfall, the less so for the constant reminders that
his frequent contact with the Swami provided.

On 21–22 January 1947 Isherwood flew alone from New York
to London after an absence of eight years. In 'Coming to London'

(E 150–56) he has written of his first impressions that January—the shabbiness of the people and the buildings, the atmosphere of friendliness, the docility towards regulations, above all the deprivations during the severest winter in living memory leading to food shortages and fuel cuts more severe than any experienced during the war. He went straight to John Lehmann's home where he was greeted by a party of friends including Plomer, Robson-Scott and Berthold Viertel. Robson-Scott remembers how he was brick-red with the Californian sun and spoke with a strong American accent[6] (which has since reverted to a mixture of north-country, ex-public school and West Coast dialects). For Isherwood the reunion with old friends—including Forster the next day—had a dream-like unreality about it: 'You enter the room and there they all are. . . . Here I am, here is X. For eight years I have been living as a ghost in his memory, and he as a ghost in mine' (E 143).

Within two days he had joined his mother, brother and the family nurse in Wyberslegh. His mother he found tremendously energetic for seventy-eight, running the household and even waiting on his decrepit old nanny. Richard appeared withdrawn. Cheshire was even colder than London—'snow all around, and the gas-fire shrunk to a dim Arctic glow on the horizon'.[7] Cooped up in the dank family home, Isherwood made the best of his misfortune by producing articles on England as he found it on his return, the trip to Mexico, and Los Angeles (for *Horizon*). After five weeks at Wyberslegh, he spent a hectic fortnight in London, staying first with Forster at his flat in Chiswick and also seeing Upward (to whose sixth-formers he ad-libbed about Hollywood), John Lehmann and his friend Alexis Rassine (whose dancing he was pleasantly impressed by), Gerald Hamilton (unchanged) and Stephen Spender (married since 1941 to Natasha Litvin, a concert pianist whom Isherwood now met for the first time). Then in mid-March he visited Olive Mangeot who was sharing a house with Jean Ross and her seven-year-old daughter by Claud Cockburn in Cheltenham. When they visited a theatre during a gale, Isherwood—hardly surprisingly—failed to calm Olive's fears by suggesting that one should think of it as an air-raid instead. Back at Wyberslegh by 20 March, he caught cold amid the almost continuous rain which was slowly helping to melt the snow. On 14 April, with some relief, he left for

London where he spent two riotous days at John Lehmann's place before catching a boat to New York and Bill Caskey on 16 April.

On 1 May he and Caskey were able to move into a New York apartment at 207 East 52nd Street belonging to James and Tania Stern who were off to Europe until September. His plan was to spend the rest of the year in New York, completing his novel. After that he and Caskey would catch a boat for South America as he had received more or less firm offers from Methuen and Random House for a South American travel book illustrated with Caskey's photographs. In the event things did not work out this way. For a start the novel stuck despite the numerous draft outlines he prepared. It was provisionally called 'The School of Tragedy' after a remark made by Josef Stern, one of the refugees at Haverford, about the mess another refugee couple had left their room in ('Such people are not fit for the school of tragedy').[8] The title, he explained to Upward, refers to the refugee hostel itself and to 'the whole experience of persecution, imprisonment, flight and emigration under the Hitler terror'.[9] The novel foundered on the admixture of reportage with purely invented material. Because he was writing about events that had occurred only five years earlier he was forced to disguise their origins or manufacture new incidents which removed much of the material from the realm of his own experience with fatal results. The narrator, then called Charles Monk, a character who is faced with a choice between war service or pacifism, proved the greatest obstacle of all, as he was and was not based on Isherwood. Moreover, to add to his difficulties, he was determined to write in the third person for the first time since *The Memorial*. As the summer heat grew more oppressive Isherwood succumbed to the same antagonistic atmosphere in New York that had demoralised him in 1939. In early September he wrote irritably of 'this hellish city, the dirt, the noise and THE PEOPLE' in the same letter in which he announced that he had abandoned the novel for the time being.[10]

Perhaps New York also offered too many social distractions. In early May he saw much of Forster on his first visit to the States, administering fatally large Manhattans to him and driving him down to Bryn Mawr to talk to a thousand students there. He also saw John van Druten who was in New York for the rehearsals of *The Druids' Circle* and, of course, Auden, who had grown stouter by 1947 and was spending much of the summer at his shack on Fire Island where Caskey and Isherwood spent many of their weekends. Spender, looking more distinguished than ever, according to Isherwood, 'with his Shelley eyes and his father's beautiful prophetic voice',[11] joined them there briefly in early September before going to teach at Sarah Lawrence College in Bronxville. Isherwood and Caskey also got to know the twenty-two-year-old Truman Capote that summer, spending two weeks with him on Nantucket Island in mid-July. Isherwood genuinely admired Capote's first novel *Other Voices, Other Rooms* which he had recently completed, readily endorsing it for the publisher; subsequently Capote may have reciprocated this admiration for Isherwood if Holly Golightly in *Breakfast at Tiffany's* is modelled on Sally Bowles. From Nantucket, where Isherwood went on to spend almost another week boating, he wrote to Dodie Smith '*Nothing* written, I'm sorry to say. I can't work in New York and will never live there again.'[12]

Instead, he brought forward the date of the South American trip. Armed with a typewriter, cameras and a smattering of Spanish, he and Caskey left New Jersey on 19 September for Columbia. During the six months they spent in South America they travelled down the west coast through five countries, breaking across to Buenos Aires in the east through Bolivia and Argentina. They travelled by every conceivable means, tending to stay for extended periods in the larger cities *en route*. Isherwood has described their journey in considerable detail in *The Condor and the Cows*, although the book is inevitably a great deal more restrained than some of his contemporaneous letters. In Bogota where he stayed for two weeks in mid-October he felt continuously depressed by the ever-present rain and the altitude. As he confessed in the book, in the mornings he felt tense, restless and uneasy; in the afternoons lazy, exhausted and sad (p 46). Quito in Equador is even higher than Bogota (9,200 feet) and his letters from Quito where he was for much of November show him severely disenchanted with the entire continent:

There is a dreadful squalor, a kind of evil laziness and despair, beneath everything. The Church seems almost wholly evil,

like a great black toad on the Indian's back. The Indians are
incredibly energetic, lively and often gay, but they are worked
like beasts, and their masters look on with their weary old
syphilitic eyes of imperial Spain. . . . The whole place is rotten
with guilt.[13]

While staying in Quito he also made an expedition to Shell's
exploratory oil wells in the Amazon jungle where he found an
entire 'Little Britain, with tea and RAF slang and Churchill
pinups and talk about the royal wedding'.[14]

His next major stop was Lima in Peru where he stayed from
14 December to 8 January 1949. For much of the time he was
suffering from dysentery. In what he called this 'kind of un-
inspired Paris' he detected an equally depressing and more
dangerous situation—'a tiny rich chic ruling class sitting daintily
on top of a volcano, which may blow up almost any day and
overwhelm them in an avalanche of Indians and enraged
llamas'.[15] While he was in Lima Gore Vidal, another aspiring
young American novelist who had greatly admired *Prater Violet*,
wrote to him sending him a copy of *The City and the Pillar*, his
second novel. Isherwood liked Vidal's frank, unpornographic
treatment of homosexuality in the book, but told him that he
thought the tragic ending would only confirm the typical liberal
reader's heterosexual prejudice: 'This is what homosexuality
brings you to, he will say: tragedy, defeat and death.'[16] Meanwhile back in New York James Laughlin of New Directions had
followed up the publication of *The Berlin Stories* (in 1945) with
the first American edition of *Lions and Shadows*; Marcel Rodd had
issued a revised edition of Isherwood's translation of Baudelaire's
Intimate Journals with a new introduction by Auden; and the
Vedanta Press had brought out Shankara's *Crest-Jewel of Discrimination* which he had translated with Prabhavananda the
previous year.

By 20 January Isherwood and Caskey reached La Paz in Bolivia
where once more the altitude produced in him the symptoms
of 'pseudo-heart-attacks, pseudo-appendicitis and pseudo-
dysentery'.[17] Obviously by this stage of the journey he was
feeling oppressed by the need to garner relevant facts for the
book. Even the Carnival began to wear thin after 'three days
on the shore of Lake Titicaca observing and photographing

drunken Indians in masks from point-blank range, and getting alternately scowled at and embraced'.[18] On 13 February they left La Paz for Buenos Aires by train. 'We had grown weary, weary to the bone', Isherwood wrote in the book, 'of those inhumanly gigantic mountains, that sombre plateau haunted by its Incaic ghosts, that weird rarified manic-depressive atmosphere' (p 163). They reached Buenos Aires late on 16 February where they were met by Berthold Szczesny or 'Bubi' as Isherwood used to call his first German boyfriend. Berthold had reached South America in the thirties only after Eric Falk had first prevailed on the Head of British Immigration to allow him into Britain on his personal guarantee and had then overcome the Argentinian Embassy's bureaucracy by suggesting to them that Berthold travel first class.[19] Now Berthold was engaged to be married. Isherwood also met another figure from his life in the thirties, Rolf Katz, the economist. By 1948, Isherwood noted, Katz had lost his Marxist dogmatism but was otherwise the same theoretical diagnostician of the times that he had been in Berlin, Paris and London.

On 27 March Caskey and Isherwood caught a boat for Le Havre. From there they went to Paris where they met Gore Vidal and spent much of their time there in his company. He left Isherwood with the manuscript of a new play he had written and asked for his comments (in the event unfavourable). They also called on Denny Fouts who was squatting in Peter Watson's flat at 33 rue du Bac. They found him in bed, deathly pale, hooked on opium, his only companion Trotsky the dog. Later that year Denny underwent an unsuccessful cure and left France for Rome. There he was talking of going to England or America for psychiatric help when he died unexpectedly that December of a heart attack, in the manner of Paul in *Down There on a Visit*.

In London they saw all Isherwood's old friends, ran into Auden briefly on his way to Ischia having just finished the libretto of *The Rake's Progress*, and strengthened his friendship with Henry Green during a drunken evening at his home. In May Isherwood took Caskey to Wyberslegh to meet his family. While he was there he wrote the first two chapters of *The Condor and the Cows*. In early July he went to the Aldeburgh music festival at the invitation of Benjamin Britten. Back in London

later that month a party was held for Isherwood at which
Tennessee Williams, according to Gore Vidal who was also
present, blithely assumed that E. M. Forster, whom both Isherwood and Vidal revered, was the creator of Captain Horatio
Hornblower.[20] Although Isherwood was planning to spend some
time in Ireland before returning to the States in August, shortage
of money forced him to curtail his stay and leave for New York
on 9 July when he received a screenwriting offer from Gottfried
Reinhardt at M-G-M.

Only stopping long enough to pay Dodie Smith and Alec
Beesley a fleeting visit in Doylestown, Pennsylvania, Isherwood
left Bill Caskey in New York and flew back to Los Angeles to
begin work on *The Great Sinner*, a film that set out to show what
happened to Dostoevsky while he was writing *The Gambler*. It
had been originally thought up by a Hungarian screenwriter,
Ladislas Fodor, who had already worked on the script before
Isherwood with his own quite different ideas was brought in.
Later he wryly commented, 'the very best things in the film are
Dostoevsky's own.'[21] Nevertheless with its strong casting
(Gregory Peck, Ava Gardner and Walter Huston) it received
mainly favourable reviews when it was released in 1949. The
film job lasted until the end of September. During this period
Isherwood stayed in Ocean Park compensating for Caskey's
absence by drinking large quantities of whisky and leading a
fairly wild night-life. In October, however, Caskey returned
and found them a house at 333 East Rustic Road, Santa Monica,
which was to serve as the model for Jim's house in *A Single
Man*. It turned out to be haunted, but this affected his friends
more than Isherwood himself. He described it to Gore Vidal as
'Rustic. Sycamores. A bridge over a creek. A little wooden
house, exquisitely furnished and as filthy as the worst hotel in
Ecuador.'[22]

While Caskey painted, carpentered and cooked Isherwood
settled down to the task of writing *The Condor and the Cows*.
Early in 1949 he was interrupted by short bouts of additional
work for M-G-M on *The Great Sinner* and four weeks' work on
a script about the young Elizabeth Tudor for Sidney Franklin.
There was also spasmodic work on a new translation of Patanjali's *Yoga Aphorisms* which he began with Prabhavananda in
January and was to appear serially in *Vedanta and the West* from

March/April 1949 to January/February 1953. *The Condor and the Cows* proved burdensome, partly because, as he explained to John Lehmann, 'the truth is that South America *bored* me, and I am ashamed that it bored me, and I hate it for making me feel ashamed.'[23] Half-way through it by the end of 1948, he still found it irksome: 'I should really have approached it in the spirit of The Air-Conditioned Nightmare, but my fatal politeness gripped my pen, and anyhow one cannot insult all kinds of people who sincerely tried to please us and probably thought us as dreary as we thought them.'[24] Undoubtedly Isherwood was partly motivated by the resentment most people experience when they have to work off an advance of money. He fell back on sheer professionalism which helped him complete the book by 4 April 1949. At least, he confessed on completing it, it avoided the extremes of politeness and boredom to be found in the South American travel articles he had sold in the interim to magazines like *Horizon, Illustrated* and *Vogue*.[25]

When *The Condor and the Cows* was published later the same year Isherwood was rather surprised at the success it enjoyed, especially in Britain where it was made the *Evening Standard*'s Book of the Month and the Book Society's Alternative Choice for November. Later in life he came to view this book more benevolently: 'I now see (it) is one of my best books', he told Stanley Poss in 1960. 'I managed to put an enormous amount of things into it that I wanted to say.'[26] Nevertheless, he has also admitted, the book fails to satisfy what he considers to be the fundamental criterion of any travel book, the need for a goal, for a reason for having gone anywhere in the first place. 'The ideal travel book', he has said, 'should be perhaps a little like a crime story in which you're in search of something and then either find it or find that it doesn't exist in the end'.[27] *The Condor and the Cows* certainly lacks any such thread of interest. Nor, as his Foreword suggests, does it aim to arm the reader with a mass of facts about the countries covered.

Instead the book is unashamedly subjective and impressionistic, which is what finally distinguishes it from the average work in this genre. Even while he was still in South America he found that everything he wrote about the country sounded 'either coy or pompous or quaint'. 'I think I will have to make it quite

7*

frankly personal', he concluded, 'with S. America in the background and my thoughts and meditations in the foreground.'[28] This is precisely how it reads—as a series of brief essays and character sketches occasioned by his wanderings through the Andes and Argentinian plains. In it he finds time to reflect on subjects as diverse as the spiritual basis of consent underlying secular codes of ethics, man's escapist dream of voluntary exile, the significance that T. E. Lawrence holds for his generation, electric shock treatment, the effects of colonial conquest and, above all, the raging contradictions that constitute his own identity.

Invariably what lifts his brief disquisitions above the mundane is the honesty with which he responds to everything he encounters. Of course the Garcia Moreno Prison ought to be demolished and modern methods of psychological and social rehabilitation introduced. Then why does he find himself, despite his liberal principles, filled with admiration for the way no one had tried to humiliate the prisoners, most of them murderers, by making them feel that they were social misfits or outcasts? He does not know the answer and does not attempt to conceal the gap separating his principles from his gut reactions. Inevitably there are occasional examples of the special brand of masochistic breast-beating that Isherwood has always fallen back on as a kind of defence mechanism against potential attacks by some imaginary enemy sometime in the future. But on the whole he has been remarkably successful at disposing of the conventional reactions which so many travel writers appear to consider it their duty to experience. As V. S. Pritchett shrewdly observed in his review of the book, 'one has to be trained to be natural—and Mr Isherwood is himself because he is trained.'[29]

In particular Isherwood's painfully acquired stylistic facility provides the perfect example of the way in which he achieved the effects of spontaneity by the application of pure craftsmanship. For every subjective mood he wants to convey he can summon up an equivalent mode of expression so appropriate that it rarely intrudes despite the variety of his linguistic originality. Motoring up into a particularly awesome part of the Andes for a picnic, he is forced to confess that his friend's conversation claimed much the largest part of his attention. There follows a small gem of an aphorism: 'Tourists carry their own conversation along with them, like their sandwiches, and can only spare a few moments for the scenery between mouthfuls' (p 118). Because it belongs firmly to its context it has none of the self-conscious cleverness of an epigram from Oscar Wilde. Behind the witty conceit in which conversation and mastication become indistinguishable, lies a personalised observation about the paradoxical nature of travel which few enough writers or travellers are willing to admit either to themselves or others. Even his generalisations avoid over-simplification by embracing the contradictory nature of the spirit of place. Isherwood calls Cuzco, for example, where the Spaniards tore down the Inca temples and grafted their own magnificent buildings on to the foundations, 'one of the most beautiful monuments to bigotry and sheer stupid brutality in the whole world' (p 129). He is drawing here on the same resistance to moral dogma which enabled him to portray the criminal Mr Norris as a lovable human being. A more light-hearted example of this occurs after he has just admitted the extent to which he cannot help respecting the Incas. Nevertheless, he continues, 'I find them, as we used to say during the Evelyn Waugh period, madly ungay' (p 130). The slight touch of camp humour is enough to humanise the grudging awe with which he views the monumental ruins of their civilisation.

The Condor and the Cows is itself a monument to Isherwood's professionalism as a writer. Yet the enforced politeness which he felt obliged to adopt restrains the subjective diarist from indulging in the indiscretions, the occasional bitchiness, the irrational responses of the moment which in the long run infuse that particular literary form with its own special insights. There are too many people whose hospitality has to be repaid by a courteous gesture, too many moral debts to be settled, too much discretion to be shown for political or legal or (in the case of Berthold Szczesny, for instance) purely private reasons. Isherwood is being just a little too nice to be able to compensate with the personal, impressionistic, even spiteful approach for the absence of any other *raison d'être* for the book. As Peter Fleming, himself the archetypal travel-writer of Isherwood's generation, observed in his review of the book, 'his gentle, tolerant, hyper-civilised approach produces in the long run a slightly anaemic effect, as though he had done a water-colour of a bull-fight.' He

concludes that 'in its admirable objectivity it contrives to be—
let us face it—rather flat.'[30] Whether this element of self-repression
was partly due to Isherwood's submersion in the teachings of
Vedanta is hard to tell; but it is significant that a similar reluctance
to stick as closely as he might have done to his subjective
experience of life at Haverford was primarily responsible for all
the difficulties he was to encounter during the following four
and a half years in which he struggled with his next novel, *The
World in the Evening.*

A Period of Uncertainty

Once he had finished *The Condor and the Cows* in April 1949, Isherwood immediately returned to his novel, 'The School of Tragedy'. On re-reading his outline for it he realised at once that something was integrally wrong with it. Stephen, the hero, in particular was neither objective nor subjective enough.[1] As Dodie Smith and Alec Beesley had just returned to Beverley Hills from Pennsylvania he was able to talk to them at length about his problems. Determined to avoid the use of an auto-biographical narrator yet again, he was also set upon writing what he called 'a comic religious novel',[2] a quite different mode from any he had employed in his previous fiction. His work on the novel that eventually became *The World in the Evening*, or his failure to work on it, dominated everything else he did between April 1949 and December 1953 when it was finally revised for publication the following year. The fact that he was elected a member of the US National Institute of Arts and Letters in 1949 may have further strengthened his resolve to finish the book.

Apart from seeing much of the Beesleys and spending time with their mutual friend John van Druten at his desert ranch at Indio, near Palm Springs, Isherwood was visited in June by Stephen Spender who was currently at work on his auto-biography, *World Within World*. Extracts from it had already appeared in the *Partisan Review* which, Isherwood told Upward, made him feel as if he were being featured in the Kinsey Report.[3] Nevertheless he urged Spender to finish it, no matter how indiscreet he had to be. When it was completed he was wildly enthusiastic about it both in private and in his review of it for the *Twentieth Century* in May 1951, although, he confessed to Upward, 'there is something in it to enrage everybody, myself and yourself included.'[4]

During 1949 he also became one of the few close friends of Igor and Vera Stravinsky whom he had met through Aldous Huxley. He quickly warmed to Stravinsky's physically demonstrative nature (he called him 'the wildest camp'),[5] his anti-intellectual disposition and his capacity for hard drinking. 'We have often been drunk together', Stravinsky told Robert Craft, '—as often as once a week, in the early 1950s, I should think—in such different climes as Sequoia Park and Santa Monica beach.'[6] On his first visit to the Stravinskys' home he fell asleep when someone started playing a recording of the host's music, which is when Stravinsky claims that his affection for him began.[7] According to Isherwood both the Stravinskys projected such a degree of cosiness that he felt quite free with them not simply to go to sleep but even to pass out drunk on the floor.[8] Robert Craft has recalled a typical vegetarian lunch at the Farmers' Market in August 1949, with Isherwood, the Stravinskys and the Huxleys, where Isherwood appeared to him a curious mixture of the humorous raconteur with a liberal smattering of Americanisms like 'heck!', 'swell!' and 'gee-whiz!', and, on the other hand, of the remote listener and observer penetrating beyond the superficialities of their conversation to the essential matter of life.[9]

Later that year Isherwood and Huxley, whose English royalties had been reduced by the devaluation of the pound, drifted into collaboration with Lesser Samuels on an original story for the movies. Isherwood had already been driven to try his hand at a screen story of his own earlier that year (to the detriment of the novel). When this would not sell he joined Huxley and Samuels in concocting a story called 'Below the Equator' concerned with revolutionary violence in South America and featuring a Hungarian character very similar to Mr Norris. By the summer of 1950 it had become clear that this story also was not going to be sold, despite the encouragement John Huston had given Huxley beforehand.[10]

Caskey was meanwhile passing through what Isherwood called 'a rather tiresome drinking phase, involving automobile accidents in the dead of night, police-courts and fines'.[11] In mid-November Caskey left to visit his sister in Florida. While there his father died and he had to go on to Kentucky to see to family business. When he returned in April 1950 after five months' absence, he had a very small income of his own which must have been a relief to Isherwood, now hard-pressed for money and depressed by his inability to make the novel work or sell his stories to the movies. That April he helped Ivan Moffat, a fellow screen-writer, escort Dylan Thomas on a brief inebriated visit round Hollywood, introducing him to Shelley Winters (whose breasts Thomas had to touch to reassure himself that they were real) and Charlie Chaplin whom he revered, although this did not stop him making a fool of himself in his cups.[12] That summer Isherwood also got to know a fellow writer and diarist, Anais Nin. She has described him as he was at that time in her Journal: 'He has an adolescent smile, a wonderful broad grin which seems to touch the tip of his ear, locks of hair which fall over his forehead like those of a schoolboy bending over his homework, something delightfully whimsical and youthful about him.'[13]

Unable to get properly started on the novel because he still could not satisfactorily overcome the block he had developed over using the first-person for a narrator other than himself, Isherwood jumped at the opportunity that the periodical *Tomorrow* offered him of undertaking long essay-reviews. Besides providing him with a small source of income, they also allowed him to try his hand at 'criticism rather than advertising' as he put it in *Exhumations* (p 15) where he reprinted six of the seven essays he wrote between October 1950 and July 1951. When *Tomorrow* turned into a journal of extra-sensory perception in 1951 his days as a regular book-critic were over, although the *Observer* did ask him in 1951 to produce occasional articles for them on US authors. He was also still collaborating with Swami Prabhavananda on the Patanjali translation as well as editing a second collection of articles culled from *Vedanta and the West* which was completed by March 1951 and published the same year as *Vedanta for Modern Man*. Apart from the short Intro-duction, Isherwood included two of his own articles, 'Religion without Prayers' and 'The Problem of the Religious Novel'. The latter article, which he republished in *Exhumations*, offers a particularly illuminating commentary on the three novels in which he portrays saintly figures, the novel on which he was currently working, the 'Paul' section of *Down There on a Visit* and *A Meeting by the River*.

By the autumn of 1950 Caskey had reverted to his heavy drinking habits.[14] Isherwood was also spending a great deal of time at Hollywood parties (there is a glimpse of him introducing Alexis Rassine, John Lehmann's friend and a leading dancer of the Royal Ballet Company on tour in America, to the glittering social world of the film stars and their entourage in *The Ample Proposition*).[15] When his novel finally came to life towards the end of that year, he rented an inexpensive house in sleepy South Laguna, about an hour and a half's drive down the coast, and deliberately shut himself off there to try to finish the novel, if only 'as an interesting failure'.[16] There, perched on the hillside covered with flowering shrubs and oleanders overlooking the Pacific, he had nothing but the sunsets to distract him from his work. They were so impoverished at this time that Caskey even took a job as a gardener that spring. Meanwhile the book was progressing. At this stage it was still obviously much closer to his own experiences at Haverford than the final version, as is apparent from his description of it in a letter to Upward:

> It is becoming much more like a Freudian analysis, and I'm far more interested to see what I shall discover about myself than to see how it will develop as an artwork. . . . Certainly, all the obstruction shows that there's *something* I'm very unwilling to admit.[17]

In January 1951 Speed Lamkin, yet another young American writer who admired Isherwood's work, arrived from Louisiana to obtain background material for his second novel, *The Easter-Egg Hunt*, about old movie stars which he was writing. (When published in 1954 it was dedicated to Isherwood and contained a minor character called Sebastian Saunders modelled on him.) With Lesser Samuels, Speed Lamkin and Isherwood started collaborating on a dramatisation of 'Sally Bowles'. When this attempt to raise money failed, Dodie Smith and her husband Alec hatched a successful plot to interest John van Druten in undertaking the dramatisation, secure in the knowledge that if he did, his reputation would be sufficient to ensure that it reached the stage. One day that spring at van Druten's desert ranch, after leading the talk round to adaptations of novels for the theatre, Alec Beesley casually said to van Druten, 'I bet you can't write a play about Sally Bowles.' Van Druten took the bait and sat down the same day to block out the first part of what became *I am a Camera*, a dramatic adaptation of 'Sally Bowles' and parts of 'The Landauers' and 'A Berlin Diary (Autumn 1930)'.[18] 'Almost everything in the play is his', Isherwood has said, apart from an autobiographical line or two.[19] Van Druten invented the character of Sally's mother, made up the Fritz-Natasha sub-plot, supplied Frl Schneider with an anti-semitic streak (which made Isherwood feel bad) and gave the material its dramatic shape. By early June he had completed it. By September he had obtained financial backing to cast it and direct it himself.

Meanwhile Isherwood, still desperately short of money, decided to spend three months during the late summer of 1951 at the Huntington Hartford Foundation in Pacific Palisades (about twenty miles from Hollywood) working on his first draft of the novel. Founded in 1949 by a chain-store multi-millionaire to assist artists, writers and musicians with three months' free room and board, it offered him a studio apartment where he could concentrate exclusively on his writing. By August he had discovered that he had two novel themes entangled, one about his own involvement with the Quakers at Haverford, the other a more invented story surrounding the past history of the semi-autobiographical character of Stephen Monk. The more he invented incidents in Stephen's past life (instead of sticking to the facts surrounding his own life) which would explain how he became involved with the Quaker hostel, the less relevant became his own experiences with the refugees at Haverford. Finally, when a friend confessed that the refugees bored him to death, he threw all of them except Gerda out of the novel and concentrated his new draft on Stephen, who by this stage was as much an invented character in his own right as a disguised autobiographical portrait.[20]

When it became certain that *I am a Camera* was to be staged in November, Isherwood obtained an advance of $1,500 on his unwritten novel from Linscott and in early October went to New York where rehearsals were about to start. He left Caskey, who was about to embark on a new life as a merchant seaman, to close up the house in his absence. In New York he found that van Druten had cast Julie Harris in the role of Sally after the actress already cast withdrew when her agents warned her she would never again get work on Broadway if she appeared in the play. Julie Harris, with what van Druten called her 'extra-ordinary luminosity of innocence', ensured the success of the play. It opened out of town on 8 November at Hartford, Connecticut and transferred to the Empire Theatre in New York on 28 November. The play was a sell-out and Julie Harris became a star overnight. Although this meant an end to Isherwood's money problems as long as the play ran, he actually received only about two and a half per cent of the royalties, plenty to live on, but not enough to prevent him having to earn a living again once the play ended its tour in 1953.

In December 1951 he went by ship to London to spend Christmas with his mother and brother at a hotel in Kensington. On the day George VI died he took part in the second programme of John Lehmann's literary magazine for BBC radio, *New Soundings*, reading a piece he had written on six up-and-coming young American writers all of whom he knew personally, Ray Bradbury, Truman Capote, William Goyen, Speed Lamkin, Norman Mailer and Calder Willingham. On 5 February he also gave a public reading of the first two chapters of his work-in-progress at the Institute of Contemporary Arts. On 10 February he flew to Berlin on an assignment for the *Observer* to write about his reactions to a city he had not revisited since his departure on Hitler's accession to power in 1933. He found Berlin devastated; but the spirit of the Berliners was still amazingly buoyant. He looked up Heinz who had learnt to speak English while a prisoner of war with the Americans and met his wife and son. They accompanied him when he paid a surprise visit on his old landlady Frl Thurau. 'As was to be expected', Isherwood has written in *Christopher and his Kind*, 'she was now enthusiastically pro-American; the Nollendorfstrasse was in the American occupation sector' (p 103). Perhaps the fact that this energetic old woman in her seventies had had to pretend to be hunch-backed and lame to avoid rape by the Russian soldiers immediately after the war finished had something to do with her pro-American feelings. She told him that 'Bobby', the bartender, had fought on the Russian front and survived unharmed. 'Otto Nowak', he wrote in his *Observer* article, 'that eternal spiv, had shown up recently at the flat, wanting to buy Frl Schroeder's carpets.'[21] After being back in London for a little over a week, he caught the *Queen Elizabeth* on 27 February for New York.

'I had a good time in England', he wrote to Gerald Hamilton, 'but came away with a real burning homesickness for California, and even wept on sighting the Statue of Liberty, like you're supposed to!'[22]

From New York he went to Bermuda for a holiday in March, where, in between swimming and cycling, he even managed to restart the novel, thanks mainly to his boyfriend's insistence that neither of them should drink anything alcoholic during their stay there. The highlight of his visit was a meeting with James Thurber, who compensated for the fact that he was almost blind with his warmth and an endless repertoire of amusing anecdotes. By mid-April Isherwood was back in Los Angeles from where he retired temporarily to the Vedanta monastery in Trabuco Canyon (Heard had finally given it to the Vedanta Society of Southern California in 1949 after his own attempts to run an inter-denominational school of meditation had come unstuck). There he completed the Patanjali translation and the first long section of *The World in the Evening*. Dodie Smith and Alec Beesley were by this time living back in the East and Isherwood sorely missed the advice they had been giving him on his difficulties with the novel. Nevertheless he continued to consult them regularly by post and his correspondence with them offers a detailed insight into the laborious evolution of *The World in the Evening*. The first chapter of the novel appeared in *New World Writing* that spring, although the generally poor reviews this new venture received hardly offered him much encouragement.

Apart from swimming (for which he had had a crew-cut) and writing, Isherwood spent a quiet summer alternating between Trabuco (where Prabhavananda was living at the time) and a garden house at 400 South Saltair Avenue in the grounds of his friends Evelyn Hooker, a group psychologist who was making a particular study of homosexuality, and her husband Edward, a professor at UCLA who had just embarked on his massive critical edition of Dryden. When in Los Angeles he continued to see his old friends, the Huxleys and Gerald Heard. 'The Huxleys', he wrote that autumn, 'are strong for hypnotism and have become ardent meat-eaters. . . . Gerald, blazing with triumph over the (flying) saucers . . . seems younger and healthier than he ever did.'[23] He also saw much of John Gielgud who was in

Hollywood shooting *Julius Caesar* with Marlon Brando as Mark Antony, as well as Julie Harris when *I am a Camera* reached Los Angeles in early December on tour. And whenever Caskey was between boat trips he spent time with him. In November they both took Isherwood's new open car, a Sunbeam Talbot bought out of the continuing bonanza from *I am a Camera*, on a two-week trip down the west coast of Mexico via Nogales as far as Guaymas, and that Christmas they again went a little way over the border to Ensenada.

In mid-September he was half-way through his rough draft of the novel. By late January 1953 it was finished—'that is to say, about five-twelfths are very rough and seven-twelfths merely unsmooth', he informed Bob Linscott, his American publisher. 'I now have several months' work ahead of me, getting the whole thing into shape (I've only just discovered what it's actually about). . . .'[24] He spoke disparagingly of it to all his friends, quoting Aldous Huxley's description of his own *Time Must Have a Stop* as more appropriate to his own book—'A curiously *trivial* story, told in *considerable* detail, with a certain amount of *squalor*.' In the same letter he explains why it seems so thin: 'because it's turned into a novel of situations and character-collisions instead of that kind of atmosphere-embroidery I've always specialised in before.'[25] In early February he nearly found himself back where he had started when the garage adjoining his garden-house burned down in the middle of the night. In his anxiety to rouse the Hookers he completely forgot to rescue the manuscript of his novel, but the firemen arrived just in time to save his part of the building.

That winter Isherwood first took notice of Don Bachardy, an eighteen-year-old college student who was accompanying his elder brother Ted (whom Isherwood already knew) to parties and outings to the beach where their crowd normally met. Isherwood found him extremely attractive and by February they had set up housekeeping together. Because of the wide discrepancy in their ages, the Hookers, fearing a scandal, asked Isherwood if he could find somewhere else to live. So he took a small apartment just below Sunset Strip for them to live in, retaining the Hookers' garden-house as an office for work in the daytime. He continued to visit John van Druten at his ranch, the Huxleys at North Kings Road (where Aldous was writing *The*

Doors of Perception after trying mescalin for the first time that May), Gerald Heard and Prabhavananda: 'Swami is a great mainstay, as always', he wrote that spring. 'Sometimes I feel he is just hauling me along with a sort of hardboiled good humour, like a swimming instructor pulling a hopeless pupil on a rope.'[26] In June Stephen Spender came to Los Angeles for a short visit and persuaded Isherwood to resurrect the brief memoir of Ernst Toller which he had written shortly after Toller had committed suicide in New York in May 1939. Spender published it in the first number of his new magazine *Encounter* that October and it reappears in *Exhumations*.

When *I am a Camera* ended its tour in the spring Isherwood's main source of income disappeared. Since he was supporting Don Bachardy at college by this time he soon found himself short of money once more. Apart from collaborating with a writer friend, Gus Field, on a farcical television story about a great novelist modelled on Maugham, he doggedly stuck to the task he had set himself of rewriting his novel over which he still had a powerful psychological block. With Don Bachardy helping him do the typing he finished it on 5 August and immediately sent it off to Dodie Smith and her husband for their comments. They reassured him that it was far from a fiasco. Dodie Smith, however, did object to a scene in which Stephen went to bed with Gerda, both of them 'knowing' nevertheless that it was unimportant. Alec Beesley found the dialogue in the scenes in which Stephen, Charles and Bob are together embarrassingly coy in places. After altering the scenes criticised by the Beesleys, he sent off *The World in the Evening* to both his publishers. Despite having written at least three versions of it, he still harboured a suspicion that it might turn out to be worthless. 'Art', he observed to Upward at the time, 'is just another kind of yoga, and I think that one might become very wise even in the process of writing something quite bad.'[27]

Once the manuscript was off his hands, Isherwood went to San Francisco with Don Bachardy for a ten-day holiday. In late September he received the reactions of both his publishers, his agent and friends like Speed Lamkin. Alan White at Methuen, having consulted L. A. G. Strong, cabled Isherwood 'We all have greatest admiration for absolutely first rate novel. Best yet.'[28] The only alteration he requested was a small expurgation in the homosexual encounter between Stephen and Michael. Robert Linscott at Random House also liked it on the whole, but felt that Stephen's character appeared hollow and lacking in sympathy, disliked the inclusion of *two* homosexual episodes, criticised Bob's false heartiness and asked Isherwood whether he could not remove some of the 'let's all part friends' patness in Part III.[29] Speed Lamkin echoed Linscott's feelings about Bob and Part III, and advised Isherwood to remove even the intention of a sex-act with Gerda.[30] By early October he had made up his mind on what revisions he would undertake: 'I shall rewrite everything about Charles and Bob, and shall slightly expurgate the Michael-Stephen scenes (some of them), and shall take out the Gerda-Stephen sex-scene, and rewrite the final scene with Jane.'[31] He decided to leave Stephen's character unaltered apart from removing some of his priggishness at the end, and insisted that the inclusion of two homosexual episodes was integral to the balance of the book.

Almost immediately he fell sick with stomach trouble for most of October (Auden would have made an interesting psychosomatic diagnosis of this outbreak at an earlier stage of their careers). By the end of November the revisions were finished. By way of celebration Isherwood and Bachardy spent Christmas and the New Year in New York. Then in early January he flew back to Los Angeles to face the realities of earning a living once more and to await the verdict of the critics on his first full-length work of fiction since *Goodbye to Berlin*.

21

The World in the Evening

When it was published in June 1954 *The World in the Evening*
received a primarily hostile reception from the critics. Even
Upward, Lehmann and Spender felt compelled to express major
reservations about it in their private correspondence with Isherwood. As for Isherwood himself, he accepted the general verdict
and subsequently became one of the book's most perceptive
critics. '*The World in the Evening* is a failure', he wrote to Upward
the year it was published. 'But an interesting one, I hope, and a
necessary one, I'm *sure* for me.'[1] Many of its failings are attributable to the circumstances surrounding its evolution outlined in
the previous chapter. Yet just because there is so much to criticise
in the novel it would be helpful to begin by considering what it is
attempting to achieve, especially as a number of critics failed to
discern any overall significance in it whatsoever.

The title of the book, although reminiscent of the pre-war
newspaper *Die Welt am Abend*, is borrowed from the title of one
of Elizabeth Rydal's novels which she explains is an adaptation
from a line in the first stanza of Donne's *The Progress of the Soul*.
The stanza begins, 'I sing the progress of a deathless soul', and
ultimately this also provides Isherwood with his ambitious
theme, even if he insists on handling it, like Elizabeth, by trans-
posing everything he writes about into his own kind of micro-
cosm (cf p 134). The soul whose progress he traces belongs to
a spoilt rich young man called Stephen Monk who, like the
refugee couple at Haverford, is unworthy of the school of
tragedy to which Gerda and Elizabeth more fittingly belong.
The choice of an unheroic hero is appropriate, however, if one
views the book, as Alan Wilde does, as 'less a novel than a fable
of redemption'.[2] The tripartite structure of the book illustrates
its thematic concern with the progress by which Stephen stops
running away from himself in 'An End', undergoes a prolonged

period of self-examination in 'Letters and Life', and embarks on a new selfless phase of living in 'A Beginning'.

The brilliant opening chapter—too exciting if anything, according to Isherwood, because whatever follows is bound to be an anti-climax[3]—provides a perfect symbol of the ephemeral and deceptive nature of the glamorous party-going life which has become Stephen's empty mode of existence by this period in his career. Drawing on his intimate knowledge of the Hollywood social scene, he economically constructs an insubstantial world of surface values. On the first page the Novotnys' house, including its occupants, 'looked as if it had been delivered, all ready equipped, from a store' (p 11). In such a setting even the grotesquely dressed Stephen's 'masquerade as a musical-comedy-Hollywood character passed entirely unnoticed' (p 12). Stephen's own house is equally sham, another tiny part of 'the enormous cheap-gaudy nightscape of Los Angeles which sparkled away out to the horizon like a million cut-rate engagement-rings' (p 16). This is the world of *maya* with a vengeance.

In the midst of 'this jibbering jungle of phonies' stands the despairing hero 'like an animal trapped in a swamp' (p 16). At the climax of the opening chapter he discovers his wife committing adultery in the children's giant doll-house in the garden, a feature which is intended to emphasise the infantile nature of Stephen's sexual fantasies. Stephen, it turns out, has avoided the responsibilities of adulthood by seeking out a succession of motherly women whom he has cleverly forced to make all the unpleasant decisions for him in his life. He gets Elizabeth to declare her love for him (instead of risking rebuff by telling her of his love for her) by behaving as a child would towards its mother, crying 'like a baby' and being comforted by the stooping figure of Elizabeth running her hand through his hair (p 106). When he is trying to persuade Jane to marry him, she draws the same parallel: 'What you need, Steve, is a mother or a nurse' (p 280). Nevertheless she finally gives in to him because she feels sorry for him. It takes Gerda to show him the egotistical motivation underlying his adoption of infantile charm:

'People will always be kind to you Stephen. You can make them feel sorry for you, with your look like a little boy. But this is bad, also. Because you know quite well what it is you are doing to them. I think perhaps it is you who are heartless.'

(p 136)

Stephen's heartless manipulation of everyone else in his life manifests itself repeatedly. He leaves it to Elizabeth to break with those friends of hers whom he dislikes and to bring his affair with Michael to an end. He waits for Sarah to exile herself to America. He forces Jane to have an abortion on her own initiative when he is the one who wants to get rid of this potential threat to his own role as spoilt child. He even leaves it to Jane to compromise herself openly with another man so that he does not have to bear the responsibility for the break-up of their marriage. This life-long accumulation of evasions ends in a panic-stricken flight back to the parental arms of Sarah, from whom in turn he is about to escape when he has a psychosomatic accident that prevents him from being able to run any further for at least ten weeks in which he is incarcerated in plaster. The image of Stephen 'physically and mentally encased in plaster, and smelling', as Frank Kermode has aptly described him,[4] gives powerful expression to the way in which Stephen has imprisoned himself beneath the atrophying layers of his surface ego.

Yet, due to the ingenious time scheme of the novel, Isherwood has been able to suggest from the beginning the presence of an impersonal self or 'deathless soul' as Donne calls it locked away somewhere deep inside Stephen. On his flight to the East Coast in Chapter Two he passes over the Arizona desert 'which makes some people think of God or Michelangelo, and which others find merely disgusting and dull because it seems to exclude their egos so completely' (p 25). When he finds that its 'absolute otherness' makes him happy he is unconsciously identifying with the former teleological viewpoint. His flight to Tawelfan is also a return to his birthplace, an instinctual search for rebirth into Heard's 'intentional living', unsupported by others, freed of addictions, possessions and pretensions, especially pretensions.

His prolonged confinement in bed affords the perfect fictional embodiment of the discipline of meditation. Stephen is compelled by his circumstances to take stock of himself and his past actions. The insight he obtains is similar to that obtained from meditation: he learns to recognise the presence of the Atman or the impersonal self within him. When he wakes up in his sick-room he is aware of all the pieces of his life lying scattered outside him, but 'what was aware of this was a simple consciousness that had no name, no face, no identity of any kind' (p 109). Moreover this consciousness suffered none of the neurotic guilt-feelings which had been responsible for some of Stephen's most unlikeable qualities: 'It felt no relation to my acts. It knew no feelings, except the feelings of being itself; and that was the deepest, quietest, most mysterious kind of happiness' (p 110). In this selfless mode of existence Stephen discerns the possibility of an internal peace that has eluded him in his ego-bound past. Without undergoing any explicit religious conversion he is shown to have found personal contentment by learning to view life from what is essentially a Vedantist point of view.

All the other characters in the novel fulfil roles that contribute to Stephen's progress of the soul. His first wife, Elizabeth Rydal, with her weak heart is forced to confront the imminence of her own death and to learn to face it unsupported by others. Reading her last letters during his convalescence, Stephen is made aware of the tragic irony of her situation during their final year together, compelled as she is by him to support all his weaknesses yet determined not to ask him for any reciprocal help in her fight to control her fear of dying alone. In the last letter she wrote before her death, Elizabeth informs Mary (and therefore Stephen) how she had overcome her fear during one of her attacks by recognising that she was 'two quite distinct people', a sick animal and a deeper will or consciousness tending that animal. This experience finally convinced her of the presence within her as well as all around her of a divine reality: 'At least I'm sure now (I used not to be) that there's a source of life within me—and that It can't be destroyed. I shall not live on, but It will' (p 260). No longer afraid of having to face life and death by herself, Elizabeth obviously offers Stephen an example of how he might similarly escape from his dependence on others.

Sarah comes closest to saintliness in the novel. In other words she has achieved such a degree of non-attachment that she has the power to inspire others (like Gerda) with her own ability to overcome pain and despair. Since Stephen is specifically shown to be a victim of his own despair in Part One, she obviously has a function to fulfil in his recovery, one which she performs overtly only in Part Three when for an instant the Atman in her looks out at Stephen through her eyes, 'as if through the eyeholes in a mask. And its look meant: Yes, I am always here' (p 323). Wisely Isherwood shows Stephen too frightened of the implications at the time to ask her who is always there. But it is clear that he will sooner rather than later be forced to face that question in his own life. Most of the remaining characters—Gerda, Jane, Michael, Bob and Charles belong firmly to the world of *maya*, although they all display a self-containment and a commitment to some form of purposive (usually socially purposive) existence which is absent from Stephen's life until he makes a new beginning of it at the end of the book by joining a civilian ambulance unit going out to the war-front in North Africa.

Yet some of these characters appear to have a very peripheral role in Stephen's development. What has Bob's homosexual militancy to do with Stephen? What part does Charles Kennedy play in his metamorphosis? Even Gerda's function is marginal— an example of courage and independence certainly, but her emotional impact on Stephen has been reduced to the level of rather banal exchanges about bed-pans since her sexual liaison with him was removed from the penultimate draft. When one further begins to question how successfully Isherwood has given his thematic skeleton fictional flesh reservations follow thick and fast. Is Sarah's potential saintliness convincing? In fact, aren't all the assertions of religious insight mere assertions on the part of the author? Is the reader ever made to experience the inevitability of Stephen's salvation, a fact that is assumed by all the characters he encounters in Part Three? Isn't Elizabeth Rydal's flash of illumination presented in epistolary form in order to avoid the necessity of testing it dramatically? The novel appears to be suffering from an excess of schematised plotting to which considerations of psychological probability have been invariably subordinated.

This is precisely the charge that Isherwood himself levelled against the novel once it had appeared in print. In 1953 he was still proud of what he called its 'incredibly complicated and highly Ibsenized construction',[5] 'more like *The Memorial* than anything else'.[6] By the following year he realised that he had been so engrossed in getting the technical part of it right that he had lost control over the characterisation.[7] Behind this obsession with plotting lay his decision to graft on to an autobiographically-based first-person narrator a mainly invented past history which, Isherwood has since confessed, 'wasn't interesting to me really because it wasn't anything I'd ever experienced'.[8] Stephen is too close to Isherwood himself in many respects for the author to be sufficiently detached from him. One constantly catches glimpses of the real Isherwood in various aspects of Stephen's past circumstances—they are both the same age, both lost their father in childhood, both have tasted Berlin during the final years of the Weimar Republic, climbed the mountains of Las Palmas and Tenerife, sampled the Hollywood scene, had first-hand experience of the Quakers at Haverford and so on. At times the degree of identification can lead to an embarrassing lack of self-criticism on Isherwood's part. Stephen's final lines in the novel, for example, in which he gratuitously forgives himself, come straight out of Isherwood's own diary where self-forgiveness forms part of a lengthy process of religious education. The other problem with Stephen is that he admits having committed unbelievably despicable acts of selfishness and dishonesty without any of the normal person's attempt at concealing the extent of his culpability from himself or the reader. He positively wallows in his confessions of guilt, which cause one to suspect that Isherwood himself is working off his unconscious aggression towards a character whom he has since called a 'dead limb grafted on a live tree'.[9] One can understand what Kingsley Amis meant when he called Stephen 'a sentimental hysteric (very imperfectly glimpsed as such by the author)'.[10]

Compared to Stephen some of the 'good' characters in the novel are even more ostensibly victims of Isherwood's obsessional plotting. Elizabeth Rydal, he has said, is modelled from Katherine Mansfield's journals and consequently suffers from this purely literary antecedent. He has also suggested that the ease with which he wrote her letters was suspect from the start.[11] Angus Wilson has probably analysed most acutely what is wrong with characters like Elizabeth and Sarah in a long review he wrote for *Encounter*. What he objected to was the 'self-deprecating facetiousness in which his "good" characters talk'.[12] Behind what he calls Sarah's 'cosiness' we should be able to discern an inward grace of wisdom and strength, and we do not. According to Isherwood, Alan Watts (a popular exponent of eastern philosophy and mysticism somewhat akin to Gerald Heard) repeatedly quoted the passage in which Sarah comforts Gerda by the strength of her silence as an example of spiritual insight.[13] But Alan Watts was already among the converted, and his use of this episode merely underlines the intrusion of dogma in the novel. It is the dialogue itself, however, which most frequently suggests a failure of nerve on Isherwood's part, a fear of sounding too sanctimonious. Sarah's exchanges with Stephen sometimes remind one of two giggly girls at their most embarrassing stage of adolescence. For example there is the occasion when Sarah explains to Stephen how her dog came to be named Saul after his biblical namesake, ending:

'Of course, I don't tell that story to everybody—'
'I should hope not! They'd put you out of Meeting.'
Sarah giggled. 'Why, Stephen! You wouldn't tell on me? I can trust *you*, surely?'
'I'll have to think it over. At any rate, I've got something on you, now.' (p 32)

There are simply far too many embarrassing examples of this kitsch style of writing in the book, something which is completely absent from any of his earlier books.

Then there are the two quite separate homosexual liaisons between Stephen and Michael and between Bob and Charles. Isherwood justified the inclusion of two rather than one homosexual strands to his worried American publisher on the grounds that the novel's 'working-title is really "Ghosts", and everything has to happen twice or be somehow echoed or repeated in another key.'[14] Like other technical devices he drew on for the novel, he toyed with this idea but failed to apply it to much effect. In fact, as V. S. Pritchett pointed out at the time, the 'homosexual theme appears in Sunday suit.'[15] In other words all three homosexual characters are idealised for propaganda purposes beyond the scope of the novel. To blacken Stephen's character, Isherwood has subsequently explained, Michael, his victim, 'became altogether just too nice for words'.[16] Behind this error of judgement lay the author's own desire to vent his spleen, as he told John Lehmann, 'against wicked bisexuals who break the hearts of innocent queens and then go waltzing back to Wifey'.[17] This concealed motive induces Isherwood to condone such examples of homosexual chauvinism as Michael's assertion that no woman ever looks at a man properly (p 225).

Bob and Charles are extraordinarily gauche representatives of homosexual respectability. Bob is little more than a mouthpiece for Isherwood's own growing militancy against the heterosexual majority. Charles only once comes to life when he gives expression to Isherwood's definition of Low and High Camp. Although Angus Wilson called his outline of High Camp 'a nice, cosy substitute for thought',[18] in this instance Isherwood was ahead of his time in giving voice to an area of life that had previously passed unnoticed because undefined. Until Susan Sontag produced her brilliant series of 'Notes on Camp' ten years later[19] this brief section of the novel remained the only attempt to articulate this phenomenon in words. But the entire digression is irrelevant to the thematic development of the novel, while the relationship between Bob and Charles is a particularly awful example of repressed Low Camp.

Ultimately one is left wondering whether Isherwood was not inhibited by sharing Elizabeth's view of the falsity of traditional fictional characterisation. If novelists insist on seeing characters as well-rounded complete entities when they really believe that human beings 'can be anything or everything' who 'have no shape, rounded or otherwise' (p 261), then their novels are bound to be second-rate, as Elizabeth's turned out to be. *The World in the Evening* is probably of more interest as a stage in the development of Isherwood's craft as a novelist than as a work of art in its own right. Yet one shouldn't ignore the fact that it entered the bottom of the US best-seller lists for two weeks, and that readers as divergent as Colin Wilson[20] and Thom Gunn[21] have considered it his best novel up to that date. Finally one has to bear in mind the fact that no one has criticised the novel more vigorously or in greater detail than Isherwood himself. As he wrote to Upward in the same letter in which he confessed that he considered it a failure: 'I had to break the spell and write that full-length contraption novel. Now I'm allowed to do as I please again.'[22]

22

The Return of Self-confidence

In January 1954, as if in answer to his monetary needs, came an unsolicited offer from Edwin Knopf of M-G-M to invent an original story for the movies about Henri II of France, Diane de Poitiers and Catherine de Medici. Because he was given a free hand he thoroughly enjoyed the project, stealing liberally from Balzac, Dumas and the whole field of French historical fiction. 'I think it comes under the heading of permissible melodramatic camp', he wrote at the time.[1] By mid-May the studio had approved the story and asked him to write the screenplay which took him till September to complete. In the meantime his financial position had been further improved by British royalties from *I am a Camera* which had proved a smash hit in London, and by the sale of the reprint rights of *The World in the Evening* for $7,000. This enabled him to rent a small house in Santa Monica Canyon that February for a year and a half where he and Don Bachardy could live together more comfortably, although he continued to keep on his garden-house at the Hookers for office purposes. While he was working on the film he still had time to see all his normal LA friends, as well as Cecil Beaton, Edith Sitwell, Gore Vidal and Julie Harris who was doing a film part in Kazan's version of *East of Eden*.

His involvement with *Diane* prevented him to his regret from accepting an offer to write the screenplay of *I am a Camera*. Henry Cornelius, the director of *Passport to Pimlico* and *Genevieve*, had already asked John van Druten to do it, but he refused. However both van Druten and Isherwood warmly recommended John Collier, a friend of Isherwood's, for the job. Isherwood's hopes for the film ran high when Julie Harris accepted the lead role. When he saw the film the following year, however, he was particularly angered at the introduction of a romance between Christopher and Sally. 'For the record', he wrote Lehmann, 'I found it disgusting ooh-la-la near-pornographic trash—a shameful exhibition.'[2]

Although Isherwood was hoping to use his large earnings at M-G-M to pay for a trip to England that autumn with Don Bachardy it had to be postponed partly because Bachardy did not hear until late that year that he was not going to be drafted. Instead they flew to Key West in November to watch Anna Magnani and Burt Lancaster making a film of Tennessee Williams' *The Rose Tattoo*. Tennessee Williams outdid even Auden in the speed with which he wrote additional scenes to order, much to the admiration of Isherwood who added his own small contribution by playing a bit-part in the film. 'Let's face it', he told one reporter, 'I'm a bit of a ham.'[3] That December they both took off again with two friends, Jo and Ben Masselink, on a month's car trip down the west coast of Mexico as far as Mexico City. Although he preferred Mexico to any other Latin American country, he came away with a certain distaste for it: 'Their way is not our way', he decided.[4]

Out of this realisation came the germ of his next novel, variously called 'The Lost', 'The Forgotten', 'Down There on a Visit' and 'the Mexican fantasy novel'. By the following summer he had worked out a rough outline of it:[5]

> The basic idea is of a conducted tour, similar to Dante's tour of the Inferno. But this Inferno is more of a Purgatorio, because nobody in it is permanently damned—only temporarily self-detained . . .

The tour was to be a journey by car across the Arizona border to the west coast of Mexico ending in Mexico City.

> The temporarily 'damned' are all aliens: exiles, expatriates and permanent tourists— . . . my cousin the British consul, Francis Turville-Petre . . . the inmates of the refugee hostel, a character named Paul whom I wanted to write a book about called Paul is Alone.

Dante, whom Isherwood always disliked intensely as a character, was to be some kind of unofficial minister with a shrewd eye for investments and the main chance, while Virgil was originally 'the author of a pseudo-religious work that Dante admires, but *he* now sees to be bogus'. Thinking him depraved, Dante considers it his mission to save him, whereas Virgil is actually trying to do the same for Dante—unsuccessfully in the event.

He had no more time than to sketch out this brief outline of the novel that year. In January casting and then shooting began on *Diane*. The Studio Front Office managed to sabotage the film by disastrous casting. Isherwood suggested Ingrid Bergman for Diane, Julie Harris for Catherine and John Williams for Francis I. Instead they chose Lana Turner (a disaster), Marisa Pavan and Pedro Armendariz. It was a blow to Isherwood who had been given a completely free hand with the script. When it was released the critics tended to blame him for the actors' failure to deliver the lines in the way he had intended. 'Christopher Isherwood', ran one review for instance in the *Manchester Guardian*, 'incidentally, wrote the script, but not noticeably.'[6] However, most of his time between January and September of 1955 was spent writing a screenplay based on an earlier script by Robert Hardy Andrews about the early life of the Buddha which was sponsored by the Indian and Japanese governments who had made some unholy deal with M-G-M. In the end nothing came of it partly because, according to Isherwood, the studios took fright at the cost involved in one scene in which the king was sitting on a throne fashioned of gold and obsidian.[7]

Apart from a brief visit to Philadelphia to see Tennessee Williams' *Cat on a Hot Tin Roof*, Isherwood was tied down by M-G-M until September. Meanwhile Don Bachardy, who was completing his time at college, was still unsure of what career he most wanted to pursue. At the time he was still contemplating making a life in the theatre. Once the studio work was finished, Isherwood and Bachardy moved temporarily to a lonely house up the coast in Malibu until it was time to leave in mid-October on their long-awaited trip to Europe—Bachardy's first time there.

From New York, their first main port of call was Tangier where Paul and Jane Bowles were living. Paul Bowles has written of how they visited him one stormy night in late October when Ahmed, their Moroccan servant, gave them enough *majoun* to send them out into the gale in a state of disorientation.[8] Isherwood had an extremely disagreeable trip during which he experienced the sensation that time had come to a stop: 'I understood in a very plastic way what was meant by eternity, which of course is hell if you're having a bad time.'[9] Out of this episode grew his idea for the finale of the Mexican fantasy novel: Dante would be given hashish by a character called Anselm Oakes (a figure primarily modelled on Alistair Crowley) and in his drugged state would finally understand the difference between good and evil.[10] Isherwood only abandoned this ending for his novel at the proof stage six years later; even then he preserved it as a separate story, 'A Visit to Anselm Oakes', which is printed in *Exhumations*.

In November they travelled through Italy enjoying an Indian summer; December they spent making their leisurely way through France; by early January 1956 they reached England. Apart from looking up all Isherwood's old friends (who invariably warmed to Don Bachardy on first meeting him) and sampling the London theatrical fare (Scofield's disastrous *Hamlet* and *Waiting for Godot* defying the critics with its long run), he saw Richard and his mother, still full of vitality at eighty-seven, and paid his last visit to Marple Hall, 'a gutted ruin, stripped naked of its ivy, with black staring window-holes' (*KF* 233). Three years later the council demolished it, a victim of the one brother's resentment of the past and the other's sheer indifference. On the eve of their departure for the States in mid-March, Isherwood announced to the Beesleys: 'As regards the novel, I have started it—half a page! Virgil is definitely to be Denny Fouts.'[11]

Back in California Isherwood spent April house-hunting in the Santa Monica Canyon area. He also met for the first time Aldous Huxley's new wife, Laura, when he went to dinner at the Stravinskys.[12] In May they moved into the first house Isherwood had ever owned himself at 434 Sycamore Road, Santa Monica: 'It's really nice', he wrote, '—a door in the wall on the street, then a patio all overgrown with roses, then the house itself, then a terraced garden on the hillside behind; but all quite manageably small.'[13] The move was complicated by the fact that Don Bachardy was in hospital with hepatitis. No sooner had he been discharged than Isherwood went down with it too. As a result neither could drink any alcohol for a year. Despite his brief stay in hospital Isherwood did manage to get three different literary projects started that spring—the Mexican fantasy novel, the preparatory work for a life of Ramakrishna that Swami Prabhavananda had been urging him to do for a long time, and an anthology of English stories for Dell. He also wrote a prologue at Gerald Hamilton's request to *Mr Norris and I* which Hamilton typically proceeded to place in the *New Statesman* without Isherwood's permission to boost the sales of his book. His first draft of the Mexican fantasy, unlike the previous novel, almost wrote itself. It was a technique he was to use for all his novels in the sixties: 'Never again will I take trouble over a first draft. For me, that's the strangling of inspiration.'[14] By the beginning of September his anthology was finished and by the end of November he had completed the first draft of his novel.

At the beginning of July Don Bachardy decided to enrol at art school beginning that summer semester. As time went on he discovered that he had a genuine aptitude for art and committed himself increasingly to making it his vocation. In mid-September Isherwood was forced to seek more work in the studios, Twentieth Century Fox this time. Jerry Wald asked him to produce a treatment of Romain Rolland's ten-volume *roman-fleuve*, *Jean-Christophe*, about a German musical genius who makes his second home in France. Isherwood spent the next nine months reducing this opus down to manageable proportions only to have the studio drop the option shortly after he had completed work on it in early June 1957, partly because they could not persuade Marlon Brando to play the lead part. According to Gavin Lambert, who was also working for Jerry Wald in 1957 on *Sons and Lovers*, *Jean-Christophe* was turned down as too expensive.[15] The younger writer was introduced to Isherwood by a fellow screenwriter at Fox, Ivan Moffat. At the time Lambert was at work on *The Slide Area* which was written under the influence of *The Berlin Stories*. They quickly became friends and took to asking each other's advice on work in progress.

Once *Jean-Christophe* was definitely finished with and Don Bachardy had completed his summer semester at art college, they planned to make a round-the-world trip via India (where Isherwood wanted to obtain background material for his book on Ramakrishna) and England. Until they left that autumn Isherwood was working steadily on the second draft of his Mexican fantasy novel, writing the whole thing as a dialogue between Dante (William) and Virgil (Paul), as he explained to Upward:

I now have the idea that they are two halves of one person. Or say that they represent two ways of life that this one person could have taken. Broadly, Dante is successful, respectable, corrupt; Virgil is unsuccessful, scandalous, unashamed. . . . The secret titles of the novel are Là-Bas, The Un-Americans or How The Other Half Lives.[16]

The different episodes correspond to phases of Dante/William's early life. When he meets the Consul he treats William like a boy of nineteen 'until he feels as if he *were* and goes through, relives, all the ghastly humiliations of the young.' Apart from the episode set on Francis Turville-Petre's island, there is also 'a female Quaker who loathes Art and is condemned to run an artists' and writers' colony, and a countess who loathes children and has to run a children's hospital.' There is also a wealthy art collector who buys and presents to museums only works of art which he considers to be utterly worthless, and a magician who believes in neither magic nor evil. The second draft was less than half finished when Isherwood and Bachardy left in mid-October for their three-month round trip.

They flew to Hawaii, continued by boat to Japan and then on to Hong Kong, Bali and Bangkok, where Isherwood became so ill that he confined the Indian part of his trip to the Calcutta area where Ramakrishna had spent most of his life. As soon as he had obtained the material he needed for the book they made straight for London in December where his (psycho-somatic?) tropical cough quickly disappeared. There was a succession of visits and parties ending in frantic last-minute meetings with old friends (Stephen Spender, Henry Green, John and Beatrix Lehmann, and the Beesleys);[17] next a short stop-off in New York where they saw much of Julie Harris and Speed Lamkin; then back to Santa Monica at the end of January.

During their absence John van Druten had died, having suffered from the results of a stroke for the past year. In April 1958 Isherwood's mother also had a stroke which paralysed her arm for a time. After some indecision over whether to visit her he stayed put, deciding there was nothing he could do in the circumstances.[18] While Bachardy returned to art school (supplemented by private lessons from 'Vernon' who had become a serious artist by this time) Isherwood began work on the Ramakrishna book. He decided to begin it with a few chapters explaining how he became a devotee of the cult of Ramakrishna. But after writing some seventy pages he abandoned this approach as too egotistical and started again. Five years later he revised the abandoned opening and published it as a religious memoir, *An Approach to Vedanta*. During the summer he also spent three months working for David O. Selznick on 'Mary Magdalene' before the project was abandoned.

Apart from half-hearted attempts to write up their world trip in diary form, Isherwood spent much of his time tussling with the Mexican fantasy novel. Early in October he realised that once more he was trying to write two novels as one, 'a heartless gossipy wandering rats piece of picaresque and a poignant short dialogue between two sundered familiars, rather along the lines of Dante's talk with Brunetto Latini in the Inferno'.[19] Jettisoning the picaresque autobiographical episodes, he started again on the fantasy. But by early 1959 he had abandoned the fantasy mid-way in favour of a different solution, reminiscent of his treatment of 'The Lost' and reverting to the autobiographical approach. He decided to break the original material up into three (not yet four) big pieces which would nevertheless be related to each other. Unlike *The World in the Evening*, the new book was to subordinate structural considerations to autobiographical veracity, treated fictionally of course. 'All in all, to date', he informed his English publisher that March, 'I have seven beginnings of drafts plus one complete (but most crude) draft, totalling about one hundred and seventy thousand words.'[20] By the end of March 1959 he had completed the rough draft of 'Mr Lancaster' and by mid-April he had sent the finished episode off to his New York agents to try selling it to a magazine. When the *New Yorker* rejected it he withdrew it and sent it off to Upward for his opinion. When he expressed his approval (apart from reservations about the treatment of the 1928 Isherwood) Isherwood asked him to send the episode to John Lehmann who published it in his *London Magazine* that October.

During the winter of 1958–9 Isherwood and Don Bachardy worked on the first of their many subsequent collaborations— a dramatisation of *The World in the Evening*, concentrating on the characters of Elizabeth and Stephen after whom it was called *The Monsters*—'an effort to restate what was mis-stated in The World in the Evening',[21] Isherwood explained to the Beesleys. When they reacted unfavourably to it, the project was allowed to lapse. He paid two visits to New York that winter and spring, one during the first half of February to see friends and catch Tennessee Williams' new play *Sweet Bird of Youth*, the other in mid-April to discuss with Auden and Chester Kallman the possibility of collaborating over a musical version of the Berlin Stories, a project which came to nothing for lack of a financial backer. Back in Los Angeles, Isherwood was becoming a familiar face on Oscar Levant's television talk-show on which he would reminisce and recite poetry, concealing his essentially private nature, according to Gavin Lambert, behind an entertaining public façade.[22] He also tried making money by collaborating with Gavin Lambert and Lesser Samuels on a film treatment of *The Vacant Room* which nearly sold but not quite.

Late that summer Isherwood and Bachardy made a lightning trip to England and France, stopping off at Lincoln Kirstein's apartment in New York in both directions. Isherwood spent four days with his mother whose powerful directing will was still much in evidence despite her recent stroke and blindness in one eye. It was to be his last meeting with her before she died the following summer at the age of ninety-one. From Wyberslegh he went down to Stratford to see Charles Laughton as Lear, a part which Laughton had discussed with him at length the previous February.[23] At the beginning of September they spent five days with Somerset Maugham at Cap Ferrat. By 9 September they had rushed back to Santa Monica in order to move into a new house Isherwood had bought in Adelaide Drive, where they live to this day. The new one-storey house was perched below the level of the street looking across Santa Monica Canyon with the Pacific breaking in the bay below to the left. There was enough room for a study for Isherwood and for a studio to be fixed up behind the garage for Don Bachardy. By this stage Bachardy was already specialising in portraits (he had sold his first one to Gerald Heard the previous year). That winter he was doing portraits to accompany interviews appearing in *The Paris Review* as well as continuing his studies at art school.

Unable to earn money at the studios, Isherwood had accepted a post as visiting professor in the English Department of California State College on the other side of town. Brand new, it was built according to its staff, in late supermarket. He taught there for two semesters from September 1959 to May 1960, talking twice weekly about his literary friends and other favourite writers, and aiming more to amuse than to instruct, as was expected of a celebrity. 'It seems strange', he remarked, 'after running away from Cambridge to avoid becoming a don, that now I am a real professor!'[24] He soon found himself enjoying his new role, especially as it left him plenty of time to get on with his own work. He saw much more of Aldous Huxley during this period, helping him to resolve a problem he was having that February in writing *Island*[25] and planning to go with him to the Governor of California to plead for the life of Caryl Chessman who was nevertheless executed after eight reprieves. He also spent a lot of time with Charles Laughton during the spring and summer of 1960 working on a theatrical version of the Dialogues of Plato based on the life of Socrates. Laughton was of course to play Socrates and they intended the entire project to be staged as a cross between a dramatic reading and a full-scale play, reaching a natural dramatic climax in the third act with Socrates' imprisonment and death. Laughton's own ill-health and early death, however, prevented the scheme from being realised.[26]

The first instalment of Isherwood's life of Ramakrishna had appeared in the March–April 1959 issue of *Vedanta and the West*. All twenty episodes were serialised in the Vedanta Society's magazine, appearing as and when he found time for them, until the task was completed with the appearance of the last instalment in May–June 1964. By February 1960, when he had finished seven chapters, he confessed to the Beesleys: 'I still have Ramakrishna's life on my back. Oh God, what a labour of duty!'[27] He continued to view the writing of this book as the repayment of a debt to Prabhavananda and he never wrote of it with the same degree of interest and enthusiasm that he showed when discussing the two novels he wrote concurrently with it.

Down There on a Visit was meanwhile taking the shape in which we know it. By June 1959 he had decided to leave the fantasy as an unfinished Kafkaesque work-in-progress. 'The other book', he informed Upward, 'is far more interesting and I see that I can steal quite large bits of the later part of the fantasy for use in it.'[28] He is obviously referring to 'Paul', the final episode of the published novel, as it was in May that he announced that it would now consist of four instead of three episodes.[29] While working on 'Ambrose', which gave him a lot of trouble, he outlined the entire novel as he then saw it to Dodie Smith:[30] '. . . it's about me, at four different ages, with four different attitudes'. In 'Mr Lancaster' he sees Berlin as 'the desirable Sodom of my fantasies'. In 'Ambrose', disenchanted yet highly politicised by his four years in Berlin, he joins Ambrose on his island where he gradually feels drawn to his Zen Buddhist way of life only to be told gently that he does not belong in Ambrose's world. 'I have to go back to my world of political paranoia, with all its restlessness and excitement. In the third episode, we see me in the midst of a sort of group hell: the Munich crisis in London.' 'Paul' is to be about Isherwood's relations with Denny Fouts during the war: 'it will be both farcical and serious, and finally tragic, because there will be an epilogue in Berlin in the early nineteen-fifties, when Denny is dying as the result of dope, etc. While I am in Berlin, I visit Waldemar, who is now a married man, living in the Russian zone, amidst the post-war ruins.'

In March 1960 he sent the completed 'Ambrose' off to Spender for possible publication in *Encounter*, but Melvin Lasky vetoed it. 'Waldemar' was finished by early summer and 'Paul', much the longest episode, by 19 August. There was still much work to be done, he informed Upward at that point: 'The last two have to be drastically rewritten and then I have to reconstruct the whole "I" framework—the interrelation of the different phases of myself, around them. This will mean doing a good deal to Mr Lancaster, too.'[31] 'Waldemar' was revised by late November of that year and 'Paul' by March 1961. The readjustment of the first-person structure was completed by June when it went off to both of his publishers.

In September 1960 Isherwood succeeded Huxley as visiting professor at the University of California at Santa Barbara, about a hundred miles up the coast from Santa Monica, where he spent two days a week during the first semester. The eight public lectures he delivered under the title of 'A Writer and His World' were also broadcast in the New Year by KPFK.[32] Apart from lecturing and writing, he also spent time tightening up Dylan Thomas's film script of Stevenson's *The Beach of Falesa*. Don Bachardy was by this stage drawing portraits of many of their friends resident in Los Angeles that year—Joan Plowright, Mary Ure, John Osborne, Charles Laughton, Tennessee Williams, Gore Vidal, the Stravinskys, Tony Richardson and others. Isherwood was immensely stimulated by Bachardy's capacity for hard work, and claimed that September that because of him it had proved one of the most creative periods in his life.[33] When Bachardy was offered a six-months' grant, he decided to spend it studying at the Slade under Sir William Coldstream, an old friend of Isherwood's. He left in late January for London where Richard Burton and his wife let him have their house in Hampstead while they were in New York involved with *Camelot*.

Isherwood was tied down in Los Angeles until March delivering three lectures at UCLA and revising 'Paul'. In early April he joined Bachardy in London. There he discussed the possibility of writing the screenplay for the film version of *England Made Me* with Graham Greene. He also resuscitated the idea of collaborating on a musical based on the Berlin material with Auden and Kallman, which Tony Richardson was anxious to stage at the Royal Court. But nothing materialised from either of these projects. In June he was interviewed by Upward for BBC radio and took part in a confrontation between writers of the thirties and the new literary generation on Granada television. In July he heard from Simon and Schuster, his new American publishers, who felt that 'Paul' was less carefully worked than the other three episodes especially in its final pages. Apart from inserting a short extra scene, Isherwood refused to make further changes at this stage. But in October, when he was checking the proofs, he suddenly decided to eliminate the penultimate episode in which Paul takes the narrator to see Anselm Oakes, mainly because it focused too much attention on the narrator when the entire section is in fact centred on Paul. After spending ten days in mid-September in the South of France with Tony Richardson seeing John Osborne and Somerset Maugham, Isherwood returned to London for the opening of Don Bachardy's first one-man show at the Redfern Gallery on 3 October. Then on 15 October he returned to Santa Monica after six months' absence, leaving Bachardy in London until the end of November fulfilling the numerous commissions he had been given as a result of the show.

23

Down There on a Visit

Isherwood has described *Down There on a Visit* as 'a loosely constructed fictional autobiography, something in the manner of *Goodbye to Berlin*'.[1] It represents a return not just to the form but to the excellence of his earlier novel. It is striking that he went through a similar process of extricating his characters from the ponderous design of an over-ambitious earlier draft in both cases. 'As soon as some of them had escaped into the later version', he told a correspondent about *Down There on a Visit*, 'and been released from the necessity of representing something or other, they immediately revived and turned into human beings.'[2] By reverting from the sheer subjectivity of invented events, to the encounter between the objective and the subjective which occurred when he used actual events and then interpreted them, he felt able to capture the life which had eluded him in the various versions of his Mexican fantasy.[3] The fragmentation of modern life resists too much artistic neatness. So Isherwood decided to use a loose episodic structure to render the time-span covered by this novel (1928–53). The alternative, which Isherwood was to employ in his next novel, is to confine the novel to a limited moment in time during which he can create at least a semblance of order.

Does this necessarily mean, then, that structural unity is automatically sacrificed in the process? Is *Down There on a Visit* an integrated novel or four separate novelettes featuring the same narrator? Isherwood himself has fluctuated ambiguously between the former and latter view of the book. During and immediately after the period in which he was writing *Down There* he was convinced of its essential cohesion. When he first announced to his English publisher that he had broken up the material into several pieces, he went on to stress how they would nevertheless relate to each other 'loosely but efficiently to give the whole a unity and make it something one could describe as a novel'.[4] By the time he had finished the book he was even more convinced of this, explaining: 'Its real continuity, I think, is as an autobiography—though largely a fictional one. The four episodes are in fact much more tightly tied together than in my *Goodbye to Berlin*, because the narrator of this present book is made into more of a character in his own right.'[5] Subsequently, however, he suggested that 'the entire claim that this has a kind of unity was very dubious'.[6] At least one critic, Francis King, obviously shared this view when he described the book as 'not an organic growth but a skilful assembly'.[7]

If one ignores the controlling presence of the narrator and the incidental presence of Waldemar in all four episodes, is there any overall thematic cohesion that can still be discerned in the book? Certainly Isherwood spoke of it at the time as if all the episodes were connected by a common viewpoint. In September of 1960 when he had completed a rough draft of all four episodes, he told the Beesleys that he wanted to call the novel 'In the Face of the Enemy' because 'each of the four main characters in it is in a minority of one, fighting The Others.'[8] Similarly he told his English publisher that the book was primarily 'about loneliness, alienation, aggression, minority-psychology and the difference between personal and public ethics'.[9] This provides a far more helpful idea of what the novel is concerned with than does its title or blurb, both of which, Isherwood later realised, were mainly leftovers from the Mexican fantasy: 'When I wrote the final version of it I had long since abandoned the idea of describing a visit to a modern Hell, or Purgatory.'[10]

Nevertheless one has to admit that without the presence of the slowly maturing narrator this connective link is fairly slender. Isherwood showed that he recognised the importance of the structural function performed by the narrator when he explained that the second of the novel's twin themes was 'about the attitudes to life which one individual can hold at different times—engagement versus disengagement, to use the French post-war jargon'.[11] In the opening section the narrator is engaged with nothing, unless one takes seriously his spurious ideal of Art. In the next section he is paradoxically attracted to a different kind of disengagement, the anarchic non-attachment of Ambrose to the outside world. In the third section he becomes obsessively engaged with European politics, only to retreat in the final section to a position of non-attachment in a specifically religious sense, which ironically involves him more directly in the life of another individual than has been the case in any of his previous phases. One can also discern a growing maturity in his successive attachments: Art gives way to world-weariness; when this fails he throws himself feverishly into politics; ultimately he commits himself to a deeper belief in a divine reality that underlies all these lesser forms of engagement. The young man of twenty-three is unwittingly instrumental in pushing Mr Lancaster over the edge into suicide: the older man of thirty-six alters his entire life style in his attempt to prevent Paul from doing likewise.

In temporal terms the novel looks back to a past self that bears little relation to the middle-aged author writing the book. By stages it draws together the first-person protagonist and the narrator until both seem to share the latter's vision (voiced in the opening pages of the novel) of the relativity of the self. *Down There on a Visit* is consequently about more than what one reviewer called 'the narrator's maturing response to the (four) victims of loneliness'.[12] It is equally about 'Christopher's' gradual penetration beneath the various strata of the ego to the 'awareness of being conscious' which 'belongs to everybody' and 'isn't a particular person' (p 14). Loneliness can lead to suicide as happens in Mr Lancaster's case. But loneliness can equally lead to the realisation that the reality of life can only be discovered through the loss of self, a viewpoint which 'Christopher' has come to share with Augustus Parr in the final episode of the book where Paul is introduced specifically to test this proposition. In the course of the novel 'Christopher' comes to experience similar feelings of loneliness and despair to those of his four pseudonymous heroes; but he also emerges from his dark night of the soul with a transcendental view of existence that has controlled the narrative viewpoint from the opening paragraph.

At the beginning of the novel Isherwood announces his discovery that Mr Lancaster can only be presented in his entirety by showing how his meeting with him was the first of a series of chapters in his life. What is implied here is that each of the four characters only acquires meaning within the context of the narrator's life. As Malcolm Bradbury suggested when he reviewed the book, all of the four main characters 'represent to us facets of Isherwood himself', not necessarily 'versions of his own degradation' as Bradbury went on to suggest,[13] but rather unrealised though potential solutions to a predicament which the narrator shares with all four characters. Like them he has confronted isolation and despair. Each of the four episodes describes his visits to their separate worlds, invariably ending in his or their departure. Their way is not for him. Yet, but for them, he might have succumbed to despair like Mr Lancaster, or to an escapist fantasy-world like Ambrose; he too could have become a pawn on the political chessboard like Waldemar or gambled for heaven or hell as Paul did. No moral judgements are involved, which should hardly surprise one by this stage in Isherwood's career. The pattern of the book is that of a life, the narrator's life. The incidents that Isherwood has selected acquire their significance from the light they throw on his subjective growth to the standpoint from which the novel is told, so that its development appears to justify its structure.

This neat aesthetic device led Stephen Spender to complain that Isherwood thereby 'deprives the reader of perspectives by which he can judge the Isherwood world. At every turn the reader finds himself being unable to separate the views and personality which are Isherwood from the view of life which is the novel.'[14] This is the age-old problem with all novels controlled by a first-person narrator based on the writer himself. Obviously the protagonist's response to Mr Lancaster is subject to the maturer narrator's disapproval. But what is one to make of Paul who is seen only through the eyes of a narrator who appears to be almost identified with the protagonist? To readers like the critic of the *New York Times*, who found Paul 'a despicable individual', the narrator's insistent sympathy for him causes the critic to denounce the entire episode as 'the least impressive and the most sickening'.[15] On the other hand Cyril Connolly, while equally 'indignant at Mr Isherwood's gullibility' in rendering Paul so sympathetically, admits that 'without it, this would not have been the best part of the book'.[16] Such antithetical responses are the result of Isherwood's highly ambiguous resort to irony in the final section as a means of maintaining his distance from the protagonist, and irony has a nasty potential for being overlooked by the reader. Nevertheless Isherwood's intention was to maintain a minimal aesthetic distance from his subject-matter. The degree to which he has succeeded is difficult to determine, especially in the last episode, mainly because the reader can never be quite sure how identified with, or detached from, the narrator the writer is at any given moment, let alone how detached the narrator is from the protagonist.

In 'Mr Lancaster' narrator and protagonist are separated by twenty-six years. Consequently Isherwood has no difficulty in maintaining a sufficient distance from what he considers virtually a former incarnation of himself:

> The Christopher who sat in that taxi is, practically speaking, dead; he only remains reflected in the fading memories of us who knew him. I can't revitalise him now. I can only reconstruct him from his remembered acts and words and from the writings he has left us. (p 14)

Even the use of the first-person plural suggests a recognition of the multiplicity of roles adopted by the ego, something which the 'Christopher' of 1928 was completely blind to. Little wonder, either, when one realises that in this first episode we are again meeting that Byronic poseur from *Lions and Shadows*, 'Isherwood the Artist'. Chronologically 'Mr Lancaster' belongs to the gap in time which occurs between Chapters Six and Seven of *Lions and Shadows*. But the narrator is some fourteen years older and has a quite different perspective on the same young protagonist. 'Christopher's' play-acting, his retreat from reality into the 'comfort and safety' of 'the world of epic myth' (p 15) is no longer seen as the product of neurotic fear as it was in *Lions and Shadows*. In *Down There on a Visit* it is clearly a symbol of his extreme attachment to the world of *maya*.

In fact both 'Christopher' and Mr Lancaster share what Isherwood in *Lions and Shadows* called the 'Epic Myth. . . . People's attitudes to their own Coriolanus-myth' (*LS* 206). Mr Lancaster, it emerges by the end of the episode, also converts everyday experience into a myth in which he features as the epic hero. Like Coriolanus (after whom the company boat on which 'Christopher' makes his Stygian crossing is appropriately named), Mr Lancaster has developed an inflated idea of his own significance until he can hear nothing but 'his own reverberations, his epic song of himself' (p 63). Like Coriolanus, too, his egotistical pride is the cause of his death. When the distance between reality and epic myth becomes impossible to bridge, Mr Lancaster ceases 'to believe in the epic any more' (p 63), is overtaken by despair and puts an end to his life with the forgotten revolver which 'Christopher' had unwittingly brought to his attention, 'a gross metallic fact in the midst of his world of fantasy' (p 48). Mr Lancaster has become so attached to the charade he has mistaken for reality that he can only stop acting out his role by opting out of life itself.

For 'Christopher' the parallel is all too clear. To commit oneself entirely to the world of *maya* is to invite despair when the play comes to an end. In fact the entire episode demonstrates 'Christopher's' failure to convert the world around him into epic myth, luckily for him. Even his 'entrance upon Act One of the drama was lacking in style' (p 16). 'Mr Lancaster' relies for its simple ironical effect on 'Christopher's' realisation by the end that, after he has allotted to Mr Lancaster the role of Enemy in his own epic myth in which only the young can be heroes, he is human after all. When he tries, however, to re-cast him in the role of rebel hero against society his mythopoeic powers fail him: 'I wanted to make a saga around Mr Lancaster's protest. I wanted to turn him into a romantic figure. But I couldn't. I didn't know how' (p 62). His impotence here exposes the sham nature of his concept of Art which is unable to incorporate too much reality.

Between 'Mr Lancaster' and 'Ambrose' lurks the ghostly presence of Isherwood's four years in Berlin and the two books he wrote out of that experience. Mr Lancaster's lurid description of this modern Sodom determined 'Christopher' to go there as soon as possible. During his four years in Berlin the sadism of 'the "cruel" ladies in boots' (who featured in *Mr Norris*) had turned into the brutalities of 'the young thugs in Nazi uniforms' (p 73). What 'Christopher' mistook for a new sense of political commitment on his part in Berlin turned out to be another charade when Hitler came to power: 'I have to admit to myself that I have never been a real partisan; only an excited spectator' (p 74). Once more reality has intruded and 'Christopher' is in a state of psychological confusion: 'I must stop wondering what I ought to think, how I ought to feel' (p 75), he concludes as he sits in the train taking him to Ambrose's Greek island of St Gregory. He longs for Waldemar's guiltless, selfish attitude to life: 'I don't want anything of him, except that he shall remain young and fearless and silly. In fact', he concludes, 'I want the impossible' (p 75). But it takes him the whole summer on St Gregory to realise that a purely animal response is no solution for his particular predicament.

Where 'Mr Lancaster' took its controlling metaphor from *Coriolanus*, 'Ambrose' evokes the world of *The Tempest*. Ambrose is twice called 'one of Shakespeare's exiled beings' (pp 109 and 113) and his resemblance to Prospero in particular is made clear when he is described as 'the only person who knows what the spirit of the island wants at any given moment' (p 101). Isherwood has confessed that while he was writing this episode he was haunted by a line from *The Tempest*, 'The isle is full of noises.'[17] The noises are mainly hallucinatory as far as the narrator is concerned, just as the island offers him an illusory prospect of retreat from the Future and the Past which so terrified him in 'Mr Lancaster':

> Spread-eagled on my back on the surface of the water, looking up into the sky, I know almost nothing but now and here. . . . Normally, I'm very much aware of my age, because my mind is busy with anxiety about the future and regrets about the past. But not now, not here. (p 106)

This state of mindless bliss which 'Christopher' momentarily experiences appears to be enjoyed continuously by Ambrose. In his attempt to escape from his guilt-ridden, time-bound self, 'Christopher' sees Ambrose as a potential Messiah. Even when he first meets him he reflects: 'He could have posed for a portrait of a saint' (p 77). In the boat on their way to St Gregory he tells Ambrose with drunken admiration that he could imagine him 'getting out and walking on the water' (p 96).

But Ambrose, like his namesake, is a natural ascetic, one who possesses 'the sort of indifference to discomfort and hardship which you would expect to find in a great hero or saint' (p 109). This is quite the opposite of the self-indulgent laid-back fantasies of escapism harboured by 'Christopher', who finds himself by the end of his sojourn in a state of alienation from himself. After Maria has disrupted Ambrose's homosexual dictatorship and absconded with Geoffrey for whom Ambrose concocted his wildest fantasies, 'Christopher' feels himself obliged to assume the roles of the departed members of the group until, as he puts it, 'I almost ceased being myself, or anybody else in particular' (p 142). Beneath his frenzied participation in this charade of what life is like exists a fear of being alone. This is what distinguishes Ambrose who gently rebukes 'Christopher' on their last drunken night together: 'But one's *always* alone, ducky. Surely you know that?' (p 147). The narrator's fear of confronting his real self on his own is what sends him scurrying from the island. He is not ready to renounce the world yet. But he has become aware of the existence of an imprisoned inner self which does not belong to the world at all and which, we learn on the last page of 'Ambrose', he sometimes glimpses from the mirror.

The next time the narrator sees his reflection five years have passed and he has exchanged the revels and insubstantial pageant of St Gregory for the social-realist drama of the Munich crisis in London. In 'Waldemar' he is still an actor in the drama of *maya*, if anything more committed to the transient present than before, living through what Balzac called 'a day without to-morrow' (p 155). Having become a success and thereby won a hollow victory over the Past (which the Others always used to invoke to his detriment), he is desperately evading the fears that the Future holds in store by involving himself in the Present with an energy bred of despair. Isherwood's use of the diary form with its sense of immediacy for this episode is particularly appropriate. Critics have tended to dismiss 'Waldemar' as little more than an edited version of Isherwood's own diaries. This is hardly the case, as he made clear to one interviewer whom he told that he 'was putting into it ("Waldemar") many other times of great anxiety, many of the post-war crises and things that other people have said . . . they felt about such crises'.[18] He also utilised material he had once planned using for a novel based on a fanatical worker-worshipping Englishwoman he knew who worked at the communist headquarters in Berlin and a German carpenter she married and travelled around with.[19]

In 'Waldemar' Isherwood attempts to draw a series of parallels between three crises—the narrator's predicament at this time, the break-up of Waldemar and Dorothy, and the wider political drama of the Munich crisis. Political commitment as a *raison d'être* in itself is explored and found wanting in the course of this episode. Against the background of Chamberlain's well-intentioned but ineffectual attempts to replace the fear of war by the security of peace, Waldemar exposes the emptiness of 'Christopher's' political posturing (another act induced by his own private fears), unconsciously helping the narrator to penetrate to a deeper layer of his feelings. 'Christopher' vacillates with the European crisis between hope and despair, but beneath his despair at the political situation he discovers a more profound sense of spiritual *malaise*. Towards the end of 'Waldemar' he admits to Dorothy he can see no meaning in life at all. But this realisation is a necessary prelude to any possibility of change. He is brought to realise that despair cannot be evaded by immersion in tomorrowless politics or tomorrowless love affairs. And he does discover that for him personally 'nothing is worth a war' (p 201). Like Dr Fisch he ends up opting for the private life and the New World where the Past and the Others hold no power over him—only the Future.

When Isherwood sent 'Waldemar' to Upward he commented: 'This is the least complete-in-itself of the four episodes; it relates a lot to Paul, which follows it.'[20] Subsequently he explained that 'it was necessary for purely artistic reasons to have a period of despair in the novel . . . to have some black there to balance the white.'[21] In 'Paul' the narrator has already taken the all-important step from despair to religious belief, although he is still a mere initiate in the search for God. E.M. (Forster) the secular figure of saintliness to whom 'Christopher' looked for guidance in 'Waldemar' has been succeeded by the specifically religious figure of Augustus Parr, a character based on Gerald Heard who fulfils the role actually played by Swami Prabhavananda in Isherwood's own life. Like the other major characters in the novel, Paul parallels 'Christopher'—in his sexually promiscuous earlier life and his sudden plunge into despair after he has caught sight of himself at the end of his tether in the mirror of a downtown bar. (Mirrors form a leading motif throughout the novel.) Like the other major characters, too, he acts as a mirror himself in which 'Christopher' can see himself reflected. 'Paul', Isherwood has said, 'is a touchstone of sincerity, without meaning to be. . . . Without being

any better himself, he has the most awful faculty of exposing that tiny little bit of untruth that there is in almost all of
us.'[22]

According to Isherwood the title of *Down There on a Visit*
'is a reference to Huysmans' *Là-Bas*, because it is partly a novel
about hell'.[23] The parallel to *Là-Bas* only really holds good in
'Paul', the final episode of the book. Both Huysmans himself and
the hero of his novel arrive at their religious conviction through
a belief in Satanism. Paul comes close to the pattern of the
sinner-saint, someone who achieves sanctity through a conscious
immersion in evil, but the novel never actually discloses how
close to sanctity Paul has come before he dies prematurely.
Besides, his dramatic function is to act as litmus paper in testing
the sincerity of the religious converts in this episode, especially
of 'Christopher' and Augustus Parr. Paul's uncompromising
entry into the religious life quickly exposes 'Christopher's'
tentative and partial involvement in it, just as his despair, unlike
the narrator's, is total: 'Not helpless, negative despair. Dynamic
despair. The kind that makes dangerous criminals, and, very
occasionally, saints' (p 260). Meditation and the search for union
with God is far too entangled with the play-world of *maya* for
the narrator, as the language he uses reveals: 'Now, at last—
I tell myself—I'm playing *my* game, not the game of The
Others . . .' (p 219). On his last meeting with Paul, Paul spells
out the difference between them: 'You know, you really *are* a
tourist, to your bones. I bet you're always sending postcards
with "down here on a visit" on them. That's the story of your
life' (p 349). The accusation sticks, especially as it is virtually
identical to that levelled against 'Christopher' by Maria, a
fellow 'monster'. It is a pity Isherwood removed the powerfully
written visit to Anselm Oakes that immediately followed this
scene, because the narrator's terrifying experience of eternity or
timelessness in this segment redeems him from this charge
and offers hope for him in the future. It also leaves the reader
in no doubt about whether Paul has attained spiritual insight
through his drug-induced immersion into the depths.

Isherwood means to leave us in no doubt about Augustus
Parr's sanctity. Paul is allowed to use all the weapons in his
armoury of scepticism to try to dent Parr's image. In fact Paul
corresponds to 'the Joneses' in Isherwood's prescription for

the fictional portrayal of a saint in his essay, 'The Problem of the Religious Novel':

> How am I to prove that X is not merely insane when he turns his back on the whole scheme of pleasures, rewards, and satisfactions which are accepted by the Joneses, the Smiths, and the Browns, and goes in search of super-conscious, extra-phenomenal experience? The only way I can see how to do this is with the help of the Joneses themselves. I must show that the average men and women of this world are searching, however unconsciously, for the same fundamental reality of which X has already had a glimpse. (E 118)

Paul is a rather exceptional example of the Joneses. But he is certainly searching for the reality of which Parr has already had a glimpse. His final verdict on Parr after his last visit to him is, 'Miss Parr is still the biggest saint in show business' (p 335), where, Isherwood has later explained, the operative word is 'saint'.[24]

Isherwood obviously wrote 'Paul' in reaction to his sentimental treatment of religion in *The World in the Evening*. Sarah has become the much more human Augustus Parr, while Stephen's role has been split between Paul and 'Christopher'. Isherwood almost succeeds in 'Paul' where he clearly failed in the earlier novel. But there are still too many passages in which the same somewhat embarrassing handling of religious aspects that marred the previous novel recurs. They are mainly to be found in exchanges between 'Christopher' and Paul when an unmistakably schoolboy set of moral attitudes appear to be accepted without reservation. This element of immature morality accompanied by a worldly tone that is meant to gain it acceptance is most obtrusive during the retreat at Eureka Beach when they all, to use Paul's words, act 'like a bunch of old maids around a converted whore' (p 281). In fact Isherwood is attempting to draw an ironic distinction between Paul's genuine search for reality and characters like 'Christopher's' confusion between the genuine and the extraneous (and often puritanical) elements of the religious quest. Some of 'Christopher's' diary entries at Eureka Beach are intended to have a purely ironic effect on the reader: 'Ratlike preoccupation with my comfort: avoided the broken chair. So Grace had to take it' (p 301). But although passages like this make the reader squirm with embarrassment, they fail to differentiate clearly enough between the protagonist's and writer's viewpoints. Consequently Parr and even Paul are frequently in danger of becoming tainted with this small-minded attitude to religion which is meant to stand in ironic contrast to their more spiritual understanding of it.

'Paul' might be flawed, but it is by no means a failure, especially when it is viewed in the light of the three preceding episodes. *Down There on a Visit* in its entirety is an extraordinary return to Isherwood's powers of the late thirties. The writing is elegant and economical, the portraiture vivid, and the novel as a whole more integrated than *Goodbye to Berlin*. It is perhaps a sign that his confidence had returned to him that, once *Down There* was completed, he determined to renounce the use of an autobiographical persona for good and revert to a third-person narrative. As the last of a series, *Down There on a Visit* is a brilliant final offering in a sequence that includes much of his best fiction and deserves—what it has not received to date—the same critical attention that has been devoted to *Goodbye to Berlin*.

24

The Professor: *A Single Man*

By mid-October 1961 Isherwood was back in Santa Monica on his own, hard at work on the seemingly never-ending biography of Ramakrishna. He also spent considerable time with Charles Laughton, who had moved into the house next door, working on their projected dramatisation of the Socratic Dialogues. Although Laughton was a sick man by this stage, both men derived a lot of enjoyment from the sheer act of collaboration. While waiting for Bachardy to rejoin him at the end of November Isherwood also met Colin Wilson, then lecturing at Long Beach University, who brought Henry Miller along to meet Isherwood. The three spent the afternoon with Huxley and went on to have drinks with Laughton. According to Colin Wilson both Huxley and Laughton tended to treat Isherwood with a kind of affectionate protectiveness, as if he were still the shy young man of *Goodbye to Berlin*.[1] In mid-December Isherwood joined Don Bachardy in New York. There they stayed with Julie Harris and attended the opening of Bachardy's first New York show in January 1962 at which he sold more than half his drawings and had to stay on to attend to all the commissions that arose from it. Isherwood still found New York antipathetic: 'a maze of canyons without perspectives', he reported; 'everywhere one feels the presence of hysteria.'[2] Late in January he was obliged to return home on his own to take up teaching again for two days a week at California State College where he had begun his part-time career as a visiting professor two years earlier.

Within two months of starting teaching the idea for a new short novel was born in which 'Christopher Isherwood', an English professor at Cal State, comes to meet the major female protagonist through one of his students who is her son. The novel, originally called *An Englishwoman*, was conceived under the influence of Willa Cather, whose work he was enthusiastically reading at the time. The Englishwoman of the title originally married a GI at the end of the war after getting pregnant by him and settled in California. By the time the narrator meets her she has turned into an eccentric, while her husband who has lost most of his earlier wildness is about to leave her for another more conventional woman. The son meanwhile invokes his teacher's help as a fellow Englishman in persuading his mother that he is not ungrateful to her in wanting to leave her to go and live with his girlfriend. The mother is a composite portrait that nevertheless owes something to Iris Tree and more to a GI bride whom Isherwood came to know after the war.[3] By May he had begun work on this version. But he was already having doubts by August as to whether 'the wretched little thing is pregnant and will die but give birth to something more robust.'[4] The following month he wrote to Upward: 'Behind it I glimpse something, a quite new approach to middle age.'[5] Once more it was to prove a case for surgery—the removal of the novel that evolved into *A Single Man* from *An English-woman*.

1962 was occupied mainly by teaching and writing, including *Ramakrishna*, 'a labour of sheer willpower' as he described it to Forster, 'and not very sheer either'.[6] Don Bachardy was having a highly successful year with shows at Los Angeles in September and Santa Barbara the following January. Perhaps Bachardy's enforced absences were in small part responsible for the way *A Single Man* developed into a study of middle-aged loneliness. That spring they also had a studio built for Bachardy adjoining the car port, and a balcony perched on the steep side of the canyon. As Gavin Lambert has pointed out it is typical of Isherwood's 'unsafe and sound' approach to life that he should have added to the vertical drop when he is susceptible to vertigo.[7] That summer he accompanied Aldous Huxley on a visit to an aeronautical plant in Los Angeles where they were working on the Apollo moon-shot capsules. Huxley, true to form, denounced the project as a waste of money and discomforted everyone by suggesting that the astronauts could well return with a virus that would wipe out everybody.[8] Anais Nin also offers a funny glimpse of Isherwood at her friend Oliver Evans's house lined up with Bachardy, Lambert and other writers on a couch facing a row of professors in silent opposition and mutual incomprehension.[9] In December Charles Laughton died and with him the Socratic dramatisation. Isherwood delivered an oration at his funeral.

By December 1962 Isherwood had performed the operation on his new novel and started work on the second quite different draft which had 'evolved so suddenly', he told Upward, 'that it was as if another part of my mind had been getting it ready as a surprise'.[10] The new version, he announced to the Beesleys, 'is fundamentally about me, at my present age, living right here in the Canyon, but under rather different circumstances. . . . It isn't in the first person!'[11] Written under the remote influence of Virginia Woolf whom he was re-reading at this time, it was to be a study of middle age and its extraordinary variety of behaviour patterns. In fact the new idea for the novel was at least partly triggered off by one of those rash impulsive acts to which middle age is susceptible. The night before he embarked on the second draft Isherwood had gone swimming in the Pacific in the middle of the night under similar circumstances to those in which George does in the novel.[12] He realised that what really fascinated him was the semi-autographically based figure of the professor, not Charlotte, the pseudonymous heroine of the first draft. So he pushed her into the background, turned the son into Kenny and concentrated on 'a day (early in December 1962) in the life of a middle-aged Englishman who lives in this town, teaches at a local college and is queer'.[13] By making his hero not just middle-aged but also homosexual and a foreigner Isherwood was also able to introduce the whole question of the loneliness and alienation experienced by members of any minority group, a subject about which he had felt strongly all his life.

In the spring of 1963 he once more turned professor. On this occasion he was invited to give a series of lectures at Berkeley and was lent a house overlooking the Bay in San Francisco itself. He called the lectures 'The Autobiography of My Books' and talked about his work as surviving evidence of the different epochs through which he had lived. These lectures were to prove the initial spark for what became *Kathleen and Frank*. By August he was telling Upward that the next book he would like to try was 'a different approach to autobiography'.[14] But before he could come to write *Kathleen and Frank* he realised that he 'needed to study his Family and his own childhood in depth' (*KF* 362). Meanwhile a further novel was to intervene.

By the end of July he had finished the second draft of *A Single Man*, as the novel was now called at Bachardy's suggestion, and sent it to Upward for his verdict. Because it was written in such a new manner Isherwood was more unsure of himself than usual and was immensely relieved when Upward wrote back to say he liked it. He did, however, suggest that Isherwood might re-examine the scene with Charlotte which failed to show the close kind of relationship between her and George that the early-morning telephone conversation led one to expect. Gore Vidal also criticised this scene and during the following two months Isherwood typed the final draft of the novel, rewriting the scene with Charlotte and the ending, as well as making other smaller alterations throughout the novel. On 21 October he sent the book off to his publishers, convinced that he had 'broken new ground in it, technically and emotionally'.[15] 'I think it is the best I have done', he wrote to John Lehmann, 'and at worst it is quite a bit different from anything else.'[16] Despite breaking a rib in a car accident that August he also managed to finish *Ramakrishna and his Disciples* in October although some revision still remained to be done. 'I fear that has a streak of institutional goodygoodyness,' he confessed to Spender.[17] The book owes more to Isherwood's feelings of loyalty to Swami Prabhavananda than to any direct inspiration or enthusiasm on his part.

The year ended sadly for him with the loss of Aldous Huxley on the same day that President Kennedy was assassinated. The last time he saw him was in the Cedars of Lebanon hospital where Huxley, for all his physical disabilities, appeared to talk his condition away for the duration of the visit. Despite his fears to the contrary he was able to go on working up to the day before he died, painfully dictating with his impaired voice the last portion of an article on Shakespeare and Religion. Huxley was cremated without a service of any kind. The only ceremony held by the family was a walk, in which Isherwood joined, along Huxley's traditional route around the Hollywood Reservoir.

Completed in his fifty-ninth year, *A Single Man* is a quite astonishing *tour de force*. Isherwood still likes it best of all his novels and so did Auden. It is even less widely known than *Down There on a Visit* which helps to explain why Isherwood, despite his literary renaissance in the sixties, is still commonly associated with his writing in the thirties. When it was published in 1964 the book had a mixed reception from the critics, but even the most favourable reviews reveal a misunderstanding of what a radical departure from his earlier books this novel represented—especially the Berlin books to which everyone inevitably compared it.

Almost everything about *A Single Man* is different—its conception of character, its narrative viewpoint, and its temporal structure. Underlying these changes is the elementary presupposition which the Vedantist shares with anyone who believes that life of some sort continues after death—that the everyday conception of the self is an illusion. Isherwood described the novel as 'an attempt to study this individual (George) in depth, as a sort of constellation of impulses which only jells into a "personality" at certain times of the day and in the presence of other people'.[18] For the first two pages the hero remains anonymous and impersonal, referred to as 'it'. When it wakes up first it becomes part of the flux of time, 'saying *am* and *now*' (p 7); next it enters the confines of space, 'here' and more specifically 'at home'. Isherwood throws an interesting sidelight on this passage when he reveals that it is adapted from a passage in his own diary.[19] He is writing out of personal experience, not dogma.

Slowly George's body is assembled to confront the image of its own *karma* in the bathroom mirror, 'the mess it has somehow managed to get itself into during its fifty-eight years' (p 8). The Vedantic presupposition is unobtrusively present in this creature's multiplicity of past selves 'preserved like fossils on superimposed layers' in its face, in the description of it as 'this live dying creature', above all in its fear of 'being rushed' to its inevitable extinction (p 8). By the third page it is given a gender and a name, but these are attached to it in a deliberately arbitrary manner to emphasise a teleological viewpoint that is cleverly attributed to a ghostly Jim who might observe from 'the vast outdoors of his freedom' his former lover inside the house, 'a prisoner for life' (p 12). George, then, is stuck together as a recognisable personality (or set of personalities) at the beginning of the novel. But the package is always in danger of coming undone. When he visits Doris on the verge of death in hospital she treats him as if he were George only for the sake of convenience. For her 'the line between reality and hallucination is getting very thin' (p 81); within the context of the book the normal interpretation of this statement becomes reversed: 'George' is the illusion.

The deceptive nature of personality is amply demonstrated within the course of George's day as he exchanges one role for another. By making him middle-aged, Isherwood was able to dramatise the diversity of his hero's supposed identity with more credibility. On his drive to work a persona detaches itself from him, 'an impassive anonymous chauffeur-figure with little will or individuality of its own, the very embodiment of muscular coordination, lack of anxiety, tactful silence, driving its master to work' (p 27). Meanwhile he fantasises about the revenge he would wreak on his enemies as 'Uncle George', the anonymous head of a secret organisation that has unmistakable similarities with the Mafia. At San Tomas State, where his students are granted their particular identities by IBM cards, he assumes a different part, in which he 'could just as well be a severed head, carried into the classroom to lecture to them from a dish' (p 41). His lecture is consistently described in theatrical terms. He carefully stages his entrance and preserves his 'provocative melodramatic silence' (p 49) until he has won his audience's attention. He then launches into his performance varying his tone from the 'hammy harmonies' of his opening speech (p 50), to that of 'the voice of a judge, summing up and charging the jury' (p 53), only to become (during the discussion) 'an attendant at a carnival booth, encouraging the crowd to throw and smash their targets' (p 56). Finally he muffs his exit when he overruns the prescribed time. But this does not prevent him from continuing to throw himself into the charade of life with gusto.

Isherwood's use of this theatrical metaphor to emphasise the deceptive nature of the world of *maya* is reminiscent of *Down There on a Visit* where 'Christopher' himself had difficulty recognising his own past selves. The difference between 'Christopher' and George is that George is firmly committed to the parts he has chosen to play on the stage of life, while 'Christopher' becomes a convert to the transcendental view of existence that transfuses both novels. George is an indefatigable 'contender' in this life, playing out his various roles with equal conviction. Before entering his class he is all 'eagerness for the play to begin' (p 35); later that morning, during a different kind of performance at lunch, when he is interrupted in mid-flight, he is compared to a trapeze-artist left to hurry past his audience to the exit. George enjoys his balancing act on the tight-rope of life. He is an expert quick-change artist. Through him the reader catches glimpses of a whole range of microcosmic societies which at the naturalistic level are typical of the way Los Angeles functions but which also serve to emphasise the multiplicity of the lives one individual can lead.

Isherwood has pointed out in *Ramakrishna and His Disciples* that 'Maya' is only 'illusory in a relative sense; namely that the universe which is made of it is impermanent and other than Brahman, the Reality' (p 15). George, as we have seen, is firmly committed to the play-world of *maya*. Isherwood has called him a 'stoic' who 'bases his entire defence on sheer agnostic courage, without the support of religious belief'.[20] But since George and the world with which he contends are nevertheless products of Brahman's power, he is unconsciously part of a Reality that the narrative takes for granted and which even he dimly intimates at times—on first waking up, on visiting Doris, on confronting a particularly large wave in the ocean. It is this double perspective which allows Isherwood near the end of the novel to introduce a marvellously controlled image which explicitly establishes George's relation to the greater Reality which the Hindus call Brahman. George, the impersonal narrative voice hypothesises, could be like the rock-pool which retains its separate identity at low tide but merges with the ocean at high tide and is left separate (but who can say the same?) when it ebbs once more.

George, as Alan Wilde has suggested, becomes in the course of the novel 'a type of everyman'.[21] Or at least he is meant to. Why then does Isherwood make him a member of the homosexual minority? Sybille Bedford, when she reviewed the novel, felt that his homosexuality constitutes 'the book's main artistic flaw because it impairs what might have been the august universality of the theme'.[22] Isherwood, however, has said that in the book 'homosexuals are used as a sort of metaphor for minorities in general'.[23] George belongs not just to the homosexual minority but to the minority of foreigners, as does Lois, Kenny's Japanese girlfriend. In fact everybody ultimately belongs to what George calls 'the ranks of that marvellous minority, The Living', he having 'freshly returned from the icy presence of The Majority, which Doris is about to join' (p 87). What gives everyone a sense of identity is membership of a minority. It segregates the living from the dead. It also isolates individual consciousness from universal consciousness. It is responsible for George's courage in confronting the worst that life can offer him and for his loneliness, which is everyone's courage and everyone's loneliness.

Isherwood has said that he was partly modelling *A Single Man* on *Peer Gynt*. George's day is a life-day in which 'you have the ages of man all revealed in one day.'[24] George vacillates between moments of youthful irresponsibility (of which the midnight swim is the most spectacular example) and times when he turns into a pathetic old man shuffling his way out to the parking lot, for instance. His first moments of consciousness in the morning are described as a form of birth (or rebirth) just as loss of consciousness with sleep becomes virtually indistinguishable from the optional death described at the end. Isherwood has said that he used Dr A. T. W. Simeons's description of a coronary occlusion in *Man's Presumptuous Brain* for his hypothetical death-scene. But he has employed this medical knowledge to disassemble his prototype, to show how naturally he comes unstuck. Personality, identity or the ego is revealed as the most fragile and temporary of constructs. In this final scene of the novel, Isherwood explained to Dodie Smith, 'it is made quite clear that only part of the thing is dead; the rest is, so to speak, dispersed.'[25] Anthony Burgess showed an understanding unusual among reviewers at the time of why the ending constitutes a natural climax to the novel: 'After the metaphorical death of the orgasm, the sham death of sleep, comes the true, but hypothetical, death of the body. The trilogy of deaths is the final ritual of stripping.'[26]

Nothing could be more appropriate to the establishment of a teleological perspective than Isherwood's adoption of a disembodied and totally detached narrative voice. Remembering his short-lived career as a medical student, he adopted the clinical tone of a surgeon observing and commenting on his patient's (i.e. George's) reactions. The result, as Isherwood observed, is that he has invented 'a very close third person; almost an old man of the sea sitting on the character's shoulders'.[27] Combined with his use of the historic present this unusual narrative technique simultaneously manages to render, often comically, George's frantic time-bound struggles to survive and yet to view him *sub specie aeternitatis*. The tone is equally dual purpose, combining clinical detachment, as David Daiches noted, 'with a touch of sharply disciplined compassion'.[28]

Consequently Isherwood remains completely in control of his material and is able to parallel George's quixotic changes of mood and behaviour with appropriate changes in tone and style. 'I wanted', he has said, 'to give the feeling of the rhythm of a day in a man's life, the feeling that there are different passages with different tempi.'[29] He has used this analogy to a musical composition or tone-poem more than once when discussing *A Single Man*. George's harangue to Cynthia in the faculty dining room was built up from a few suggestions in the Mexican fantasy he wrote into what he has called 'a sort of aria'.[30] Similarly the fortissimo language used during the scene in which George and Kenny go swimming at night 'becomes quite hysterical—deliberately so'.[31] And yet, despite the much greater variety of styles to be found in *A Single Man* than perhaps anywhere else in his oeuvre, he appears completely in control throughout. Judged in technical terms the book is almost flawless; in artistic terms it remains among the finest of his achievements. *A Single Man* could yet become, what Gavin Lambert has forecast, as legendary as *The Berlin Stories*.[32]

25

Between Two Worlds:
A Meeting by the River

Just before Christmas 1963 Isherwood accompanied Prabhavananda, at the Swami's urging, on a flying visit to Calcutta where they were celebrating Vivekananda's centenary. He stayed at the chief monastery of the Belur Math order on the Ganges. As his contribution to the celebration, he gave a talk in English to a crowd of thousands most of whom understood nothing of what he was saying. Also during his stay John Yale and another American from Los Angeles took their final monastic vows. It was very much a duty visit. Yet on the plane back to Rome, where he stopped off to see Gore Vidal, the idea came to him of incorporating the basic confrontation underlying the rejected Mexican fantasy novel into the setting he had just witnessed. One of his characters could be on the point of taking his final vows in a monastery on the Ganges where he is visited by his polar opposite, rather like Christ and Satan in the wilderness, or like Paul and Peter in the original version of the Mexican fantasy.

By 24 January he was back at Santa Monica where he awaited the arrival of Tony Richardson who held out the prospect of some much-needed film work. Meanwhile he completed the final typescript of what he called his 'weary old *Ramakrishna and his Disciples* . . . a necessary work of popular biographical journalism'.[1] He had felt cramped throughout by the fact that the Ramakrishna Order had sanctioned it, vetting its accuracy chapter by chapter. Ramakrishna, as far as Isherwood was concerned, was a figure inseparable from camp and camp could hardly be incorporated in an 'official' life. During the summer he continued to tinker with the final version, mainly, he told Upward, to 'suck out some of the sweetness and switch off some of the light'.[2]

That February he was also prompted into undertaking an anthology of his uncollected articles and stories by an offer from an English enthusiast of his work to edit such a volume for him. As Isherwood told his English publisher, he had long had in mind the idea of such a collection, to be linked by a series of autobiographical passages—which necessitated his undertaking the editing himself. Typically for him he envisaged his book of odds and ends as an addition to his many works of partial autobiography, a collection of exhibits from his past which with morbid humour he decided to call *Exhumations*.

He was destined to work on *Exhumations* in his spare moments because in March Tony Richardson engaged him to collaborate with Terry Southern on the filmscript of Evelyn Waugh's *The Loved One*. It was a relief to be back in the bustle of the studios, especially as Isherwood thoroughly enjoyed working for Tony Richardson. When the film was being shot later that year he also played a bit part in it as a mourner of the strangulated John Gielgud. By July he was at work writing an entire screenplay for Richardson based on Carson McCullers's *Reflections in a Golden Eye*. Because the book was so fully visualised it lent itself to the screen with little alteration. By September he had finished it and spent the following four months writing a further screenplay for Richardson, an adaptation of Marguerite Duras's *Le Marin de Gibraltar* which Jeanne Moreau had persuaded him to direct with her in the lead role.

None of these three projects proved successful for Isherwood. *The Loved One* received a poor press when it was released the following year. John Russell Taylor in *Sight and Sound* attributed its failure to the conflict between the Southern—Isherwood script 'written . . . as a roaring farcical burlesque' and Richardson's direction of it 'as straight social satire'.[3] When Richardson decided not to direct *Reflections in a Golden Eye* John Huston was engaged as director and commissioned another script. As for *The Sailor from Gibraltar*, this was an unmitigated disaster for which Richardson accepted responsibility. Isherwood had doubts about its suitability from the start, which is perhaps why Richardson brought in Don Magner to help him alter the script when it was being shot the following year.

That spring Isherwood met the young David Hockney through a mutual friend. Both of them were artists and homosexuals

from the north of England who loved California. 'We hit it
off', Hockney has said, from the start.[4] Since 1964 Hockney
has become one of Isherwood's and Bachardy's closer friends,
sharing holidays with them during which he obsessively photographs them and everything else of interest, painting them and
being himself drawn by Bachardy, and matching Isherwood's
camp wit with his own zanier form of camp humour. Don
Bachardy was in the meantime continuing his successful career
as an artist, with a one-man show at the Banfer Gallery in New
York that autumn.

For Christmas 1964 Isherwood and Bachardy went to New
Mexico to watch the Indians' celebrated deer dance. January
was spent completing the film script of *The Sailor from Gibraltar*
and also finishing *Exhumations* in which he refused to improve
on his occasional writing from the past, however bad he felt
it to be, since he saw the entire collection as 'a sort of True
Confessions'.[5] The reason for the rush was that in February
he began a semester at UCLA as Regents' Professor, chiefly
reading students' manuscripts and commenting on them individually, but also delivering a series of lectures expanding
on his Berkeley series of 1963 which were to help shape *Kathleen
and Frank*, a future project that he frequently mentions in his
correspondence at this time.

In April 1965 *Ramakrishna and his Disciples* was published. It
is significant that it was the only book he wrote which he didn't
send to Upward and he was in a state of some trepidation when
it appeared. He told his UCLA students that all he had attempted
to do was to write 'a popular biography that summarises a
whole lot of material that you can find elsewhere, but . . . very
badly needed rearranging and summarising'.[6] Although he confesses his own lack of partiality in the first chapter he still
manages to display a rather naïve credulity in the accuracy of
his two principal sources who, he claims, reproduced the 'words
and deeds Ramakrishna indubitably spoke and did' (p 1). The
tone represented here by the presence of 'indubitably' elicited
mainly polite but sceptical responses from the critics. Malcolm
Muggeridge conceded that 'it is still a pleasure to read him,
even on this out-of-the-way subject, whose treatment has forced
him to accept more or less at their face value the pious reminiscences of Ramakrishna's disciples.'[7] Frank Kermode commented

bitingly that 'it matters less as an account of the saint than as a hint of what it is that comes over Hindu thought when it moves west.'[8] Isherwood also chose to use a style deliberately reminiscent of the St James' Bible, perhaps to help his western readers feel more at home. John Whitehead, who liked the book, nevertheless admitted that it 'at times read like a version of the New Testament written by the author of Kim'.[9] 'Yes', Isherwood admitted to the Beesleys after reading the reviews, 'the book was a chore and I offered it up, fairly gladly, but chiefly glad to have finished it.'[10]

During his term as visiting professor at UCLA Isherwood also managed to get started on the first draft of his last novel to date, *A Meeting by the River*. In May he told the Beesleys: 'It is very experimental (for me) because it is entirely told in letters and a diary.' He was fascinated by the technical problems this new form presented, reporting that currently 'the number of offstage characters—ie people the one brother writes to—is in danger of increasing alarmingly.'[11] After describing to John Lehmann the plot, which is loosely reminiscent of the situation in *Les Liaisons Dangereuses*, he added, 'Doesn't that sound like the least-likely-to-succeed story of the year?'[12] Behind his obvious enjoyment in writing the book can perhaps be detected a conviction that within a fictional framework he would have the freedom of expression that he had had to deny himself when treating the subject of Hinduism in his life of Ramakrishna. By the end of June he had finished the first rough draft and put it aside for a month. Between August and October he wrote a complete second draft, structurally similar to the published book but still somewhat raw in its psychological handling of the two brothers' relationship (it ends, for instance, with the bald realisation on Oliver's part: 'I love my Brother').[13] In mid-October he sent his second draft to Upward for his comments.

The summer of 1965 had been marred for Isherwood by the riots in the black ghetto of Watts. Although a member of the American Civil Liberties Union, he felt powerless in the face of the growing tide of violence in America the root cause of which lay in the Vietnamese war. Since he undertook another semester's teaching as a visiting professor at the Riverside campus of the University of California in the spring of 1966 he couldn't help but identify with his students' fear and anger at their enforced participation in the war. 'Most are just disgustingly resigned', he told John Whitehead. 'It makes you sick at heart to listen to them and feel so unable to help.'[14]

The teaching stint slowed down the writing of the third and final draft of the novel which he had begun work on in December 1965 after receiving Upward's criticisms of the second draft. Upward suggested that Patrick appeared to be undermined in his efforts to convert Oliver from his religious calling by a lack of determination in pursuing his purpose. Isherwood responded by heightening the tension between the two brothers and postponing Oliver's dream vision to the confrontation scene after Tom's drunken phone call when Patrick almost succeeds in diverting Oliver from his chosen course—a scene which he completely re-wrote. Towards the end of June the third draft was completed and sent off, first to John Yale (now a Swami) for his professional advice as someone who had taken his final vows like Patrick, then to Upward. At Upward's suggestion he added a paragraph in Oliver's second letter to Patrick which pre-dates Oliver's doubts and despair about his life of social dedication to before his meeting with the Swami. Within a month it had been accepted by both his publishers without requests for any significant alterations.

Ostensibly *A Meeting by the River* describes a confrontation between two representative figures who hold utterly opposed sets of values. Patrick revels in the world and the flesh; Oliver renounces it. Patrick is an atheist; Oliver believes in God. Patrick is the personification of the ego; Oliver views his with humorous distaste. Yet to see the book simply in terms of dichotomies is a falsification of Isherwood's subtle presentation of his two protagonists. For a start the two are brothers locked until the finale in a love-hate relationship that emphasises their similarities far more than their differences. Each, for example, claims to detect in the other signs of weariness from the pursuit of his chosen path of life (pp 50–1 and 57). Being brothers, heredity, as Oliver observes, has made them 'part of the same circuit' (p 95). Their differences, such as they are, are attributed to the roles their mother tried to impose on them and are consequently less deep-seated, at least in Isherwood's view. Because of their common heritage each shares more of the other's characteristics than at first either dares admit. 'At moments', Oliver writes, 'I can actually feel and think like him, and that scares me, of course. I get afraid that I'll start behaving like him and lose my identity altogether' (p 95).

At least one reviewer at the time—Stanley Kauffman—suggested that the entire book 'can be seen as a symbolic mono-drama: within one man', an interpretation that has since been echoed by Francis King and others.[15] In psychological terms both share a common fixation with a parental archetype. In Patrick's case it is the mother. 'I see Patrick', Isherwood wrote to the Beesleys, 'as an arrested juvenile who has married a mother-figure. His homosexuality is really only his way of trying to escape into a world, a still juvenile world, outside the safety of mother-marriage.'[16] John Gross has made the parallel suggestion that 'Oliver is a son in search of an ideal father, casting the Swami for the role in which earlier mentors . . . have failed.'[17] But this doesn't necessarily imply that both brothers share the same identity. Isherwood expresses the matter in different terms when he shows within the space of two pages first Patrick and then Oliver discovering within themselves the dual nature of their identity. Each has a vain monkey-like ego which performs tricks that pass for reality (just as Patrick mimics others). But each also has another half which, as even Patrick confesses, 'watches and is merely curious to see what'll happen' (p 93). Within the perspective of Vedanta philosophy the ego is what separates the individual from the fundamental Reality that embraces all individuals, whereas the detached self is virtually undifferentiated from other detached selves. In their separate ways both brothers turn out to be searching for a sense of unity with others, and, more especially, with each other.

Brotherhood, as Isherwood has pointed out on more than one occasion, is a dominant metaphor in *A Meeting by the River*.[18] Patrick admits to Tom, his latest lover, that he has been searching for a brother all his adult life (p 109), ever since, in fact, he and Oliver grew apart during their childhood. In this search he embodies Tom in a Whitmanesque dream of brotherhood between men which he elaborates in the 'vision' he has of a shared future life without taboos. This 'vision' of his is paralleled by Oliver's vision in which he becomes mystically united with his Swami—and Patrick: 'I was aware', Oliver writes, 'that he was an established part of our life, the three of us belonged together intimately and I accepted this as a matter of course' (p 146). Oliver has chosen the brotherhood of fellow-monks, Patrick that of male lovers. But both are inspired by an identical desire for an ideal of universal brotherhood that will transcend the limitations of the everyday ego. What each brother does for the other is to help overcome the neuroses which have prevented them from meeting each other in a spirit of love, whether human or supra-human. Thanks to Patrick, Isherwood explained to one correspondent, Oliver 'overcomes the feelings of inferiority and jealousy which he has always been plagued with, feelings which have caused him to doubt'.[19] Thanks to Oliver, Patrick is able to understand his mother-fixated behaviour. In his final letter to Penelope he sees in their life together the possibility of 'safety and freedom', just as Oliver sees in his life in the monastery safety and freedom of a different kind.

It would be wrong, however, to leave the impression that the confrontation between the brothers is entirely illusory. Their very similarities place Patrick in the position of offering a genuine threat to the foundations of Oliver's new-found Hindu beliefs. Isherwood has said of the novel that 'in pattern it alludes to the temptations of Jesus in the wilderness'[20]—which imbues Patrick with self-confessed satanic qualities. But his temptations are effective precisely because he represents characteristics also inherent in Oliver. As Oliver admits to himself Patrick is 'a monster I've raised up' (p 44), an able spokesman for the lures of the life of the ego. Just as Satan tempts Jesus, after his fast of forty days and nights, to turn stones into bread, Patrick urges Oliver to attend more to his bodily needs, and further offers him the temptations of the flesh when he exercises naked before him. Patrick's most powerful temptation, however, comes towards the end of the book when he diagnoses qualities of leadership in Oliver that make it inevitable, in his view, that Oliver will become pre-eminent in whatever field he chooses to put his energies into. This, of course, parallels Satan's offer to give Jesus power over all the kingdoms of the world.

The outcome of this trial of strength is intended to be left in doubt. Isherwood has described the book as 'like a trial in which all the evidence is presented on both sides, but there's no verdict. . . . Both parties leave the court . . . with a feeling that they've won the case.'[21] In other words Oliver is convinced that Patrick is spiritually saved by being under the Swami's protection even though he doesn't realise it, just as Patrick is convinced that Oliver will eventually abandon his vocation as a monk in favour of the role of a Gandhi or a Nehru. Seen in terms of a conflict, neither wins but both are changed. Or, at least, that is Isherwood's intention. He has even gone so far as to claim that, if anything, he is far more Patrick than he is Oliver.[22] Nevertheless most readers cannot avoid the impression that the author has stacked the cards in Oliver's favour. He is given the final word. Moreover his standpoint is endorsed by the various swamis. Because their beliefs, as Alan Wilde has pointed out, are never called into question 'an affirmation is clearly intended',[23] an affirmation of Vedanta.

The episode of Oliver's 'vision' also tends to give added narrative authority to his viewpoint. Not that this was Isherwood's intention. He deliberately handled the entire incident in such a way that the reader could either believe that some form of divine visitation had occurred or could simply attribute it to self-delusion on Oliver's part. As he explained to Upward, there should be no authorial intervention at any point: 'This novel must be rigorously subjective throughout.'[24] 'Artistically speaking', he later elaborated, 'no final philosophical statements are being made here, on either side; all that is being presented is an interplay of opposing attitudes and personalities.'[25] In Hindu eyes *sub specie aeternitatis* neither side can be in the right since God is not interested in man's righteousness or his sins. But the average Western reader, bringing his Christian prejudices with him, is bound to interpret Oliver's vision as an endorsement of his viewpoint which is by no means counter-balanced by Patrick's 'vision', a vision which is at any rate negated later in the novel by his rejection of Tom. In fact, as John Gross observed when reviewing the book, 'the psychological patterns of the story are worked out more energetically than the spiritual design.'[26]

On balance one has to admit that the novel as a whole is badly flawed. Theoretically the use of letters by the chameleon-like Patrick and diary entries by the introspective Oliver is highly appropriate. In practice, however, the epistolary form often seems the least natural form of expression for Patrick, the jet-age executive used to the conveniences of modern telecommunications. Worse still, Patrick's letters are frequently characterised by what Gerald Sykes called a 'gushiness' that 'does himself and Mr Isherwood a genuine disservice each time he takes his pen in hand.'[27] He not only acts but reports himself as acting towards Oliver like a gauche schoolgirl, apologising for touching him on the arm, lying unconvincingly, inventing excuses for telling his wife—what she must already have known—Oliver's early history, and even providing explanations for various Hindu practices when he is supposed to be utterly opposed to all 'this languid supercilious oriental negativism' (p 87). Oliver too at times adopts a false chumminess in his dealings with Patrick and tends to treat his loyalty to his new-found religion with the immaturity of a public school boy supporting a bad home team.

One might be tempted to attribute this ring of insincerity to Isherwood's attempt to treat his religious subject matter with humour (an application of what Gerald Heard called 'meta-comedy'), were it not for the fact that this comic element assumes far greater prominence in the dramatised version of the novel that he and Bachardy wrote in 1968, which is a considerable artistic improvement over the novel. Isherwood himself told W. I. Scobie that he thought the play 'far more realised than the book: it plays out the undecided duel between the two brothers more intensely, and so the nature of the comedy comes out more clearly.'[28] Although it has been produced in the States, the play remains unpublished to date. It certainly reads as less gauche, tighter and more effective for the device the authors employ throughout of bringing all the characters including the Mother, Penelope and Tom on stage, irrespective of geographical distances, where they talk directly at each other. In this way the play is able to expose the ineffectuality of Patrick's epistolary lies, where the novel gives the impression that they were swallowed whole by their recipients. For example in the Second Act Patrick reads out part of his letter to his mother who is listening on stage and commenting aloud on what he says/ writes to her:

PATRICK—I only hope that Oliver's complicated meditations will bring him the same serene happiness that you've found by simply leading a normal and natural life.

MOTHER—How *dare* he talk to me about happiness! I'm full of hate, and I'm old and I'm lonely.[29]

At another point in the play the Mother and Penelope take turns at reading out utterly conflicting reports from Patrick on Oliver's condition.

At the same time the play further tips the balance of the scales in Oliver's direction. His vision is represented by an objective change in the stage lighting, first darkening almost to blackness then slowly flooding with light, followed by Oliver's assertion 'Yes. I saw him. He was here, right beside me.' Patrick's future salvation is also made that much more of a certainty, partly by Penelope's and the Mother's reaction to the news that Oliver has become a monk ('We're all saved!'), partly by the crisis about to overtake Patrick when he finds Tom waiting for him in Singapore, the first of many incidents ahead that are destined to make him dissatisfied with his chosen way of life now that he is, as Oliver claims, 'in a state of grace'. Oliver might be deluded about this, but the play endorses his opinion. Strangely enough this imbalance might have been less obvious had Oliver been able to counter-tempt Patrick to turn Hindu (and ostensibly fail); but the nature of Hindu belief prevents Oliver from attempting any form of direct conversion. Nonetheless the play does work more satisfactorily as a meta-comedy ending with both brothers and the swamis all laughing at the cosmic joke in which they have participated.

In 1973 Isherwood and Bachardy rewrote the play for the first of a number of times as a filmscript. Forced to abandon the expressionist form of the stage-play for the more naturalistic conventions of the cinema, they brought all the characters to India, Tom as Patrick's assistant camera-man, Penelope flying out to persuade Oliver to stay in the monastery (rather than leave it, the usual female role in a celibate's life) to keep their love pure. Calcutta was to feature as the principal setting, held in balance with the foreground drama. For instance Oliver has his vision in bed in a Calcutta hotel where he sees himself and Patrick sitting beside the dead swami on his seat, an image of the insignificance of good and evil in the face of the knowledge of Reality.[30] To date the film, like so many of Isherwood's other scripts, remains unmade. But he has plans to publish both the play and the filmscript together one day. Until then *A Meeting by the River* can only be assessed in its fictional form which might well come to be seen as an early, not entirely satisfactory draft of its subsequent metamorphosis for stage and screen.

26

Towards Autobiography:
Kathleen and Frank

Almost as soon as he had finished writing the final draft of
A Meeting by the River Isherwood was offered his first television
assignment in July 1966 writing part of the script for an ABC
Christmas Special for Daniel Mann, the director, who was a
friend. He was asked to concoct a story about how the carol
'Silent Night' came to be written in 1818 for the church at
Arnsdorf-Salzach, Austria, as a fill-in when the organ broke
down. The work entailed an expenses-paid trip to Austria
where the film was to be shot. After working for ten days there
on the film, he spent the whole of October in England. He
stayed for most of the time in Cheshire with his brother Richard
sorting through his parents' letters. During the remainder of
his stay he looked up many of his old friends whom he had not
seen since 1961, including Forster and Spender with whom he
stayed. But he had to fly back to California at the beginning of
November to complete the filmscript. In the event almost all
of his contribution was cut in favour of some sentimental footage
showing Kirk Douglas talking to children of all nationalities
who then sang 'Silent Night' outside, needless to say, the United
Nations building. Furious, Isherwood tried unsuccessfull
have his name removed from the cre

In November *Cabaret*, the
Camera, with Joel Grey, L
in New York. Isherwood
script to the producer,
his own team of writers
bodings were realised when
was being provided with a
'Christopher' was to hav

pregnant by him. He took the advice of his friends and never went to see this malformed offspring of his original invention. To add insult to injury it was discovered that the producer of *I am a Camera* hadn't been paid for her share of the royalties from the stage play, thus reducing his own share in *Cabaret* to about 0.4 per cent.

After spending Christmas in Santa Monica at a long succession of parties given by Tony Richardson and Vanessa Redgrave, and Rex Harrison and his wife, Isherwood started work on the first draft of his long-planned autobiographical book. The idea for the book originated with his Santa Barbara lectures in 1960 called 'The Writer and his World' which he re-structured at Berkeley in 1963 as 'The Autobiography of My Books' and expanded in 1965 at UCLA. That year he explained to one correspondent that the autobiography was to be 'a sort of Jungian study of the main characters in my mythology, as opposed to the real people in my life', which he thought of calling 'Hero-Father, Demon-Mother'.[1] Apart from his two parental figures, some of the subjects from his personal mythology which he had in mind for the book were 'the Home-image, the romance of distant places, loneliness, homosexuality, the cult of being an Outsider, the anti-Hero, Vedanta as anti-Religion, High Camp, etc.'[2]

The main reason for his visit to England in October 1966 was to read through his father's letters to his mother which she and then his brother had preserved intact. They convinced him that his parents, his brother and he were all part of the same weave. So, regardless of the inevitable complications, he decided to try writing the book entirely in the present tense, moving backwards and forwards in time to demonstrate how his parents' actions and personalities reflected themselves in the behaviour of h⋯ ⋯ his brother.[3] In between correcting ⋯ nd writing an introduction to ⋯ ures, *Religion in Practice*, he ⋯ ring.

⋯ would have to return to ⋯ of the story. Gradually ⋯ ecoming subordinated to the ⋯ due to the wealth of material ⋯ house when he returned to

England that May. He spent most of his time sorting through the family archives, but took time off to attend a pre-publication reception laid on by his publishers and to pay fleeting visits to some of his friends, including Forster and Joe Ackerley who died just before Isherwood left for California on 9 June.

For the next year and a quarter he settled down to the laborious —one might say masochistic—task of copying out and editing his mother's diaries and his father's letters which he had brought back with him. By the time he had finished what he called this 'spade work', he had become convinced that 'the source-material is really very good and shouldn't be too much jazzed up.'[4] The book had moved that much further along the spectrum from autobiography to biography. The arduous editorial task was also prolonged by the need to make money when opportunities offered themselves. In 1968 he was involved in writing a dramatised adaptation of Bernard Shaw's story 'The Adventures of the Black Girl in Her Search for God' which was produced early the following year at the Mark Taper Forum, an experimental theatre in Los Angeles, where it ran for a respectable period and was reviewed favourably by the *L A Times*. He was also adapting, at Anthony Page's request, Wedekind's two Lulu plays, *Earth Spirit* and *Pandora's Box* for possible production at the Royal Court Theatre, London. His major commitment in the second half of 1968, apart from the book, was the adaptation of *A Meeting by the River* with Don Bachardy for possible stage production in America.

One catches glimpses of his social persona during this period. In 1967 Auden came to stay with him and Isherwood was delighted to find that 'underneath the great structure of his public image the friend was still absolutely there.'[5] His relations with Auden had always been complex, more personal, emotional and volatile than with any of his other friends from his youth, with the possible exception of Spender. 'Somehow', he now reflected, 'I've failed to grow old monumentally like Wystan. His face really belongs in the British Museum.'[6] Isherwood saw much of Stravinsky during his closing years. He was one of Stravinsky's few surviving close friends, addressing him as 'Igor' unlike almost everyone else but his wife, getting drunk with him or falling asleep in front of the television while Stravinsky listened to some of his music with Robert Craft, and periodically leavening the more serious conversation with his deflationary wit ('like a supervisory imp, more often mischievous than demolishing' according to Lillian Libman).[7] He also saw much of David Hockney, especially in the spring and summer of 1968 when he was painting his celebrated portrait of Isherwood and Bachardy at home. When Bachardy was away in London for two months Isherwood would frequently drop round at Hockney's studio, five minutes away, where he confessed on one occasion how much he was missing Bachardy, but also expressed his determination never to become possessive of him.[8]

In October 1968 Isherwood began writing *Kathleen and Frank*, a task that, because of interruptions and a certain natural antipathy on his part to the composition of all forms of non-fiction, took him until the end of 1970 to complete. 'I now see how to write it', he told Upward after he had started it. 'Christopher is a character exactly like the others, and the author is a sort of don, sifting evidence and following clues and annotating diary and letter quotations with historical asides.'[9] Interrupted first by the production of the Shaw adaptation and then by the need to write the film story of *Cabaret* (for producers who, when they ran out of money, transferred the property to new producers who commissioned a different script), the book was about a third-written by the summer of 1969. On 20 July 1969 Isherwood and Bachardy flew to Australia, via Tahiti, Bora Bora, Samoa and New Zealand to discuss with Tony Richardson the screen-play he wanted them to write for his next projected film to be based on Robert Graves's *I, Claudius* and *Claudius the God*. They returned to Santa Monica within a month and worked non-stop on the script until early November when they sent it off to Richardson. However, nothing more came of the project, although they were paid for the work they did.

Another abortive project brought Isherwood to London from February to April of 1970. Clifford Williams proposed staging *A Meeting by the River* if the authors could expand it. Both Isherwood and Bachardy worked frantically to produce the necessary additional scenes. Bachardy had to fly back in mid-February for a show of his work in Los Angeles, but Isherwood remained until the end of April when it became certain that the production would have to be postponed. During his stay he managed to snatch a few days in the south of France with David Hockney who preferred to keep out of the way until his retrospective exhibition opened at the Whitechapel Gallery. He also saw a number of his friends for the last time, unbeknown to him—Robert Moody, Jean Ross and E. M. Forster (who didn't even recognise him at first when he visited him in his rooms at Cambridge).[10] When Forster died that summer he left Isherwood the rights in *Maurice*, his long-suppressed homosexual novel. In accordance with Forster's wishes, Isherwood promptly made over the royalties earned by the book to the National Institute of Arts and Letters in the States for the establishment of a fund to help British writers to visit America. Gerald Hamilton, whom Isherwood had helped bail out from another of his recurrent financial crises as recently as 1967, also died that summer.[11]

Back in California Isherwood, determined to finish *Kathleen and Frank*, spent his main energies writing the last half of the book between May and November of 1970. Although he had reduced his typed-out extracts from his parents' letters and diaries to one tenth of their size, it was still extremely long, about 370 typewritten pages, and he was not in the least surprised when his English agent suggested that it would need cutting. Eventually he did condense the elaboration of the number of obstacles which his parents had encountered to their proposed marriage. By January 1971 the revisions were completed. The book was published in England that October and in the States the following January.

In order to maintain a satisfactory distance from a subject in which he was intimately involved Isherwood adopted the egalitarian convention of calling all his characters by their Christian names and referring to all of them in the third person including the earlier self. As a result, he told Thomas Lask, he almost felt as if he were dealing with characters in fiction— 'fascinating but a little remote.'[12] Simultaneously the present-day narrator of the book, who never admits to having any connection with the character of Christopher, adopts what Isherwood has called 'a sort of anonymous professor voice'.[13] In many ways it is an ingenious device for telling his own family story. But there is an element of self-delusion in his claim to treat Christopher, like all the other characters, 'entirely from the outside'.[14] Much of the information with which the narrator supplies us about Christopher's feelings implies, indeed depends on, a sense of identity between past and present selves. Consequently wherever this sense of identity becomes apparent in the book the reader's attention is drawn to the artificiality of the narrator's donnish pose and to a coyness in his refusal to admit any kind of common identity between himself and Christopher. As Frederick Raphael has suggested, his arch references to himself in the third person are rather 'like a self-effacing Caesar'.[15]

The other narrative device which Isherwood employs for the book is that of a double time scheme and this works brilliantly. The story of his mother's and father's life is told through their letters and her diary in a strictly chronological fashion. Chapter I uses her spasmodically-kept 1883 diary as an introduction to the book. Chapters 2 to 17 cover the period 1891 when his mother started regularly keeping a diary to 1915 when his father was killed in the war, followed by seven additional pages of diary extracts up to 1919 to show how fixated she had become in the past. Chapter 18 briefly covers the rest of his mother's long life up to 1960, and an Afterword enables Isherwood to examine the extent to which Christopher's character is inherited from his parents and family. Simultaneously there is an editorial commentary that deliberately jumps backwards and forwards in time to enable him to draw the parallels and conclusions that make the book break outside the conventions normally observed by biographies. Within the first two pages he has already revealed the fact that his father died in 1915 and that his mother lived to a ripe old age. Isherwood described it as 'a somewhat Proustian kind of structure because the past is literally recaptured and certain things that were already stated at the beginning of the book are restated at the end.'[16]

With the help of this double time scheme Isherwood is able to add two additional dimensions to his biography—those of social history and of autobiography. As he explained to his American publisher, it is not simply a love-story, but 'a *period* love-story, in that Kathleen and Frank take the attitudes of their class and express the ideas of their period—the sense of duty, the snobbery, the inhibitions, the romanticism, the conservatism.'[17] As a Jamesian study of late Victorian and Edwardian England the book makes fascinating reading and offers numerous small but genuinely revealing insights into what one reviewer called 'the mores, the staggering blindnesses, the hypocrisies and the blessed stability of an era when to be well-off and equipped with anesthetized social conscience enabled a minority of British folk to direct their entire nervous energy toward self-indulgence on a truly monumental scale.'[18] Any reader in the 1970s has been conditioned to accept generalisations of this kind, but the type of social commentary Isherwood provides arises from historically verifiable minutiae and allows his reader to form his own more sensitively registered conclusions. When Kathleen, for instance, writes in her diary, 'la cuisine dit que sa homme veut beaucoup le marie dans septembre', the narrator immediately explains: 'The habit of speaking French (usually as incorrect as the above) to conceal information from the servants was a characteristic vulgarity of the period' (p 250). The book is full of such telling insights. It also contains informative asides on Whistler's introduction to England of 'Japonisme' from France, Oscar Wilde's trial, Roentgen's discovery of X-rays, the revival of interest in El Greco, Harold Monroe's Poetry Bookshop, Shackleton's expedition to the Antarctic, as well as considerable background information on the Boer War, the Irish situation and the opening stages of the First World War.

The editorial commentary also enables Isherwood to make comparisons between past and present, principally in order to demonstrate 'how heredity and kinship create a woven fabric', as he claims in the Afterword. 'Christopher has found that he is far more closely interwoven with Kathleen and Frank than he had supposed, or liked to believe' (p 363). In fact, he has since explained, he was amazed at how his empathy with his parents helped him to read between the lines of his parents' letters and diaries so that the concepts underlying the book virtually declared themselves.[19] Isherwood was himself sixty-seven by the time the book was published which meant that he could view atemporally two, sometimes three generations of the family and discern patterns of heredity in them with some confidence. To a great extent he saw most of his feline and artistic instincts originating in his father, as well as his father's interest in eastern religion. What he claims to have derived from his mother's side of the family is 'a counter-force which gave him strength' (p 361). Elsewhere he has justified this idea that one can inherit as much by opposition to a parent as by imitation by reference to Vedanta philosophy which claims that the physical world is composed of three forces or 'gunas', the inspiration, the principle of force and the principle of inertia or resistance.[20] Kathleen provides the necessary resistance to impel him into opposing motion. It is a dubious argument, since it provides him with virtually a *carte-blanche* to trace everything he chooses to see as characteristic of himself either to its similarity or its dissimilarity to one of his parents.

To some extent he counters such an objection by demonstrating how his youthful opposition to his mother's cult of the Past not only depended on powers of obstinacy which he had inherited from her but also resolved itself in his old age into a parallel cult of the Past—his and hers. For *Kathleen and Frank* is almost as much about its author as it is about his parents. He suggests as much himself in the final paragraph when he reminds the reader of Kathleen's diary entry about her five-year-old son: 'After tea, C dictated a story called *The Adventures of Mummy and Daddy*, chiefly about himself!' (p 247). Isherwood has recently claimed that the book 'is really autobiography', principally 'because it's all explanations about why I am the way I am'.[21] The original idea of writing 'The Autobiography of My Books' still survives, severely repressed, in its biographical offspring.

The kind of autobiography Isherwood had in mind was heavily influenced by Jung's own autobiography, *Memories, Dreams, Reflections* in which he explains in the Prologue that his intention is to tell his personal myth: 'I can only make direct statements, only "tell stories". Whether or not the stories are "true" is not the problem. The only question is whether what I tell is *my* fable, *my* truth.'[22] 'The real truth to the writer', Isherwood has suggested in talking about this passage from Jung, 'is not the same as what actually happens to him. He only uses his experiences to create a myth which corresponds to his inner reality.'[23] In his case the inner reality was that of a son whose widowed mother ostensibly cared more for his dead father than for him, holding him out to her son as a Hero-Father against whom he inevitably rebelled. The rest followed naturally. 'By denying your duty toward the Hero-Father you deny the authority of the Flag, the Old School Tie, the Unknown Soldier, The Land That Bore You and the God of Battles' (p 357). Later he sought to reconcile himself to his father by turning him into an 'Anti-Heroic Hero', a figure who appears in disguised fashion in so many of his books: Mr Norris, Bergmann, Ambrose, and E.M. are all paternalistic figures in secret revolt against the establishment. When Isherwood extends the myth backwards in time, however, to embrace his regicidal ancestor, Judge Bradshaw, one gets the impression that he is beginning to make intellectual play with this concept. But the story of his myths has provided him with his principal guideline in selecting and editing his parents' diaries and letters. The shape he has given to *Kathleen and Frank* is as much the result of his own mythopoeic needs as of the need to tell his parents' story.

Perhaps the most telling criticism that has been levelled against the book is Spender's observation that 'in *Kathleen and Frank* the painful effort to be nice about his mother made him less sympathetic than when he was being very nasty about her in *The Memorial*.' Spender has explained that because Isherwood has warmth, 'if he sees a person's faults he's capable of understanding them in a way that ultimately puts them in a sympathetic light.'[24] Equally, because he is, however unconsciously, attempting to lessen or excuse his mother's faults in *Kathleen and Frank* she loses part of her humanity in the portrait he draws of her in his editorial comments. He also claims for her diaries a literary status and level of interest beyond anything that the extracts he provides afford. To suggest that 'she could invest minor domestic events with an epic quality' (p 2) is to devalue the traditional meaning of 'epic', just as to call her diary 'her masterpiece' (p 2) implies the presence of exceptional powers of observation on her part, whereas, as Auden observed in reviewing the book, in fact 'her remarks are too typical of her class to be considered her own'.[25] One also tends to side with the young Christopher who was enraged by Kathleen's description of a book as 'soothing' (p 19) as opposed to the elderly benevolent narrator who appears to regard this habit of hers from the perspective of the present as a mere foible. Surely Christopher was right in thinking that it betrayed 'Kathleen's subconscious contempt for all literature', in which case the author, a professional writer, still ought to find the adjective offensive.

Kathleen and Frank is a book in which Isherwood attempts to reconcile himself with his parents, what Angus Wilson has called 'an act of empathy designed to atone for a lifetime of rebellion'.[26] In seeking to forgive them he is simultaneously seeking forgiveness for himself. Obviously the temptation to draw an over-indulgent portrait of his parents was inherent in the undertaking. But the ingenious structure he has invented for himself has largely saved him from this pitfall. Perhaps he is overly kind to his biographical subjects at times, but this is only natural. Perhaps he has allowed himself the luxury of prolixity under the mistaken impression that what is obviously fascinating to him must be of similar interest to the reader. The fact remains that *Kathleen and Frank* is so much more than a personal memoir, that it tells us about attitudes and patterns of life during a crucial period of English history as well as providing fascinating insights into a writer's personal mythology, none of which would have been possible without the firm control Isherwood exercised over the tone and format of his material by means uniquely his own.

27

The Seventies: *Christopher and his Kind*

With *Kathleen and Frank* off his hands, Isherwood once again turned to Hollywood for work. Through Hunt Stromberg Jr, the producer, he and Don Bachardy were commissioned by Universal Studios to write a television script about Frankenstein. They began work in February 1971, assured by Stromberg that they would have a free hand in the treatment and casting of the teleplay. Isherwood and Bachardy drastically altered Mary Shelley's version, turning it into a romantic melodrama by making the creature beautiful at first so that his creator, instead of immediately running away from him in horror, enters into a father–son or near homosexual relationship with him.[1] 'It's a very touching relationship', Isherwood wrote, 'and is really a fable about birth control and the generation gap.'[2] Completed by September, the project was destined to be sabotaged in various ways—requests for additional material, the choice of Jack Smight as director and Leonard Whiting as Frankenstein in place of John Boorman and Jon Voight, the author's nominees, and finally cuts and rewrites over which they had no control. Before this had become apparent, however, Isherwood and Bachardy accepted a further commission in January 1972 to write an Egyptian thriller for Universal Television called 'The Lady from the Land of the Dead', a modern story of reincarnation which again took them till September to complete and which, although paid for, was never made.[3]

Meanwhile Isherwood was spending his time reconstructing his journals for the period 1945–53 when he only kept the sparsest of an events diary, unlike the war years during which he had kept a detailed journal which he had written up, almost in finished book form, shortly afterwards. 'This has incidentally got me into sexual memoirs', he told Upward, '—an attempt, influenced by Jung, to explore one's personal sexual mythology and identify one's sexual archetypes.'⁴ Out of these memoirs was eventually to emerge the idea for *Christopher and his Kind*.

During 1971 two of his closest friends in California died, Stravinsky and Gerald Heard. Michael Barrie reports that at exactly the time Stravinsky died in New York Heard, instead of going to sleep as usual, tried but couldn't speak to Barrie but lay gazing fixedly over his shoulder with a look of concern.⁵ Heard himself died in Santa Monica four months later after his thirty-first stroke, having undergone a slow decline since 1966.

Isherwood was prevented by an operation on a crooked finger from accepting an offer by Methuen to pay his expenses for a trip to London to coincide with the publication there of *Kathleen and Frank* in October 1971. But he did go to New York early in February 1972 for the book's American launching. He appeared on two major talk-shows and gave a television interview in which he openly talked in public for the first time about his homosexuality. While there he saw a private showing of *Cabaret*, the much-improved film version of the musical for which Liza Minnelli won an Oscar. The final incarnation of Sally Bowles had transformed Isherwood's third-rate actress into a dazzling performer. Between her and Joel Grey, however, Isherwood rightly commented, the cabaret 'would have attracted half of Europe. You wouldn't have been able to get in for months on end.'⁶ During 1972 he and Bachardy were also involved in James Bridges's production of their play, *A Meeting by the River*, which premiered in Los Angeles that April and later was brought briefly to New York as one of the Phoenix Theatre's 'Side-shows' where it was equally well received.

Early in February 1973 both of them were called to England at short notice where *Frankenstein: the true story* was being filmed. After their departure they discovered to their disgust the extent to which the producer and director had altered their script, especially in the second half, while they had been forced to stand idly by because of a strike by the Screen-writers' Guild to which they both belonged. After a brief spell at Pinewood Studios they took the opportunity of visiting Salka Viertel in Switzerland and Gavin Lambert (who had left California the previous year) and Gore Vidal in Rome, Vidal arranging an impromptu champagne party to celebrate Isherwood and Bachardy's twentieth anniversary together.⁷ *Frankenstein* was eventually shown on British and American television and received mainly bad notices. Annoyed at the way they had been treated, Isherwood and Bachardy insisted on the publication of their original filmscript in December 1973 by Avon Books in New York. In 1976 *Frankenstein* won a prize for the best scenario at the International Festival of Fantastic and Science Fiction Films in Paris. Back in Santa Monica they spent much of the summer of 1973 writing the first version of their screenplay of *A Meeting by the River*.

More friends died that year—Jean Ross, Robert Moody, William Plomer, and, the biggest loss, W. H. Auden, the news of whose death on 29 September was rather cruelly sprung on Isherwood by a brisk call from Reuter's wanting an off-the-cuff comment. Perhaps it was the increasing momentum with which so many of his friends were becoming figures of history which stimulated him to begin work on what was to evolve into his next book. In October 1973 he announced that he had embarked on 'another autobiographical book' based on his American diaries of 1939–44. 'Am trying to cut down on mere gossip', he informed Upward, 'and concentrate on a fairly small group of representative characters in different areas.' He added: 'Am at present writing about myself in those days as "Christopher" and saying "I" when I speak as the present-day author.'[8] He appropriated the approach he had adopted in writing up his post-war journals for the new venture: 'My book aims at being rather internal', he told Spender, 'and when I describe people I will try to concentrate on their myths, the myths I made about them.'[9] Within a month he realised that he would have to start his story much earlier than his departure for America in order to explain why he went there: because he had become a chronic wanderer, came the answer, ever since he had taken off to Berlin in 1929 where he began his search for a sexual homeland. This in turn presented him with the problem of reconstructing his life (with the help of his friends) between 1929 and 1939, having destroyed his diaries for this period once he had completed *Goodbye to Berlin*. By May 1974 he had completed a rough draft of the first ten years of a book he still thought might cover 1929–44. But he decided to revise the 1929–39 section first in its final form in order to see whether he would have space for the war period.

The revision went slowly, interrupted by a trip to New Orleans in the spring to lecture there and further work on the screenplay of *A Meeting* after James Ivory had shown interest in it. That August he celebrated his seventieth birthday. 'I must say', he told Upward, 'if I had known when I was 21, that I should be as happy as I am now, I should have been sincerely shocked. They promised me wormwood and the funeral raven.'[10] To celebrate his birthday he broke with his agent, Curtis Brown, in New York, whom he held responsible for the fact that almost all his work apart from the Berlin books was unavailable in the States. He and Bachardy spent the last two weeks of the year in New York where he talked at the Modern Language Association convention on 'Homosexuality and Literature'. Regarded as a daring innovation by the organisers, it actually turned out to be a case of preaching to the converted.

Work on the revision of his autobiography to which he gave the working title of 'Wanderings' was again interrupted during 1975 by a filmscript he wrote with Don Bachardy for NBC Television, an adaption of Scott Fitzgerald's *The Beautiful and the Damned*. Yet again the film was never made because, according to Isherwood, the Scott Fitzgerald vogue suddenly died.[11] By August, when he had completed just over two-thirds of his autobiography for 1929–39, he decided to limit the book to these ten years, partly for reasons of length, partly because, as he explained to the Beesleys, 'the form is different as soon as the American diary starts.'[12] Even then he did not finish the book until early May 1976. *Christopher and his Kind*, as he called this autobiography, was the final product of considerable emotional turmoil for Isherwood who confessed to Carolyn Heilbrun that he couldn't even meditate with the required detachment until the book was completed.[13]

Later that May Isherwood and Bachardy left for London where the National Portrait Gallery had organised an exhibition of Young Writers of the Thirties, including himself. Accompanied by David Hockney, they called on Benjamin Britten (who was already very ill and died the following December) at Aldeburgh. Shortly before his return to California Isherwood was dismayed to learn that Swami Prabhavananda had died on 4 July.

The publication of *Christopher and his Kind*, first in New York in November, then in London in March involved him in another gruelling round of press interviews and appearances on radio and television. But to his mild surprise the book was generally well received on both sides of the Atlantic and had better initial sales than any other book he had written. Because of its frank treatment of his homosexual life he had half-expected the kind of vicious attack which in the event only one or two reviewers such as Rebecca West delivered who denounced the book as 'one long symphony of squalor'.[14] It was rather as he had forecast the year before in a letter announcing its completion: 'Oh, one always thinks one has dropped an H-bomb, and in fact one is lucky if it isn't mistaken for a burst tyre or a car back-firing.'[15]

Isherwood opens *Christopher and his Kind* somewhat misleadingly by claiming that *Lions and Shadows* was not truly autobiographical because it concealed important facts about its author and over-dramatised many episodes, whereas this book 'will be as frank and factual' as he can make it, especially about himself (p 9). The implication is that *Lions and Shadows* is too fictional in its methodology to qualify as true autobiography which is more akin to history. Yet anyone who has followed Isherwood's career knows that such a strict division between fact and fiction is quite alien to his way of thinking. Even while he was at work on the book he informed his English agent that it belonged together with both *Lions and Shadows* and *Kathleen and Frank*.[16] After completing it he wrote even more explicitly to his English publisher that the book 'isn't historical' but 'highly impression-istic and subjective'.[17] In other words what he really means by being 'factual' is being true to himself, his personal myths, his memories of how things were. As he told Upward when he was still reconstructing the sequence in which events occurred in his life during the thirties: 'As soon as I've arranged all these dates in order, I can start to remember—or to invent, it doesn't matter which.'[18]

Isherwood has always constructed his fiction on a foundation of fact and has constantly reiterated his conviction that what interests him is the interpretation of existing experience rather than the invention of new experience. This holds true of his latest autobiography, as he has made quite clear in an interview with W. I. Scobie:

If *Christopher and his Kind* does in fact read like a novel, perhaps it's because I've always felt very little difference between fiction and non-fiction. What matters is what you say about a given situation. Maybe you can explain its reality better by heightening its drama, by way of comment on it. Fiction enters the garden in a serpentine way.[19]

One might be inclined to ignore the opening two paragraphs of *Christopher and his Kind* if one didn't also encounter a number of places in the book where he appears to imply that his fiction would have been improved had it adhered more closely to the original facts. Stephen Spender has commented on this tendency in the book for Isherwood to assume that characters like Natalia and Bernhard Landauer would have been improved as fictional *dramatis personae* had they more closely resembled Gisa Solo-weitschik and Wilfred Israel on whom they were modelled. Yet, Spender points out, both sets of characters, whether they appear in *Goodbye to Berlin* or *Christopher and his Kind* are fictitious portrayals. The real gulf remains—'between the person who exists but has not been written about, and the same person when he has been written about by Isherwood.'[20]

Here again Isherwood has specifically acknowledged the fictitious quality of his portraits in *Christopher and his Kind*, pointing out, for example, to his English publisher that he had confined the number of named characters in the book to a minimum, because he 'wanted it to read more like a novel than a memoir.'[21] Since many of the characters are friends most of whom are still alive he has also falsified some of the facts to avoid hurting anyone's feelings. Curiously enough this sometimes has the effect Spender observed in the case of Kathleen's portrait in *Kathleen and Frank*, of depriving his characters of a three-dimensional quality which they have in his fiction where he feels free to combine a love for them with an element of normal bitchiness that makes them human. The transcript of the television interview which Alan Wallis shot at his home in 1976 contains a fascinating scene at the beginning during which Isherwood is discussing a draft section of *Christopher and his Kind* with Don Bachardy who has just read it. Bachardy recommends him to reinsert Stephen Spender's comments about John Lehmann's 'pale quizzing eyes'. Isherwood replies that he can't because it's hardly flattering. In reply Bachardy echoes Spender's argument by pointing out that to keep dwelling on people's beauty eventually becomes a send-up of them.[22] In the event this rather innocuous description found its way back into the book. But the incident reflects the scrupulous way in which Isherwood has censored most of his character-portraits.

There is one obvious exception, however. Christopher, his younger self, is treated with no such scruples. Isherwood makes a point of sparing Christopher nothing. At one point in the book he quotes a diary entry in which Christopher determines after a quarrel that, if he and Heinz have to part, it will be he who does the leaving when it suits him best. Isherwood comments: 'here I am confronted by the reality of Christopher's monster behaviour—his tears followed by cold calculation—and it shocks me, it hurts my self eseem, even after all these years! The more reason for recording it' (p 112). The reason for recording it is not just fictional (to ensure that the character of Christopher is portrayed in the round); it also represents the present-day Isherwood's Vedantist desire for detachment from the vanities of the ego. But, as James Fenton has pointed out, the device by which Isherwood treats Christopher as an independent character within the book breaks down here, since Isherwood clearly still identifies with Christopher at this moment. Fenton is not the only reviewer to find his use of Christopher as a separate persona irritating.[23] Anthony Powell thought it ran the risk of archness[24] and Francis King found it whimsical.[25]

Yet this device has enabled Isherwood to say some things about his relations with his friends which might otherwise have been too offensive to include. For instance, when reporting his quarrel with Spender, he can attribute to Christopher the bitchy reply to Spender's suggestion that they might at least part like men ('but, Stephen, we *aren't* men', p 86), without accepting present responsibility for it, even castigating Christopher for his evasive response. By this means he manages to have it both ways at once, recording offensive remarks without offending. There is the further theoretical justification for the use of Christopher as the fictional hero of the book, which Peter Conrad perceptively pointed out in his review of the book. 'He cannot write an autobiography', Conrad wrote, 'because he doesn't know himself well enough: even looking in the mirror, he shares the biographer's plight of having to penetrate a fugitive individuality different from himself, a creature lost in the past and protected by the dishonesty of his own recollections.'[26] The use of 'Christopher' serves as a constant reminder to the reader that Isherwood sees his earlier self as a stranger, the major protagonist in a scenario that he is fictionally reconstructing from such historical facts as he can collect at forty years' distance in time.

Besides, what interests him is his personal mythology, past and present. Like any novel, *Christopher and his Kind* is controlled by a number of thematic motifs. 'The absolutely basic themes in my book', he wrote to Spender when he still intended covering the war years as well, 'are being queer and being political and being a pacifist Quaker and being a movie writer and being a Vedantist.'[27] Despite curtailing the duration of his autobiography, these themes remain virtually unchanged. The dominant theme is the effect that his homosexuality had on every aspect of his life—turning him into a rebel against English society (and so turning him into a chronic wanderer), against his class (and so inducing him to espouse the cause of the left) and against the Anglican Church (thereby persuading him to think of himself as an atheist for almost twenty years of his life). He even suggests that he chose homosexuality in the first place as a way of rebelling against his Mother and all the Others. But the fact remains that his homosexuality kept him firmly in the ranks of the rebels. If it was responsible for his life as an artist it was also responsible for the years he spent deluding himself that he was a political activist and atheist with a natural urge to keep travelling.

In fact—and it is part of the strategy of the book to show this—his eventual abandonment of his thirties self for a settled life in California where politics has been supplanted by Vedanta is potentially present during these earlier years. The book reflects the manner of its evolution, being an account of why he went to the States. Consequently he has shaped the material accordingly. Whenever there is any mention of America, for instance, as he told Paul Bailey, he strikes it like a note in a symphony.[28] He includes a trivial plan of Jean Ross's to go to America (p 68); makes much of Viertel's descriptions of his house in Santa Monica Canyon (pp 119–20), just as he emphasises his first involvement with Viertel in the movies from which he is to make so much of his living in America; quotes a letter from Spender in which he suggests to Isherwood that he should emigrate to the States in 1935 (p 151); gives details of his numerous attempts to get Heinz and himself to South America; has frequent switches forward in time to his period of residence in California; and ends the book confronting the Statue of Liberty. This is merely one example of the way in which Isherwood consciously shapes his autobiography by artistic means. One could similarly identify a mounting note of impending personal crisis which he strikes almost from the beginning of the book.

On completing the book he wrote to Dodie Smith: 'It "tells all" and is perhaps over-aggressive.'[29] Certainly some of the critics found it so. Francis King, reviewing the book for *Gay News* felt it destroyed some of the mystery and magic which the Berlin books acquired just because Isherwood was compelled to conceal his narrator's homosexuality in them.[30] Philip Toynbee echoed this sentiment in his *Observer* review, noting the presence of a strident note in the book which, he claimed, is a recognisable feature of members of minority groups of any kind.[31] Artistically speaking, Isherwood's insistence on the primacy of his homosexuality affords the only instances in the book where life is clearly distorted to fit into a pre-arranged pattern. Actually, as Peter Conrad pointed out, Isherwood's 'lacerating frankness about his sexual truancies is as evasive and oblique as Auden's reticence was a coy technique of self-dramatisation.'[32] We don't learn any more about Isherwood including his homosexuality in his autobiography of the thirties than we did about Isherwood without a sex life in his autobiography of the twenties. Or rather, we learn a lot about him in both books. And just as *Lions and Shadows* concentrated on the formation of Isherwood the artist, so, as Upward remarked of *Christopher and his Kind*, 'to be a writer was even more essential to him than to be a homosexual . . . though he never explicitly says so in the book.'[33] For Christopher's kind do consist of more than homosexuals, as his lifelong friendship with the heterosexual Upward and his closeness to numerous other heterosexual artistic friends demonstrate within the book itself.

In some ways his career can be seen to have led him inevitably to the autobiographical mode which, paradoxically, offers him the greatest opportunities for subjective expression and creative interpretation. Since late 1976 he has been at work on a personal account, gleaned from his diaries, of his long association with Prabhavananda, a subjective memoir that might well offer another chapter of concealed autobiography in the manner of *Kathleen and Frank*. At present, he writes, 'my idea is that it should deal almost exclusively with the relation between the two of us and therefore refer only briefly to others.'[34] Also waiting to see the light of day some time in the future are his already-once-written autobiography of the war years and his written-up journal covering 1945–53. Obviously no final estimation of the man or his work is possible or even desirable at this stage. He continues to look half his age, to live a vigorous life, to make money from filmscripts when he needs to, and, of course, to go on creating that inextricable and fascinating admixture of fact and fiction, experience and interpretation which is to be found in all of Isherwood's imaginative writing.

APPENDIX

An unpublished poem written by
W. H. Auden for Isherwood in 1937

(Auden wrote the following poem for and about Isherwood on the first three blank pages of a copy of D. H. Lawrence's *Birds, Beasts and Flowers*, William Heinemann Ltd, London, new edition, 1931. Since it has never been published in full I reproduce it here, as transcribed by Edward Mendelson, partly for the light it throws on Auden's view of Isherwood towards the end of their period of close collaboration.)

Who is that funny-looking young man so squat with a top-heavy head
A cross between a cavalry major and a rather prim landlady
Sitting there sipping a cigarette?
A brilliant young novelist?
You don't say!

Sitting in the corner of the room at a party, with his hair neatly brushed,
    quite clean
Or lying on the beach in the sun
Just like the rest of the crowd
Just as brown, no, browner
Anonymous, just like us.

Wait a moment

Wait till there's an opening in the conversation, or a chance to show off
And you strike like a lobster at a prawn
A roar of laughter. Aha, listen to that
Didn't you fool them beautifully,
Didn't they think you were nobody in particular,
That landlady

That major
Sold again.

With your great grey eyes taking everything in,
And your nicely creased trousers
Pretending to be nobody, to be quite humdrum and harmless
All the time perfectly aware of your powers
You puff-adder
You sham.

And your will, my word!
Don't you love to boss just everybody, everybody
To make all of us dance to your tune
Pied Piper
At an awkward moment.
Turning on your wonderful diplomacy like a fire-hose
Flattering, wheedling, threatening,
Drenching everybody.
Don't you love being ill,
Propped up on pillows, making us all dance attendance.
Do you think we don't see
Fussy old Major
Do you think we don't know what you're thinking
'I'm the cleverest man of the age
The genius behind the scenes, the anonymous dictator
Cardinal Mazarin
Myecroft Holmes
Lawrence of Arabia
Lady Asquith
Always right.'

And if anything goes wrong,
If absolutely the whole universe fails to bow to your command
If there's a mutiny in Neptune
A revolt in one of the farthest nebulae
How you stamp your bright little shoe
How you pout
House-proud old landlady
At times I could shake you
Il y a des complaisances que je déteste.

Yet how beautiful your books are
So observant, so witty, so profound
And how nice you are really
So affectionate, so understanding, so helpful, such wonderful company
A brilliant young novelist?
My greatest friend?
Si, Signor.

Standing here in Dover under the cliffs, with dotty England behind you
And challenging the provocative sea
With your enormous distinguished nose and your great grey eyes
Only 33 and a real diplomat already
Our great ambassador to the mad.

Use your will. We need it.

Dover. Sept 3 1937

Notes

(See Bibliography for the editions of Isherwood's works referred to and for abbreviations of their titles used throughout this book. All unascribed letters are in the possession of their addressees. ALS = Autograph letter signed. AMS = Autograph manuscript. APCS = Autograph postcard signed. CI = Christopher Isherwood. TLS = Typed letter signed.)

INTRODUCTION

1. cf. CI, 'Reflections of an Anglo-Californian' (interview with Jon Bradshaw), *Vogue*, December 1974, p. 84.
2. Leon Edel, *Literary Biography*, Indiana University Press, 1973, p. 3.
3. James L. Clifford, *From Puzzles to Portraits*, University of North Carolina Press, Chapell Hill, 1970, p. 102.

CHAPTER ONE: FAMILY

1. CI, 'The Writer and His World'. Lectures delivered at the University of California at Santa Barbara, 1960–61.
2. CI, Interview with Brian Finney at CI's home in Santa Monica, 1 July 1975 (hereafter all my interviews with CI in Santa Monica will be referred to as 'CI, Interview', followed by the date).
3. David Lambourne, 'The Novelist Between the Wars: Post-modernist Fiction from 1918–1939 in its Social, Political and Historical Context', PhD Thesis, University of Hull, 1973, p. 733.
4. CI, Interview, 1 July 1975.
5. W. H. Auden and CI, 'Preliminary Statement', AMS, 3 pp., in the possession of the late Mr Sylvain Mangeot.
6. CI, 'Isherwood Plays a Guessing Game' (Interview with B. Lehane), *Daily Telegraph* (Colour Supplement), 7 August 1970, p. 20.

CHAPTER TWO: CHILDHOOD

1. CI, Interview, 1 July 1975.

2. Rachel Natzio (*née* Monkhouse), Interview with Brian Finney at her home in Marton, Cheshire, 7 May 1977.
3. cf. CI, Interview with Robert Wennerstein on 28 September 1971, *Transatlantic Review* 42–43, Spring/Summer 1972, p. 19.

CHAPTER THREE: ST EDMUND'S PREPARATORY SCHOOL

1. Cyril Connolly, *Enemies of Promise*, George Routledge & Sons, 1938, p. 206.
2. Sonia Orwell and Ian Angus (eds.), 'Such, Such Were the Joys', *The Collected Essays, Journalism and Letters of George Orwell*, Penguin Books, 1970, Vol. 4, pp. 379–422.
3. Graham Greene (ed.), *The Old School*, Jonathan Cape, 1934, p. 133.
4. CI, 'CI: An Interview' (with Winston Leyland), *Gay Sunshine* (San Francisco), No. 19, September/October 1973, p. 2.
5. Stephen Spender (ed.), *W. H. Auden: A Tribute*, Weidenfeld and Nicolson, 1975, p. 31.
6. Ibid., p. 35 and *LS* 13.
7. Mrs Rosamira Bulley (*née* Morgan Brown), 'Memoir' (written for Brian Finney), 1976.
8. Graham Greene (ed.), *The Old School*, op. cit., p. 185.
9. Sonia Orwell and Ian Angus (eds.), 'Such, Such Were the Joys', op. cit., p. 419.
10. Both poems are in the private possession of Mrs Rosamira Bulley.
11. Samuel Hynes, *The Auden Generation*, Bodley Head, 1976, p. 23.
12. Stephen Spender (ed.), *W. H. Auden: A Tribute*, op. cit., p. 34.
13. W. H. Auden, Interview with Michael Newman, *Writers at Work: The Paris Review Interviews: Fourth Series* (ed. G. Plimpton), Secker & Warburg, 1977, p. 249.
14. Stephen Spender (ed.), *W. H. Auden: A Tribute*, op. cit., p. 36.
15. W. H. Auden, 'As It Seemed to Us', *Forewords and Afterwords* (ed. E. Mendelson), Faber and Faber, 1973, p. 505; and *LS* 184.
16. CI, Interview, 5 September 1976.
17. Mrs Rosamira Bulley, 'Memoir', op. cit.

CHAPTER FOUR: REPTON

1. Graham Greene (ed.), *The Old School*, op. cit., p. 11.
2. Ibid., p. 105.
3. Ibid., p. 132.
4. Ibid., p. 17.
5. Edward Upward, Telephone conversation with Brian Finney, 15 May 1977.
6. CI, Interview, 5 September 1976.
7. Ibid.

8. Ibid.

9. Eric Falk, Telephone conversation with Brian Finney, 16 May 1977.

10. Form and subject grades supplied by W. Downing, librarian of Repton.

11. CI, Interview, 5 September 1976.

12. CI, Interview with Kenneth Allsop, *Daily Mail*, 7 August 1961 (where CI compares Fisher unfavourably with Prabhavananda).

13. Edward Upward, *The Spiral Ascent: No Home But the Struggle*, Heinemann, 1977, p. 661.

14. CI, 'Minora', *The Reptonian*, February 1922, p. 190.

15. Michael Davie (ed.), *The Diaries of Evelyn Waugh*, Weidenfeld and Nicholson, 1976, p. 29 (entry for 16 October 1919).

16. Report of debate held on 17 November 1922, *The Reptonian*, December 1922, p. 53.

17. CI, Interview, 5 September 1976.

18. Cyril Connolly, *Enemies of Promise*, op. cit., p. 325.

19. CI, ALS to Edward Upward, 22 March 1923.

20. Patrick Monkhouse, Telephone conversation with Brian Finney, 15 November 1976.

21. Allan Monkhouse, *My Daughter Helen*, Jonathan Cape, 1922, pp. 39 and 46.

22. CI, ALS to Eric Falk, 30 May 1923.

23. CI, ALS to Eric Falk, 20 July 1923.

CHAPTER FIVE: CAMBRIDGE

1. Edward Upward, *The Spiral Ascent: No Home But the Struggle*, op. cit., p. 673.

2. CI, 'Mortmere: Introductory Dialogue', AMS, 19 pp., in the possession of Edward Upward.

3. CI, Two AMSS, 1 p. and 3 pp., in the possession of Edward Upward.

4. David Lambourne, 'The Novelist Between the Wars', op. cit., p. 785.

5. CI, 'The Writer and His World', op. cit.

6. Edward Upward, *The Spiral Ascent: No Home But the Struggle*, op. cit., pp. 670, 671.

7. Ibid., p. 169.

8. For a fuller account of CI's and Upward's Mortmere material, see Brian Finney, 'Laily, Mortmere and All That', *Twentieth Century Literature*, Vol. 22, October 1976, pp. 286–302.

9. CI, Interview, 5 September 1976.

10. CI, ALS to Edward Upward, 7 April 1925.

11. Martin Green, *Children of the Sun*, Basic Books, New York, 1976, p. 45.
12. cf. Cecil Day Lewis, *The Buried Day*, Chatto and Windus, 1960, p. 158; John Lehmann, *The Whispering Gallery*, Longman's Green, 1955, p. 139; Michael Roberts (ed.), *New Country*, Hogarth Press, 1933, p. 9.
13. Roger Burford, Interview with Brian Finney at R.B.'s home in London, 16 September 1977.
14. cf. Roland Mathias, *Vernon Watkins 1906–67*, University of Wales Press, Cardiff, 1974.
15. CI, AMS, 6 pp., in the possession of Edward Upward.

CHAPTER SIX: LONDON

1. CI, ALS to Edward Upward, 1 July 1925.
2. Eric Falk, Interview with Brian Finney at E.F.'s home in London, 29 October 1975.
3. Sylvain Mangeot, Interview with Brian Finney at S.M.'s home in Cresswell Place, 11 May 1976.
4. Fowke Mangeot, Interview with Brian Finney at Cresswell Place, 10 June 1976.
5. CI and Sylvain Mangeot, 'People One Ought to Know', bound AMS, 32 pp., in the possession of the late Mr Sylvain Mangeot.
6. cf. CI, ALS to Olive Mangeot, postmarked 18 January 1932.
7. Edward Upward, Interview with Brian Finney at E.U.'s home in Sandown, Isle of Wight, 2 October 1976.
8. Sylvain Mangeot, Interview with Brian Finney at S.M.'s home in London, 11 March 1976.
9. 'I hate you all', AMS, 1 p., in the possession of Alan Clodd.
10. CI, AMSS, 2 pp. and 1 p., in the possession of Edward Upward.
11. Edward Upward, *The Spiral Ascent: No Home But the Struggle*, op. cit., p. 714.
12. Stephen Spender, *World Within World*, Hamish Hamilton, 1951, p. 50.
13. Ibid., p. 61.
14. W. H. Auden, 'I chose this lean country', *Poems 1928*, Stephen Spender, privately printed, 1928, Poem II.
15. Stephen Spender, Interview with Brian Finney at S.S.'s home in London, 7 December 1976.
16. W. H. Auden, 'Birthday Poem', *Collected Shorter Poems 1930–1944*, Faber and Faber, 1950, p. 32.
17. Edward Upward, 'Remembering the Earlier Auden', *Adam International Review*, Nos. 379–84, 1973–4, pp. 17–22.
18. W. H. Auden, ALS to Edward Upward, 6 October 1930.
19. CI, ALS to Olive Mangeot, 11 August 1926 (in the possession of

Fowke Mangeot); and Edward Upward, Interview with Brian Finney at E.U.'s home in Sandown, Isle of Wight, 2 October 1976.
20. CI, ALS to Roger Burford, 2 September (1926).
21. W. H. Auden, *Collected Poems* (edited E. Mendelson), Faber and Faber, 1976, p. 55 (originally in AMS 'Preliminary Statement', op. cit.).
22. A. L. Tolley, *The Poetry of the Thirties*, Victor Gollancz, 1975, p. 87.
23. CI, 'CI: An Interview' (with Winston Leyland), op. cit., p. 3.
24. Ruth de Lichtenberg, Telephone conversation with Brian Finney, 4 and 16 April 1976.
25. W. H. Auden, *Collected Poems*, op. cit., p. 40.
26. Edward Upward, *The Spiral Ascent: No Home But the Struggle*, op. cit., pp. 744–5 and p. 762.
27. cf. William Plomer, ALS to Alan Clodd, 11 April 1955.
28. CI, ALS to Edward Upward, Wednesday (1 April 1928).
29. Stephen Spender, *World Within World*, op. cit., p. 102.
30. Ibid., p. 103.
31. CI, 'Autobiography of an Individualist', *The Twentieth Century*, 149, May 1951, p. 409.
32. CI, 2 ALSs to Stephen Spender, 'Tuesday' and 'Monday' (late May? 1929).
33. CI, ALS to Stephen Spender, 'Monday' (late May? 1929) and CI, Interview, 3 September 1976.

CHAPTER SEVEN: 'ALL THE CONSPIRATORS'

1. AMS, 167 pp., in the possession of Alan Clodd.
2. CI, 'A Kind of Left-Wing Direction' (Interview with David Lambourne), *Poetry Nation*, 4, 1975, p. 55.
3. Anon, *Times Literary Supplement*, 14 June 1928, p. 452.
4. CI, Interview, 1 July 1975.
5. Cyril Connolly, 'Introduction' to *All the Conspirators*, Cape's Traveller's Library Edition, 1939.
6. K. W. Gransden, *E. M. Forster*, Oliver and Boyd, Edinburgh, 1962, pp. 8–9 and 30.
7. CI, Interviews, 1 July 1975 and 28 August 1976.
8. W. H. Auden, *Collected Poems*, op. cit., p. 35.
9, Ibid., 'Paysage Moralisé', pp. 104–5.
10. Walter Allen, *Tradition and Dream*, Penguin Books, 1965, p. 256.

CHAPTER EIGHT: BERLIN

1. W. H. Auden, *The Orators*, Faber and Faber, 1932, p. 83.
2. cf. CI, Interview with Robert Wennersten, op. cit., pp. 12–13, or Interview with Paul Bailey, broadcast on BBC Radio 3, 28 March 1977.

3. Claud Cockburn, *I, Claud . . .*, Penguin Books, rev. ed., 1967, p. 56.
4. CI, Interview with W. I. Scobie, *Gay News*, No. 93, 22 April–5 May 1976, p. 17.
5. cf. John Lehmann, *In the Purely Pagan Sense*, Blond and Briggs, 1976, pp. 44–5.
6. cf. W. H. Auden, unpublished 'Journal', 1929, in the possession of Edward Mendelson; also Margaret Gardiner, 'Auden: A Memoir', *The New Review*, Vol. 3, No. 28, July 1976, pp. 9–11, and Interview with Brian Finney at M.G.'s home in London, 28 March 1976.
7. CI, ALS to John Layard, 2 July 1929, in the possession of Richard Layard.
8. CI, Interview, 1 July 1975; and *E* 14.
9. W. H. Auden, *Collected Poems*, op. cit., p. 48 (cf. '1929' on p. 50: lines 20–22 also refer to Layard).
10. CI, ALS to Roger Burford, 9 August (1929).
11. Sylvain Mangeot, Interview with Brian Finney at S.M.'s home in London, 11 May 1976.
12. CI, 'CI: An Interview' (with Winston Leyland), op. cit., p. 2.
13. Stephen Spender, Interview with Brian Finney at S.S.'s home in London, 7 December 1976.
14. W. H. Auden, 'An early poetical notebook', BM MS 52430, pp. 76–7, at the British Library.
15. CI, ALS to Stephen Spender, Sunday (October 1931?).
16. cf. 'My financial troubles are worse than ever before': CI, ALS to Stephen Spender, 28 August (1930).
17. Stephen Spender, 'On Being a Ghost in Isherwood's Berlin', *Mademoiselle*, Vol. 79, September 1974, pp. 139 and 197.
18. Stephen Spender, *World Within World*, op. cit., p. 122.
19. Iain Johnstone, 'The Real Sally Bowles', *Folio*, Autumn 1975, p. 33.
20. Sylvain Mangeot, Interview with Brian Finney at S.M.'s home in London, 11 May 1976.
21. Paul Bowles, *Without Stopping*, Peter Owen, 1972, p. 114.
22. Stephen Spender, 'On Being a Ghost in Isherwood's Berlin', op. cit., pp. 139 and 197.
23. cf. Interviews between Brian Finney and Professor A. H. Campbell (7 June 1976), Fowke Mangeot (10 June 1976), Sylvain Mangeot (11 March and 11 May 1976), Rachel Natzio (*née* Monkhouse) (7 May 1977) and telephone conversation with Ann McNaughton (23 May 1976).
24. Professor A. H. Campbell, TLS to Brian Finney, 15 October 1975 and Interview with Brian Finney in London, 7 June 1976.
25. W. H. Auden, 'Birthday Poem', op. cit., p. 33.
26. CI, ALS to Roger Burford, Himmelfahrt, 1931.
27. cf. CI, ALS to Stephen Spender, Monday (?June 1931).

28. cf. Gerald Hamilton, *Mr Norris and I*, Allan Wingate, 1956; Peter Burton, 'Meetings with Mr Norris' (unpublished memoir); and Robin Maugham, 'I worked the perfect crime', *The People*, 13 February 1966.

29. Sir Moore Crosthwaite, Interview with Brian Finney at M.C.'s home in London, 4 January 1977.

30. John Symonds, *Conversations With Gerald*, Duckworth, 1974, p. 122.

31. CI, ALS to Stephen Spender, Friday (September 1931).

32. Paul Bowles, *Without Stopping*, op. cit., p. 110.

33. CI, ALS to Stephen Spender, Friday (September 1931).

34. John Symonds, *The Great Beast*, Mayflower Books, 1973, p. 431.

35. William Robson-Scott, Interview with Brian Finney at W.R.-S.'s home in London, 15 December 1975; cf. CI, Interview, 1 July 1975.

36. John Lehmann, 'Two of the Conspirators', *Twentieth Century Literature*, Vol. 22, October 1976, p. 265; cf. CI, ALS to Edward Upward, 8 July 1932.

37. CI, ALS to Stephen Spender, Sunday (October 1931).

38. CI, ALS to Edward Upward, Friday (?8 July 1932).

39. CI, 'Back to Berlin', *The Observer*, 23 March 1952, p. 2.

40. John Lehmann, *The Whispering Gallery*, op. cit., pp. 180–81.

41. Paragraph based on Jay Michael Barrie, 'Some Reminiscences of Gerald Heard', typescript in his possession; cf. Gerald Heard, *The Ascent of Humanity*, Jonathan Cape, 1929.

42. E. M. Forster, ALS to William Plomer, 12 December 1957, (King's College, Cambridge).

43. Stephen Spender, Interview with Brian Finney at S.S.'s home in London, 7 December 1976.

44. CI, ALS to Stephen Spender, Tuesday (?October 1931).

45. CI, ALS to E. M. Forster, Tuesday (October 1932).

46. John Lehmann, 'Two of the Conspirators', op. cit., p. 266.

47. CI, ALS to William Plomer, Thursday (10 November 1932) (Durham University Library).

48. CI, ALS to Stephen Spender, Saturday (?7 January 1933).

49. CI, 'The Writer and His World', op. cit.

50. John Lehmann, 'Two of the Conspirators', op. cit., p. 267.

CHAPTER NINE: 'THE MEMORIAL'

1. W. H. Auden, 'Get there if you can . . .', *Poems*, Faber and Faber, 1930, p. 73.

2. W. H. Auden, 'Consider this and in our time', *Poems*, op. cit., p. 87.

3. Edward Upward, *The Spiral Ascent: In the Thirties*, op. cit., p. 18, and *No Home But the Struggle*, p. 779.

4. CI, Interview, 3 September 1976.

5. Hena Maes-Jelinek, *Criticism of Society in the English Novel between*

the Wars, Société d'Editions 'Les Belles Lettres', Paris, 1970, p. 457;
Goronwy Rees, *The Oxford Outlook*, Vol. 12, May 1932, p. 141;
Angus Wilson, 'The New and the Old Isherwood,' *Encounter*, Vol. 3,
August 1954, p. 63.
6. Lloyd Morris, 'Englishman in a Dissolving World', *New York
Herald Tribune Weekly Book Review*, 5 January 1947, p. 6.
7. CI, Interview, 3 September 1976.
8. CI, TLS to Mrs Hector Mackenzie-Wintle, 27 December (1934).
9. Alan Wilde, *Christopher Isherwood*, Twayne Publishers, New York,
1971, p. 49.
10. Lloyd Morris, 'Englishman in a Dissolving World', op. cit., p. 6.
11. CI, ALS to Edward Upward, Tuesday (?September 1931).
12. Edith R. Mirrielees, 'A Bewildering English Family', *New York
Times Book Review*, 24 November 1946, p. 7.
13. Frank Kermode, *Puzzles and Epiphanies*, Routledge and Kegan
Paul, 1962, pp. 125–6.
14. V. S. Pritchett, 'Books in General', *New Statesman and Nation*,
Vol. 44, 23 August 1952, p. 214.
15. W. H. Auden, 'The Novelist', *Collected Poems*, op. cit., p. 147.

CHAPTER TEN: THE EARLY WANDER YEARS

1. Margaret Gardiner, 'Auden: A Memoir', op. cit., p. 14.
2. CI, TS of 'Ambrose', 84 pp., in the possession of Edward Upward.
3. CI, ALS to John Lehmann, 19 August (1933).
4. CI, ALS to Stephen Spender, 23 June (1933).
5. CI, TLS to Olive Mangeot, 28 July (1933), in the collection of
Fowke Mangeot.
6. Professor A. H. Campbell, Interview with Brian Finney in
London, 15 October 1975.
7. cf. DM, 'Forecasts and Side Glances', *Theatre Arts*, March 1952,
p. 13.
8. Berthold Viertel, 'Christopher Isherwood and Dr Friedrich
Bergmann', *Theatre Arts*, Vol. 30, May 1946, pp. 295–8.
9. CI, Lecture at the University of California at Los Angeles, 4 May
1965.
10. CI, Interview, 1 July 1975.
11. CI, Interview, 4 September 1976.
12. CI, Lecture at UCLA, 4 May 1965.
13. CI, ALS to William Plomer, 2 October 1934 (Durham University
Library).
14. CI, ALS to E. M. Forster, 5 April (1934).
15. CI, TLS to Stephen Spender, 9 May (1934).
16. CI, 'A Kind of Left Wing Direction' (Interview with David
Lambourne recorded early in 1970), op. cit., p. 56.

17. CI, Interview, 1 July 1975.
18. CI, TLS to Stephen Spender, 12 July (1934).
19. CI, ALS to John Lehmann, 22 July (1934).
20. CI, TLS to Hector and Donne Wintle, 24 October (1934).
21. cf. John Lehmann, 'Two of the Conspirators', op. cit., p. 269.
22. CI, TLS to E. M. Forster, 26 August (1934).
23. CI, TLS to John Lehmann, 26 August (1934).
24. cf. Edward Mendelson, 'The Auden–Isherwood Collaboration', *Twentieth Century Literature*, Vol. 22, October 1976, pp. 278–9.
25. CI, TLS to Stephen Spender, 7 February (1935).
26. W. H. Auden, ALS to T. S. Eliot, Monday (?February 1935) (Mrs Valerie Eliot); cf. Auden's ALS to Stephen Spender, Friday (?June 1935), quoted on p. 158.
27. CI, ALS to John Lehmann, 19 August 1933, quoted in *The Whispering Gallery*, op. cit., p. 212.
28. CI, ALS to William Plomer, 2 October 1934 (Durham University Library).
29. CI, TLS to Stephen Spender, 20 November (1934).
30. Stephen Spender, *World Within World*, op. cit., p. 137.
31. Edward Upward, 'A Conversation with Edward Upward', *The Review*, Nos. 11–12, 1964, p. 65.
32. cf. Geoffrey Grigson, 'Breaking Out of the Shell', *Country Life*, 29 December 1977, p. 1988.

CHAPTER ELEVEN: 'MR NORRIS CHANGES TRAINS'
('THE LAST OF MR NORRIS')

1. CI, 'A Conversation on Tape' (Interview with Stanley Poss), *The London Magazine*, Vol. 1, June 1961, p. 43.
2. CI, 'The Autobiography of My Books', the first of three tape-recorded lectures at the University of California at Berkeley, given in April/May 1963.
3. Ibid.
4. CI, Interview, 1 July 1975.
5. CI, talk delivered at a meeting of the Modern Language Association on 27 December 1974, quoted by Alan Wilde in 'Language and Silence: Isherwood and the Thirties', *Contemporary Literature*, Vol. 16, Autumn 1975, p. 481.
6. Gore Vidal, 'Art, Sex and Isherwood', *The New York Review of Books*, Vol. 23, 9 December 1976, p. 14.
7. CI, 'CI: An Interview' (with Winston Leyland), op. cit., p. 1.
8. John Symonds, *Conversations with Gerald*, op. cit., p. 18.
9. Alan Wilde, *Christopher Isherwood*, op. cit., p. 62.
10. David P. Thomas, 'Goodbye to Berlin: Refocusing Isherwood's Camera', *Contemporary Literature*, Vol. 13, Winter, 1972, p. 50.

11. John Whitehead, 'Christophananda: Isherwood at Sixty', *The London Magazine*, Vol. 5, July 1965, p. 94.
12. Cyril Connolly, 'New Novels', *New Statesman and Nation*, Vol. 9, 2 March 1935, p. 284.
13. Samuel Hynes, *The Auden Generation*, op. cit., p. 178.
14. cf. CI 'A Kind of Left-Wing Direction' (interview with David Lambourne), op. cit., p. 60; and 'CI: An Interview' (with Winston Leyland), op. cit., p. 1.
15. Cyril Connolly, *Enemies of Promise*, op. cit., p. 94.
16. Ibid.
17. Alan Wilde, *Christopher Isherwood*, op. cit., pp. 14–20 and 63.
18. Richard Mayne, 'The Novel and Mr Norris', *The Cambridge Journal*, Vol. 6, June 1953, p. 564.
19. cf. E. M. Forster, ALS to CI, 11 May 1935 (King's College, Cambridge).
20. Cyril Connolly, *Enemies of Promise*, op. cit., p. 94.

CHAPTER TWELVE: THE LAST YEARS WITH HEINZ

1. Francis King, 'Down there for the harvest', *The Listener*, Vol. 75, 17 March 1966, p. 407.
2. CI, 'Christopher Isherwood: An Interview' (with Carolyn Heilbrun), *Twentieth Century Literature*, Vol. 22, October 1976, p. 258.
3. W. H. Auden, ALS to Stephen Spender, Friday (late June? 1935).
4. cf. Margaret Gardiner, 'Auden: A Memoir', op. cit., pp. 12–13.
5. John Lehmann, *The Whispering Gallery*, op. cit., p. 232.
6. CI, APCS to John Lehmann, 6 December 1934; cf. CI, Interview, 1 July 1975.
7. cf. Martin Green, *Children of the Sun*, Basic Books, N.Y., 1976.
8. CI, TLS to Stephen Spender, 2 September (1935).
9. Humphrey Spender, Interview with Brian Finney in London, 26 October 1976.
10. Humphrey Spender, MS diary entry for Monday, 20 January 1936.
11. Stephen Spender, Interview with Brian Finney at S.S.'s home in London, 7 December 1976.
12. CI, ALS to Stephen Spender, 20 April (1936).
13. CI, TLS to Stephen Spender, 12 May (1936).
14. CI, TLS to Stephen Spender, 31 May (1936).
15. CI, APCS to John Lehmann, 20 November 1935.
16. cf. John Lehmann, 'Two of the Conspirators', op. cit., pp. 271–2.
17. W. H. Auden and Louis MacNeice, *Letters from Iceland*, Faber and Faber, 1937, p. 30.
18. Heinz N—, ALS to Stephen Spender, 15 October (1936).
19. CI, TLS to Stephen Spender, 15 November 1936.

20. P. N. Furbank, *E. M. Forster, A Life*, Vol. 2, Secker and Warburg, 1978, p. 213.
21. E. M. Forster, ALS to Christopher Isherwood, 27 February 1937 (King's College, Cambridge).
22. Cyril Connolly, 'Appointment with . . .', Granada Television broadcast, 29 June 1961.
23. Heinz N—, ALS to Stephen Spender, 25 September 1946.
24. Stephen Spender, Interview with Brian Finney at S.S.'s home in London, 7 December 1976.
25. CI, TLS to John Lehmann, 15 September (1937).

CHAPTER THIRTEEN: 'LIONS AND SHADOWS'

1. CI, ALS to John Lehmann, quoted in John Lehmann's 'Two of the Conspirators'. op. cit., p. 265 (c. early April 1932).
2. CI, 'Autobiography of an Individualist', op. cit., p. 405.
3. CI, ALS to Leonard Woolf, 15 October 1937 (Hogarth Press).
4. Anon., 'Novelist's Youth', *Times Literary Supplement*, 19 March 1938, p. 185.
5. CI, 'An Interview' (with George Wickes), *Shenandoah*, Vol. 16, Spring 1965, p. 51.
6. CI, TLS to Alan Clodd, 7 December 1953.
7. Jon Bradshaw, 'Reflections of an Anglo-Californian'. op. cit., p. 84.
8. CI, TLS to Stephen Spender, 15 November 1936.
9. CI, TLS to Alan Clodd, 7 December 1953.
10. CI, Interview, 1 July 1975.
11. CI, TLS to James and Tania Stern, 17 November 1936.
12. CI, TLS to Stephen Spender, 15 November 1936.
13. Hugh Brogan, 'Lions and Shadows', *Twentieth Century Literature*, Vol. 22, October 1976, p. 303.
14. Alan Wilde, *Christopher Isherwood*, op. cit., p. 20.
15. Evelyn Waugh, 'Author in Search of a Formula', *Spectator*, Vol. 160, 25 March 1938, p. 538.
16. Alan Wilde, *Christopher Isherwood*, op. cit., pp. 23–4.
17. E. M. Forster, ALS to CI, 17 February 1938 (King's College, Cambridge).
18. Samuel Hynes, *The Auden Generation*, op. cit., p. 325.

CHAPTER FOURTEEN: THE BREAK WITH EUROPE

1. W. H. Auden, ALS to Bennett Cerf, 11 September 1937 (cf. B. C. Bloomfield and Edward Mendelson, *W. H. Auden: A Bibliography, 1924–1969*, University of Virginia Press, Charlottesville, 1972, p. 35).

2. CI, ALS to Rupert Doone, 1 September (1937) (Berg Collection, New York Public Library).

3. CI, ALS to Stephen Spender, 23 September (1937).

4. W. H. Auden, ALS to J. M. Keynes, 9 October 1937 (Keynes Collection, King's College, Cambridge).

5. CI, 'A Kind of Left-Wing Direction' (interview with David Lambourne), op. cit., p. 51.

6. CI, holograph note on ALS from Bob Buckingham to E. M. Forster (28 June 1937) (King's College, Cambridge).

7. P. N. Furbank, Interview with Brian Finney, London, 28 October 1976.

8. Stephen Spender, *World Within World*, op. cit., p. 238.

9. CI, ALS to Stephen Spender, 5 July (1938).

10. Ibid.

11. CI, TLS to John Lehmann, 24 February (1938).

12. CI, ALS to Stephen Spender, 5 July (1938).

13. cf. Christopher Hassall, *Edward Marsh, Patron of the Arts, A Biography*, Longmans, 1959, p. 611.

14. William Empson, Telephone conversation with Brian Finney, 7 January 1977.

15. CI, TLS to John Lehmann, 24 February (1938).

16. CI, TLS to Stephen Spender, 27 April (1938).

17. CI, 'China in Wartime', *The Listener*, Vol. 20, 10 November 1938, p. 989.

18. W. H. Auden, ALS to Stephen Spender (early July? 1938).

19. CI, 'A Kind of Left-Wing Direction' (interview with David Lambourne), op. cit., p. 52.

20. cf. John Auden, 'A Brother's Viewpoint' in *W. H. Auden: A Tribute*, op. cit., p. 28; cf. *CK* 235.

21. CI, TLS to Stephen Spender, 29 August (1938).

22. cf. John Lehmann, *The Whispering Gallery*, op. cit., p. 331.

23. CI, TLS to Richard de la Mare, 17 December (1938) (Faber and Faber).

24. Robert Medley, Telephone conversation with Brian Finney, 28 September 1976.

25. Mirko Jurak, 'English Political Verse Drama of the Thirties: Revision and Alteration', *Acta Neophilologica*, Vol. 1, 1968, p. 77.

26. C. Day Lewis, Review of *On the Frontier*, *The Listener*, Vol. 20, 24 November 1938, p. 1145.

27. W. H. Auden, 'Ode to the New Year (1939)', AMS (Estate of W. H. Auden).

28. cf. Gerald Hamilton, ALS to James Stern, 9 January 1939.

29. Cyril Connolly, 'Comment', *Horizon*, Vol. 1, No. 2, February 1940, p. 68.

CHAPTER FIFTEEN: 'GOODBYE TO BERLIN'

1. John Lehmann, 'Christopher Isherwood and Berlin', *New Writing in England*, Critics Group Press, New York, 1939, p. 25.
2. Frederick Karl, *A Reader's Guide to the Contemporary English Novel*, Thames & Hudson, 1963, p. 291.
3. CI, Interview, 1 July 1975.
4. Carolyn Heilbrun, *Christopher Isherwood*, Columbia University Press, 1970, p. 20.
5. cf. CI, 'An Interview on Tape', op. cit., p. 43, and Samuel Hynes, *The Auden Generation*, op. cit., p. 355.
6. G. S. Fraser, *The Modern Writer and His World*, Penguin, rev. ed., 1964, pp. 133, 137–9.
7. CI, 'An Interview with CI' (interview with David J. Geherin), *Journal of Narrative Technique*, March 1972, p. 146.
8. Harvey Breit, *The Writer Observed*, Alvin Redman Ltd, 1957, p. 215.
9. Norman Friedman, 'Point of View in Fiction: The Development of a Critical Concept', *PMLA*, Vol. 70, December 1955, pp. 1178–9.
10. David Thomas, 'Goodbye to Berlin: Refocusing Isherwood's Camera', op. cit., p. 48.
11. Alan Wilde, *Christopher Isherwood*, op. cit., pp. 72–3.
12. David Thomas, 'Goodbye to Berlin: Refocusing Isherwood's Camera', op. cit., p. 51.
13. Anon., *Times Literary Supplement*, 4 March 1939, p. 133.
14. CI, ALS to Stephen Spender, 5 July (1938).
15. Thomas Lask, 'Isherwood Looks At an English Era', *New York Times*, 15 February 1972, p. 26.
16. John Lehmann, *New Writing in Europe*, Penguin Books, 1940, p. 51.
17. CI, TLS to John Lehmann, 16 January (1936).
18. CI, TLS to John Lehmann, 2 January (1937).
19. Alan Wilde, *Christopher Isherwood*, op. cit., p. 71.
20. Geoffrey Grigson, 'Rum Tum Tum on a Broken Drum', *New Verse*, Vol. 1, May 1939, p. 54.
21. Henry Hewes, 'Christopher Isherwood's Snapshots', *Saturday Review*, Vol. 35, 12 April 1952, p. 38.
22. Colin Wilson, 'An Integrity Born of Hope: Notes on Christopher Isherwood', *Twentieth Century Literature*, Vol. 22, October 1976, p. 321.

CHAPTER SIXTEEN: THE COLLABORATIONS WITH AUDEN

1. Mardi Valgemae, 'Auden's Collaboration with Isherwood on *The Dog Beneath the Skin*', *The Huntingdon Library Quarterly*, Vol. 31, August 1968, p. 374.
2. Ibid.

3. CI, 'Some notes on the early poetry', *W. H. Auden: A Tribute*, op. cit., p. 77.

4. TS in the possession of CI.

5. CI, Interview, 1 July 1975.

6. W. H. Auden in *Writers at Work: The Paris Review Interviews: Fourth Series*, op. cit., p. 260.

7. CI, Lecture at UCLA, 27 April 1965.

8. Stephen Spender, 'The Poetic Dramas of W. H. Auden and Christopher Isherwood', *New Writing, New Series* 1, Autumn 1938, Hogarth Press, pp. 102–3 (reprinted in *The Thirties and After*, Macmillan, 1978).

9. Rupert Doone, 'The Theatre of Ideas', *Theatre Newsletter* VI, No. 131, 29 September 1951, p. 5.

10. Rupert Doone, 'I Want the Theatre to Be', printed in programme for the Group Theatre's production of Jean Giono's *Sowers of the Hills* at the Westminster Theatre, 29 October 1935 (Theatre Museum, London).

11. cf. Edward Mendelson, 'The Auden–Isherwood Collaboration', op. cit., pp. 278–9.

12. cf. Mardi Valgemae, 'Auden's Collaboration with Isherwood on *The Dog Beneath the Skin*', op. cit., note 14 on p. 376.

13. cf. carbon TS of *The Chase* at the library of Exeter College, Oxford.

14. CI, ALS to Stephen Spender, 16 June 1935.

15. Mardi Valgemae, 'Auden's Collaboration with Isherwood on *The Dog Beneath the Skin*', op. cit., pp. 378, 380–1.

16. W. H. Auden, 'I Want the Theatre to Be' from Group Theatre programme for *The Dance of Death* and *Sweeney Agonistes*, 25 February and 4 March 1934, reprinted in Samuel Hynes, *The Auden Generation*, op. cit., p. 399.

17. Julian Symons, *The Thirties: A Dream Revolved*, Faber and Faber, 1975, p. 76.

18. W. H. Auden, 'I Want the Theatre to Be', op. cit.; cf. CI, Lecture at UCLA, 27 April 1965.

19. Stephen Spender, 'The Poetic Dramas of W. H. Auden and Christopher Isherwood', op. cit., p. 104.

20. cf. John Willett, *The Theatre of Bertholt Brecht*, Methuen, 1967, pp. 220–21; CI, 'German Literature in England', *The New Republic*, Vol. 98, 5 April 1939, p. 255.

21. CI, Lecture at UCLA, 27 April 1965.

22. W. H. Auden, ALS to Stephen Spender, Friday (late June? 1935).

23. Barbara Everett, *W. H. Auden*, Oliver and Boyd, Edinburgh, 1964, p. 55.

24. CI, ALS to Stephen Spender, 16 June (1935).

25. Robert Medley, Interview with Brian Finney at R.M.'s home in London, 28 October 1975.

26. Cyril Connolly, 'The Muse's Off Day', *New Statesman*, Vol. 11, 8 February 1936, p. 188.

27. cf. Mirko Jurak, 'English Political Verse Drama of the Thirties: Revision and Alteration', *Acta Neophilologica*, Vol. 1, 1968, pp. 69–70.

28. Mardi Valgemae, 'Auden's Collaboration with Isherwood on *The Dog Beneath the Skin*', op. cit., p. 382.

29. Robert Medley, Interview with Brian Finney at R.M.'s home in London, 28 October 1975.

30. Cyril Connolly, 'The Muse's Off Day', op. cit., p. 188.

31. Derek Verschoyle, 'The Theatre: *The Dog Bebeath the Skin*', *Spectator*, Vol. 156, 7 February 1936, p. 211.

32. DP, 'The Dog Beneath the Skin', *The Sunday Times*, 2 February 1936, p. 7.

33. CI, Interview, 4 September 1976.

34. cf. Forest Earl Hazard, 'The Auden Group and the Group Theatre: The Dramatic Theories and Practices of Rupert Doone, W. H. Auden, Christopher Isherwood, Louis MacNeice, Stephen Spender and Cecil Day Lewis', PhD dissertation, The University of Wisconsin, 1964.

35. Shirley K. Hood, 'Interview with Christopher Isherwood Concerning His Play *The Ascent of F6*', 24 March 1966, TS, pp. 20–21 (Department of Special Collections, UCLA).

36. CI, Lecture at UCLA, 27 April 1965.

37. Ibid.

38. Stephen Spender, 'Fable and Reportage', *Left Review*, Vol. 2, November 1936, pp. 781 and 782.

39. E. M. Forster, 'The Ascent of F6', *The Listener*, Vol. 16, 14 October 1936, Supplement p. VII (reprinted in *Two Cheers for Democracy*, Edward Arnold, 1951).

40. CI, TLS to E. M. Forster, 25 October (1936).

41. cf. E. M. Forster, ALS to CI, 27 February 1937 (King's College, Cambridge); and B. C. Bloomfield and E. Mendelson, *W. H. Auden: A Bibliography 1924–1969*, op. cit., p. 21.

42. EBH, 'The Ascent of F6', *Cambridge Review*, Vol. 58, 30 April 1937, p. 354.

43. CI, Lecture at UCLA, 27 April 1965.

44. cf. TS, prompt copy of *The Ascent of F6* (Berg Collection, New York Public Library).

45. Stephen Spender, 'The Poetic Dramas of W. H. Auden and Christopher Isherwood', op. cit., p. 107.

46. Monroe K. Spears, *The Poetry of W. H. Auden*, Oxford University Press, New York, 1963, p. 102.

47. 'The Ascent of F6', *Group Theatre Paper*, No. 6, December 1936, p. 5; quoted in Samuel Hynes, *The Auden Generation*, op. cit., p. 239.

48. Louis MacNeice, *Modern Poetry: A Personal Essay*, Oxford University Press, 1938, p. 173.

49. cf. Howard Griffin, 'A Dialogue with W. H. Auden', *The Hudson Review*, Vol. 3, Winter 1951, p. 583; and *E* 13.

50. W. H. Auden, 'T. E. Lawrence', *Now and Then*, No. 47, Spring 1934, p. 30.

51. F. R. Leavis, 'Mr Auden's Talent', *Scrutiny*, Vol. 5, December 1936, p. 327.

52. Stephen Spender, 'Fable and Reportage', *Left Review*, op. cit., pp. 779–82; C. Day Lewis, 'Paging Mankind', *Poetry*, Vol. 49, January 1937, p. 227.

53. Stephen Spender, 'W. H. Auden and His Poetry', *The Atlantic Monthly*, Vol. 192, July 1953, p. 77.

54. CI, 'A Conversation on Tape' (interview with Stanley Poss), op. cit., p. 51.

55. Harvey Breit, *The Writer Observed*, op. cit., p. 216.

56. cf. Mirko Jurak, 'English Political Verse Drama of the Thirties: Revision and Alteration', op. cit., p. 77.

57. T. S. Eliot, ALS to J. M. Keynes, 15 November 1938 (Keynes Collection, King's College Library, Cambridge).

58. cf. Katherine B. Hoskins, *Today the Struggle*, University of Texas Press, Austin, 1969, p. 177.

59. C. Day Lewis, 'On the Frontier', *Listener*, Vol. 20, 24 November 1938, p. 1145.

60. Anon., 'A Poetic Drama of Today', *Times Literary Supplement*, 29 October 1938, p. 689.

61. CI, 'A Writer and His World', op. cit.; cf. W. H. Auden, ALS to Stephen Spender (July 1938).

62. cf. John Lehmann, *New Writing in England*, op. cit., p. 35.

63. Louis MacNeice, 'The Theatre', *Spectator*, Vol. 161, 18 November 1938, p. 858.

64. F. McEachran, 'Topical Drama', *Adelphi*, Vol. 15, January 1939, p. 202.

65. Evelyn Waugh, 'Mr Isherwood and Friend', *Spectator*, Vol. 162, 24 March 1939, p. 496.

66. G. W. Stonier, 'Auden and Isherwood', *New Statesman*, Vol. 17, 18 March 1939, p. 428.

67. Evelyn Waugh, 'Mr Isherwood and Friend', op. cit., p. 498.

CHAPTER SEVENTEEN: THE WAR YEARS

1. cf. CI, TLS to Bennett Cerf, 1 May (1939) (Columbia University Library).

2. CI, ALS to Stephen Spender, 14 November (1939).

3. CI, Interview, 5 September 1976.

4. CI, TLS to Edward Upward, 6 August (1939).
5. CI, TLS to Stephen Spender, 28 April (1939).
6. CI, TLS to E. M. Forster, 29 April (1939).
7. CI, 'A Fortunate Happy Life' (Interview with Derek Hart), *The Listener*, Vol. 83, 2 April 1970, p. 450.
8. CI, TLS to John Lehmann, 26 December (1940).
9. CI, TLS to John Lehmann, 7 July (1939).
10. cf. Jay Michael Barrie, 'Introduction' to Gerald Heard's *Training for the Life of the Spirit*, Strength Books, NY, 1975.
11. CI, TLS to E. M. Forster, 14 February (1941).
12. E. M. Forster, TLS to William Plomer, 26 February 1944 (Durham University Library).
13. CI, 'Discovering Vedanta', *The Twentieth Century*, Vol. 70, Autumn 1961, p. 71.
14. Ibid.
15. Sybille Bedford, *Aldous Huxley, A Biography*, Vol. 2, Chatto and Windus, 1974, p. 6.
16. CI, TLS to John Lehmann, 7 July (1939).
17. Sybille Bedford, *Aldous Huxley, A Biography*, op. cit., p. 206.
18. Ibid.
19. CI, ALS to James Stern, 13 November (1939).
20. cf. Jonathan Fryer, *Christopher Isherwood*, New English Library, 1977, pp. 203–4.
21. CI, Interview, 5 September 1976.
22. CI, TLS to James Stern, 9 November (1940).
23. Sybille Bedford, *Aldous Huxley, A Biography*, op. cit., p. 10.
24. Julian Huxley (ed.), *Aldous Huxley 1894–1963: A Memorial Volume*, Chatto and Windus, 1966, pp. 91–3.
25. Cyril Connolly, 'Comment', *Horizon*, Vol. 1, No. 2, February 1940, p. 69.
26. Harold Nicolson, 'People and Things', *Spectator*, No. 5834, 19 April 1940, p. 555.
27. Stephen Spender, Letter to the Editor, *Spectator*, No. 5835, 26 April 1940, p. 596.
28. WRM, 'To Certain Intellectuals Safe in America', *Spectator*, No. 5843, 21 June 1940, p. 833.
29. E. M. Forster, Letter to the Editor, *Spectator*, No. 5845, 5 July 1940.
30. CI, Interview, 1 July 1975.
31. Klaus Mann, *The Turning Point*, Victor Gollancz, 1944, pp. 258–9.
32. cf. Truman Capote, 'Unspoiled Monsters', *Esquire*, Vol. 8, May 1976, pp. 60–62.
33. CI, TLS to E. M. Forster, 14 February (1941).
34. CI, ALS to John Lehmann, 29 December (1941) (University of Texas at Austin).

35. CI, 'The Day at La Verne', *Penguin New Writing*, Vol. 14, September 1942, pp. 12–14.
36. CI, AMS to E. M. Forster, 11 January (1942).
37. W. H. Auden, TLS to Stephen Spender, 13 March 1941.
38. Grover Smith (ed.), *Letters of Aldous Huxley*, Chatto and Windus, 1969, p. 470.
39. CI, TLS to E. M. Forster, 8 July (1942).
40. Sybille Bedford, *Aldous Huxley, A Biography*, op. cit., pp. 42–3.
41. CI, TLS to John Lehmann, 9 January (1943), quoted in John Lehmann, *I Am My Brother*, Longmans Green & Co, 1960, p. 153.
42. Donald Hayne, *Batter My Heart*, Hutchinson, 1963, p. 226.
43. Tennessee Williams, *Memoirs*, W. H. Allen, 1976, p. 77.
44. Dodie Smith and Alec Beesley, Interview with Brian Finney at their home in Essex, 21 April 1976.
45. cf. *Time*, Vol. 45, 12 February 1945, p. 94.
46. Dodie Smith and Alec Beesley, Interview, op. cit.; Michael Barrie, Interview with Brian Finney at Trabuco Monastery, 17 August 1976.
47. CI, TLS to Gerald Hamilton, 11 August 1943 (Alan Clodd).
48. CI, TLS to Gerald Hamilton, 12 June 1944 (Alan Clodd).
49. CI, TLS to E. M. Forster, 29 July (1944).
50. cf. TS of 'Jacob's Hands', 102 pp. (Mrs Laura Archera Huxley).
51. cf. CI, 'Isherwood in Hollywood' (interview with Gilbert Adair), *Sight and Sound*, Vol. 46, Winter 1976/77, p. 25; Grover Smith (ed.), *Letters of Aldous Huxley*, op. cit., pp. 510–11; CI, Interview, 5 September 1976.
52. CI, ALS to John Lehmann, 15 November (1944).
53. Sybille Bedford, *Aldous Huxley, A Biography*, op. cit., p. 59.

CHAPTER EIGHTEEN: 'PRATER VIOLET'

1. CI, TLS to James Stern, 17 April (1945).
2. CL, TLS to John Lehmann, 9 May (1942).
3. cf. *Time*, Vol. 46, 5 November 1945, p. 102.
4. Diana Trilling, 'Fiction in Review', *The Nation*, Vol. 161, 17 November 1945, p. 530.
5. Edmund Wilson, 'Books', *The New Yorker*, Vol. 21, Part 3, 10 November 1945, p. 97.
6. cf. CI, 'A Conversation on Tape' (interview with Stanley Poss), op. cit., p. 52.
7. CI, Interview, 1 July 1975.
8. cf. CI, 'An Interview' (with George Wickes), op. cit., pp. 48–9; CI, Lecture at UCLA, 4 May 1965.
9. Theodore M. Purdy, 'Isherwood Again', *Saturday Review of Literature*, Vol. 28, 17 November 1945, p. 34.

CHAPTER NINETEEN: TRAVELLING: 'THE CONDOR AND
THE COWS'

1. CI, TLS to James Laughlin, 10 November (1945) (New Directions Publishing Corporation).
2. CI, TLS to Bennett Cerf, 8 April (1946) (Columbia University Library).
3. CI, TLS to Henry Heckford, 18 October (1949).
4. CI, APCS to Mr Commins, 23 November (1946) (Columbia University Library).
5. Shankara, *Crest-Jewel of Discrimination* with *A Garland of Questions and Answers*, translated by Swami Prabhavananda and CI, New American Library, 1970, p. 124.
6. W. Robson-Scott, Interview with Brian Finney at W.R.S.'s home in London, 15 December 1975.
7. CI, TLS to Dodie Smith, 29 January (1947).
8. CI, TLS to Dodie Smith, 3 May (1947).
9. CI, TLS to Edward Upward, 20 August (1947).
10. CI, TLS to Dodie Smith and Alec Beesley, 4 September (1947).
11. CI, TLS to Edward Upward, 2 September (1947).
12. CI, APCS to Dodie Smith, 23 July (1947).
13. CI, TLS to James Stern, 20 November (1947).
14. CI, TLS to E. M. Forster, 20 November (1947).
15. CI, ALS to William Plomer, 21 December (1947) (Durham University Library).
16. CI, TLS to Gore Vidal, 19 December (1947) (State Historical Society of Wisconsin).
17. CI, TLS to Gore Vidal, 6 February (1948) (State Historical Society of Wisconsin).
18. Ibid.
19. Eric Falk, Interview with Brian Finney at E.F.'s home in London, 29 October 1975.
20. Gore Vidal, 'The Art of Fiction', *The Paris Review*, Vol. 15, Fall 1974, p. 147.
21. CI, 'Isherwood on Hollywood' (interview with Charles Higham), *London Magazine*, Vol. 8, April 1968, p. 35.
22. CI, ALS to Gore Vidal, 3 February (1949) (State Historical Society of Wisconsin).
23. CI, TLS to John Lehmann, 6 November (1948).
24. CI, TLS to Dodie Smith and Alec Beesley, 27 December (1948).
25. CI, TLS to Henry Heckford, 7 April (1949).
26. CI, 'A Conversation on Tape', op. cit., p. 52.
27. CI, 'The Autobiography of My Books', Third lecture at the University of California at Berkeley, May 1963.

28. CI, ALS to Gore Vidal, 6 January (1948) (State Historical Society of Winconsin).

29. V. S. Pritchett, 'Books in General', *New Statesman*, Vol. 38, 19 November 1949, p. 585.

30. Peter Fleming, 'Mild Earthquakes', *Spectator*, Vol. 183, 9 December 1949, p. 828.

CHAPTER TWENTY: A PERIOD OF UNCERTAINTY

1. CI, TLS to Dodie Smith, 28 March (1949).

2. CI, TLS to Henry Heckford, 7 April (1949).

3. CI, TLS to Edward Upward, 19 May (1949).

4. CI, TLS to Edward Upward, 24 January (1951).

5. CI, TLS to Stephen Spender, 27 March (1951).

6. Igor Stravinsky and Robert Craft, *Dialogues and A Diary*, Faber and Faber, 1968, p. 93.

7. Ibid.

8. CI in *Writers at Work: The Paris Review Interviews: Fourth Series*, op. cit., p. 232.

9. Robert Craft, *Stravinsky: Chronicle of a Friendship*, Victor Gollancz, 1972, pp. 11–12.

10. cf. CI, 'Isherwood in Hollywood' (interview with Gilbert Adair), op. cit., p. 25.

11. cf. TLS to William Plomer, 11 October (1949) (Durham University Library).

12. cf. Paul Ferris, *Dylan Thomas*, Hodder and Stoughton, 1977, p. 247.

13. Gunther Stuhlmann (ed.), *The Journals of Anais Nin*, Vol. 5, Peter Owen, 1974, p. 58.

14. cf. CI, ALS to Rupert Doone, 12 September (1950) (Berg Collection, New York Public Library).

15. John Lehmann, *The Ample Proposition*, Eyre and Spottiswoode, 1966, pp. 125–6.

16. CI, ALS to Edward Upward, 5 December (1950).

17. CI, TLS to Edward Upward, 24 January (1951).

18. Dodie Smith and Alec Beesley, Interview with Brian Finney, 16 May 1976.

19. Henry Hewes, 'Christopher Isherwood's Snapshots', *Saturday Review*, op. cit., p. 38.

20. CI, Interview, 1 July 1975.

21. CI, 'Back to Berlin', *Observer*, 23 March 1952, p. 2.

22. CI, TLS to Gerald Hamilton, 20 May (1952) (Humanities Research Center, University of Texas at Austin).

23. CI, ALS to Alec Beesley, 5 October (1952).

24. CI, TLS to Robert Linscott, 29 January (1953) (Columbia University Library).

25. CI, TLS to Dodie Smith and Alec Beesley, 10 March (1953).
26. CI, TLS to Dodie Smith and Alec Beesley, 3 April (1953).
27. CI, ALS to Edward Upward, 31 August (1953).
28. Alan White, Cable to CI, 28 September 1953 (Eyre Methuen).
29. Robert Linscott, TLS to CI, 17 September 1953 (Columbia University Library).
30. CI, TLS to Dodie Smith, 23 September (1953).
31. CI, TLS to Robert Linscott, 6 October (1953) (Columbia University Library).

CHAPTER TWENTY-ONE: 'THE WORLD IN THE EVENING'

1. CI, ALS to Edward Upward, 16 September (1954).
2. Alan Wilde, *Christopher Isherwood*, op. cit., p. 110.
3. CI, Lecture at UCLA, 11 May 1965.
4. Frank Kermode, *Puzzles and Epiphanies*, op. cit., p. 123.
5. CI, ALS to Edward Upward, 31 August (1953).
6. CI, TLS to Alan Clodd, 7 December 1953.
7. cf. CI, TLS to Stephen Spender, 22 July (1954).
8. CI, Interview, 1 July 1975.
9. CI, Lecture at UCLA, 11 May 1965.
10. Kingsley Amis, 'Book Notes', *Twentieth Century*, Vol. 156, July 1954, p. 88.
11. CI, 'A Conversation on Tape', op. cit., p. 50.
12. Angus Wilson, 'The New and the Old Isherwood', *Encounter*, Vol. 3, August 1954, p. 64.
13. CI, Interview, 4 September 1976.
14. CI, TLS to Robert Linscott, 6 October (1953) (Columbia University Library).
15. V. S. Pritchett, Review of *The World in the Evening*, *New Statesman*, Vol. 47, 19 June 1954, p. 803.
16. CI, Lecture at UCLA, 11 May 1965.
17. CI, TLS to John Lehmann, 17 May (1954).
18. Angus Wilson, 'The New and the Old Isherwood', op. cit., p. 326.
19. Susan Sontag, 'Notes on Camp', *Partisan Review*, Vol. 31, Fall 1964, pp. 515-30.
20. Colin Wilson, 'Notes on Christopher Isherwood', op. cit., p. 326.
21. Thom Gunn, Review of *The World in the Evening*, *The London Magazine*, Vol. 1, October 1954, p. 85.
22. CI, ALS to Edward Upward, 16 September (1954).

CHAPTER TWENTY-TWO: THE RETURN OF SELF-CONFIDENCE

1. CI, TLS to John Lehmann, 17 May (1954).
2. CI, TLS to John Lehmann, 14 September (1955).

3. CI, 'Here on a Visit' (interview with Philip Oakes), *Sunday Times*, 15 February 1970.
4. CI, TLS to Dodie Smith and Alec Beesley, 12 January (1955).
5. CI, TS accompanying TLS to Edward Upward, 20 August (1955).
6. Review of *Diane*, *Manchester Guardian*, 28 January 1956.
7. CI, 'The Writer and his World', Lectures delivered at the University of California at Santa Barbara, 1960–1.
8. Paul Bowles, *Without Stopping*, op. cit., p. 331.
9. CI, Interview, 1 July 1975.
10. CI, Interview, 18 August 1976.
11. CI, ALS to Dodie Smith and Alec Beesley, 11 March (1956).
12. Robert Craft, *Stravinsky, Chronicle of a Friendship*, op. cit., p. 48.
13. CI, ALS to Dodie Smith and Alec Beesley, 12 May (1956).
14. CI, TLS to Dodie Smith and Alec Beesley, 15 July (1956).
15. Gavin Lambert, Interview with Brian Finney in London, 20 May 1976.
16. CI, TLS to Edward Upward, 12 August 1957.
17. Don Bachardy, ALS to Dodie Smith and Alec Beesley, 15 January (1958).
18. CI, TLS to Dodie Smith, 10 September (1958).
19. CI, TLS to Edward Upward, 19 December (1958).
20. CI, TLS to Alan White, 20 March (1959) (Eyre Methuen).
21. CI, ALS to Dodie Smith and Alec Beesley, 10 February (1959).
22. Gavin Lambert, Interview with Brian Finney in London, 20 May 1976.
23. cf. Charles Higham, *Charles Laughton, An Intimate Biography*, W. H. Allen, 1976, pp. 212–13.
24. CI, TLS to Dodie Smith, 18 October (1959).
25. cf. Grover Smith (ed.), *Letters of Aldous Huxley*, op. cit., p. 886.
26. cf. Charles Higham, *Charles Laughton, An Intimate Biography*, op. cit., pp. 219–21.
27. CI, TLS to Dodie Smith and Alec Beesley, 8 February (1960).
28. CI, TLS to Edward Upward, 14 July (1959).
29. CI, TLS to Edward Upward, 23 May (1959).
30. CI, TLS to Dodie Smith, 18 October (1959).
31. CI, TLS to Edward Upward, 21 August (1960).
32. CI, TLS to Tom Willis, 27 January (1961) (Department of Special Collections, University of California at Santa Barbara).
33. CI, TLS to Dodie Smith and Alec Beesley, 3 September 1960.

CHAPTER TWENTY-THREE: 'DOWN THERE ON A VISIT'

1. CI, 'Here on a Visit' (interview with Denis Hart), *Guardian*, 22 September 1961, p. 11.
2. CI, TLS to Henry Heckford, 21 March 1967.

3. CI, Interview, 18 August 1976.
4. CI, TLS to Alan White, 20 March (1959) (Eyre Methuen).
5. CI, TLS to Alan Collins, 20 June (1961) (Columbia University Library).
6. CI, Interview, 1 July 1975.
7. Francis King, *Christopher Isherwood*, Longman Group Ltd (for the British Council), 1976, p. 19.
8. CI, TLS to Dodie Smith and Alec Beesley, 3 September (1960).
9. CI, TLS to Alan White, 9 April (1962) (Eyre Methuen).
10. CI, TLS to Henry Heckford, 21 March 1967.
11. CI, TLS to Dodie Smith, 18 October (1959).
12. Julian Jebb, Review of *Down There on a Visit*, *London Magazine*, Vol. 2, April 1962, p. 88.
13. Malcolm Bradbury, 'New Novels', *Punch*, Vol. 242, 4 April 1962, pp. 549 and 550.
14. Stephen Spender, 'Isherwood's Heroes', *New Republic*, Vol. 146, 16 April 1962, p. 24.
15. Herbert Mitgang, 'Books of the Times', *New York Times*, 23 March 1962, p. 31.
16. Cyril Connolly, 'The Inferno of Herr Issyvoo', *Sunday Times*, 11 March 1962, p. 33.
17. CI, Lecture delivered at UCLA on 15 May 1965.
18. CI, 'An Interview with Christopher Isherwood' (by George Wickes), op. cit., p. 31.
19. CI, Interview, 4 September 1976.
20. CI, TLS to Edward Upward, 30 November (1960).
21. CI, Interview, 1 July 1975.
22. CI, Lecture delivered at UCLA on 15 May 1965.
23. CI, 'A Conversation on Tape' (Interview with Stanley Poss), op. cit., p. 46.
24. CI, Interview, 1 July 1975.

CHAPTER TWENTY-FOUR: THE PROFESSOR: 'A SINGLE MAN'

1. Colin Wilson, ALS to Brian Finney, 18 November 1975.
2. CI, TLS to Dodie Smith and Alec Beesley, 18 January (1962).
3. cf. CI, 'An Interview with CI' (by David Geherin), op. cit., p. 150; and CI, Interview, 5 September 1976.
4. CI, TLS to Edward Upward, 22 August (1962).
5. CI, TLS to Edward Upward, 9 September (1962).
6. CI, TLS to E. M. Forster, 6 April (1962).
7. Gavin Lambert, 'Christopher Isherwood' in *Double Exposure* (ed. Roddy McDowall), Delacorte Press, NY, 1966, p. 107.
8. CI in *Aldous Huxley 1894–1963: A Memorial Volume*, op. cit., p. 161.

9. Gunther Stuhlmann (ed.), *The Diary of Anais Nin 1955-1966*, Harcourt Brace Jovanovich, NY, 1976, pp. 312-13.
10. CI, TLS to Edward Upward, 13 August (1963).
11. CI, TLS to Dodie Smith and Alec Beesley, 13 December (1962).
12. CI, Lecture delivered at UCLA, 18 May 1965; cf. CI, 'A Meeting by Another River' (interview with Norma McLain Stoop), *After Dark*, Vol. 7, April 1975, p. 62.
13. CI, TLS to Cyril Connolly, 31 May (1963) (Tulsa University).
14. CI, TLS to Edward Upward, 13 August (1963).
15. CI, TLS to Alan White, 20 October 1963 (Eyre Methuen).
16. CI, TLS to John Lehmann, 22 October 1963.
17. CI, TLS to Stephen Spender, 1 December 1963.
18. CI, TLS to Dodie Smith, 26 May (1963).
19. CI, Lecture delivered at UCLA, 25 May 1965.
20. CI, 'Interview with CI' (by Robert Wennerstein), *Transatlantic Review*, op. cit., p. 11.
21. Alan Wilde, *Christopher Isherwood*, op. cit., p. 128.
22. Sybille Bedford, 'Poor Old Chap!', *Spectator*, Vol. 213, 11 September 1964, p. 343.
23. CI, 'An Interview with CI' (by George Wickes), op. cit., p. 52.
24. CI, Lecture delivered at UCLA, 25 May 1965.
25. CI, TLS to Dodie Smith, 26 May (1963).
26. Anthony Burgess, 'Why, this is Hell', *Listener*, Vol. 72, 10 October 1964, p. 514.
27. CI, TLS to Dodie Smith, 26 May (1963).
28. David Daiches, 'Life Without Jim', *New York Times Book Review*, Section 7, 30 August 1964, p. 5.
29. CI, Lecture delivered at UCLA, 25 May 1965.
30. CI, Interview, 5 September 1976.
31. CI, 'A Kind of Left Wing Direction' (interview with David Lambourne), op. cit., p. 55.
32. Gavin Lambert, 'Christopher Isherwood' in *Double Exposure*, op. cit., p. 107.

CHAPTER TWENTY-FIVE: BETWEEN TWO WORLDS:
'A MEETING BY THE RIVER'

1. CI, TLS to Dodie Smith and Alec Beesley, 19 February (1964).
2. CI, TLS to Edward Upward, 11 June (1964).
3. John Russell Taylor, 'The Loved One', *Sight and Sound*, Vol. 35, Spring 1966, p. 93.
4. Nikos Stangos (ed.), *David Hockney by David Hockney*, Thames and Hudson, 1976, p. 98.
5. CI, TLS to Alan White, 1 March (1965) (Eyre Methuen).
6. CI, Lecture delivered at UCLA, 1 June 1965.

7. Malcolm Muggeridge, 'Swamis go West', *Observer*, 11 April 1965, p. 30.
8. Frank Kermode, 'The Old Amalaki', *New York Review of Books*, Vol. 4, 17 June 1965, p. 20.
9. John Whitehead, 'Christophananda: Isherwood at Sixty', *London Magazine*, op. cit., p. 99.
10. CI, TLS to Dodie Smith and Alec Beesley, 16 June (1965).
11. CI, TLS to Dodie Smith and Alec Beesley, 2 May 1965.
12. CI, TLS to John Lehmann, 26 April 1965.
13. CI, TS, 115 pp., in the private collection of Edward Upward.
14. CI, TLS to John Whitehead, 28 March 1966.
15. Stanley Kauffman, 'A Meeting by the River', *New Republic*, Vol. 156, 15 April 1967, p. 38; cf. Francis King, *Christopher Isherwood*, op. cit., p. 21.
16. CI, TLS to Dodie Smith and Alec Beesley, 26 March 1967.
17. John Gross, 'A Question of Upbringing', *New York Review of Books*, Vol. 8, 18 May 1967, p. 36.
18. CI, 'CI: An Interview' (with Winston Leyland), *Gay Sunshine*, op. cit., p. 2; cf. CI, 'Lively Arts' (interview with Karl Miller), BBC Radio, 31 May 1967.
19. CI, ALS to Marshall Bean, 3 April 1966 (Alan Clodd).
20. CI, 'CI in Conversation with Nicola Thorne', *Vogue*, November 1971, p. 155.
21. CI, 'CI' (interviewed by Robert Wennersten), *Transatlantic Review*, op. cit., p. 9.
22. CI, 'An Interview with CI' (interview with David J. Geherin), *Journal of Narrative Technique*, op. cit., p. 152.
23. Alan Wilde, *Christopher Isherwood*, op. cit., p. 146.
24. CI, TLS to Edward Upward, 28 March 1966.
25. CI, TLS to Alan White, 21 April 1967 (Eyre Methuen).
26. John Gross, 'A Question of Upbringing', op. cit., p. 36.
27. Gerald Sykes, 'Tom Spilled the Beans', *New York Times Book Review*, Sect. 7, 25 June 1967, p. 41.
28. CI in *Writers at Work: The Paris Review Interviews: Fourth Series*, op. cit., p. 216.
29. CI and Don Bachardy, *A Meeting by the River* (play), TS, 84 pp.
30. CI, Interview, 18 August 1976.

CHAPTER TWENTY-SIX: TOWARDS AUTOBIOGRAPHY:
'KATHLEEN AND FRANK'

1. CI, TLS to Alan Clodd, 16 November (1965).
2. CI, TLS to Dodie Smith, 22 July (1965).
3. CI, ALS to Marshall Bean, 19 January (1967) (Alan Clodd).

4. CI, TLS to Richard Simon, 30 September 1968 (Curtis Brown, London).
5. CI, TLS to John Lehmann, 4 April 1967.
6. CI, ALS to Dodie Smith and Alec Beesley, 25 August (1968).
7. cf. Robert Craft, *Stravinsky: Chronicle of a Friendship*, op. cit., pp. 356, 369; Lillian Libman, *And Music at the Close*, Macmillan, 1972, pp. 290–91.
8. cf. Nikos Stangos (ed.), *David Hockney by David Hockney*, op. cit., p. 157.
9. CI, TLS to Edward Upward, 30 November 1968.
10. cf. P. N. Furbank, *E. M. Forster, A Life*, Vol. 2, op. cit., p. 324.
11. cf. CI, TLS to Gerald Hamilton, 12 April 1967 (University of Texas at Austin).
12. Thomas Lask, 'Isherwood Looks At an English Era', *New York Times*, 15 February 1972, p. 26.
13. CI, TLS to Dodie Smith and Alec Beesley, 1 February (1969).
14. Ibid.
15. Frederick Raphael, Review of *Kathleen and Frank*, *Sunday Times*, 24 October 1971, p. 36.
16. CI, 'An Interview with CI' (by David J. Geherin), *Journal of Narrative Technique*, op. cit., p. 150.
17. CI, TLS to Peter Schwed, 13 October 1971 (Simon & Schuster).
18. R. F. Delderfield, 'Seventy years of English Foibles', *Life*, Vol. 72, 28 January 1972, p. 18.
19. CI, Interview, 1 July 1975.
20. CI, 'An Interview with CI' (by David J. Geherin), *Journal of Narrative Technique*, op. cit., p. 149.
21. CI, Interview, 3 September 1976.
22. C. G. Jung, *Memories, Dreams, Reflections*, Collins, 1967, p. 17.
23. CI, 'Mightier than the Sword' (interview with Hale Sparks), University of California, Radio-Television Administration, Broadcast 7161-VE1919, 25 April 1965 (Dept. of Special Collections, UCLA).
24. Stephen Spender, Interview with Brian Finney in London, 3 March 1976.
25. W. H. Auden, 'The Diary of a Diary', *New York Review of Books*, Vol. 18, 27 January 1972, p. 19.
26. Angus Wilson, 'Issyvoo and his parents', *Observer*, 24 October 1971, p. 36.

CHAPTER TWENTY-SEVEN: THE SEVENTIES:
'CHRISTOPHER AND HIS KIND'

1. cf. Gilbert Adair, 'Isherwood in Hollywood', *Sight and Sound*, op. cit., p. 25.

2. CI, ALS to Dodie Smith and Alec Beesley, 29 March 1971.

3. CI, TLS to Brian Finney, 7 October 1975.

4. CI, TLS to Edward Upward, 11 March 1973.

5. Jay Michael Barrie, 'Some Reminiscences of Gerald Heard', op. cit.

6. CI, 'An Interview with CI' (by David J. Geherin), *Journal of Narrative Technique*, op. cit., p. 147.

7. Jonathan Fryer, *Christopher Isherwood*, op. cit., p. 282.

8. CI, ALS to Edward Upward, 9 October 1973.

9. CI, TLS to Stephen Spender, 11 November 1973.

10. CI, ALS to Edward Upward, 2 September 1974.

11. CI, Interview, 5 September 1976.

12. CI, TLS to Dodie Smith and Alec Beesley, 7 September 1975.

13. CI, 'CI: An Interview' (with Carolyn Heilbrun) *Twentieth Century Literature*, op. cit., p. 263.

14. Rebecca West, 'A Symphony of Squalor', *Sunday Telegraph*, 3 April 1977, p. 15.

15. CI, TLS to Dodie Smith, 9 May 1976.

16. CI, TLS to Peter Gose, 14 November 1974 (Curtis Brown, London).

17. CI, TLS to John Cullen, 29 July 1976 (Eyre Methuen).

18. CI, TLS to Edward Upward, 29 December 1973.

19. CI, 'The Youth that was "I"' (interview with W. I. Scobie), *London Magazine*, Vol. 17, April/May 1977, p. 24.

20. Stephen Spender, 'Notebook—XII', *London Magazine*, Vol. 17, April/May 1977, p. 50.

21. CI, TLS to John Cullen, 29 July 1976 (Eyre Methuen).

22. Alan Wallis, 'Aquarius', Thames Television, London, 5 February 1977.

23. James Fenton, 'A Backward Love', *New Review*, Vol. 3, March 1977, p. 41.

24. Anthony Powell, 'I am my own camera', *Daily Telegraph*, 31 March 1977, p. 14.

25. Francis King, 'Behind the Scenes', *Gay News*, No. 116, 7–20 April 1977, p. 29.

26. Peter Conrad, 'The trouble with Christopher', *Spectator*, Vol. 238, 2 April 1977, p. 20.

27. CI, TLS to Stephen Spender, 11 November 1973.

28. cf. Paul Bailey, Interview with CI, BBC Radio 3, 28 March 1977.

29. CI, TLS to Dodie Smith, 9 May 1976.

30. Francis King, 'Behind the Scenes', *Gay News*, op. cit., p. 29.

31. Philip Toynbee, 'Herr Issyvoo comes clean', *Observer*, 3 April 1977, p. 26.

32. Peter Conrad, 'The trouble with Christopher', *Spectator*, op. cit., p. 20.

33. Edward Upward, 'The Resolute Anti-Hero', *New Statesman*, 1 April 1977, p. 434.

34. CI, ALS to Brian Finney, 12 August 1977.

Select Bibliography

(Unless otherwise stated the place of publication is London. *Indicates the text referred to in this book. Bracketed abbreviations of titles are those used in the text.)

(A) BOOKS BY CHRISTOPHER ISHERWOOD

INDIVIDUAL WORKS

All the Conspirators (*AT*). Jonathan Cape, 1928; *1957 (new edition with a Foreword by CI). New Directions, N.Y., 1958

The Memorial. *Hogarth Press, 1932. New Directions, Norfolk, Conn., 1946

Mr Norris Changes Trains. Hogarth Press, 1935. W. Morrow & Co., N.Y., 1935 (as *The Last of Mr Norris*)

Sally Bowles. Hogarth Press, 1937 (subsequently incorporated in *Goodbye to Berlin*)

Lions and Shadows (*LS*). Hogarth Press, 1938; reissued by *Methuen, 1953. New Directions, Norfolk, Conn., 1947

Goodbye to Berlin. Hogarth Press, 1939. Random House, N.Y., 1939

Prater Violet (*PV*). Random House, N.Y., 1945. *Methuen, 1946

The Condor and the Cows (*CC*). Random House, N.Y., 1949. *Methuen, 1949

The World in the Evening. Random House, N.Y., 1954. *Methuen, 1954

Down There on a Visit (*DTV*). Simon and Schuster, N.Y., 1962. *Methuen, 1962

An Approach to Vedanta (*AV*). Vedanta Press, Hollywood, 1963

A Single Man. Simon and Schuster, N.Y., 1964. *Methuen, 1964

Ramakrishna and his Disciples. Methuen, 1965. *Simon and Schuster, N.Y., 1965

Exhumations (*E*). *Methuen, 1966. Simon and Schuster, N.Y., 1966

A Meeting by the River. Simon and Schuster, N.Y., 1967. *Methuen, 1967

Essentials of Vedanta. Vedanta Press, Hollywood, 1969

Kathleen and Frank (*KF*). *Methuen, 1971. Simon and Schuster, N.Y., 1972
Christopher and his Kind (*CK*). Farrar, Straus and Giroux, N.Y., 1976. *Eyre Methuen, 1977

COLLECTIONS

The Berlin Stories (re-issue of *The Last of Mr Norris* and *Goodbye to Berlin*). New Directions, N.Y., 1945
The Berlin of Sally Bowles (re-issue of *Mr Norris Changes Trains* and *Goodbye to Berlin*). *Hogarth Press, 1975

COLLABORATIONS WITH W. H. AUDEN

The Dog Beneath the Skin. *Faber and Faber, 1935. Random House, N.Y., 1935
The Ascent of F6. Faber and Faber, 1936. Random House, N.Y., 1937
On the Frontier. Faber and Faber, 1938. Random House, N.Y., 1939
Journey to a War. *Faber and Faber, 1939. Random House, N.Y., 1939
Ascent of F6 and On the Frontier. *Faber and Faber, 1958
Two Great Plays by W. H. Auden and Christopher Isherwood: The Dog Beneath the Skin and The Ascent of F6. Random House, N.Y., 1959

TRANSLATIONS

Intimate Journals by Charles Baudelaire. Blackamore Press, 1930 (Introduction by T. S. Eliot). Random House, N.Y., 1930 (Introduction by T. S. Eliot). Marcel Rodd, Hollywood, 1947 (Introduction by W. H. Auden). Methuen, 1949 (Introduction by W. H. Auden; Preface by Isherwood)
A Penny for the Poor by Bertolt Brecht. R. Hale, 1937 (translated by Desmond Vesey; verses translated by Isherwood). Hillman-Curl, N.Y., 1938 (translated by Desmond Vesey; verses translated by Isherwood). Grove Press, N.Y., 1956 (under new title: *Threepenny Novel*)

TRANSLATIONS WITH SWAMI PRABHAVANANDA

The Song of God: Bhagavad-Gita. Marcel Rodd, Hollywood, 1944. Phoenix House, 1947. Harper, N.Y., 1951
Shankara's Crest-Jewel of Discrimination. Vedanta Press, Hollywood, 1947
How to Know God: The Yoga Aphorisms of Patanjali. Harper, N.Y., 1953. Allen and Unwin, 1953. Vedanta Press, Hollywood, 1962

EDITINGS

Vedanta for the Western World. Marcel Rodd, Hollywood, 1945.
Vedanta Press, Hollywood, 1946. Allen and Unwin, 1948
Vedanta for Modern Man. Harper, N.Y., 1951. Allen and Unwin, 1952
Great English Short Stories. Dell Publishing Co., N.Y., 1957

UNCOLLECTED INTRODUCTIONS, PREFACES AND
    CONTRIBUTIONS

The Railway Accident by Allen Chalmers (i.e. Edward Upward). New
    Directions, N.Y., 1949
The Railway Accident & Other Stories by Edward Upward. Heinemann,
    1969. Penguin Books, 1972
Teachings of Swami Vivekananda by Swami Vivekananda. Advaita
    Ashrama, Mayavati, India, 1948
Toward the Goal Supreme by Swami Virajananda. Harper, N.Y., 1950
A Man of God by Swami Vividishananda. Sri Ramakrishna Math,
    Mylapore, Madras, 1957
What Vedanta Means to Me, a Symposium, edited by John Yale. Double-
    day, N.Y., 1960
What Religion Is in the Words of Swami Vivekananda, edited by John Yale.
    Phoenix House, 1962. Julian Press, N.Y., 1962
Religion in Practice by Swami Prabhavananda. Allen and Unwin, 1968
Narada's Way of Divine Love, The Bhakti Sutras, trans. by Swami
    Prabhavananda. Vedanta Press, Hollywood, 1971
Meditation and Its Methods according to Swami Vivekananda by Swami
    Vivekananda. Vedanta Press, Hollywood, 1976

INTERVIEWS

Adair, Gilbert, 'Isherwood in Hollywood', *Sight and Sound,* Vol. 46,
    Winter 1976/77, p. 25
Aitken, Will, 'Up here on a visit', *Body Politic* (Toronto), No. 32,
    April 1977, pp. 12–14
Allsop, Kenneth, 'That Other Me', *Daily Mail,* 7 August 1961, p. 6;
    'The World of Books', BBC Home Service, 6 June 1967
Amory, Cleveland, 'Trade Winds', *Saturday Review,* Vol. 55, 19
    February 1972, p. 10
Anon., 'Candid Camera', *Sunday Times,* 16 January 1977, p. 35
Bailey, Paul, 'Interview with Christopher Isherwood', BBC Radio 3,
    28 March 1977
Bell, Arthur, 'Christopher Isherwood: No Parades', *New York Times
    Book Review,* 25 March 1973, pp. 10–14
Bradshaw, Jon, 'Reflections of an Anglo-Californian', *Vogue,* Vol.
    131, Whole No. 2107, December 1974, pp. 72, 76, 84, 86, 91

Breit, Harvey, 'Talks with Mr Isherwood', *New York Times Book Review*, 16 December 1951, p. 18; reprinted in expanded form in *The Writer Observed*, World Publishing Co., N.Y., 1956; Alvin Redman Ltd., 1957, pp. 215–17

Coven, Edwina, 'Christopher Isherwood', *She*, May 1970, p. 140

Day, James, 'Day at Night', *PBS*, Spring 1974

Delfino, Rita, 'The Camera Speaks', *New York Post*, 17 February 1972, p. 45

Dolbier, Maurice, 'Out of a Certain Foreignness', *New York Herald Tribune Books*, 11 March 1962, p. 5

Edwards, Sydney, 'Sally: Still No. 1 with Isherwood', *Evening Standard*, 4 February 1972, p. 18

Finney, Brian, 'Christopher Isherwood—A Profile', *New Review*, Vol. 2, August 1975, pp. 17–24

Fleming, Anne Taylor, 'Christopher Isherwood, He Is A Camera', *LA*, Vol. 23, 9 December 1972, pp. 14–16

Ford, Christopher, 'Christopher's Jungle Book', *Guardian*, 30 March 1977, p. 10; 'Christopher Isherwood Speaks out', *Gay Scene*, Vol. 5, February 1975, pp. 4–5

Geherin, David J., 'An Interview with Christopher Isherwood', *Journal of Narrative Technique*, Vol. 2, March 1972, pp. 143–58

Halpern, Daniel, 'A Conversation with Christopher Isherwood', *Antaeus*, Vols. 13/14, Spring/Summer 1974, pp. 366–88

Hanscom, Leslie, 'The Boys in Berlin', *Guardian*, 4 January 1977, p. 6

Hart, Denis, 'Here on a Visit', *Guardian*, 22 September 1961, p. 11

Hart, Derek, 'A Fortunate, Happy Life', *Listener*, Vol. 83, 2 April 1970, pp. 449–50; 'Now Read On', BBC Radio 4, 20 October 1971

Heilbrun, Carolyn G., 'Christopher Isherwood: An Interview', *Twentieth Century Literature*, Vol. 22, October 1976, pp. 253–63

Hewes, Henry, 'Christopher Isherwood's Snapshots', *Saturday Review*, Vol. 35, 12 April 1952, pp. 38–40

Higham, Charles, 'Isherwood on Hollywood', *London Magazine*, Vol. 8, April 1968, pp. 31–8

Hood, Shirley K., 'Interview with Christopher Isherwood Concerning His Play *The Ascent of F6*', (24 March 1966), typescript, 32 pp. at UCLA Department of Special Collections.

Jebb, Julian, 'Success Story', BBC1 Television, 22 April 1974 (cf. 'Out of the Air (Sally and Issyvoo)', *Listener*, Vol. 91, 16 May 1974, p. 635)

Johnstone, Iain, 'Bowles Players', *Radio Times*, 18 April 1974, pp. 54–9; 'The Real Sally Bowles', *Folio*, Autumn 1975, pp. 32–8

Lambourne, David, 'An Interview with Christopher Isherwood', Appendix A of 'The Novelist between the Wars: Post-Modernist Fiction from 1918–1939 in its Social, Political and Historical Context', PhD thesis, University of Hull, 1973. Reprinted in shortened form as 'A Kind of Left Wing Direction', *Poetry Nation*, Vol. 4, 1975, pp. 47–62

Lask, Thomas, 'Isherwood Looks at an English Era', *New York Times*, 15 February 1972, p. 26

Lehane, B., 'Isherwood Plays a Guessing Game', *Daily Telegraph* (Colour Supplement), 7 August 1970, pp. 18–20

Lewis, Peter, 'My Berlin Days and the Real Sally Bowles', *Daily Mail*, 31 March 1977, p. 7

Leyland, Winston, 'Christopher Isherwood. An Interview', *Gay Sunshine*, San Francisco, Vol. 19, September–October 1973, pp. 1–2

Mason, Michael and Burton, Peter, 'A Figure-head, not a Leader', *Gay News*, No. 126, 8–21 September 1977, pp. 17–18, 24

Miller, Karl, 'The Lively Arts', BBC Radio, 31 May 1967

Muggeridge, Malcolm, 'Appointment With . . .', Granada Television, Manchester, England, 29 June 1961

Newquist, Roy, 'Christopher Isherwood', *Conversations*, Rand McNally & Co. (NP), 1967, pp. 169–81; 'Where are they now?', *Newsweek*, Vol. 68, 5 December 1966, p. 20

Oakes, Philip, 'Here on a Visit', *Sunday Times*, 15 February 1970, p. 52; 'From a Conversation with Christopher Isherwood', *Performing Arts*, Vol. 3, No. 4, April 1969, pp. 23 and 31

Phelps, Robert, 'Happy Birthday, Herr Issyvoo', *Washington Post*, 16 August 1964, Book Week, p. 2

Poss, Stanley, 'A Conversation on Tape', *London Magazine*, Vol. 1, June 1961, pp. 41–5

Reuven, Ben, 'Christopher Isherwood: reading the sands of time', *Los Angeles Times: West View*, 5 December 1976, p. 3

Ring, Francis, 'Isherwood—A Writer in Many Mediums', *Los Angeles Times*, 21 August 1966, p. 9

Robinson, Robert, 'Domestic Occasion', *Spectator*, Vol. 203, 23 October 1959, p. 544 (shortened version of a BBC Television interview for 'Monitor', broadcast 8 November 1959)

Russo, Tony, 'Christopher Isherwood', *Christopher Street*, Vol. 1, March 1977, pp. 7–10

Scheuer, Philip K., 'Ado About Novel Amuses Author', *Los Angeles Times*, 13 January 1946, Part III, pp. 1 and 3

Scobie, W. I., 'The Homosexual Revolt', *London Magazine*, Vol. II, June/July 1971, pp. 57–9; 'The Art of Fiction: Christopher Isherwood', *Paris Review*, Vol. 14, Spring 1974, pp. 138–82; reprinted in *Writers at Work. Fourth Series* (edited by George Plimpton), Secker and Warburg, 1977, pp. 209–42; 'Christopher Isherwood, A Lively Exchange with One of Our Greatest Living Writers', *The Advocate*, Vol. 179, 17 December 1975, pp. 6–8; reprinted in *Gay News*, No. 93, 22 April–5 May 1976, pp. 16–17; 'The Youth that was "I",' *London Magazine*, Vol. 17, April/May 1977, pp. 23–32

Smith, Sarah and Marcus, 'To Help Along the Line', *New Orleans Review*, Vol. 4, No. 4, 1975, pp. 307–10

Solway, Clifford, 'An Interview with Christopher Isherwood', *The Tamarisk Review*, Toronto, Spring 1966, pp. 22–34 (broadcast on CBC TV, 30 May 1965)

Sparks, Hale, 'Mightier than the Sword', University of California TV, 25 April 1965

Stanley, Richard, 'Isherwood', *In Touch*, No. 24, July–August 1976, p. 28

Stoop, Norma McLain, 'Christopher Isherwood: A Meeting by Another River', *After Dark*, Vol. 7, April 1975, pp. 60–65

Thorne, Nicola, 'Christopher Isherwood in Conversation with Nicola Thorne', *Vogue*, Vol. 15, November 1971, pp. 154–5

Times Diary, 'Isherwood on Novel as Play', *The Times*, 10 February 1970, p. 10

Upward, Edward, 'New Comment', BBC Third Programme, 15 June 1961

Wallis, Alan, 'Aquarius', Thames Television, London, 5 February 1977

Weatherby, W. J., 'W. J. Weatherby meets Christopher Isherwood', *Guardian*, 17 November 1960, p. 8

Wennersten, Robert, 'Interview with Christopher Isherwood', *Transatlantic Review*, Vols. 42 and 43, Spring–Summer 1972, pp. 5–21

Wickes, George, 'An Interview with Christopher Isherwood,' *Shenandoah*, Vol. 16, Spring 1965, pp. 22–52

(B) BOOKS ABOUT CHRISTOPHER ISHERWOOD

BIBLIOGRAPHY

Westby, Selmer and Clayton M. Brown, *Christopher Isherwood, A Bibliography 1923–1967*, California State College at Los Angeles, 1968

BIOGRAPHY

Fryer, Jonathan, *Isherwood, A Biography of Christopher Isherwood*, New English Library, 1977

CRITICAL

Heilbrun, Carolyn G., *Christopher Isherwood* (Columbia Essays on Modern Writers), Columbia University Press, N.Y., 1970

Wilde, Alan, *Christopher Isherwood* (Twayne's United States Authors Series), Twayne Publishers Inc, N.Y., 1971

King, Francis, *Christopher Isherwood* (Writers and their Work), Longman Group for the British Council, 1976

Heilbrun, Carolyn G. (ed.), *Twentieth Century Literature* (Christopher Isherwood Issue), Vol. 22, No. 3, October 1976

Piazza, Paul, *Christopher Isherwood: Myth and Anti-Myth*, Columbia University Press, 1978

Index